Egerton Castle, Theodore Brown Hapgood

The Light of Scarthey

A Romance

Egerton Castle, Theodore Brown Hapgood

The Light of Scarthey
A Romance

ISBN/EAN: 9783744776240

Printed in Europe, USA, Canada, Australia, Japan

Cover: Foto ©Thomas Meinert / pixelio.de

More available books at **www.hansebooks.com**

The
LIGHT
of
SCARTHEY

A Romance

By EGERTON CASTLE
Author of
"The Pride of Jennico," "Young
April," etc.

"Take whichsoever way thou wilt—the ways are all alike;
But do thou only come—I bade my threshold wait thy
coming.
From out my window one can see the graves, and on
my life
The graves keep watch." *Luteplayer's Song.*

New York
FREDERICK A. STOKES COMPANY
MCM

FOURTH EDITION.

¶ Dedicate

THIS BOOK TO THE

MEMORY OF

FREDERICK ANDREWS LARKING

OF THE ROCKS, EAST MALLING, KENT

THAT, SO LONG AS ANYTHING OF MINE SHALL ENDURE,

THERE MAY ENDURE ALSO

A RECORD OF OUR FRIENDSHIP AND OF

MY SORROW

PREFACE TO THE AMERICAN EDITION.

Among the works of every writer of Fiction there are generally one or two that owe their being to some haunting thought, long communed with—a thought which has at last found a living shape in some story of deed and passion.

I say one or two advisedly: for the span of man's active life is short and such haunting fancies are, of their essence, solitary. As a matter of fact, indeed, the majority of a novelist's creations belong to another class, must of necessity (if he be a prolific creator) find their conception in more sudden impulses. The great family of the " children of his brain" must be born of inspirations ever new, and in alluring freshness go forth into the world surrounded by the atmosphere of their author's present mood, decked in the colours of his latest imaginings, strengthened by his latest passional impressions and philosophical conclusions.

In the latter category the lack of long intimate acquaintance between the author and the friends or foes he depicts, is amply compensated for by the enthusiasm appertaining to new discoveries, as each character reveals itself, often in quite unforeseen manner, and the consequences of each event shape themselves inevitably and sometimes indeed almost against his will.

Although dissimilar in their genesis, both kinds of stories can, in the telling, be equally life-like and equally alluring to the reader. But what of the writer? Among his literary family is there not one nearer his heart than all the rest—

his dream-child? *It may be the stoutest of the breed or it may be the weakling; it may be the first-born, it often is the Benjamin. Fathers in the flesh know this secret tenderness. Many a child and many a book is brooded over with a special love even before its birth.—Loved thus, for no grace or merit of its own,* this book is *my dream-child.*

. . . .

Here, by the way, I should like to say my word in honour of Fiction—*"fiction" contradistinguished from what is popularly termed "serious" writing.*

If, in a story, the characters and the events are truly convincing; if the former are appealingly human and the latter are so carefully devised and described as never to evoke the idea of improbability, then it can make no difference in the intellectual pleasure *of the reader whether what he is made to realise so vividly is a record of fact or of mere fancy. Facts we read of are of necessity past: what is past, what is beyond the immediate ken of our senses, can only be realised in imagination; and the picture we are able to make of it for ourselves depends altogether on the sympathetic skill of the recorder. Is not Diana Vernon, born and bred in Scott's imagination, to the full as living now before us as Rob Roy Macgregor whose existence was so undeniably tangible to the men of his days? Do we not see, in our mind's eye, and know as clearly the lovable "girl John Ridd" of* Lorna Doone *the romance as his contemporaries, Mr. Samuel Pepys of the hard and uncompromising* Diary *or King James of* English Annals?

Pictures, alike of the plainest facts or of the veriest imaginings, are but pictures: it matters very little therefore whether the man or the woman we read of but never can see in the flesh has really lived or not, if what we do read raises an emotion in our hearts. To the novelist, every character, each in his own degree, is almost as living as a personal acquaintance; every event is as clear as a personal experience. And if this be true of the story written à la grâce de la plume, where both events and characters unfold themselves like the buds of some unknown plant, how much more strongly is it the case of the story that has so long been mused over that one day it had *to be told! Then the marking events of the actors' lives, their adventures, whether of sorrow or of joy, their sayings and doings, noble or bright or mistaken, recorded in the book, are but a tithe of the adventures, sayings and doings with which the writer seems to be familiar. He might write or talk about them, in praise or vindictiveness as he loves or dreads them, for many a longer day—but he has one main theme to make clear to his hearers and must respect the modern canons of the Story-telling Art. Among the many things therefore he could tell, an he would, he selects that only which will unravel a particular thread of fate in the tangle of endless consequences; which will render plausible the growth of passions on which, in a continuous life-drama, is based one particular episode.*

Of such a kind is the story of Adrian Landale.

The haunting thought round which the tale of the sorely tempest-tossed dreamer is gathered is one which, I think, must at one time or other have occurred to many a man as he neared the maturity of middle-life:—What form of turmoil would come into his heart if, when still in the strength of his age but after long years of hopeless separation, he were again brought face to face with the woman who had been the one passion of his life, the first and only love of his youth? And what if she were still then exactly as he had last seen her—she, untouched by years even as she had so long lived in his thoughts: he, with his soul scarred and seamed by many encounters bravely sustained in the Battle of Life?

The problem thus propounded is not solvable, even in fiction, unless it be by "fantastic" treatment. But perhaps the more so on this account did it haunt me. And out of the travail of my mind around it, out of the changing shadows of restless speculation, gradually emerged, clear and alive, the being of Adrian Landale and his two loves.

Here then was a man, whose mind, moulded by nature for grace and contemplation, was cast by fate amid all the turmoils of Romance and action. Here was one of those whose warm heart and idealising enthusiasm must wreathe the beauty of love into all the beauties of the world; whose ideals are spent on one adored object; who, having lost it, seems to have lost the very sense of love; to whom love never could return, save by some miracle. But fortune, that had been so cruelly hard on him, one day in her blind way brings back to his door the miraculous restitution—and there leaves him to struggle along the new path of his fate! It is there also that I take up the thread of the speculation, and watch through its vicissitudes the working of the problem raised by such a strange circumstance.

The surroundings in a story of this kind are, of the nature of things, all those of Romance. And by Romance, I would point out, is not necessarily meant in tale-telling, a chain of events fraught with greater improbability than those of so-called real life. (Indeed where is now the writer who will for a moment admit, even tacitly, that his records are not of reality?) It simply betokens, a specialisation of the wider genus Novel; a narrative of strong action and moving incident, in addition to the necessary analysis of character; a story in which the uncertain violence of the outside world turns the course of the actors' lives from the more obvious channels. It connotes also, as a rule, more poignant emotions—emotions born of strife or peril, even of horror; it tells

*of the shock of arms in life, rather than of the mere diplo-
macy of life.*

Above all Romance *depends upon picturesque and varied
setting ; upon the scenery of the drama, so to speak. On
the other hand it is not essentially (though this has sometimes been advanced) a narrative of mere adventures as contrasted to the observation and dissection of character and
manners we find in the true " novel." Rather be it said
that it is one in which the hidden soul is made patent under
the touchstone of blood-stirring incidents, of hairbreadth
risks, of recklessness or fierceness. There are soaring passions, secrets of the innermost heart, that can only be set
free in desperate situations—and those situations are not
found in the tenor in every-day, well-ordered life: they
belong to Romance.*

*Spirit-fathers have this advantage that they can bring
forth their dream-children in what age and place they list:
it is no times of now-a-days, no ordinary scenery, that would
have suited such adventures as befell Adrian Landale, or
Captain Jack, or " Murthering Moll the Second."*

*Romantic enough is the scene, which, in a manner,
framed the display of a most human drama ; and fraught
it is, even to this day, in the eyes of any but the least
imaginative, with potentialities for strange happenings.**
*It is that great bight of Morecambe ; that vast of brown and
white shallows, deserted, silent, mysterious, and treacherous
with its dreaded shifting sands ; fringed in the inland distance by the Cumbrian hills, blue and misty ; bordered out-*

---

* *Those who like to associate fiction with definite places may be interested to know that the prototype of Scarthey is the* Piel of Foudrey,
*on the North Lancashire coast, near the edge of Morecambe Bay, and that
Pulwick was suggested by Furness Abbey. Barrow-in-Furness was then
but a straggling village. A floating light, facing the mouth of the Wyre,
now fulfils the duties devolving on the beacon of Scarthey at the time of
this story.*

*wards by the Irish sea, cold and grey. And in a corner of
that waste, the islet, small and green and secure, with its
ancient Peel, ruinous even as the noble abbey of which it was
once the dependant stronghold; with its still sturdy keep,
and the beacon, whose light-keeper was once a Dreamer of
Beautiful Things.*

*And romantic the times, if by that word is implied a freer
scope than can be found in modern years for elemental passions, for fighting and loving in despite of every-day conventions; for enterprise, risks, temptations unknown in the
atmosphere of humdrum peace and order. They are the
early days of the century, days when easy and rapid means
of communication had not yet destroyed all the glamour of
distance, when a county like Lancashire was as a far-off
country, with a spirit, a language, customs and ideas unknown to the Metropolis; days when, if there were no life-
boat crews, there could still be found rather experienced
"wreckers," and when the keeping of a beacon, to light a
dangerous piece of sea, was still within the province of a pub-
lic-spirited landlord. They are the days when the spread of
education had not even yet begun (for weal or for woe) its
levelling work; days of cruel monopolies and inane prohibi-
tions, and ferocious penal laws, inept in the working, baleful
in the result; days of keel-hauling and flogging; when the
"free-trader" still swung, tarred and in chains, on conspicuous points of the coast—even as the highwayman
rattled at the cross-road—for the encouragement of the
brotherhood; when it was naturally considered more logical
(since hang you must for almost any misdeed) to hang for
a sheep than a lamb, and human life on the whole was held
rather cheap in consequence. They are the days when in
Liverpool the privateers were daily fitting out or bringing in
the "prizes," and when, in Lord Street Offices, distant car-
goes of "living ebony" were put to auction by steady, in-*

tensely respectable, Church-going merchants.   But especially they are the days of war and the fortunes of war; days of pressgangs, to kidnap unwilling rulers of the waves; of hulks and prisons filled to overflowing, even in a mere commercial port like Liverpool, with French prisoners of war.

A long course of relentless hostilities, lasting the span of a full-grown generation, had cultivated the predatory instinct of all men with the temperament of action, and seemed to justify it.   Venturesome, hot-spirited youths, with their way to make in the world (who in a former age might have been reduced to "the road)" took up privateering on a systematic scale.   In such an atmosphere there could not fail to return a belief in the good old border rule, "the simple plan: that they should take who have the power, and they should keep who can."   And it must be remembered that an island country's border is the enemy's coast!   On that ethical understanding many privateer owners built up large fortunes, still enjoyed by descendants who in these days would look upon high-sea looting of non-combatants with definite horror.

The years of the great French war, however, fostered a species of nautical enterprise more venturesome even than privateering, raiding, blockade-running and all the ordinary forms of smuggling that are usual when two coast lines are at enmity.   I mean that smuggling of gold specie and bullion which incidentally was destined to affect the course of Sir Adrian's life so powerfully.

. . . .

As Captain Jack's last venture may, at this distance of time, appear a little improbable, it is well to state here some little-known facts concerning the now rather incomprehensible pursuit of gold smuggling—a romantic subject if ever there was one.

The existence at one time of this form of " free-trade " is all but forgotten. Indeed very little was ever heard of it in the world, except among parties directly interested, even at the time when it played an important part in the machinery of governments. Its rise during the years of Napoleonic tyranny on the continent of Europe, and its continuance during the factitious calm of the First Restoration in France, were due to circumstances that never existed before and are little likely to occur again.

The accumulation of a fund of gold coin, reserved against sudden contingency, was one of Bonaparte's imperial ideas. In a modified and more modern form, this notion of a " war-chest," untouched and unproductive in peace-time, is still adhered to by the Germans: they have kept to heart many of their former conqueror's lessons, lessons forgotten by the French themselves—and the enormous treasure of gold bags guarded at Spandau is a matter of common knowledge. Napoleon, however, in his triumphant days never, and for obvious reasons, lacked money. It was less an actual treasure that he required and valued so highly for political and military purposes, than an ever ready reserve of wealth easily portable, of paramount value at all times; " concentrated," so to speak. And nothing could come nearer to that description than rolls of English guineas. Indeed the vast numbers of these coins which fitfully appeared in circulation throughout Europe justified the many weird legends concerning the power of " British Gold "—l'or Anglais !

There is every reason to believe that, in days when the national currency consisted chiefly of lumbering silver écus, the Bourbon government also appreciated to the full the value of a private gold reserve. At any rate it was at the time of the first Restoration that the golden guinea of England found in France its highest premium.

Without going into the vexed and dreary question of single or double standard, it will suffice to say that during the early years of the century now about to close, gold coin was leaving England at a rate which not only appeared phenomenal but was held to be injurious to the community.

As a matter of fact most of it was finding its way to France, whilst Great Britain was flooded with silver. It was then made illegal to export gold coin or bullion. The prohibition was stringently, indeed at one time, ruthlessly, enforced. In this manner the new and highly profitable traffic in English guineas entered the province of the "free-trader"; the difference introduced in his practice being merely one of degree. Whereas, in the case of prohibited imports, the chief task lay in running the illicit goods and distributing them, in the case of guinea-smuggling its arduousness was further increased by the danger of collecting the gold inland and clearing from home harbours.

Very little, as I said, has ever been heard of this singular trade, and for obvious reasons. In the first place it obtained only for a comparatively small number of years, the latter part of the Great War: the last of it belonging to the period of the Hundred Days. *And in the second it was, at all times, of necessity confined to a very small number of free-trading skippers. Of adventurous men, in stirring days, there were of course a multitude. But few, naturally, were the men to whose honour the custody of so much ready wealth could safely be intrusted. "That is where," as Captain Jack says sometimes in this book, " the ' likes of me ' come in."*

The exchange was enormously profitable. As much as thirty-two shillings in silver value could, at one time, be obtained on the other side of the water for an English guinea. But the shipper and broker, in an illegal venture where contract could not be enforced, had to be a man whose simple word was warranty—and indeed, in the case of large con-

signments, this blind trust had to be extended to almost every man of his crew.   What a romance could be written upon this theme alone!

In the story of Adrian Landale, however, it plays but a subsidiary part. Brave, joyous-hearted Captain Jack and his bold venture for a fortune appear only in the drama to turn its previous course to unforeseen channels; just as in most of our lives, the sudden intrusion of a new strong personality— transient though it may be, a tempest or a meteor—changes their seemingly inevitable trend to altogether new issues.

.   .   .   .
.   .   .   .

It was urged by my English publishers that, in " The Light of Scarthey," I relate two distinct love-stories and two distinct phases of one man's life; and that it were wiser (by which word I presume was meant more profitable) to distribute the tale between two books, one to be a sequel to the other.   Happily I would not be persuaded to cut a fully composed canvas in two for the sake of the frames. " It is the fate of sequels," as Stevenson said in his dedication of Catriona, " *to disappoint those who have waited for them." Besides, life is essentially continuous.—It may not be inept to state a truism of this kind in a world of novels where the climax of life, if not indeed its very conclusion, is held to be reached on the day of marriage! There is often, of course, more than one true passion of love in a man's life; and even if the second does not really kill the memory of the first, their course (should they be worth the telling) may well be told separately.   But if, in the story of a man's love for two women, the past and the present are so closely interwoven as were the reality and the " might-have-been " in the mind of Adrian Landale, any separation of the two phases, youth and maturity, would surely have stultified the whole scheme of the story.*

I have also been taken to task by some critics for having, the tale once opened at a given time and place, harked back to other days and other scenes: an inartistic and confusing method, I was told. I am still of contrary opinion. There are certain stories which belong, by their very essence, to certain places. All ancient buildings have, if we only knew them, their human dramas: this is the very soul of the hidden but irresistible attraction they retain for us even when deserted and dismantled as now the Peel of Scarthey. For the sake of harmonious proportions, and in order to give it its proper atmosphere, it was imperative that in this drama —wherever the intermediate scenes might be placed, whether on the banks of the Vilaine, on the open sea, or in Lancaster Castle—the Prologue should be witnessed on the green islet in the wilderness of sands, even as the Crisis and the Closing Scene of rest and tenderness.

E. C.,

49, Sloane Gardens,

London, S. W.

October 1899.

TABLE OF CONTENTS

PART I

SIR ADRIAN LANDALE, LIGHT-KEEPER OF SCARTHEY

PART II

"MURTHERING MOLL THE SECOND"

xix

xx

CONTENTS

PART III

"CAPTAIN JACK," THE GOLD SMUGGLER

CHAP.   PAGE

XVII. Gold Smuggler and the Philosopher.................. 191

XVIII. "Love Gilds the Scene and Woman Guides the Plot".. 211

XIX. A Junior's Opinion................................. 224

XX. The Quick and the Dead........................... 244

XXI. The Dawn of an Eventful Day..................... 252

XXII. The Day: Morning................................ 262

XXIII. The Day: Noon.................................. 276

XXIV. The Night...................................... 294

XXV. The Fight for the Open.......................... 309

XXVI. The Three Colours............................... 323

XXVII. Under the Light Again: The Lady and the Cargo...... 335

XXVIII. The End of the Thread.......................... 349

XXIX. The Light Goes Out............................. 364

XXX. Husband and Wife............................... 375

XXXI. In Lancaster Castle............................. 382

XXXII. The One He Loved and the One Who Loved Him..... 393

XXXIII. Launched on the Great Wave.................... 406

XXXIV. The Gibbet on the Sands........................ 413

XXXV. The Light Rekindled............................. 430

PART I

SIR ADRIAN LANDALE, LIGHT-KEEPER
OF SCARTHEY

We all were sea-swallowed, though some cast again ;
And by that destiny to perform an act,
Whereof what's past is Prologue.

THE TEMPEST

THE LIGHT OF SCARTHEY

CHAPTER I

THE PEEL OF SCARTHEY

He makes a solitude and calls it peace.

BYRON.

ALONE in the south and seaward corner of the great bight on the Lancastrian coast—mournfully alone some say, gloriously alone to my thinking—rises in singular unexpected fashion the islet of Scarthey ; a green oasis secure on its white rocky seat amidst the breezy wilderness of sands and waters.

There is, in truth, more sand than water at most times round Scarthey. For miles northward the wet strand stretches its silent expanse, tawny at first, then merging into silver grey as in the dim distance it meets the shallow advance of briny ripple. Wet sand, brown and dull, with here and there a brighter trail as of some undecided river seeking an aimless way, spreads westward, deep inland, until stopped in a jagged line by bluffs that spring up abruptly in successions of white rocky steps and green terraces.

Turn you seaward, at low tide there lies sand again and shingle (albeit but a narrow beach, for here a depth of water sinks rapidly) laved with relentless obstinacy by long, furling, growling rollers that are grey at their sluggish base and emerald-lighted at their curvetting crest. Sand yet again to the south, towards the nearer coast line, for a mile or perhaps less, dotted, along an irregular path, with grey rocks that look as though the advance guard of a giant army had attempted to ford its insecure footing, had sunk into its treacherous shifting pits, and left their blanching skull-tops half emerging to record the disaster.

On the land side of the bight, far away beyond the grandly desolate, silent, yellow tract, a misty blue fringe on the horizon heralds the presence of the North Country ; whilst beyond the nearer beach a sprinkling of greenly ensconced homesteads cluster round some peaceful and paternal looking church tower. Near the salty shore a fishing village scatters its greystone cabins along the first terrace of the bluffs.

Outwards, ever changing in colour and temper roll and fret the grey waters of the Irish Sea, turbulent at times, but generally lenient enough to the brown-sailed ketches that break the regular sweep of the western horizon as they toil at the perpetual harvest of the deep.

Thus stands Scarthey. Although appearing as an island on the charts, at low tides it becomes accessible dry-foot from the land by a narrow causeway along the line of the white shallow reefs, which connect the main pile to the rocky steps and terraces of the coast. But woe betide man or beast that diverges many feet from the one secure path ! The sands of the great bay have already but too well earned their sinister reputation.

During the greater part of the day, however, Scarthey justifies its name—Skard- or Scarth-ey, the Knoll Island in the language of the old Scandinavian masters of the land.

In fair weather, or in foul, whether rising out of sunny sands when the ebbing waters have retired, or assailed on all sides by ramping breakers, Scarthey in its isolation, with its well-preserved ruins and its turret, from which for the last hundred years a light has been burning to warn the seafarer, has a comfortable look of security and privacy.

The low thick wall which in warlike times encompassed the bailey (now surrounding and sheltering a wide paddock and neat kitchen gardens) almost disappears under a growth of stunted, but sturdy trees ; dwarf alders and squat firs that shake their white-backed leaves, and swing their needle clusters, merrily if the breeze is mild, obstinately if the gale is rousing and seem to proclaim : "Here are we, well and secure. Ruffle and toss, and lash, O winds, the faithless waters, *we* shall ever cling to this hospitable footing, the only kindly soil amid this dreariness ; here you once wafted our seed ; here shall we live and perpetuate our life."

On the sea front of the bailey walls rise, sheer from the steep rock, the main body and the keep of the Peel. They are ruinous and shorn of their whilom great height, humbled more by the wilful destruction of man than by the decay of time.

But although from a distance the castle on the green island seems utterly dismantled, it is not, even now, all ruin. And, at the time when Sir Adrian Landale, of Pulwick, eighth baronet, adopted it as his residence, it was far from being such.

True, the greater portion of that mediæval building. half monastic, half military, exposed even then to the searching winds many bare and roofless chambers ; broken vaults filled with driven sands ; more than one spiral stair with hanging steps leading into space. But the massive square keep had been substantially restored. Although roofless its upper platform was as firm as when it was first built ; and in a corner, solidly ensconced, rose the more modern turret that sheltered the honest warning light.

The wide chambers of the two remaining floors, which in old warlike days were maintained bare and free, and lighted only by narrow watching loopholes on all sides, had been, for purposes of peaceful tenanncy, divided into sundry small apartments. New windows had been pierced into the enormous thickness of stone and cement ; the bare coldness of walls was also hidden under more home-like panellings. Close-fitting casements and solid doors insured peace within ; the wind in stormy hours might moan or rage outside this rocky pile, might hiss and shriek and tear its wings among the jagged ruins, bellow and thunder in and out of opened vaults, but it. might not rattle a window of the modern castellan's quarters or shake a latch of his chamber door.

There, for reasons understood then only by himself, had Sir Adrian elected, about the "year seven" of this century and in the prime of his age, to transplant his lares and penates.

The while, this Adrian Landale's ancestral home stood, in its placid and double pride of ancient and settled wealth, only some few miles away as the bee flies, in the midst of its noble park, slightly retired from the coast-line ; and from its upper casements could be descried by day the little green patch of Scarthey and the jagged outline of its ruins on the yellow or glimmering face of the great bay, and by night the light of its turret. And there he was still living, in some kind of happiness, in the "year fourteen," when, out of the eternal store of events, began to shape themselves the latter episodes of a life in which storm and peace followed each other as abruptly as in the very atmosphere that he then breathed.

For some eight years he had nested on that rock with no other companions but a dog, a very ancient housekeeper who cooked and washed for "t' young mester" as she obstinately persisted in calling the man whom she had once nursed upon her knee, and a singular sturdy foreign man (René L'Apôtre in the language of his own land, but known as Renny Potter to the land of his adoption) ; which latter was more than suspected of having escaped from the Liverpool Tower, at that time the lawful place of custody of French war prisoners.

His own voluntary captivity, however, had nothing really dismal for Adrian Landale. And the inhabited portions of Scarthey ruins had certainly nothing prison-like about them, nothing even that recalled the wilful contrition of a hermitage.

On the second floor of the tower (the first being allotted to the use, official and private, of the small household), clear of the surrounding walls and dismantled battlements, the rooms were laid out much as they might have been up at Pulwick Priory itself, yonder within the verdant grounds on the distant rise. His sleeping quarters plainly, though by no means ascetically furnished, opened into a large chamber, where the philosophic light-keeper spent the best part of his days. Here were broad and deep windows, one to the south with a wide view of the bay and the nearer coast, the other to the west where the open sea displayed her changeable moods. On three sides of this room, the high walls, from the white stone floor to the time-blackened beams that bore the ceiling, almost disappeared under the irregular rows of many thousand of volumes. Two wooden armchairs, bespeaking little aversion to an occasional guest, flanked the hearth.

The hearth is the chief refuge of the lone thinker; this was a cosy recess, deep cut in the mediæval stone and mortar; within which, on chilly days, a generous heap of sea-cast timber and dried turf shot forth dancing blue flames over a mound of white ash and glowing cinders; but which, in warmer times, when the casements were unlatched to let in with spring or summer breeze the cries of circling sea-fowls and the distant plash of billows, offered shelter to such green plants as the briny air would favour.

At the far end of the room rose in systematical clusters the pipes of a small organ, built against the walls where it bevelled off a corner. And in the middle of the otherwise bare apartment stood a broad and heavy table, giving support to a miscellaneous array of books, open or closed, sundry philosophical instruments, and papers in orderly disorder; some still in their virginal freshness, most, however, bearing marks of notemaking in various stages.

Here, in short, was the study and general keeping-room of the master of Scarthey, and here, for the greater part, daily sat Sir Adrian Landale, placidly reading, writing. or thinking at his table; or at his organ, lost in soaring melody; or yet, by the fireside, in his wooden armchair musing over the events of that strange world of thought he had made his own; whilst the aging black retriever with muzzle stretched between his paws slept his light, lazy sleep, ever and anon opening an eye of inquiry upon his master when the latter spoke aloud his thoughts (as solitary men are wont to do), and then with a deep, comfortable sigh, resuming dog-life dreams.

CHAPTER II

THE LIGHT-KEEPER

He who sits by the fire doth dream,
Doth dream that his heart is warm.
But when he awakes his heart is afraid for the bitter cold.
                                    Luteplayer's Song.

THE year 1814 was eventful in the annals of the political world. Little, however, of the world's din reached the little northern island ; and what there came of it was not willingly hearkened to. There was too much of wars past and present, too many rumours of wars future about it, for the ear of the recluse.

Late in the autumn of that red-letter year which brought a short respite of peace to war-ridden Europe—a fine, but rather tumultuous day round Scarthey—the light-keeper, having completed the morning's menial task in the light-turret (during a temporary absence of his factotum) sat, according to custom, at his long table, reading.

With head resting on his right hand whilst the left held a page ready to turn, he solaced himself, pending the appearance of the mid-day meal, with a few hundred lines of a favourite work—the didactic poems, I believe, of a certain Doctor Erasmus Darwin, on the analogies of the outer world.

There was quite as little of the ascetic in Adrian Landale's physical man as of the hermitage in his chosen abode.

With the exception of the hair, which he wore long and free, and of which the fair brown had begun to fade to silver-grey, the master of Scarthey was still the living presentment of the portrait which, even at that moment, presided among the assembly of canvas Landales in the gallery of Pulwick Priory. Eight years had passed over the model since the likeness had been fixed. But in their present repose, the features clear cut and pronounced, the kindly thoughtful eyes looked, if anything, younger than

6

their counterfeit ; indeed, almost incongruously young under the flow of fading hair.

Clean shaven, with hands of refinement, still fastidious, his long years of solitude notwithstanding, as to general neatness of attire, he might at any moment of the day have walked up the great stair of honour at Pulwick without by his appearance eliciting other remarks than that his clothes, in cut and colour, belonged to fashions now some years lapsed.

The high clock on the mantelshelf hummed and gurgled, and with much deliberation struck one. Only an instant later, lagging footsteps ascended the wooden, echoing stairs without, and the door was pushed open by the attendant, an old dame. She was very dingy as to garb, very wrinkled and feeble as to face, yet with a conscious achievement of respectability, both in appearance and manner, befitting her post as housekeeper to the " young master." The young master, be it stated at once, was at that time fast approaching the end of his second score years.

" Margery," said Adrian, rising to take the heavy tray from the knotted, trembling hands ; " you know that I will not allow you to carry those heavy things upstairs yourself." He raised his voice to sing-song pitch near the withered old ear. " I have already told you that when Renny is not at home, I can take my food in your kitchen."

Margery paused, after her wont, to wait till the sounds had filtered as far as her intellect, then proceeded to give a few angry headshakes.

" Eh ! Eh ! It would become Sir Adrian Landale o' Pulwick—Barrownite—to have 's meat i' the kitchen—it would that. Nay, nay, Mester Adrian, I'm none so old but I can do my day's work yet. Ah ! an' it 'ud be well if that gomerl, Renny Potter, 'ud do his'n. See here, now, Mester Adrian, nowt but a pint of wine left ; and it the last," pointing her withered finger, erratically as the palsy shook it, at a cut-glass decanter where a modicum of port wine sparkled richly under the facets. " And he not back yet, whatever mischief's agate wi' him, though he kens yo like your meat at one." And then circumstances obliged her to add : " He is landing now, but it's ower late i' the day."

"So—there, Margery," sang the "Squire," giving his old nurse affectionate little taps on the back. "Never fash yourself; tides cannot always fit in with dinner-hours, you know. And as for poor Renny, I believe after all you are as fond of him, at the bottom of your heart, as I am. Now what good fare have you got for me to-day?" bending from his great height to inspect the refection, "Ah—hum, excellent."

The old woman, after another pause for comprehension, retired battling with dignity against the obvious pleasure caused by her master's affectionate familiarity, and the latter sat down at a small table in front of the south window.

Through this deep, port-hole-like aperture he could, whilst disposing of his simple meal, watch the arrival of the yawl which did ferrying duty between Scarthey and the mainland. The sturdy little craft, heavily laden with packages, was being hauled up to its usual place of safety high on the shingle bank, under cover of a remnant of walling which in the days of the castle's strength had been a secure landing-place for the garrison's boats, but which now was almost filled by the cast-up sands and stone of the beach.

This was done under the superintendence of René, man of all work, and with the mechanical intermediary of rollers and capstan, by a small white horse shackled to a lever, and patiently grinding his steady rounds on the sand.

His preliminary task achieved, the man, after a few friendly smacks, set the beast free to trot back to his loose pasture: proceeding himself to unship his cargo.

Through the narrow frame of his window, the master, with eyes of approval, could see the servant dexterously load himself with a well-balanced pile of parcels, disappearing to return after intervals empty-handed, within the field of view, and select another burden, now heavier now more bulky.

In due course René came up and reported himself in person, and as he stopped on the threshold the dark doorway framed a not unstriking presentment; a young-looking man for his years (he was a trifle junior to his master), short and sturdy in build, on whose very broad shoulders sat a phenomenally fair head—the hair short, crisp, and curly, in colour like faded tow—and who, in smilingly respectful silence, gazed into the room out of small, light-blue eyes, brimful of alertness and intelligence, waiting to be addressed.

" Renny," said Adrian Landale, returning the glance with one of comfortable friendliness, "you will have to make your peace with Margery ; she considers that you neglect me shamefully. Why, you are actually twenty minutes late after three days' journeying, and perils by land and sea ! "

The Frenchman answered the pleasantry by a broader smile and a scrape.

"And, your honour," he said, "if what is now arriving on us had come half an hour sooner, I should have rested planted there " (with a jerk of the flaxen head towards the mainland), "turning my thumbs, till to-morrow, at the least. We shall have a grain, number one, soon."

He spoke English fluently, though with the guttural accent of Brittany, and an unconquerable tendency to translate his own jargon almost word for word.

In their daily intercourse master and man had come for many years past to eschew French almost entirely ; René had let it be understood that he considered his proficiency in the vernacular quite undeniable, and with characteristic readiness Sir Adrian had fallen in with the little vanity. In former days the dependant's form of address had been *Monseigneur* (considering, and shrewdly so, an English landowner to stand in that relation to a simple individual like himself); in later days "Monseigneur" having demurred at the appellation, "My lord," in his own tongue, the devoted servant had discovered "Your honour" as a happy substitute, and adhered to this discovery with satisfaction.

"Oh, we are going to have a squall, say you," interpreted the master, rising to inspect the weather-glass, which in truth had fallen deep with much suddenness. " More than a squall, I think ; this looks like a hurricane coming. But since you are safe home, all's well ; we are secure and sound here, and the fishing fleet are drawing in, I see," peering through the seaward window. "And now," continued Adrian, laying down his napkin, and brushing away a few crumbs from the folds of a faultless silk stock, "what have you for me there—and what news ? "

" News, your honour ! Oh, for that I have news this

time," said Mr. Renny Potter, with an emphatic nod, "but if your honour will permit, I shall say them last. I have brought the clothes and the linen, the wine, the brandy, and the books. Brandy and wine, your honour, I heard, out of the last prize brought into Liverpool, and a Nantes ship it was, too "—this in a pathetically philosophical tone. Then after a pause : " Also provisions and bulbs for the devil's pot, as Margery will call it. But there is no saying, your honour eats more when I have brought him back onions, eschalot, and *ail ;* now do I lie, your honour ? May I ?" added the speaker, and forthwith took his answer from his master's smile ; " may I respectfully see what the old one has kitchened for you when I was not there ? "

And Adrian Landale with some amusement watched the Frenchman rise from the package he was then uncording to examine the platters on the table and loudly sniff his disdain.

"Ah, ah, boiled escallops again. Perfectly—boiled cabbage seasoned with salt. Not a taste in the whole affair. Prison food—oh, yes, old woman ! Why, we nourished ourselves better in the Tower, when we could have meat at all. Ah, your honour," sighed the man returning to his talk ; "you others, English, are big and strong, but you waste great things in small enjoyment !"

"Oho, Renny," said the light-keeper squire, as he leant against the fireplace leisurely filling a long clay pipe, "this is one of your epigrams ; I must make a note of it anon ; but let me see now what you really have in those parcels of books—for books they are, are they not ? so carefully and neatly packed."

"Books," assented the man, undoing the final fold of paper. "Mr. Young in the High Street of Liverpool had the packets ready. He says you must have them all ; and all printed this year. What so many people can want to say, I for my count cannot comprehend. Three more parcels on the stairs, your honour. Mr. Young says you must have them. But it took two porters to carry them to the Preston diligence."

Not without eagerness did the recluse of Scarthey bend over and finger the unequal rows of volumes arrayed on the table, and with a smile of expectation examine the labels.

" The Corsair" and "Lara" he read aloud, lifting a small tome more daintily printed than the rest. " Lord Byron. What's this? Jane Austen, a novel. ' Roderick, last of the Goths.' Dear, dear," his smile fading into blankness ; "tiresome man, I never gave him orders for any such things."

René, battling with his second parcel, shrugged his shoulders.

" The librarian," he explained, " said that all the world read these books, and your honour must have them."

" Well, well," continued the hermit, " what else ? ' Jeremy Bentham,' a new work ; Ricardo, another book on economy ; Southey the Laureate, 'Life of Nelson.' Really, Mr. Young might have known that naval deeds have no joy for me, hardly more than for you, Renny," smiling grimly on his servant. " ' Edinburgh Review,' a London magazine for the last six months ; ' Rees's Cyclopædia,' vols. 24–27 ; Wordsworth, 'The Recluse.' Ah, old Willie Wordsworth ! Now I am anxious to see what he has to say on such a topic."

" Dear Willie Wordsworth," mused Sir Adrian, sitting down to turn over the pages of the " Excursion," " how widely have our lives drifted apart since those college days of ours, when we both believed in the coming millennium and the noble future of mankind—noble mankind ! "

He read a few lines and became absorbed, whilst René noiselessly busied himself in and out of the chamber. Presently he got up, book in hand, slowly walked to the north window, and passively gazed at the misty distance where rose the blue outline of the lake hills.

" So my old friend, almost forgotten," he murmured, "that is where you indite such worthy lines. It were enough to tempt me out into men's world again to think that there would be many readers and lovers abroad of these words of yours. So, that is what five and twenty years have done for you—what would you say to what they have done for me . . . . ? "

It was a long retrospect.

Sir Adrian was deeply immersed in thought when he became aware that his servant had come to a standstill, as if waiting for a return of attention. And in answer to the mute appeal he turned his head once more in René's direction.

"Your honour, everything is in its place," began the latter, with a fitting sense of his own method. "I have now to report that I saw your man of business in Lancaster, and he has attended to the matter of the brothers Shearman's boat that was lost. I saw the young men themselves this morning. They are as grateful to Sir Adrian as people in this country can express." This last with a certain superiority.

Sir Adrian received the announcement of the working of one of his usual bounties with a quiet smile of gratification.

"They also told me to say that they would bring the firewood and the turf to-morrow. But they won't be able to do that because we shall have dirty weather. Then they told me that when your honour wants fish they begged your honour to run up a white flag over the lantern—they thought that a beautiful idea—and they would bring some as soon as possible. I took on myself to assure them that I could catch what fish your honour requires; and the prawns, too . . . . but that is what they asked me to say."

"Well, well, and so you can," said the master, amused by the show of sub-acute jealousy. "What else?"

"The books of the man of business and the banker are on the table. I have also brought gazettes from Liverpool." Here the fellow's countenance brimmed with the sense of his news' importance. "I know your honour cares little for them. But this time I think you will read them. Peace, your honour, it is the peace! It is all explained in these journals—the 'Liverpool Mercury.'"

Renny lifted the folded sheets from the table and handed them with contained glee. "There has been peace these six months, and we never knew it. I read about it the whole way back from the town. The Emperor is shut up on an island—but not so willingly as your Honour, ah, no!—and there is an end of citizen Bonaparte. Peace, France and England no longer fighting, it is hard to believe—and our old kings are coming back, and everything to be again as in the old days."

Sir Adrian took the papers, not without eagerness, and glanced over the narrative of events, already months old, with all the surprise of one who, having wilfully shut himself out from the affairs of the world, ignored the series of disasters that had brought about the tyrant's downfall.

"As you say, my friend, it is almost incredible," he said, at length. Then thoughtfully : "And now you will be wanting to return home?" said he.

René, who had been scanning his master's face with high expectation, felt his heart leap as he thought he perceived a hidden tone of regret in the question.

He drew himself up to his short height, and with a very decided voice made answer straightway :

"I shall go away from your honour the day when your honour dismisses me. If your honour decides to live on this rock till my hour, or his, strikes—on this rock with him I remain. I am not conceited, I hope, but what, pray, will become of your honour here without me?"

There was force in this last remark, simply as it was pronounced. Through the mist of interlacing thoughts suggested by the word Peace ! (the end of the Revolution, that distant event which, nevertheless, had had such sweeping influence over the course of his whole life), it brought a faint smile to Sir Adrian's lips.

He took two steps forward and laid his hand familiarly on the man's broad shoulder, and, in a musing way, he said at intervals :

"Yes, yes, indeed, good Renny, what would become of me ?—what would have become of me ?—how long ago it seems !—without you? And yet it might have been as well if two skeletons, closely locked in embrace, blanched by the grinding of the waters and the greed of the crabs, now reposed somewhere deep in the sands of that Vilaine estuary. . . . . This score of years, she has had rest from the nightmare that men have made of life on God's beautiful earth. I have been through more of it, my good Renny."

René's brain was never equal to coping with his master's periodic fits of pessimism, though he well knew their first and ever-present cause. In a troubled way he looked about the room, so peaceful, so retired and studious ; and Sir Adrian understood.

"Yes, yes, you are right ; I have cut off the old life," he made answer to the unspoken expostulation, "and

that I can live in my own small world without foregoing
all my duties, I owe to you, my good friend ; but startling news like this brings back the past very livingly, dead
though it be—dead."

René hesitated ; he was pondering over the advisability
of disburdening himself of yet another strange item of
information he had in reserve ; but, as his master, rousing
himself with an effort as if to dismiss some haunting
thought, turned round again to the table, he decided that
the moment was not propitious.

"So you have seen to all these things," said Sir Adrian
wearily.   "Good ; I will look over them."

He touched the neat pile of books and papers, listlessly,
as he spoke, yet, instead of sitting down, remained as he
was, with eyes that had grown wondering, staring out
across the sea.

" Look," he said presently, in a low voice, and René
noticed a rare flush of colour rise to the thin cheeks.
"Look—is not this day just like—one we both remember
well . . . . ?   Listen, the wind is coming up as it did
then.   And look at yonder sky !"

And taking the man by the arm, he advanced slowly
with him towards the window.

In the west the heavens on the horizon had grown
threateningly dark ; but under the awe-inspiring slate-
coloured canopy of clouds there opened a broad archway
filled with primrose light—the luminous arch, well known
to seafarers, through which charge the furious south-
western squalls.   The rushing of the storm was already
visible in the distance over the grey waters, which having
been swayed for days by a steady Aquilon were now
lashed in flank by the sudden change of wind.

The two men looked out for a while in silence at the
spectacle of the coming storm.   In the servant's mind
ran various trivial thoughts bearing on the present—what
a lucky matter it was that he should have returned in
time ; only just in time it was ; from the angry look of
the outer world the island would now, for many a day
be besieged by seas impassable to such small craft as
alone could reach the reef.   Had he tarried but to the
next tide (and how sorely he had been tempted to remain
an hour more in the gatekeeper's lodge within sight and
hearing of buxom Moggie, Margery's granddaughter),

had he missed the tide, for days, maybe for weeks, would the master have had to watch and tend, alone, the beacon fire. But here he was, and all was well; and he had still the marvellous news to tell. Should he tell them now? No, the master was in one of his trances—lost far away in the past no doubt, that past that terminated on such a day as this. And Sir Adrian, with eyes fixed on the widening arch of yellow light, was looking inwards on the far-away distance of time.

Men, who have been snatched back to life from death in the deep, recall how, before seeming to yield the ghost, the picture of their whole existence passed in vivid light before the eye of their mind. Swift beyond the power of understanding are such revelations; in one flash the events of a good or an evil life leap before the seeing soul—moment of anguish intolerable or of sublime peace!

On such a boisterous day as this, some nineteen years before, by the sandy mouth of the river Vilaine, on the confines of Brittany and Vendée had Adrian Landale been drowned; under such a sky, and under the buffets of such an angry wind had he been recalled to life, and in the interval, he had seen the same pictures which now, coursing back many years in a few seconds, passed before his inward vision.

CHAPTER III

DAY DREAMS : A PHILOSOPHER'S FATE

Le beau temps de ma jeunesse . . . . quand j'étais si malheureux.

THE borderland between adolescence and manhood, in the life of men of refined aspirations and enthusiastic mettle, is oftener than not an unconsciously miserable period—one which more mature years recall as hollow, deceiving, bitterly unprofitable.

Yet there is always that about the memories of those far-off young days, their lofty dreams long since scattered, their virgin delights long since lost in the drudgery of earthly experience, which ever and anon seizes the heart unawares and fills it with that infinite weakness : that mourning for the dead and gone past, which yet is not regret.

In the high days of the Revolutionary movement across the water, Adrian Landale was a dreamy student living in one of those venerable Colleges on the Cam, the very atmosphere of which would seem sufficient to glorify the merits of past ages and past institutions.

Amidst such peaceful surroundings this eldest scion of an ancient, north-country race—which had produced many a hardy fighter, though never yet a thinker nor even a scholar—amid a society as prejudiced and narrow-minded as all privileged communities are bound to become, had nevertheless drifted resistlessly towards that unfathomable sea whither a love for the abstract beautiful, a yearning for super-earthly harmony and justice, must inevitably waft a young intelligence.

As the academical years glided over him, he accumu-lated much classical lore, withal read much latter-day philosophy and developed a fine youthful, theoretical love for the new humanitarianism. He dipped æsthetically into science, wherein he found a dim kind of help towards a more recondite appreciation of the beauties of nature. His was not a mind to delight in profound knowledge, but rather in " intellectual cream."

He solaced himself with essays that would have been voted brilliant had they dealt with things less extravagant than Universal Harmony and Fraternal Happiness ; with verses that all admitted to be highly polished and melodious, but something too mystical in meaning for the understanding of an every-day world ; with music, whereof he was conceded an interpreter of no mean order.

In fact the worship of his soul might have been said to be the Beautiful in the abstract—the Beautiful in all its manifestations which include Justice, Harmony, Truth, and Kindliness—the one indispensable element of his physical happiness, the Beautiful in the concrete.

This is saying that Adrian Landale, for all his array of definite accomplishments, which might have been a never-failing source of interest in an easy existence, was fitted in a singularly unfortunate manner for the life into which one sudden turn of fortune's wheel unexpectedly launched him.

During the short halcyon days of his opening independence, however, he was able to make himself the centre of such a world as he would have loved to live in. He was not, of course, generally popular, either at college or at home ; nor yet in town, except among that small set in whose midst he inevitably found his way wherever he went ; his inferiors in social status perhaps, these chosen friends of his ; but their lofty enthusiasms were both appreciative of and congenial to his own. Most of them, indeed, came in after-life to add their names to England's roll of intellectual fame, partly because they had that in them which Adrian loathed as unlovely—the instinct and will of strife, partly, it must be added, because they remained free in their circumstances to follow the lead of their nature. Which freedom was not allotted to him.

On one magnificent frosty afternoon, early in the year 1794, the London coach deposited Adrian Landale in front of the best hostelry in Lancaster, after more than a year's separation from his family.

This separation was not due to estrangement, but rather to the instigation of his own sire, Sir Thomas—a gentleman of the "fine old school"—who, exasperated by the, to him, incomprehensible and insupportable turn of mind developed by his heir (whom he loved well enough, notwithstanding, in his own way), had hoped, in good utilitarian fashion, that a prolonged period of contact with the world, lubricated by a plentiful supply of money, might shake his "big sawney of a son" out of his sickly-sentimental views; that it would show him that *gentlemen's* society—and, "by gad, ladies' too"—was not a thing to be shunned for the sake of "wild-haired poets, dirty firebrands, and such cattle."

The downright old baronet was even prepared, in an unformed sort of way, to see his successor that was to be return to the paternal hearth the richer for a few gentlemanly vices, provided he left his nonsense behind him.

As the great lumbering vehicle, upon the box seat of which sat the young traveller, lost in dreamy speculation according to his wont, drew clattering to a halt, he failed at first to notice the central figure in the midst of the usual expectant crowd of inn guests and inn retainers, called forward by the triumphant trumpeting which heralds the approach of the mail. There, however, stood the Squire of Pulwick, "Sir Tummus" himself, in portly and jovial importance.

The father's eyes, bright and piercing under his bushy white brows, had already detected his boy from a distance; and they twinkled as he took note, with all the pride of an author in his work, of the symmetry of limb and shoulders set forth by the youth's faultless attire—and the dress of men in the old years of the century was indeed calculated to display a figure to advantage—of the lightness and grace of his frame as he dismounted from his perch; in short of the increased manliness of his looks and bearing.

But a transient frown soon came to overshade Sir Thomas's ruddy content as he descried the deep flush (an old weakness) which mantled the young cheeks under the spur of unexpected recognition.

And when, later, the pair emerged from the inn after an hour's conversation over a bottle of burnt sherry—conversation which, upon the father's side, had borne, in truth, much the character of cross-examination—to mount the phaeton with which a pair of high-mettled bays were impatiently waiting the return homewards, there was a very definite look of mutual dissatisfaction to be read upon their countenances.

Whiling away the time in fitful constrained talk, parcelled out by long silences, they drove again through the gorgeous, frost-speckled scenery of rocky lands until the sheen of the great bay suddenly peered between two distant scars, proclaiming the approach to the Pulwick estate. The father then broke a long spell of muteness, and thus to his son, in his ringing country tones, as if pursuing aloud the tenor of his thoughts :

"Hark'ee, Master Adrian," said he, "that you are now a man of parts, as they say, I can quite see. You seem to have read a powerful lot of things that do not come our way up here. But let us understand each other. I cannot make head or tail of these far-fetched new-fangle notions you, somehow or other, have fallen in love with —your James Fox, your Wilberforce, your Adam Smith, they may be very fine fellows, but to my humble thinking they're but a pack of traitors to king and country, when all is said and done. All this does not suit an English gentleman. You think differently; or perhaps you do not care whether it does or not. I admit I can't hold forth as you do; nor string a lot of fine words together. I am only an old nincompoop compared to a clever young spark like you. But I request you to keep off these topics in the company I like to see round my table. They don't like Jacobins, you know, no more do I!"

"Nor do I," said Adrian fervently.

"Nor do you? Don't you, sir, don't you? Why, then what the devil have you been driving at?"

"I am afraid, sir, you do not understand my views."

"Well, never mind; I don't like 'em, that's short, and if you bring them out before your cousin, little Madame Savenaye, you will come off second best, my lad, great man as you are, and so I warn you!"

In tones as unconcerned as he could render them the young man sought to turn the intercourse to less personal topics, by inquiring further anent this unknown cousin whose very name was strange to him.

Sir Thomas, easily placable if easily roused, started willingly enough on a congenial topic. And thus Adrian conceived his first impression of that romantic being whose deeds have remained legendary in the French west country, and who was destined to exercise so strong an influence upon his own life.

"Who is she?" quoth the old gentleman, with evident zest. "Ay. All this is news to you, of course. Well! she *was* Cécile de Kermelégan. You know your mother's sister Mary Donoghue (murthering Moll, they called her on account of her killing eyes) married a M. de Kermelégan, a gentleman of Brittany. Madame de Savenaye is her daughter (first cousin of yours), that means that she has good old English blood in her veins and Irish to boot. She speaks English as well as you or I, her mother's teaching of course, but she is French all the same ; and, by gad, of the sort which would reconcile even an Englishman with the breed!"

Sir Thomas's eyes sparkled with enthusiasm ; his son examined him with grave wonder.

"The very sight of her, my boy, is enough to make a man's heart warm. Wait till you see her and she begins to talk of what the red-caps are doing over there—those friends of yours, who are putting in practice all your fine theories! And, bookworm as you are, I'll warrant she'll warm your sluggish blood for you. Ha! she's a rare little lady. She married last year the Count of Savenaye."

Adrian assumed a look of polite interest.

"Emigré, I presume?" he said, quietly.

"Emigré? No, sir. He is even now fighting the republican rapscallions, d—n them, and thrashing them, too, yonder in his country. She stuck by his side ; ay, like a good plucked one she did, until it became palpable that, if there was to be a son and heir to the name, she had better go and attend to its coming somewhere else, in peace. Ho, ho, ho! Well, England was the safest place, of course, and, for her, the natural one. She came and offered herself to us on the plea of relationship. I was rather taken aback at first, I own ; but, gad, boy, when I saw the woman, after hearing what she had had to go through to reach us at all, I sang another song. Well, she is a fine creature—finer than ever now that the progeny has been satisfactorily hatched ; a brace of girls instead of the son and heir, after all! Two of them ; no less. Ho, ho, ho! And she was furious, the pretty dear! However, you'll soon see for yourself. You will see a woman, sir, who has loaded and fired cannon with her own hands, when the last man to serve it had been shot. Ay, and more than that, my lad—she's brained a hulking sans-culotte that was about to pin her servant to the floor. The lad has told me so himself, and I daresay he can tell you more if you care to practise your French with master René L'Apôtre, that's the fellow! A woman who sticks to her lord and master in mud and powder-smoke until there is precious little time to spare, when she makes straight for a strange land, in a fishing-smack, with no other protector than a peasant; and now, with an imp of a black-eyed infant to her breast (Sally Mearson's got the other; you remember Sally, your own nurse's daughter?), looks like a chit of seventeen. That's what you'll see, sir. And when she sails downstairs for dinner, dressed up, powdered and high-heeled, she might be a princess, a queen who has never felt a crumpled roseleaf in her life. Gad! I'm getting poetical, I declare."

In this strain did the Squire, guiding his horses with strong, dexterous hand, expatiate to his son; the crisp air rushing past them, making their faces glow with the tingling blood until, burning the ground, they dashed up the avenue that leads to the white mansion of Pulwick, and halted amidst a cloud of steam before its Palladian portico.

What happened to Adrian the moment after happens, as a rule, only once in a man's lifetime.

Through the opening portals the guest, whose condensed biography the Squire had been imparting to his son (all unconsciously eliciting thereby more repulsion than admiration in the breast of that fastidious young misogynist), appeared herself to welcome the return of her host.

Adrian, as he retired a pace to let his father ascend the steps, first caught a glimpse of a miraculously small and arched foot, clad in pink silk, and, looking suddenly up, met fully the flash of great dark eyes, set in a small white face, more brilliant in their immense blackness than even the glinting icicles pendant over the lintel that now shot back the sun's sinking glory.

The spell was of the kind that the reason of man can never sanction, and yet that have been ever and will be while man is. This youth, virgin of heart, dreamy of

head who had drifted to his twentieth year, all unscathed
by passion or desire, because he had never met aught in
flesh and blood answering to his unconscious ideal, was
struck to the depth of his soul by the presence of one, as
unlike this same ideal as any living creature could be ;
struck with fantastic suddenness, and in that all-encompassing manner which seizes the innermost fibres of the
being.

It was a pang of pain, but a revelation of glory.

He stood for some moments, with paling cheeks and
hotly-beating heart, gazing back into the wondrous eyes.
She, yielding her cheek carelessly to the Squire's hearty
kiss, examined the new-comer curiously the while :

"Why—how now, tut, tut, what's this?" thundered
the father, who, following the direction of her eyes,
wheeled round suddenly to discover his son's strange
bearing, "Have you lost all the manners as well as the
notions of a gentleman, these last two years? Speak to
Madame de Savenaye, sir !—Cécile, this is my son ; pray
forgive him, my dear ; the fellow's shyness before ladies
is inconceivable. It makes a perfect fool of him, as you
see."

But Madame de Savenaye's finer wits had already perceived something different from the ordinary display of
English shyness in the young man, whose eyes remained
fixed on her face with an intentness that savoured in no
way, of awkwardness. She now broke the spell with a
broader smile and a word of greeting.

"You are surprised," said she in tripping words, tinged
with a distinct foreign intonation, "to see a strange face
here, Mr. Adrian—or, shall I say cousin ? for that is the
style I should adopt in my Brittany. Yes, you see in me
a poor foreign cousin, fleeing for protection to your noble
country. How do you do, my cousin ?"

She extended a slender, white hand, one rosy nail of
which, bending low, Adrian gravely kissed.

"*Mais, comment donc !*" exclaimed the lady, "my dear
uncle did you chide your son just now? Why, but these
are Versailles manners—so gallant, so courtly !"

And she gave the boy's fingers, as they lingered under
hers, first a discreet little pressure, and then a swift flip
aside.

"Ah ! how cold you are !" she exclaimed ; and then,

laughing, added sweetly: "Cold hands, warm heart, of course."

And with rapping heels she turned into the great hall and into the drawing-room whither the two men—the father all chuckles, and the son still struck with wonder —followed her.

She was standing by the hearth holding each foot alternately to the great logs flaming on the tiles, ever and anon looking over her shoulder at Adrian, who had advanced closer, without self-consciousness, but still in silence.

" Now, cousin," she remarked gaily, "there is room for you here, big as you are, to warm yourself. You must be cold. I know already all about your family, and I must know all about you, too! I am very curious, I find them all such good, kind, handsome people here, and I am told to expect in you something quite different from any of them. Now, where does the difference come in? You are as tall as your father, but in face— no, I believe it is your pretty sisters you are like in face."

Here the Squire interrupted with his loud laugh, and, clapping his hand on his stalwart son's head:

·'You have just hit it, Cécile, it's here the difference lies. Adrian, I really believe, is a little mistake of Dame Nature; his brain was meant for a girl and was tacked on to that big body by accident, ho, ho, ho! He is quite lady-like in his accomplishments—loves music, and plays, by gad, better than our organist. Writes poetry, too. I found some devilish queer things on his writing-table once, which were not *all* Latin verses, though he would fain I thought so. And as for deportment, Madame Cécile, why there is more propriety, in that hobbedehoy, at least, more blushing in him, than in all the bread-and-butter misses in the county!"

Adrian said nothing ; but, when not turned towards the ground, his gaze still sought the Countess, who now returned the look with a ripening smile open to any interpretation.

"Surely," she remarked, glancing then at the elder for an instant with some archness, "surely you English gentlemen, who have so much propriety, would not rather . . . . . there was young Mr. Bradbury, we heard talked

of yesterday, whom every farmer with a red-cheeked lass
of his own—"

"No, no!" hastily interrupted the baronet, with a
blush himself, while Adrian's cheek in spite of the recent
indictment preserved its smooth pallor—in truth, the boy,
lost in his first love-dream, had not understood the allusion. "No, I don't want a Landale to be a blackguard,
you know, but—" And the father, unable to split this
ethical hair, to logical satisfaction, stopped and entered
another channel of grumbling vituperation, whilst the
Countess, very much amused by her private thoughts,
gave a little rippling laugh, and resumed her indulgent
contemplation of the accused.

"What a pity, now, school-boy Rupert is not the
eldest; there would be a country gentleman for you!
Whereas, this successor that is to be of mine is a man of
books and a philosopher. Forsooth, a first-class bookworm; by gad, I believe the first of our race! And he
might make a name for himself, I've been told, among
that lot, though the pack o' nonsense he treats us to at
times cannot, I'm thinking, really go down even among
those college fuzzle-heads. But I am confounded if that
chap will ever be of any use as a landlord whenever he
steps into my shoes. He hates a gun, and takes more
pleasure—what was it he said last time he was here?—
oh, yes, more pleasure in watching a bird dart in the blue
than bringing it down, be it never so neat a shot. Ho,
ho! did ye ever hear such a thing? And though he can
sit a horse—I will say that for him (I should like to see a
Landale that could not!)—I have seen this big boy of
mine positively sicken, ay! and scandalise the hunt by
riding away from the death. Moreover, I believe that,
when I am gone, he will always let off any poaching
scoundrel on the plea that the vermin only take for their
necessity what we preserve for sport."

The little foreign lady, smiling no longer, eyed her big
cousin with wondering looks.

"Strange, indeed," she remarked, "that a man should
fail to appreciate the boon of man's existence, the strength
and freedom to dominate, to be up and doing, to *live* in
fact. How I should long to be a man myself, if I ever
allowed myself to long for anything; but I am a woman,
as you see," she added, rising to the full height of her

exquisite figure, "and must submit to woman's lot—and that is just now to the point, for I must leave you to go and see to the wants of that *mioche* of mine which I hear whining upstairs. But I do not believe my uncle's account of you is a complete picture after all, cousin Adrian. I shall get it out of you anon, catechise you in my own way, and, if needs be, convert you to a proper sense of the glorious privileges of your sex."

And she ran out of the room.

"Well, my lad," said Sir Thomas, that evening, when the ladies had left the two men to their decanter, "I thought my Frenchwoman would wake you up, but, by George, I hardly expected she would knock you all of a heap so quick. Hey! you're winged, Adrian, winged, or this is not port."

"I cannot say, sir," answered Adrian, musing.

The old man caught up the unsatisfactory reply in an exasperated burlesque of mimicry : "I cannot say, sir— you cannot say? Pooh, pooh, there is no shame in being in love with her. We all are more or less ; pass the bottle. As for you, since you clapped eyes on her you have been like a man in the moon, not a word to throw to a dog, no eyes, no ears but for your own thoughts, so long as madam is not there. Enter madam, you're alive again, by George, and pretty lively, too ! Gad, I never thought I'd ever see *you* do the lady's man, all in your own queer way, of course ; but, hang it all, she seems to like it, the little minx ! Ay, and if she has plenty of smiles for the old man she's ready to give her earnest to you—I saw her, I saw her. But don't you forget she's married, sir, very much married, too. She don't forget it either, I can tell you, though you may think she does. Now, what sort of game is she making of you? What were you talking about in the picture gallery for an hour before dinner, eh?"

"To say the truth," answered the son, simply, "it was about myself almost the whole time."

"And she flattered you finely, I'll be bound, of course," said his elder, with a knowing look. "Oh, these women, these women !"

"On the contrary, sir, she thinks even less of me than you do. That woman has the soul of a savage ; we have not one thought in common."

The father burst into a loud laugh. "A pretty savage to

look at, anyhow ; a well-polished one in the bargain, ho, ho, ho ! Well, well, I must make up my mind, I suppose, that my eldest son is a lunatic in love with a savage."

Adrian remained silent for a while, toying with his glass, his young brow contracted under a painful frown. At length, checking a sigh, he answered with deliberation :

"Since it is so palpable to others, I suppose it must be love, as you say. I had thought hitherto that love of which people talk so much was a feeling of sweetness. What I feel in this lady's presence is much more kin to anguish ; for all that, as you have noticed, I appear to live only when she is nigh."

The father looked at his son and gaped. The latter went on, after another pause :

"I suppose it is so, and may as well own it to myself and to you, though nothing can come of it, good or bad. She is married, and she is your guest ; and even if any thought concerning me could enter her heart, the merest show of love on my part would be an insult to her and treason to you. But trust me, I shall now be on my guard, since my behaviour has already appeared strange."

"Tut, tut," said the Baronet, turning to his wine in some dudgeon, his rubicund face clouding as he looked with disfavour at this strange heir of his, who could not even fall in love like the rest of his race. "What are you talking about ? Come, get out of that and see what the little lady's about, and let me hear no more of this. She'll not compromise herself with a zany like you, anyhow, that I'll warrant."

But Adrian with all the earnestness of his nature and his very young fears was strenuously resolved to watch himself narrowly in his intercourse with his too fascinating relative ; little recking how infinitesimal is the power of a man's free-will upon the conduct of his life.

The next morning found the little Countess in the highest spirits. Particularly good news had arrived from her land with the early courier. True, the news were more than ten days old, but she had that insuperable buoyancy of hopefulness which attends active and healthy natures.

The Breton peasants (she explained to the company round the breakfast table), headed by their lords (among whom was her own *Seigneur et Maître*) had again crushed

the swarms of ragged brigands that called themselves
soldiers. From all accounts there was no hope for the
latter, their atrocities had been such that the whole land,
from Normandy to Guyenne, was now in arms against
them.

And in Paris, the hot pit whence had issued the storm
of foulness that blasted the fair kingdom of France after
laying low the hallowed heads of a good king and a
beautiful queen, in Paris, leaders and led were now chopping each other's heads off, *à qui mieux mieux.* "Those
thinkers, those lofty patriots, *hein, beau cousin,* for whom,
it seems, you have an admiration," commented the lady,
interrupting her account to sip her cup of cream and
chocolate, with a little finger daintily cocked, and shoot
a mocking shaft at the young philosopher from the depth
of her black eyes.

"Like demented wolves they are destroying each other
—Pray the God of Justice," quoted she from her husband's
letter, "that it may only last; in a few months, then,
there will be none of them left, and the people, relieved
from this rule of blood, will all clamour for the true order
of things, and the poor country may again know peace
and happiness. Meanwhile, all has yet to be won, by
much devotion and self-sacrifice in the cause of God and
King; and afterwards will come the reward ! . . .

"And the revenge," added Madame de Savenaye, with
a little, fierce laugh, folding the sanguine budget of news.
"Oh! they must leave us a few for revenge! How we
shall make the hounds smart when the King returns to
his own! And then for pleasures and for life again.
And we may yet meet at the mansion of Savenaye, in
Paris," she went on gaily, "my good uncle and fair
cousins, for the King cannot fail to recall his faithful sup-
porter. And there will be feasts and balls. And there,
maybe, we shall be able to repay in part some of your
kindness and hospitality. And you, cousin Adrian, you
will have to take me through pavanne and gavotte and
minuet; and I shall be proud of my northern cavalier.
What! not know how one dances the gavotte? *Fi donc!*
what ignorance! I shall have to teach you. Your hand,
monsieur," slipping the missive from the seat of war into
her fair bosom. "La! not that way; with a *grace,* if
you please," making a profound curtsey. "Ah, still that

cold hand ; your great English heart must be a very fur-
nace. Come, point your right foot—so. And look round
at your partner with—what shall I say—*admiration
sérieuse !*"

That she saw admiration, serious enough in all conscience in Adrian's eyes, there was little doubt. With
sombre heart he failed not to mark every point of this
all-human grace, but to him goddess-like beauty, the
triumph and glory of youth. The coy, dainty poise of
the adorable foot—pointed *so*—and treading the ground
with the softness of a kitten at play ; the maddening
curve of her waist, which a sacque, depending from an
exquisite nape, partly concealed, only to enhance its
lithe suppleness ; the divinely young throat and bust ;
and above all the dazzling black rays from eyes alternately mocking, fierce or caressing.

Well might his hand be cold with all his young untried
blood, biting at his heart, singing in his head. Why did
God place such creatures on His earth to take all savour
from aught else under the sun ?

"Fair cousin, fair cousin, though I said serious admiration, I did not mean you to look as if you were taking me
to a funeral. You are supposed to be enjoying yourself,
you know !"

The youth struggled with a ghastly smile ; and the
father laughed outright. But Madame de Savenaye
checked herself into gravity once more.

"Alas ! *Nous n'en sommes pas encore là*," she said,
and relinquished her adorer's hand. "We have still to
fight for it. . . . . Oh ! that I were free to be up and
doing !"

The impatient exclamation was wrung out of her, apparently, by the appearance of two nurses, each bearing
an infant in long, white robes for the mother's inspection ;
a preliminary to the daily outing.

The elder of these matrons was Adrian's own old nurse
who, much occupied with her new duties of attendant
to Madame de Savenaye and one of her babies, now beheld her foster-son again for the first time since his return.

"Eh—but you've grown a gradely mon, Mester
Adrian !" she cried, in her long-drawn Lancastrian,
dandling her bundle energetically from side to side in
the excess of her admiration, and added with a laugh of

tender delight : " Eh, but you're my own lad still, as how 'tis ! " when, blushing, the young man crossed the room and stooped to kiss her, glancing shyly the while at the white bundle in her arms.

" Well, and how are the little ones ? " quoth Madame de Savenaye, swinging her dainty person up to the group and halting by beaming Sally—the second nurse, who proudly held forth her charge—merely to lay a finger lightly on the infant's little cheek.

" Ah, my good Sally, your child does you credit !—Now Margery, when you have done embracing that fine young man, perhaps you will give me my child, *hein ?* "

Both the nurses blushed ; Margery at the soft impeachment as she delivered over the minute burden : her daughter in honest indignation at the insulting want of interest shown for her foster-babe.

" No, I was not made to play with puppets like you, mademoiselle," said the comtesse, addressing herself to the unconscious little being as she took it in her arms, but belying her words by the grace and instinctive maternal expertness with which she handled and soothed the infant. " Yes, you can go, Sarah—*au revoir*, Mademoiselle Madeleine. Fie the little wretch, what faces she pulls ! And you, Margery, you need not wait either ; I shall keep this creature for a while. Poor little one ! " sang the mother, walking up and down, and patting the small back with her jewelled hand as she held the wee thing against her shoulder, " indeed I shall have soon to leave you——"

" What's this—what's this ? " exclaimed the master of the house with sudden sharpness. He had been surveying the scene from the hearthrug, chuckling in benevolent amusement at little Madam's ways.

Yes, it was her intention to return to her place by the side of her lord, she explained, halting in her walk to face him gravely ; she had come to that resolution. No doubt her uncle would take the children under his care until better times—those good times that were so fast approaching. Buxom Sally could manage them both—and to spare, too !

Adrian felt his heart contract at the unexpected announcement ; a look of dismay overspread Sir Thomas's face.

"Why—what? what nonsense, child!" cried he again in rueful tones. "*You*, return to that place now . . . . what good do you think you could do—eh?" But here recollecting himself, he hesitated and started upon a more plausible line of expostulation. "Pooh, pooh! You can't leave the little ones, your husband does not ask you to come back and leave them, does he? In any case," with assumed authority, "I shall not let you go."

She looked up with a smile.

"Would *you* allow your friends to continue fighting alone for all you love, because you happened to be in safe and pleasant circumstances yourself?" she asked. Then she added ingenuously: "I have heard you say of one that was strong of will and staunch to his purpose, that he was a regular Briton. I thought that flattering: I am a Briton, of Brittany, you know, myself, uncle: would you have *me* be a worthless Briton? As to what a woman can do there—ah, you have no idea what it means for all these poor peasants of ours to see their lords remain among them, sharing their hardship in defence of their cause. Concerning the children," kissing the one she held and gazing into its face with wistful look, "they can better afford to do without me than my husband and our men. A strong woman to tend them till we come back, is all that is wanted, since a good relative is willing to give them shelter. René cannot be long in returning now, with the last news. Indeed, M. de Savenaye says that he will only keep him a few days longer, and, according to the tidings he brings must I fix the date for my departure."

Sir Thomas, with an inarticulate growl, relapsed into silence; and she resumed her walk with bent head, lost in thought, up and down the great room, out of the pale winter sunshine into the shadow, and back again, to the tune of "Malbrook s'en va t'en guerre," which she hummed beneath her breath, while the baby's foolish little head, in its white cap from which protruded one tiny straight wisp of brown hair, with its beady, unseeing black eyes and its round mouth dribbling peacefully, bobbed over her shoulder as she went.

Adrian stood in silence too, following her with his eyes, while the picture, so sweet to see, so strange to one who knew all that was brewing in the young mother's head and heart, stamped itself upon his brain.

At the door, at length, she halted a moment, and looked at them both.

"Yes, my friends," she said, and her eyes shot flame ; "I must go soon." The baby bobbed its head against her cheek as if in affirmative ; then the great door closed upon the pair.

CHAPTER IV

DAY DREAMS: A FAIR EMISSARY

Many guests had been convened to the hospitable board of Pulwick upon the evening which followed Adrian's return home; and as, besides the fact that the fame of the French lady had spread enthusiasm in most of the male breasts of the district and anxious curiosity in gentler bosoms, there was a natural neighbourly desire to criticise the young heir of the house after his year's absence, the county had responded in a body to the invitation.

It was a goodly company therefore that was assembled in the great withdrawing rooms, when the Countess herself came tripping down the shallow oaken stairs, and found Adrian waiting for her in the hall.

He glanced up as she descended towards him to cover her with an ardent look and feast his eyes despairingly on her beauty; and she halted a moment to return his gaze with a light but meaning air of chiding.

"Cousin!" she said, "you have very singular manners for one supposed to be so shy with ladies. Do you know that if my husband were here to notice them you might be taken to task?"

Adrian ran up the steps to meet her. The man in him was growing apace with the growth of a man's passion, and by the boldness of his answer belying all his recent wise resolutions, he now astonished himself even more than her.

"You are going back to him," he said, with halting voice. "All is well—for him; perhaps for you. For us, who remain behind there is nothing left but the bitterness of regret—and envy."

Then in silence they descended together.

As they were crossing the hall there entered suddenly to them, stumbling as he went, René, the young Breton

32

retainer, whom the lord of Savenaye had appointed as squire to his lady upon her travels, and who, since her establishment at Pulwick, had been sent to carry news and money back to Brittany.

No sooner had the boy—for such he was, though in intelligence and blind devotion beyond his years—passed into the light, than on his haggard countenance was read news of disastrous import.   Recent tears had blurred his sunburnt cheek, and the hand that tore the hat from his head at the unexpected sight of his mistress, partly in instinctive humility, partly, it seemed, to conceal some papers he held against his breast, twitched with nervous anguish.

"René!" cried the Countess, eagerly, in French. "What hast thou brought? Sweet Jesu! Bad news— bad news? Give!"

For an instant the courier looked around like a hunted animal seeking a retreat, and then up at her in dumb pleading; but she stamped her foot and held him to the spot by the imperiousness of her eye.

"Give, I tell thee," she repeated; and, striking the hat away, snatched the papers from his hand.   "Dost thou think I cannot bear ill news—My husband?"

She drew nearer to a candelabra, and the little white hands impatiently broke the seals and shook the sheets asunder.

Sir Thomas, attracted by his favourite's raised tones and uneasy at her non-appearance, opened the drawing-room door and came forward anxiously, whilst his assembled guests, among whom a sense that something of importance was passing had rapidly spread, now gathered curiously about the open doorway.

The Countess read on, unnoticing, with compressed lips and knitted brows—those brows that looked so black on the fair skin, under the powdered hair.

"My husband! ah, I knew it, my André . . . . the common fate of the loyal!" A sigh lifted the fair young bosom, but she showed no other sign of weakness.

Indeed those who watched this unexpected scene were struck by the contrast between the bearing of this young, almost girlish creature, who, holding the written sheets with firm hands to the light, read their terrible contents with dry eyes, and that of the man who had sunk, kneel-

3

ing, at her feet, all undone, to have had the bringing of the news.

The silence was profound, save for the crackling of the pages as she turned them over, and an occasional long-drawn sob from the messenger.

When she came to the end the young widow—for such she was now—remained some moments absorbed in thought, absently refolding the letter into its original neatness. Then her eyes fell on René's prostrate figure and she stooped to lay a kind hand for an instant on his shoulder.

"Bear up, my good René," she said. At her voice and touch he dragged his limbs together and stood humbly before her.

"We must be brave," she went on; "your master's task is done—ours, yours and mine, is not."

He lifted his bloodshot eyes to her with the gaze of a faithful dog in distress, scraped an uncouth bow and abruptly turned away, brushing the tears from his cheek with his sleeve, and hurrying, to relieve his choking grief in solitude. She stood a while, again absorbed in her own reflection, and of those who would have rushed to speak gentle words to her, and uphold her with tender hands, had she wept or swooned, there was none who dared approach this grief that gave no sign.

In a short time, however, she seemed to recollect herself and awaken to the consciousness of the many watching eyes.

"Good uncle," she said, going up to the old man and kissing his cheek, after sweeping the assembled company with dark, thoughtful gaze. "Here are news that I should have expected sooner—but that I would not entertain the thought. It has come upon us at last, the fate of the others . . . . André has paid his debt to the king, like many hundreds of true people before—though none better. He has now his reward. I glory in his noble death," she said with a gleam of exaltation in her eyes, then added after a pause, between clenched teeth, almost in a whisper :

"And my sister too—she too is with him—but I will tell you of it later; they are at rest now."

Jovial Sir Thomas, greatly discomposed and fairly at a loss how to deal with the stricken woman, who was so unlike any womankind he had ever yet come across, patted her hand in silence, placed it within his arm and quietly led her into the drawing-room, rolling, as he did so, uneasy eyes upon his guests. But she followed the current of her thoughts as her little feet kept pace beside him.

"That is bad—but worse—the worst of all, the cause of God and king is again crushed; everything to begin afresh. But, for the present, we "—here she looked round the room, and her eyes rested an instant upon a group of young men, who were surveying her from a corner with mingled admiration and awe—" we, that is René and I, have work to do in this country before we return. For you will keep us a little longer?" she added with an attempt at a smile.

"Will I keep you a little longer?" exclaimed the squire hotly, "will I ever let you go, now!"

She shook her head at him, with something of her natural archness. Then, turning to make a grave curtsey to the circle of ladies around her :

"I and my misfortune," she said, "have kept your company and your dinner waiting, I hardly know how long. No doubt, in their kindness they will forgive me."

And accepting again her uncle's arm which, delighted at the solution of the present difficulty, and nodding to Adrian to start the other guests, he hastened to offer her, she preceded the rest into the dining-hall with her usual alert bearing.

The behaviour of the Countess of Savenaye, had affected the various spectators in various ways. The male sex, to a man, extolled her fortitude ; the ladies, however, condemned such unfeminine strength of mind, while the more charitable prophesied that she would pay dearly for this unnatural repression. And the whispered remark of one of the prettier and younger damsels, that the loss of a husband did not seem to crush her, at any rate, met, on the whole, with covert approval.

As for Adrian, who shall describe the tumult of his soul—the regret, the hungering over her in her sorrow, the wild unbidden hopes and his shame of them? Careful of what his burning eyes might reveal, he hardly dared raise them from the ground ; and yet to keep them long from her face was an utter impossibility. The whispered comments of the young men behind him, their admiration, and astonishment drove him to desperation. And the high-nosed dowager, whom it was his privilege to escort to his father's table, arose from it convinced that Sir Thomas's heir had lost in his travels the few poor wits he ever possessed.

The dinner that evening was without doubt the most dismal meal the neighbourhood had ever sat down to at the hospitable board of Pulwick, past funeral refections not excepted. The host, quite taken up with his little foreign relative, had words only for her; and these, indeed, consisted merely in fruitless attempts to induce her to partake largely of every course—removes, relieves, side-dishes, joints, as their separate turn came round. Long spells of silence fell upon him meantime, which he emphasised by lugubriously clearing his throat. Except for the pretty courtesy with which she would answer him, she remained lost in her own thoughts—ever and anon consulting the letter which lay beside her to fall again, it seemed, into a deeper muse; but never a tear glinted between her black lashes.

More than once Adrian from his distant end of the table, met her eyes, fixed on him for a moment, and the look, so full of mysterious meanings made his heart beat in anguish, expecting he knew not what.

Among the rest of the assembly, part deference to a calamity so stoutly borne, part amazement at such strange ways, part discomfort at their positions as feasters in the midst of mourning, had reduced conversation to the merest pretence. The ladies were glad enough when the time came for them to withdraw; nor did most of the men view with reluctance a moment which would send the decanters gliding freely over the mahogany, and relieve them from this unwonted restraint.

Madame de Savenaye had, however, other interests in store for these latter.

She rose with the rest of the ladies, but halted at the door, and laying her hand upon her uncle's arm, said an earnest word in his ear, in obedience to which he bundled out his daughters, as they hung back politely, closed the door upon the last skirt, and reconducted the Countess to the head of the table, scratching his chin in some perplexity, but ready to humour her slightest whim.

She stood at her former place and looked for a moment in silence from one to another of the faces turned with different expressions of astonishment and anticipation towards her—ruddy faces most of them, young, or old, handsome or homely, the honest English stamp upon each ; and distinct from them all, Adrian's pallid, thoughtful features and his ardent eyes.

Upon him her gaze rested the longest. Then with a little wave of her hand she prayed them to be seated, and waited to begin her say until the wine had passed round.

"Gentlemen," then quoth she, " with my good uncle's permission I shall read you the letter which I have this night received, so that English gentlemen may learn how those who are faithful to their God and their King are being dealt with in my country. This letter is from Monsieur de Puisaye, one of the most active partisans of the Royal cause, a connection of the ancient house of Savenaye. And he begins by telling me of the unexpected reverses sustained by our men so close upon their successes at Chateau-Gonthier, successes that had raised our loyal hopes so high. 'The most crushing defeat,' he writes, 'has taken place near the town of Savenaye itself, on your own estate, and your historic house is now, alas ! in ruins . . . . During the last obstinate fight your husband had been wounded, but after performing prodigies of valour—such as, it was hoped or trusted, the king should in time hear of—he escaped from the hands of his enemies. For many weeks with a few hundred followers he held the fields in the Marais, but he was at last hemmed in and captured by one of the monster Thureau's *Colonnes Infernales*, those hellish legions with an account of whose deeds,' so says this gallant gentleman our friend, 'I will not defile my pen, but whose boasts are like those of Attila the Hun, and who in their malice have invented obscene tortures worthy of Iroquois savages for all who fall into their clutches, be they men, women, or children. . . . . But, by Heaven's mercy, dear Madame,' says M. de Puisaye to me, ' your noble husband was too weak to afford sport to those demons, and so he has escaped torment. He was hanged with all speed indeed, for fear he might die first of his toils and his wounds, and so defeat them at the last.' "

A rustling murmur of horror and indignation went round the table; but the little woman faced the audience proudly.

"He died," she said, "as beseems a brave man. But this is not all. I had a sister, she was very fair—like me some people said, in looks—she used to be the merry one at home in the days of peace," she gave a little smile, far more piteous than tears would be—"She chose to remain among her people when they were fighting, to help the wounded, the sick." Here Madame de Savenaye paused a moment and put down the letter from which she had been reading; for the first time since she had begun to speak she grew pale; knitting her black brows and with downcast eyes she went on : "Monsieur de Puisaye says he asks my pardon humbly on his knees for writing such tidings to me, bereaved as I am of all I hold dear, but 'it is meet,' he says, 'that the civilised world should know the deeds these followers of *liberty* and *enlightenment* have wrought upon gallant men and highborn ladies,' and I hold that he says well."

She flashed once more her black gaze round upon the men, who with heads all turned towards her and forgetting their wine, hung upon her words. "It is right that I should know, and you too ! It is meet that such deeds should be made known to the world : my sister was taken by these men, but less fortunate than my husband she had life enough left for torture—she too is dead now ; M. de Puisaye adds : Thank God ! And that is all that I can say too—Thank God !"

There was a dead silence in the room as she ceased speaking, broken at last, here and there, along the table by exclamations and groans and a deep execration from Sir Thomas, which was echoed deep-mouthed by his guests.

Adrian himself, the pacific, the philosopher, with both arms, stretched out on the table, clenched his hands, and set his teeth and gazed into space with murderous looks.

Then the clear young voice went on again :

"You, who have honoured mothers and wives of your own, and have young sweethearts, or sisters or daughters—you English gentlemen who love to see justice, how long will you allow such things to be done while you have arms to strike ? We are not beaten yet ; there are French hearts still left that will be up and doing so long as they have a drop of blood to shed.   Our gallant Bretons and Vendéens are uniting once more, our émigrés are collecting, but we want aid, brave English friends, we want arms, money, soldiers.   My task lies to my hand ; the sacred legacy of my dead I have accepted ; is there any of you here who will help the widow to maintain the fight ? "

She had risen to her feet ; the blood glowed on her cheek as she concluded her appeal ; a thousand stars danced in her eyes.

Old men and young they leapt up, with a roar ; pressing round her, pouring forth acclamations, asseverations and oaths—Would they help her ?   By God—they would die for her—Never had the old rafters of Pulwick rung to such enthusiasm.

And when with proud smiles and crimsoned face she withdraws at last from so much ardour, the door has scarcely fallen behind her before Sir Thomas proposes her health in a bellow, that trembles upon tears :

"Gentlemen, this lady's courage is such as might put most men's strength to shame.   Here is, gentlemen, to Madame de Savenaye ! "

And she, halting on the stairs for a moment, to still her high-beating heart, before she lay her babe against it, hears the toast honoured with three times three.

When the Lancastrian ladies had succeeded at length in collecting and carrying off such among the hiccupping husbands, and maudlin sons, who were able to move, Sir Thomas re-entering the hall, after speeding the last departing chariot, and prudently leaning upon his tall son —for though he had a seasoned head the night's potations had been deep and fiery—was startled well-nigh into soberness, at the sight of his niece waiting for him at the foot of the stairs.

"Why, Cis, my love, we thought you had been in bed this long while ! why—where have you been then since you ran away from the dining-room ? By George ! " chuckling, " the fellows were mad to get another glimpse of you ! "

His bloodshot eye hung over her fondly.   There was not a trace of fatigue upon that delicate, pretty face.

"I wanted to think—I have much to think on now.   I

have had to read and ponder upon my instructions here,"
—tapping her teeth with the letter, she still carried,
"Good uncle, I would speak with you—yes, even now,"
quick to notice Adrian's slight frown of disapproval (poor
fellow, he was sober enough at any rate !), "there is no
time like the present. I have my work to do, and I shall
not rest to-night, till I have planned it in my head."

Surely the brilliancy of those eyes was feverish ; the
little hands she laid upon them to draw them into the dim-
lit library were hot as fire.

"Why, yes, my pretty," quoth the good uncle, stifling
a portentous yawn, and striving to look wondrous wise,
"Adrian, she wants to consult me, sir, hic !"

He fell into an armchair as he spoke, and she sank on
her knees beside him, the firelight playing upon her eager
face, while Adrian, in the shadow, watched.

"Do you think," she asked of the old man, eagerly,
"that these gentlemen, who spoke so kindly to me a
few hours ago, will be as much in earnest in the morning?"

"Why d—n them ! if they go back on their word, I'll call
them out !" thundered Sir Thomas, in a great rage all of
a sudden. She surveyed him inquiringly, and shot a swift
keen glance from the placid, bulky figure in the chair, to
Adrian pale and erect, behind it, then rose to her feet
and stood a few paces off, as it were pondering.

"What is now required of me—I have been thinking it
well over," she said at last, "can hardly be achieved by a
woman alone. And yet, with proper help and support,
I think I could do more than any man by himself. There
is that in a woman's entreaties which will win, when a
man may fail. But I must have a knight at my side ; a
protector, at the same time as a faithful servant. These
are not the times to stand on conventional scruples. Do
you think, among these gentlemen, any could be found
with sufficient enthusiasm, for the Royal cause, here
represented by me, to attend, and support me through all
the fatigues, the endless errands, the interviews—ay, also
the rebuffs, the ridicule at times, perhaps the danger of
the conjuration, which must be set on foot in this country
—to do all that, without hope of other reward than the
consciousness of helping a good cause, and—and the
gratitude of one, who may have nothing else to give?"

She stopped with a little nervous laugh : "No, it is

absurd! no man, on reflection would enter into such a service unless it were for his own country."

As the last words fell from her lips, she suddenly turned to Adrian and met his earnest gaze.

"Or for his kindred," said the young man, coming up to her with grave simplicity, "if his kindred required it."

A gleam of satisfaction passed across her face. The father, who had caught her meaning—sharp enough, as some men can be in their cups—nodded his head with great vigour.

"Yes, why should you think first of strangers," he grumbled, "when you have your own blood, to stand by you—blood is thicker than water, ain't it? Am I too old, or is he too young, to wait on you—hey, madam?"

She extended her hand, allowing it to linger in Adrian's grasp, whilst she laid the other tenderly on the old man's shoulder.

"My good uncle! my kind cousin! Have I the choice already between two such cavaliers? I am fortunate indeed in my misfortune. In other circumstances to decide would be difficult between two men, each so good; but," she added, after a moment's hesitation, and looking at Adrian in a manner that made the young man's heart beat thickly, "in this case it is obvious I must have some one whom I need not fear to direct."

"Ay, ay," muttered the baronet, "I'd go with you, my darling, to the world's end; but there's that young philosopher of mine breaking his heart for you. And when all's said and done, it's the young fellow that'll be the most use to you, I reckon. Ay, you've chosen already, I'll be bound. The gouty old man had best stop at home. Ho, ho, ho! You've the luck, Adrian; more luck than you deserve."

"It is I who have more luck than I deserve," answered Madame de Savenaye, smiling upon her young knight as, taking heart of grace, he stooped to seal the treaty upon her hand. "To say the truth, I had hoped for this, yet hardly dared to allow myself to count upon it. And really, uncle, you give your own son to my cause?—and you, cousin, you are willing to work for me? I am indeed strengthened at the outset of my undertaking. I shall pray that you may never have cause to regret your chivalrous goodness."

She dropped Adrian's hand with a faint pressure, and moved sighing towards the door.

" Do you wonder that I have no tears, cousin ? " she said, a little wistfully; " they must gather in my heart till I have time to sit down and shed them."

Thus it was that a letter penned by this unknown M. de Puisaye from some hidden fastness in the Bocage of Brittany came to divert the course of Adrian Landale's existence into a channel where neither he, nor any of those who knew him, would ever have dreamed to see it drift.

CHAPTER V

THE AWAKENING

Oh, what hadst thou to do with cruel Death,
Who wast so full of life, or Death with thee?
                                        LONGFELLOW.

SIR ADRIAN LANDALE, in his sea-girt fastness, still absorbed in dreams of bygone days, loosed his grasp of faithful René's shoulder and fell to pacing the chamber with sombre mien ; while René, to whom these fits of abstraction in his master were not unfamiliar, but yet to his superstitious peasant soul, eerie and awe-inspiring visitations, slipped unnoticed from his presence.

The light-keeper sate down by his lonely hearth and buried his gaze in the glowing wood-embers, over which, with each fitful thundering rush of wind round the chimney, fluttered little eddies of silvery ash.

So, that long strife was over, which had wrought such havoc to the world, had shaped so dismally the course of his own life ! The monster of selfish ambition, the tyrannic, insatiable conqueror whose very existence had so long made peaceable pursuits unprofitable to mankind, the final outcome of that Revolution that, at the starting point, had boded so nobly for human welfare—he was at last laid low, and all the misery of the protracted struggle now belonged to the annals of the past.

It was all over—but the waste ! The waste of life and happiness, far and wide away among innocent and uninterested beings, the waste remained.

And, looking back on it, the most bitter portion of his own wrecked life was the short time he had yet thought happy ; three months, spent as knight-errant.

How far they seemed, far as irrevocable youth, those days when, in the wake of that love-compelling emissary, he moved from intrigue to intrigue among the émigrés in

43

London, and their English sympathisers, to bustling yet secret activity in seafaring parts !

The mechanical instrument directed by the ingenious mind of Cécile de Savenaye ; the discreet minister who, for all his young years, secured the help of some important political sympathiser one day, scoured the country for arms and clothing, powder and *assignats* another ; who treated with smuggling captains and chartered vessels that were to run the gauntlet on the Norman and Breton coast, and supply the means of war to struggling and undaunted loyalists. All this relentless work, little suited, on the whole, to an Englishman, and in a cause the rights of which he himself had, up to then, refused to admit, was then repaid a hundredfold by a look of gratitude, of pleasure even, a few sweet moments of his lady's company, before being sent hence again upon some fresh enterprise.

Ah, how he loved her ! He, the youth on the threshold of manhood, who had never known passion before, how he loved this young widowed mother who used him as a man to deal for her with men, yet so loftily treated him as a boy when she dealt with him herself. And if he loved her in the earlier period of his thraldom, when scarce would he see her one hour in the twenty-four, to what all-encompassing fervour did the bootless passion rise when, the day of departure having dawned and sunk, he found himself on board the privateer, sailing away with her towards unknown warlike ventures, her knight to protect her, her servant to obey !

On all these things mused the recluse of Scarthey, sinking deeper and deeper into the past : the spell of haunting recollection closing on him as he sat by his hearthside, whilst the increasing fury of the gale toiled and troubled outside fighting the impassable walls of his tower.

Could it have been possible that she—the only woman that had ever existed for him, the love for whom had so distorted his mind from its natural sympathies, had killed in him the spring of youth and the savour of life—never really learnt to love him in return till the last ?

And yet there was a woman's soul in that delicious woman's body—it showed itself at least once, though until that supreme moment of union and parting, it seemed as if a man's mind alone governed it, becoming

sterner, more unbendable, as hardships and difficulties
multiplied.

In the melancholy phantasm passing before his mind's
eye, of a period of unprecedented bloodshed and savagery,
when on the one side Chouans, Vendéens, and such
guerillas of which Madame de Savenaye was the moving
spirit, and on the other the *colonnes infernales* of the
revolutionary leaders, vied with each other in ferocity and
cunning, she stood ever foremost, ever the central point
of thought, with a vividness that almost a score of years
had failed to dim.

When the mood was upon him, he could unfold the
roll of that story buried now in the lonely graves of the
many, or in the fickle memories of the few, but upon his
soul printed in letters of fire and blood—to endure for
ever.

Round this goddess of his young and only love clustered
the sole impressions of the outer world that had ever
stirred his heart : the grandeur of the ocean, of the storm,
the glory of sunrise over a dishevelled sea, the ineffable
melancholy of twilight rising from an unknown strand ;
then the solemn coldness of moonlight watches, the scent
of the burnt land under the fierce sun, when all nature
was hushed save the dreamy buzz of insect-life : the green
coolness of underwood or forest, the unutterable harmony
of the sighing breeze, and the song of wild birds during
the long patient ambushes of partisan war ; the taste of
bread in hunger, of the stream in the fever of thirst, of
approaching sleep in exhaustion—and, mixed with these,
the acrid emotions of fight and carnage, anguish of suspense, savage exultation of victory—all the doings of a
life which he, bred to intellectual pleasures and high
moral ideas, would have deemed a nightmare, but which,
lived as it was in the atmosphere of his longing and devotion, yet held for him a strange and pungent joy : a
cup of cruel memories, yet one to be lingered over luxuriously till the savour of each cherished drop of bitterness
be gathered to the uttermost.

Now, in the brightness of the embers, between the
fitful flames of crumbling wood, spreads before his eyes
the dreary strand near Quiberon, immense in the gathering
darkness of a boisterous evening. Well hidden under the
stone table of a Druidical men-hir glows a small camp-fire

sedulously kept alive by René for the service of The Lady.
She, wrapped up in a coarse peasant-cloak, pensively
gazes into the cheerless smoke and holds her worn and
muddy boots to the smouldering wood in the vain hope
of warmth.

And Adrian stands silently behind her, brooding on
many things—on the vicissitudes of that desultory war
which has left them not a roof whereunder they can lay
their heads, during which the little English contingent
has melted from them one by one ; on the critical action
of the morrow when the republican columns, now hasten-
ing to oppose the landing of the great royalist expedition to Quiberon (that supreme effort upon which all their
hopes centre) must be surprised and cut off at whatever
cost ; on the mighty doings to follow, which are to complete the result of the recent sea fight off Ushant and
crown their devoted toil with victory at last. . . .

And through his thoughts he watches the pretty foot, in
its hideous disguise of patched, worn, ill-fitting leather,
and he sees it as on the first day of their meeting, in its
gleaming slipper and dainty silken stocking.

Now and then an owl-cry, repeated from point to point,
tells of unremitting guard, but for which, in the vast
silence, none could suspect that a thousand men and
more are lying stretched upon the plain all around them,
fireless, well-nigh without food, yet patiently waiting for
the morrow when their chiefs shall lead them to death ;
nor that, in a closer circle, within call, are some fifty *gars*,
remnant of the indomitable "Savenaye band," and tacitly
sworn bodyguard to The Lady who came back from ease
and safety over seas to share their peril.

No sound besides, but the wind as it whistles and moans
over the heath—and the two are together in the mist
which comes closing in upon them as if to shroud them
from all the rest, for even René has crept away, to sleep
perhaps.

She turns at last towards him, her small face in the
dying light of this sullen evening, how wan and weather-
beaten !

"Pensive, as usual, cousin ?" she says in English, and
extends her hand, browned and scratched, that was once
so exquisite, and she smiles, the smile of a dauntless soul
from a weary body.

Poor little hands, poor little feet, so cold, so battered, so ill-used! He, who would have warmed them in his bosom, given his heart for them to tread upon, breaks down now, for the first time; and falling on his knees covers the cold fingers with kisses, and then lays his lips against those pitiful torn boots.

But she spurns him from her—even from her feet:

"Shame on you!" she says angrily; and adds, more gently, yet with some contempt: "*Enfant, va !*—is this the time for such follies?"

And, suddenly recalled to honour and grim actuality, he realises with dismay his breach of trust—he, who in their earlier days in London had called out that sprightly little émigré merely for the vulgar flippancy (aimed in compliment, too, at the grave aide-de-camp), "that the fate of the late Count weighed somewhat lightly upon Madame de Savenaye;" he, who had struck that too literary countryman of his own across the face—ay, and shot him in the shoulder, all in the secret early dawn of the day they left England—for daring to remark within his hearing: "By George, the handsome Frenchwoman and her cousin may be a little less than kin, but they are a little more than kind."

But yet, as the rage of love contending in his heart with self-reproach, he rises to his feet in shame, she gives him her hand once more, and in a different voice:

"Courage, cousin," says she, "perhaps some day we may both have our reward. But will not my knight continue to fight for my bidding, even without hope of such?"

Pondering on this enigmatic sentence he leaves her to her rest.

When next he finds himself by her side the anticipated action has begun; and it is to be the last day that those beautiful burning eyes shall see the glory of the rising sun.

The Chouans are fighting like demons, extended in long skirmishing lines, picking out the cluster of gunners, making right deadly use of their English powder; imperceptibly but unflinchingly closing their scattered groups until the signal comes and with ringing cries: "*Notre Dame d'Auray !*" and "*Vive le roi!*" they charge, undismayed by odds, the serried ranks of the Republicans.

She, from the top of the druidical stone, watches the progress of the day. Her red, parted mouth twitches as she follows the efforts of the men. Behind her, the *gars* of Savenaye, grasping with angry clutch, some a new musket, others an ancient straightened scythe, gaze fiercely on the scene from under their broad felts. Now and then a flight of republican bullets hum about their ears, and they look anxiously to Their Lady, but that fearless head never bends.

Then the moment arrives, and with a fervent, " God be with you, brave people," she hurls, by a stirring gesture, the last reserve on to the fight.

And now he finds himself in the midst of the furious medley, striking mechanically, his soul away behind on that stone, with her. Presently, as the frenzy waxes wilder, he is conscious that victory is not with them, but that they are pressed back and encompassed, and that for each blue coat cast down amidst the yells and oaths, two more seem to come out of the rain and smoke ; whilst the bare feet and wooden shoes and the long hair of his peasants are seen in ever-lessening ranks. And, in time, they find themselves thrown back to the men-hir ; she is there, still calm but ghastly white, a pistol in each hand. Around her, through the wet smoke, rise and fall with sickening thuds the clubbed muskets of three or four men, and then one by one these sink to the ground too. With a wailing groan like a man in a nightmare, he sees the inevitable end and rushes to place his body before hers. A bullet shatters his sword-blade ; now none are left around them but the begrimed and sinister faces of their enemies.

As they stand prisoners, and unheeding the hideous clamour, he, with despair thinking of her inevitable fate at the hands of such victors, and scarcely daring to look at her, suddenly sees *that* in her eyes which fills his soul to overflowing.

"All is lost," she whispers, "and I shall never repay you for all you have done, cousin ! "

The words are uttered falteringly, almost plaintively.

"We are not long now for this world, friend," she adds more firmly. " Give me your forgiveness."

How often has Adrian heard this dead voice during the strange vicissitudes of these long, long years ! And, hearing it whisper in the vivid world of his brain, how often has he not passionately longed that he also had been able to yield his poor spark of life on the last day of her existence.

For the usual fate of Chouan prisoners swiftly overtakes the surviving leaders of the Savenaye "band of brigands," as that doughty knot of loyalists was termed by their arch-enemy, Thureau.

A long journey towards the nearest town, in an open cart, under the pitiless rain, amidst a crowd of evil-smelling, blaspheming, wounded republicans, who, when a more cruel jolt than usual awakens their wounds, curse the woman in words that should have drawn avenging bolts from heaven. She sits silent, lofty, tearless; but her eyes, when they are not lost in the grey distance, ever wistfully seek his face.

The day is drawing to a close; they reach their goal, a miserable, grey, draggled town at the mouth of the Vilaine, and are roughly brought before the arbiter of their lives—Thureau himself, the monstrous excrescence of the times, who, like Marat and Carrier, sees nothing in the new freedom but a free opening for the lowest instincts of ferocity.

And before this monstrous beast, bedizened in his general's frippery, in a reeking tavern-room, stand the noble lady of Savenaye and the young heir of Pulwick.

The ruffian's voice rings with laughter as he gazes on the silent youthful pair.

"Aha, what have we here; a couple of drowned rats? or have we trapped you at last, the ci-devant Savenaye and her *godam* from England? I ought really to send you as a present to the Convention, but I am too soft-hearted, you see, my pigeons; and so, to save time and make sure, we will marry you to-day."

One of the officers whispers some words in his ear, which Thureau, suddenly growing purple with rage, denies with a foul oath and an emphatic thump of his huge fist on the table.

"Hoche has forbidden it, has he? Hoche does not command here. Hoche has not had to hunt down the brigands these last two years. Dead the beast, dead the venom, I say. And here is the order," scribbling hurriedly on a page torn from a pocket-book. "It shall not be said that I have had the bitch of Savenaye in my

4

hands and trusted her on the road again. Hoche has forbidden it! Call the cantineer and hop: the marriage and quick—the soup waits."

Unable to understand the hidden meaning of the order, Adrian looks at his lady askance, to find that, with eyes closed upon the sight of the grinning faces, she is whispering prayers and fervently crossing herself. When she turns to him again her face is almost serene.

"They are going to drown us together; that is their republican marriage of aristocrats," she says in soft English. "I had feared worse. Thank heaven there is no time now for worse. We shall be firm to the last, shall we not, cousin?"

There is a pathetic smile on her worn weather-stained face, as the cantineer and a corporal enter with ropes and proceed to pinion the prisoners.

But, as they are marched away once more under the slanting rain, are forced into a worn-out boat and lashed face to face, her fortitude melts apace.

"There, my turtle-doves," sneers the truculent corporal, "another kindness of the general. The Nantes way is back to back, but he thought it would amuse you to see each other's grimaces."

On the strand resounds the muffled roll of wet drums, announcing the execution of national justice; with one blow of an axe the craft is scuttled; a push from a gaff sends it spinning on the swift swollen waters into the estuary. Adrian's lips are on her forehead, but she lifts her face; her eyes now are haggard.

"Adrian," she sobs, "you have forgiven me? I have your death on my soul! Oh, Adrian, ... I could have loved you!"

Helpless and palsied by the merciless ropes, she tries passionately to reach her little mouth to his. A stream of fire rushes through his brain—maddening frenzy of regret, furious clinging to escaping life!—Their lips have met, but the sinking craft is full, and, with a sudden lurch, falls beneath the eddies. . . . . A last roll of the drums, and the pinioned bodies of these lovers of a few seconds are silently swirling under the waters of the Vilaine.

And now the end of this poor life has come—with heart-breaking sorrow of mind and struggle of body, overpowering horror at the writhings of torture in the limbs

lashed against his—and vainly he strives to force his last
breath into her hard-clenched mouth.

Such was the end of Adrian Landale, aged twenty—the
end that should have been—The pity that it was not permitted!

After the pangs of unwelcome death, the misery of unwelcome return to life. Oh, René, René, too faithful
follower; thou and the other true men who, heedless of
danger, hanging on the flanks of the victorious enemy,
never ceased to watch your lady from afar. You would
have saved her, could courage and faithfulness and cunning have availed! But, since she was dead, René,
would thou hadst left us to drift on to the endless sea!
How often have I cursed thee, good friend, who staked
thy life in the angry bore to snatch two spent bodies from
its merciless tossing. It was not to be endured, said you,
that the remains of the Lady of Savenaye should drift
away unheeded, to be devoured by the beasts of the sea!
They now repose in sacred ground, and I live on! Oh,
hadst thou but reached us a minute later!—ah, God, or a
minute earlier!

Rarely had Sir Adrian's haunting visions of the past
assumed such lurid reality. Rising in torment from the
hearth to pace unceasingly the length and breadth of the
restful, studious room, so closely secure from the outer
turmoil of heaven and earth, he is once more back in
the unknown sea-cave, in front of the angry breakers.
Slowly, agonisingly, he is recalled to life through wheeling
spaces of pain and confusion, only that his bruised and
smarting eyes may see the actual proof of his own
desolateness—a small, stark figure wrapped in coarse
sailcloth, which now two or three ragged, long-haired
men are silently lifting between them.

He wonders, at first, vaguely, why the tears course
down those wild, dark faces; and then, as vainly he
struggles to speak, and is gently held down by some
unknown hand, the little white bundle is gone, and he
knows that *there* was the pitiful relict of his love—that he
will never see her again!

Sir Adrian halted in front of his seaward window, staring
at the driven rain, which bounded and plashed and spread

in minute torrents down the glass, obscuring the already darkening vision of furious sea and sky.

The dog, that for some moments had shown an anxious restlessness in singular concert with his master's, now rose at last to sniff beneath the door. No sound penetrated the roar of the blast; but the old retriever's uneasiness, his sharp, warning bark at length recalled Sir Adrian's wandering thoughts to the present. And, walking up to the door, he opened it.

Oh, God! Had the sea given up its dead?

Sir Adrian staggered back, fell on his knees and clapped his hands together with an agonised cry:

"Cécile . . . . !"

CHAPTER VI

THE WHEEL OF TIME

And to his eye
There was but one beloved face on earth,
And that was shining on him.
BYRON.

UPON the threshold she stood, looking in upon him with dark, luminous eyes ; round the small wet face tangles of raven hair fell limp and streaming ; dark raiments clung to her form, diapered with sand and sea-foam, sodden with the moisture that dripped from them to the floor ; under the hem of her skirt one foot peered forth, shoeless in its mud-stained stocking.

Sir Adrian stared up at her, his brain whirling with a frenzy of joy, gripped in its soaring ecstasy by terror of the incomprehensible.

On the wings of the storm and the wind had she come to him, his love—across the awful barriers that divide life and death ? Had his longings and the clamour of his desolate soul reached her, after all these years, in the far-beyond, and was her sweet ghost here to bid him cease from them and let her lie at rest ? Or, yet, had she come to call him from the weary world that their souls might meet and be one at last ? . . . . Then let her but lay her lips against his, as once in the bitterness of death, that his sorely-tried heart may break with the exquisite pang and he, too, may die upon their kiss.

Swift such thoughts were tossing in the turmoil of his mind when the vision smiled . . . . a young, rosy, living smile ; and then reason, memory, the wonder of her coming, the haunting of her grave went from him ; possessed by one single rapturous certainty he started up and gathered the wet form into his strong arms—yet gently as if he feared to crush the vision into void—and showered kisses on the wet face.

53

Not death—but life! A beating heart beneath his; a lithe young form under his hand, warm lips to his kisses, ... Merciful Heaven! Were, then, these twenty years all an evil, fevered dream, and was he awake at length?

She turned her face from him after a moment and put her hand against his breast to push him from her; and as she did so the wonder in the lovely, familiar eyes turned to merriment, and the lips parted into laughter.

The sound of the girlish laughter broke the spell. Sir Adrian stepped back, and passed his hand across his forehead with a dazed look.

And still she laughed on.

"Why, cousin Landale," she said, at length between the peals; "I came to throw myself upon your kindness for shelter from the storm, but—I had not anticipated such a reception."

The voice, clear and sweet, with just a tinge of outlandish intonation, struck Adrian to the heart.

"I have not heard," he faltered, "that voice for twenty years . . . . !"

Then, coming up to her, he took her hands; and, drawing her towards the firelight, scanned her features with eager, hungering eyes.

"Do not think me mad, child," he said at last; "tell me who you are—what has brought you here? Ah, God, at such a moment! Who is it," he pursued, as if to himself, whilst still she smiled mockingly and answered not; "who is it, then, since Cécile de Savenaye is dead—and I am not dreaming—nor in fever? No vision either—this is flesh and blood."

"Yes, indeed," mocked the girl with another burst of merriment; "flesh and blood, please, and very living! Why, cousin Landale, you that knew Cécile de Savenaye so well have you forgotten two babes that were born at your own house of Pulwick? I believe, 'tis true, I have somewhat altered since you saw me last."

And again the old room echoed to the unwonted sound of a girl's laughter.

Now was the hallucination clearing; but the reality evoked a new and almost as poignant tenderness. Cécile —phantom of a life-time's love, reborn in the flesh, young as on the last day of her earthly existence, coming back into his life again, even the same as she had left it! A

second wonder, almost as sweet as the first! He clung
to it as one clings to the presence of a dream, and, joy
unspeakable, the dream did not melt away, but remained,
smiling, beautiful, unchanged.

"Cécile's daughter . . . ." he murmured: "Cécile's
self again; but she was not so tall, I think," and drew
trembling, reverent hands from her head to her straight
young shoulders. And then he started, crying in a
changed voice:

"How wet and cold you are! Come closer to the fire
—sit you into this chair, here, in the warmth."

He piled up the hearth with faggots till the flames
roared again. She dropped into the proffered chair with
a little shiver; now that he recalled her to it, she was
wet and cold too.

He surveyed her with gathering concern.

"My child," he began, and hesitated, continuing, after
a short pause of musing—for the thought struck him as
strange—"I may call you so, I suppose; I that am nearly
old enough to be your father; my mind was so unhinged
by your sudden appearance, by the wonderful resemblance, that I have neglected all my duties as host. You
will suffer from this—what shall we do to comfort you?
Here, Jem, good dog! Call René!"

The old retriever who, concluding that the visitor was
welcome, had returned to his doze, here gathered his
stiff limbs together, hobbled out through the doorway to
give two or three yelping barks at some point on the
stairs, and then crawl back to his cosy corner by the
hearth.

The girl laughed again. It was all odd, new, exciting.
Adrian looked down at her. Cécile, too, had had a merry
heart, even through peril and misfortune.

And now there were hasty steps upon the stairs, creaking above the outer tumult of sea and wind; and, in accordance with the long-established custom of summoning
him, René appeared upon the threshold, holding a pair of
candles.

At the sight of the figure sitting by the fire he halted, as
if rooted to the ground, and threw up his hands, each still
clutching its candle.

"Mademoiselle . . . . !" he ejaculated. "Mademoiselle here!" Then, rapidly recovering his quick wits, he

deposited his burden of light upon the table, advanced towards the lady, made an uncouth but profound bow, and turned to his master.

"And this, your honour," he remarked, oracularly, and in his usual manner of literal adaptation, "was also part of the news I had for your honour from my last journey; but, my faith, I did not know how to take myself to it, as your honour was so much occupied with old times this evening. But I had seen Mademoiselle at the castle, as Mademoiselle can tell you herself. And if your honour," he added, with a look of astonishment, "will have the goodness to say how it is possible that Mademoiselle managed to arrive here on our isle, in this weather of all the devils—reverence speaking, and I humbly beg the pardon of Mademoiselle for using such words—when it was with pain I could land myself, and that before the storm—I should be grateful to your honour. For I avow I cannot comprehend it at all. Ah, your honour!" continued René, with an altered tone, "'tis a strange thing, this!"

The looks of master and man crossed suddenly, and in the frank blue eyes of the Breton peasant, Sir Adrian read a reflex of his own thoughts.

"Yes," he said, more in answer to the look than to the exclamation, "yes, it is a strange thing, friend."

"And his Honour cannot read the riddle any more than you yourself, René," quoth Mademoiselle de Save-naye, composedly from her corner; "and, as for me, I can give no explanations until I am a little warmer."

"Why, truly," exclaimed Sir Adrian, striking his forehead, "we are a very pair of dolts! Hurry, Renny, hurry, call up Margery, and bid her bring some hot drink —tea, broth, or what she has—and blankets. Stay! first fetch my furred cloak; quick, René, every moment is precious!"

With all the agitation of a rarely excited man Sir Adrian threw more wood on the fire, hunted for a cushion to place beneath her feet, and then, seizing the cloak from René's hands, he helped her to rise, and wrapped its ample folds round her as carefully as if she were too precious almost to be touched.

Thus enveloped she sank back in the great arm-chair with a cosy, deliberate, kitten-like movement, and stretched out her feet to the blaze, laying the little shoe-less one upon Jem's grey muzzle.

Adrian knelt beside her, and began gently to chafe it with both hands. And, as he knelt, silence fell between them, and the storm howled out yonder ; he heard her give a little sigh—that sigh which would escape from Cécile's weariness in moments of rest, which had once been so familiar and so pathetic a sound in his ear. And once more the power of the past came over him ; again he was upon the heath near Quiberon, and Cécile was sitting by him and seeking warmth by the secret fire.

"Oh, my darling," he murmured, "your poor little feet were so cold ; and yet you would not let me gather them to my breast." And, stooping slowly, he kissed the pretty foot in its torn, stained stocking with a passion he had not yet shown.

The girl looked on with an odd little smile. It was a novel experience, to inspire—even vicariously—such feel-ings as these ; and there was something not unpleasant in the sense of the power which had brought this strange handsome man prostrate before her—a maidenly tremor, too, in the sensation of those burning lips upon her feet.

He raised his eyes suddenly, with the old expectation of a rebuff ; and then, at the sight of the youthful, curious face above him, betook himself to sighing too ; and, laying the little foot back tenderly upon the cushion, he rose.

From between the huge fur collar which all but covered her head, the black eyes followed him as alertly as a bird's ; intercepting the soft melancholy of his gaze, she smiled at him, mischievous, confident, and uncommuni-cative, and snuggled deeper into the fur.

Leaning against the high mantel-board, he remained silent, brooding over her ; the clock ticked off solemnly the fleeting moments of the wonderful hour ; and ever and anon the dog drew a long breath of comfort and stretched out his gaunt limbs more luxuriously to the heat. After a while Sir Adrian spoke.

"He who has hospitality to dispense," said he, smiling down at her mutinous grace, "should never ask whence or how the guest came to his hearth . . . . and yet—"

She made a slight movement of laziness, but volunteered nothing ; and he continued, his look becoming more wist-ful as he spoke :

"Your having reached this rock, during such weather, is startling enough ; it is God's providence that there should live those in these ruins who are able to give you succour. But that you should come in to me at the moment you did—" He halted before the bold inquisitive brightness of her eyes. "Some day perhaps you will let me explain," he went on, embarrassed. "Indeed I must have seemed the most absolute madman, to you. But he who thinks he sees one returned from death in angry waters, may be pardoned some display of emotion."

The girl sat up briskly and shook herself as if in protest against the sadness of his smile and look.

"I rise indeed from a watery grave," she said lightly, "or at least from what should have been my grave, had I had my deserts for my foolishness ; as it has turned out I do not regret it now ; though I did, about midway."

The red lips parted and the little teeth gleamed. "I have found such kindness and welcome." She caressed the dog who, lazily, tried to lick her hand. "It is all such an adventure ; so much more amusing than Pulwick ; so much more interesting than ever I fancied it might be !"

"Pulwick ; you come from Pulwick ?" said Sir Adrian musing ; "true, René has said it but just now. Yet, it is of a piece with the strangeness of it all."

"Yes," said Mademoiselle de Savenaye, once more collecting her cloak, which her hurried movement had thrown off her shoulder. "Madelon and I are now at Pulwick—I am Molly, cousin, please to remember—or rather I am here, very warm now, and comfortable, and she is somewhere along the shore—perhaps—she and John, as wet as drowned rats. Well, well, I had best tell you the tale from the beginning, or else we never shall be out of the labyrinth.—We started from Pulwick, for a ride by the shore, Madelon and I. When we were on the strand it came on to rain. There was smoke out of your chimney. I proposed a canter as far as the ruins, for shelter. I knew very well Madelon would not follow ; but I threw poor Lucifer —you know Lucifer, Mr. Landale has reserved him for me ; of course you know Lucifer, I believe he belongs to you ! Well, I threw him along the causeway. John, he's the groom you know, and Madelon, shrieked after me. But it was beautiful—this magnificent tearing gallop in the

rain—I was not going to stop.—But when we were half
way, Lucifer and I, I saw suddenly that the foam seemed
to cover the sand in front of me. Then I pulled up quick
and turned round to look behind me. There was already
a frightful wind, and the sand and the rain blinded me
almost, but there was no mistake—the sea was running
between the shore and me. Oh! my God! but I was
frightened then; I beat poor Lucifer until my whip
broke, and he started away with a will. But when his
feet began to splash the water he too became frightened
and stopped. I did not know what to do; I pulled out
my broach to spur him with the pin, but, at the first prick
I gave him, he reared, and swerved and I fell right on my
face in the froth. I got up and began to run through the
water; then I came to some stones and I knew I was
saved, though the water was up to my knees and rushing
by like a torrent. When I had clambered up the beach I
thought again of poor Lucifer. I looked about and saw
him a little way off. He was shaking and tossing his dear
black head, and neighing, though I really did not hear
him, for the wind was in my ears; his body was stock
still, I could not see his legs. . . . . And gradually he
sank lower, and lower, and lower, and at last the water
passed over his head. Oh! it was horrible, horrible!"

The girl shuddered and her bright face clouded. After
a moment she resumed:

"It was only then I thought of the moving sands they
spoke of the other day at Pulwick—and that was why
Madelon and that poltroon groom would not follow me!
Yet perhaps they were wise, after all, for the thought of
being buried alive made me turn weak all of a sudden.
My knees shook and I had to sit down, although I knew I
had passed through the danger. But I was so sorry for
poor Lucifer! I thought if I had come down and led
him, poor fellow, he might have come with me. Death
is so awful, so hideous; he was so full of life and carried
me so bravely, only a few minutes before! Is it not a
shame that there should be such a thing as death?" she
cried, rebelliously, and looked up at the man above her,
whose face had grown white at the thought of the danger
she had barely escaped.

"I waited," she resumed at length, "till I thought he
must be quite dead, there below, and came up to the

ruins, and looked for an entrance. I knocked at some doors and called, but the wind was so loud, no one heard. And then, at last, there was one door I could open, so I entered and came up the stairs and startled you, as you know. And that is how I came here and how Lucifer is drowned."

As she finished her tale at last, she looked up at her companion. But Sir Adrian, who had followed her with ever-deepening earnestness of mien, remained silent; noticing which she added quickly and with a certain tinge of defiance :

"And now, no doubt, you are not quite so pleased as you seemed at first with the apparition which has caused you the loss of one of your best horses !"

"Why child," cried Sir Adrian, "so that you be safe you might have left all Pulwick at the bottom of the sands for me !" And René who entered the room at that moment, heading the advance of Dame Margery with the posset, here caught the extraordinary sound of a laugh on his master's lips, and stepped back to chuckle to himself and rub his hands.

"Who would have believed that !" he muttered, "and I who was afraid to tell his honour ! Oh, yes, there are better times coming. Now in with you, Mother Margery, see for yourself who is there."

Holding in both hands a fragrant, steaming bowl, the old crone made her slow entrance upon the scene, peering with dim eyes, and dropping tremulous curtseys every two or three steps.

"Renny towd me as you wanted summat hot for a lady," she began cautiously ; and then having approached near for recognition at last, burst forth into a long-drawn cry !

"Eh, you never says ! Eh, dear o' me," and was fain to relinquish the bowl to her fellow-servant who narrowly watching, dived forward just in time to catch it from her, that she might clasp her aged hands together once and again with ever-renewed gestures of astonishment. "An' it were truth then, an' I that towd Renny to give over his nonsense—I didn't believe it, I welly couldn't. Eh, Mester Adrian, but she's like the poor lady that's dead and gone, the spit an' image she is—e-ch, she is !"

Molly de Savenaye laughed aloud, stretched out her

hand for the bowl, and began with dainty caution to sip
its scalding contents.

"Ah, my dear Margery," said the master, "we little
thought what a guest the sea would cast up at our doors
to-night! and now we must do our best for her; when
she's finished your comforting mixture I shall give her
into your charge. You ought to put her to bed—it will
not be the first time."

"Ah! it will not, and a troublesome child she was,"
replied Margery, after the usual pause for the assimila-
tion of his remark, turning to the speaker from her palsied
yet critical survey of her whilom nursling.

"And I'll see to her, never fear, I'll fettle up a room
for her at once—blankets is airing already, an' sheets, an'
Renny he's seen to the fire, so that as soon as Miss, here,
is ready, I am."

Upon which, dropping a last curtsey with an assumed
dignity which would have befitted a mistress of the robes,
she took her departure, leaving Adrian smiling with amusement at her specious manner of announcing that his own
bedroom—the only one available for the purpose in the
ruins—was being duly converted into a lady's bower.

"It grieves me to think," mused he after a pause, while
René still bursting with ungratified curiosity, hung about
the further end of the room, "of the terrible anxiety they
must be in about you at Pulwick, and of our absolute
inability to convey to them the good news of your
safety."

The girl gave a little laugh, with her lips over the cup,
and shrugged her shoulders but said nothing.

"My God, yes," quoth René cheerfully from his corner.
"Notre Dame d'Auray has watched over Mademoiselle
to-day. She would not permit the daughter to die like
the mother. And now we have got her ladyship we shall
keep her too. This, if your honour remembers his sailor's
knowledge, looks like a three-days' gale."

"You are right, I fancy," said Sir Adrian, going over
to him and looking out of the window. "Mademoiselle
de Savenaye will have to take up her abode in our lighthouse for a longer time than she bargained. I do not
remember hearing the breakers thunder in our cave so
loud for many years. I trust," continued the light-keeper,
coming down to his fair guest again, "that you may be

able to endure such rough hospitality as ours must needs
be!"

"It has been much more pleasant and I feel far more
welcome already than at Pulwick," remarked Mademoiselle, between two deliberate sips, and in no way discomposed, it seemed, at the prospect held out to her.

"How?" cried Sir Adrian with a start, while the unwonted flush mounted to his forehead, "you, not welcome at Pulwick! Have they not welcomed a child of
Cécile de Savenaye at Pulwick? . . . . Thank God, then,
for the accident that has sent you to me!"

The girl looked at him with an inquisitive smile in her
eyes; there was something on her lips which she restrained. Surrendering her cup, she remarked demurely:

"Yes, it was a lucky accident, was it not, that there
was some one to offer shelter to the outcast from the sea?
It is like a tale of old. It is delightful. Delightful, too,
not to be drowned, safe and sound . . . . and welcome
in this curious old place."

She had risen and, as the cloak fell from her steaming
garments, again she shivered.

"But you are right," she said, " I must go to bed, and
get these damp garments off. And so, my Lord of Scarthey, ' will retire to my apartments; my Lady in Waiting
I see yonder is ready for me."

With a quaint mixture of playfulness and gravity, she
extended her hand, and Adrian stooped and kissed it—
as he had kissed fair Cécile de Savenaye's rosy finger-tip
upon the porch of Pulwick, twenty years before.

CHAPTER VII

FOREBODINGS OF GLADNESS

MOLLY de Savenaye in her improvised bedroom, wet as she was, could hardly betake herself to disrobing, so amused was she in surveying the fresh and romantic oddity of her surroundings, with their mixture of barbarous rudeness and almost womanish refinement.

Old Margery's fumbling hands were not nimble either, and it was long since she had acted as attendant upon one of her own sex. And so the matter progressed but slowly ; but the speed of Margery's tongue was apparently not affected by its length of service. It wagged ceaselessly ; the girl between her own moods of curious speculation vouchsafing an amused, half-contemptuous ear.

Presently, however, as the nurse's reminiscences wandered from the less interesting topic of her own vicissitudes, the children she had reared or buried, and the marvellous ailments she had endured, to an account of those days when she had served the French Madam and her babes, Molly, slowly peeling a clinging sleeve from her arm, turned a more eager and attentive face to her.

"Ah," quoth Margery, appraising her with blear eyes, " it's a queer thing how ye favour your mother, miss. She had just they beautiful shoulders and arms, as firm an' as white ; but you're taller, I think, and may be so, to speak, a stouter make altogether. Eh, dear, you were always a fine child and the poor lady set a deal of store on you, she did. She took you with her and left your sister with my Sally, when she was trapesing up to London and back with Mester Adrian, ay, and me with ye. And many the day that I wished myself safe at Pulwick ! And I mind the day she took leave of you, I do that, well."

Here Dame Margery paused and shook her head solemnly, then pursued in another key :

"See now, miss, dear, just step out of they wet things, will ye now, and let me put this hot sheet round ye ? "

"But I want to hear about myself," said Molly, gratefully wrapping the hot linen round her young beauty, and beginning to rub her black locks energetically. "Where was it my mother parted from me?"

"Why, I'll tell you, miss. When Madam—we allus used to call her Madam, ye know—was goin' her ways to the ship as was to take her to France, I took you after her mysel' down to the shore that she might have the very last of ye. Eh, I mind it as if it were yesterday. Mester Adrian was to go with her—Sir Adrian, I should say, but he was but Mester Adrian then—an' a two three more o' th' gentry as was all fur havin' a share o' th' fightin'. Sir Thomas himsel' was theer—I like as if I could see him now, poor owd gentleman, talkin' an' laughin' very hard an' jov'al, an' wipin' 's e'en when he thought nobody noticed. Eh, dear, yes! I could ha' cried mysel' to see th' bonny young lady goin' off fro' her bairns. An' to think she niver came back to them no more. Well, well! An' Mester Adrian too—such a fine well-set-up young gentleman as he were—and *he* niver comed back for ten year an' when he did, he was that warsened—" she stopped, shook her head and groaned.

"Well, but how about me, nurse," observed Molly, "what about *me*?"

"Miss, please it was this way. Madam was wantin' a last look at her bairn—eh, she did, poor thing! You was allus her favoryite, ye know, miss—our Sally was wet-nurse to Miss Maddyline, but Madam had you hersel'. Well, miss, I'd brought you well lapped up i' my shawl an' William Shearman—that was Thomas Shearman's son, feyther to William an' Tom as lives over yonder at Pulwick village—well, William was standin' in 's great sea-boots ready to carry her through th' surf into the boat; an' Mester Adrian—Sir Adrian, I mean—stood it might be here, miss, an' there was Renny, an' yon were th' t'other gentry. Well, Madam stopped an' took you out o' my arms, an' hugged you to her breast—an' then she geet agate o' kissin' you—your head an' your little 'ands. An' you was jumpin' an' crowin' in her arms—the wind had blown your cap off, an' your little downy black hair was standing back. (Just let me get at your hair now, miss, please— Eh! it's cruel full of sand, my word, it is.)"

"It's 'ard, when all's said an' done, to part wi' th' babe

ye've suckled, an' Madam, though there was niver nought
nesh about 'er same as there is about most women, an'
specially ladies—she 'ad th' mother's 'eart, she 'ad, miss,
an when th' time coom for her to leave th' little un, I
could see, as it were, welly burstin'.   There we stood wi'
th' wind blowin' our clothes an' our 'air, an' the waves
roarin', an' one bigger nor th' t'others ran up till th' foam
reached Madam's little feet, but she niver took no notice.
Then all of a sudden she gets th' notion that she'd like to
take you with 'er, an' she turns an' tells Mester Adrian so.
'She shall come with me,' she says, quite sharp an' determined, an' makes a sign to William Shearman to carry
'em both over. 'No, no,' says Mester Adrian, 'quite impossible,' says he, as wise as if he'd been an owd man
i' stead o' nobbut a lad, ye might say.   'It would be madness both for you an' th' child. Now,' he says, very quiet
an' gentle, 'if I might advise, I should say stay here with
the child.' Eh, I couldn't tell ye all he said, an' then Sir
Tummas coom bustlin' up, 'Do, now, my dear; think of
it,' he says, pattin' her o' th' hand. 'Stay with us,' he
says, 'ye'll be welcome as th' flowers in May!' An'
there was Kenny wi' 's 'at off, an' th' tears pourin' down
his face, beggin' an' prayin' Madam to stop—at least, I
reckoned that was what he were sayin' for it was all in 's
own outlandish gibberish. The poor lady! she'd look
from one to th' t'other an' a body a' must think she'd give
in—an' then she'd unbethink hersel' again.   An' Sir
Thomas, he'd say, 'Do now, my dear,' an' then when
she'd look at him that pitiful, he'd out wi' 's red 'andkercher
an' frown over at Mester Adrian, an', says he, 'I wonder
ye can ax her!' Well, all of a sudden off went th' big
gun in th' ship—that was to let 'em know, miss, do ye
see—an' up went Madam's head, an' then th' wind fetched
th' salt spray to her face, an' a kind o' change came over
her.   She looked at the child, then across at the ship—an'
then she fair tossed ye back to me.   Big William catched
her up in his arms just same as another bairn, an' carried
her to the boat."

"Yes," said Molly, gazing into the burning logs with
brilliant eyes, but speaking low, as if to herself, so that
her attendant's deaf ears failed to catch the meaning of
the words.   "Ah, that was life indeed! Happy mother
to have seen such life—though she did die young."

5

"As ye say, miss," answered Margery, making a guess at the most likely comment from a daughter's lips, "it was cruel hard—it was that. 'Come, make haste!' cries the other young gentlemen: my word, they were in a hurry lest Madam happen to change her mind. I could welly have laughed to see their faces when Mester Adrian were trying to persuade her to stop at Pulwick, and let the men go alone. 'T wern't for that they reckoned to go all that road to France, ye may think, miss. Well, miss, in a few minutes they was all out i' the boat wi' th' waves tossin' 'em—an' I stood watchin' with you i' my arms, cryin' and kickin' out wi' your little legs, an' hittin' of me wi' your little 'ands, same as if ye knowed summat o' what was agate, poor lamb, an' was angry wi' me for keepin' ye. Then in a little while the big, white sails o' th' ship went swellin' out an' soon it was gone. An' that was th' last we saw o' Madam. A two-three year arter you an' Miss Maddyline was fetched away, to France, as I've been towd. I doubt you didn't so much as think there was such a place as Pulwick, though many a one there minds how they dandled and played wi' you when you was a wee bairn, miss."

"Well, I am very glad to be back in England, anyhow," said Molly, nimbly slipping into bed. "Oh, Margery, what delicious warm sheets, and how good it is to be in bed alive, dry, and warm, after all!"

A new atmosphere pervaded Scarthey that night. The peaceful monotony of years, since the master of Pulwick had migrated to his "ruins," was broken at last, and happily. A warm colour seemed to have crept upon the hitherto dun and dull surroundings and brightened all the prospects.

At any rate René, over his busy work in the lantern, whistled and hummed snatches of song with unwonted blithesomeness, and, after lighting the steady watch-light and securing all his paraphernalia with extra care, dallied some time longer than usual on the outer platform, striving to snatch through the driven wraith a glance of the distant lights of Pulwick. For there, in the long distance, ensconced among the woods, stood a certain gate-lodge of greystone, much covered with ivy, which sheltered, among other inmates, the gatekeeper's blue-eyed, ripe and ruddy daughter—Dame Margery's pet grandchild.

The idea of ever leaving the master—even for the sake
of the happiness to be found over yonder—was not one
to be entertained by René.   But what if dreams of a return to the life of the world should arise after to-day in
the recluse's mind?   Ah, the master's eyes had been filled
with light! . . . . and had he not actually laughed?

René peered again through the wind, but nothing could
be seen of the world abroad, save grey, tumbling waters
foaming at the foot of the islet ; fretful waters coalescing
all around with the driven, misty air.   A desolate view
enough, had there been room for melancholy thoughts in
his heart.

Blithely did he descend the steep wooden stairs from
the roaring, weather-beaten platform, to the more secure
inhabited keep ; and, humming a satisfied tune, he entered upon Margery in her flaming kitchen, to find the
old lady intent on sorting out a heap of feminine garments
and spreading them before the fire.

René took up a little shoe, sand-soiled and limp, and
reverentially rubbed it on his sleeve.

" Well, mother," he said, cheerfully, " it is a long while
since you had to do with such pretty things.   My faith,
these are droll doings, ah—and good, too !   You will see,
Mother Margery, there will be good out of all this."

But Margery invariably saw fit, on principle, to doubt
all the opinions of her rival.

Eh, she didn't hold so much wi' wenches hersel', an'
Mester Adrian, she reckoned, hadn't come to live here all
by himsel' to have visitors breaking in on him that gate !

" There be visitors *and* visitors, mother—I tell you, I
who speak to you, that his honour is happy."

Margery, with a mysterious air, smoothed out a long
silk stocking and gave an additional impetus to the tremor
Nature had already bestowed upon her aged head.

Well, it wasn't for her to say.   She hoped and prayed
there was nowt bad a coomin' on the family again ; but
sich likenesses as that of Miss to her mother was not lucky,
to her minding ; it was not.   Nowt good had come to
Mester Adrian from the French Madam.   Ah, Mester
Adrian had been happy like with her too, and she had
taken him away from his home, an' his people, an' sent
him back wi'out 's soul in the end.

" And now her daughter has come to give it him back,"

retorted René, as he fell to, with a zest, on the savoury
mess he had concocted for his own supper.

"Eh, well, I hope nowt bad's i' the road," said Margery with senile iteration. "They do say no good ever
comes o' saving bodies from drowning ; not that one 'ud
wish the poor Miss to have gone into the sands—an' she
the babby I weaned too ! "

René interrupted her with a hearty laugh. "Yes,
every one knows it carries misfortune to save people from
the drowning, but there, you see, her ladyship, she saved
herself—so that ought to bring good fortune. Good-
night, Mother Margery, take good care of the lady. . . .
Ah, how I wish I had the care of her ! " he added simply,
and, seizing his lantern, proceeded to ascend once more
to his post aloft.

He paused once on his way, in the loud sighing stairs,
struck with a fresh aspect of the day's singular events—
a quaint thought, born of his native religious faith : The
Lady, the dear Mistress had just reached Heaven, no
doubt, and had straightway sent them the young one to
console and comfort them. Eh bien ! they had had their
time of Purgatory too, and now they might be happy.

Pleasant therefore were René's musings, up in the light
watcher's bunk, underneath the lantern, as, smoking a
pipe of rest, he listened complacently to the hissing storm
around him.

And in the master's sleeping chamber beneath him,
now so curiously turned into a feminine sanctum, pleasant thoughts too, if less formed, and less concerned with
the future, lulled its dainty occupant to rest.

Luxuriously stretched between the warm lavender-
scented sheets, watching from her pillow the leaping fire
on the hearth, Miss Molly wondered lazily at her own
luck ; at the many possible results of the day's escapade ;
wondered amusedly whether any poignant sorrow—except, indeed poor Madeleine's tears—for her supposed
demise, really darkened the supper party at Pulwick this
evening ; wondered agreeably how the Lord of the Ruined
Castle would meet her on the morrow, after his singular
reception of her this day ; how long she would remain in
these romantic surroundings and whether she would like
them as well at the end of the visitation.

And as the blast howled with increasing rage, and the

cold night drew closer on, and the great guns in the sea-cave boomed more angrily with the risen tide, she dimly began to dwell upon the thought of poor Lucifer being sucked deeper into his cold rapacious grave, whilst she was held in the warm embrace of a man whose eyes were masterful and yet gentle, whose arm was strong, whose kisses were tender.

And in the delight of the contrast, Mademoiselle de Savenaye fell into the profound slumber of the young and vigorous.

CHAPTER VIII

THE PATH OF WASTED YEARS

And I only think of the woman that weeps ;
But I forget, always forget, the smiling child.
                                        Luteplayer's Song.

THAT night, even when sheer fatigue had subdued the
currents of blood and thought that surged in his head,
Sir Adrian was too restless to avail himself of the emergency couch providently prepared by René in a corner.
But, ceasing his fretful pacing to and fro, he sat down in
the arm-chair by the hearth where she had sat—the waif
of the sea—wrapped round him the cloak that had enfolded the young body, hugging himself in the salt
moisture the fur still retained, to spend the long hours in
half-waking, firelight dreams.

And every burst of tempest rage, every lash of rain at
the window, every thud of hurricane breaking itself on
impassable ramparts, and shriek of baffled winds searching
the roofless halls around, found a strangely glad echo in
his brain—made a sort of burden to his thoughts :

Heap up the waters round this happy island, most
welcome winds—heap them up high and boiling, and
retain her long captive in these lonely ruins !

And ever the image in his mind's eye was, as before,
Cécile—Cécile who had come back to him, for all sober
reason knew it was but the child.

The child——! Why had he never thought of the
children these weary years ? They, all that remained of
Cécile, were living and might have been sought. Strange
that he had not remembered him of the children !

Twenty years since he had last set eyes upon the little
living creature in her mother's arms. And the picture
that the memory evoked was, after all, Cécile again, only
Cécile—not the queer little black-eyed puppet, even then
associated with sea-foam and salty breeze. Twenty years

during which she was growing and waxing in beauty, and unawares, maturing towards this wonderful meeting—and he had never given a thought to her existence.

In what sheltered ways had this fair duplicate of his love been growing from a child to womanhood during that space of life, so long to look back upon—or so short and transient, according to the mood of the thinker?

And, lazily, in his happier and tender present mood he tried to measure once again the cycles of past discontent, this time in terms of the girl's own lifetime.

It is bitter in misery to recall past misery—almost as bitter, for all Dante's cry, as to dwell on past happiness. But, be the past really dead, and a new and better life begun, the scanning back of a sombre existence done with for ever, may bring with it a kind of secret complacency.

Truly, mused Sir Adrian, for one who ever cherished ideal aspirations, for the student, the "man of books" (as his father had been banteringly wont to term him), worshipper of the muses, intellectual Epicurean, and would-be optimist philosopher, it must be admitted he had strangely dealt, and been dealt with, since he first beheld that face, now returned to light his solitude! Ah, God bless the child! Pulwick at least nursed it warmly, whilst unhappy Adrian, ragged and degraded into a mere fighting beast, roamed through the Marais with Chouan bands, hunted down by the merciless revolutionists, like vermin; falling, as months of that existence passed over him, from his high estate to the level of vermin indeed; outlawed, predatory, cunning, slinking, filthy—trapped at last, the fit end of vermin!

Scarcely better the long months of confinement in the hulks of Rochelle. How often he had regretted it, then, not to have been one of the chosen few who, the day after capture, stood in front of six levelled muskets, and were sped to rest in some unknown charnel! Then!—not now. No, it was worth having lived to this hour, to know of that fair face, in living sleep upon his pillow, under the safeguard of his roof.

Good it was, that he had escaped at last, though with the blood of one of his jailors red upon his hands; the blood of a perhaps innocent man, upon his soul. It was the only time he had taken a life other than in fair fight, and the thought of it had been wont to fill him with a sort of nausea ; but to-night, he found he could face it, not only without remorse, but without regret. He was glad he had listened to René's insidious whispers—René, who could not endure the captivity to which his master might, in time, have fallen a passive, hopeless slave, and yet who would have faced a thousand years of it rather than escape alone—the faithful heart !

Yes, it was good, and he was glad of it, or time would not have come when she (stay, how old was the child then ?—almost three years, and still sheltered and cherished by the house of Landale)—when she would return, and gladden his eyes with a living sight of Cécile, while René watched in his tower above ; ay, and old Margery herself lay once more near the child she had nursed.

Marvellous turn of the wheel of fate !

But, who had come for the children, and where had they been taken ? To their motherland, perhaps ; even it might have been before he himself had left it ; or yet to Ireland, where still dwelt kinsfolk of their blood ? Probably it was at the breaking up of the family, caused by the death of Sir Thomas, that these poor little birds had been removed from the nest, that had held them so safe and close.

That was in '97, in the yellow autumn of which year Adrian Landale, then French fisherman, parted from his brother René l'Apôtre upon the sea off Belle Isle ; parted one grizzly dawn after embracing, as brothers should. Oh, the stealthy cold of that blank, cheerless daybreak, how it crept into the marrow of his bones, and chilled the little energy and spirits he had left ! For a whole year they had fruitlessly sought some English vessel, to convey this English gentleman back to his native land. He could remember how, at the moment of separation, from the one friend who had loved both him and her, his heart sank within him—remember how he clambered from aboard the poor little smack, up the forbidding sides of the English brig ; how René's broken words had bidden God bless him, and restore him safely home (home !) ; remember how swiftly the crafts had moved apart, the mist, the greyness and desolateness ; the lapping of the waters, the hoarse cries of the seamen, all so full of heart-piercing associations to him, and the last vision of René's simple face, with tears pouring down it, and his open mouth spasmodically trying to give out a hearty cheer, despite the sobs that came heaving up to it. How little the simple fellow dreamed of what bitterness the future was yet holding for his brother and master, to end in these reunions at last !

The vessel which had taken Adrian Landale on board, in answer to the frantic signals of the fishing-smack, that had sailed from Belle Isle obviously to meet her, proved to be a privateer, bound for the West Indies, but cruising somewhat out of her way, in the hope of outgoing prizes from Nantes.

The captain, who had been led to expect something of importance from the smack's behaviour, in high dudgeon at finding that so much bustle and waste of time was only to burden him with a mere castaway seeking a passage home—one who, albeit a countryman, was too ragged and disreputable in looks to be trusted in his assurances of reward—granted him indeed the hospitality of his ship, but on the condition of his becoming a hand in the company during the forthcoming expedition.

There was a rough measure of equity in the arrangement, and Adrian accepted it. The only alternative, moreover, would have been a jump overboard. And so began a hard spell of life, but a few shades removed from his existence among the Chouan guerillas ; a predatory cruise lasting over a year, during which the only changes rung in the gamut of its purpose were the swooping down, as a vulture might, upon unprotected ships ; flying with superior speed from obviously stronger crafts ; engaging, with hawk-like bravery, everything afloat that displayed inimical colours, if it offered an equal chance of fight.

And this for more than a year, until the privateer, much battered, but safe, despite her vicissitudes made Halifax for refitting. Here, at the first suitable port she had touched, Adrian claimed and obtained his release from obligations which made his life almost unendurable.

Then ensued a period of the most absolute penury ; unpopular with most of his messmates for his melancholy taciturnity, despised by the more brutal as one who had as little stomach for a carouse as for a bloody fight, he left the ship without receiving, or even thinking of his share of prize-money. And he had to support existence with such mean mechanical employment as came in his way, till an opportunity was offered of engaging himself as seaman, again from sheer necessity, on a homeward-bound merchantman—an opportunity which he seized, if not eagerly, for there was no eagerness left in him, yet under the pressure of purpose.

Next the long, slowly plodding, toilsome, seemingly eternal course across the ocean.

But even a convoy, restricted to the speed of its slowest member, if it escape capture or natural destruction, must meet the opposite shore at length, and the last year of the century had lapsed in the even race of time when, after many dreary weeks, on the first of January 1801, the long low lines of sandhills on the Lancastrian coast loomed in sight. The escort drew away, swiftly southwards, as if in joyful relief from the tedious task, leaving the convoy to enter the Mersey, safe and sound.

That evening Adrian, the rough-looking and taciturn sailor, set foot, for a short while, on his native land, after six years of an exile which had made of him at five and twenty a prematurely aged and hopelessly disillusioned man.

And Sir Adrian, as he mused, wrapped in the honoured fur cloak, with eyes half closed, by his sympathetic fire, recalled how little of joy this return had had for him. It was the goal he had striven to reach, and he had reached it, that was all ; nay, he recalled how, when at hand, he had almost dreaded the actual arrival home, dreaded, with the infinite heart-sickness of sorrow, the emotions of the family welcome to one restored from such perils by flood and field—if not indeed already mourned for and forgotten—little wotting how far that return to Pulwick, that seemed near and certain, was still away in the dim future of life.

Yet, but for the fit of hypochondriacal humour which had fallen black upon him that day of deliverance and made him yearn, with an intensity increasing every moment, to separate himself from his repugnant associates and haste the moment of solitude and silence, he might have been rescued, then and for ever, from the quagmire in which perverse circumstances had enslaved him.

"Look'ee here, matey," said one of his fellow-workers to him, in a transient fit of good-fellowship which the prospect of approaching sprees had engendered in him even towards one whom all on board had felt vaguely to be of a different order, and disliked accordingly, "you don't seem to like a jolly merchantman—but, maybe, you wouldn't take more kindly to a man-o'-war.   Do you see that there ship?—a frigate she is ; and, whenever there's a King's ship in the Mersey that means that it's more wholesome for the likes of us to lie low.   You take a hint, matey, and don't be about Liverpool to-night, or until she's gone.   Now, I know a crib that's pretty safe, Birkenhead way ; Mother Redcap's. we call it—no one's ever been nabbed at Mother Redcap's, and if you'll come along o' me—why then if you won't, go your way and be damned to you for a——"

This was the parting of Adrian Landale from his fellow-workers.   The idea of spending even one night more in that atmosphere of rum and filth, in the intimate hearing of blasphemous and obscene language, was too repulsive to be entertained, and he had turned away from the offer with a gesture of horror.

With half a dozen others, in whose souls the attractions of the town at night proved stronger than the fear of the press party, he disembarked on the Lancashire side, and separating from his companions, for ever, as he thought, ascended the miserable lanes leading from the river to the upper town.

His purpose was to sleep in one of the more decent hotels, to call the next day for help at the banking-house with which the Landales had dealt for ages past, and thence to take coach for Pulwick.   But he had planned without taking reck of his circumstances.   No hotel of repute would entertain this weather-beaten common sailor in the meanest of work-stained clothes.   After failing at various places even to obtain a hearing, being threatened with forcible ejectment, derisively referred to suitable cribs in Love Lane or Tower Street, he gave up the attempt ; and, in his usual dejection of spirit, intensified by unavowed and unreasonable anger, wandered through the dark streets, brooding.   Thus aimlessly wandering, the remembrance of his young Utopian imaginings came back to him to mock him.   Dreams of universal brotherhood, of equality, of harmony.   He had already seen the apostles of equality and brotherhood at work—on the banks of the Vilaine.   And realising how he himself, now reduced to the lowest level in the social

scale, hunted with insult from every haunt above that
level, yet loathed and abhorred the very thought of asso-
ciating again with his recent brothers in degradation, he
laughed a laugh of bitter self-contempt.

But the night was piercing cold ; and, in time, the
question arose whether the stench and closeness of a river-
side eating-house would not be more endurable than the
cutting wind, the sleet, and the sharper pangs of hunger.

His roaming had brought him once more to that quarter
of the town "best suited to the likes of him," according
to the innkeeper's opinion, and he found himself actually
seeking a house of entertainment in the slimy, ill-lighted
narrow street, when, from out the dimness, running
towards him, with bare feet paddling in the sludge, came
a slatternly girl, with unkempt wisps of red hair hanging
over her face under the tartan shawl.

"Run, run, Jack," she cried, hoarsely, as she passed
by breathless, "t' gang's comin' up. . . . "

A sudden loathly fear seized Adrian by the heart.   He
too, took to his heels by the side of the slut with all the
swiftness his tired frame could muster.

"I'm going to warn my Jo," she gasped, as, jostling
each other, they darted through a maze of nameless alleys.

And then as, spent with running, they emerged at last
into a broader street, it was to find themselves in the very
midst of another party of man-of-war's men, whose brass
belt-buckles glinted under the flickering light of the oil-
lamp swinging across the way.

Adrian stopped dead short and looked at the girl in
mute reproach.

"May God strike me dead," she screamed, clapping
her hands together, "if I knew the bloody thieves were
there !   Oh, my bonny lad, I meant to save ye !"   And
as her words rang in the air two sailors had Adrian by
the collar and a facetious bluejacket seized her round the
waist with hideous bantering.

A very young officer, wrapped up in a cloak, stood a
few paces apart calmly looking on.   To him Adrian
called out in fierce, yet anguished, expostulation :

"I am a free and independent subject, sir, an English
gentleman.   I demand that you order your men to release
me.   For heaven's sake," he added, pleadingly, "give
me but a moment's private hearing !"

A loud guffaw rang through the group. In truth, if appearances make the gentleman, Adrian was then but a sorry specimen.

The officer smiled—the insufferable smile of a conceited boy raised to authority.

"I can have no possible doubt of your gentility, sir," he said, with mocking politeness, and measuring, under the glimmering light, first the prisoner, from head to foot, and then the girl who, scratching and blaspheming, vainly tried to make her escape ; " but, sir, as a free-born English gentleman, it will be your duty to help his Majesty to fight his French enemies. Take the English gentleman along, my lads ! "

A roar of approbation at the officer's facetiousness ran through the party.

" An' his mother's milk not dry upon his lips," cried the girl, with a crow of derisive fury, planting as she spoke a sounding smack on a broad tanned face bent towards her. The little officer grew pink. "Come, my men, do your duty," he thundered, in his deepest bass.

A rage such as he never had felt in his life suddenly filled Adrian's whole being. He was a bigger man than any of the party, and the rough life that fate had imposed on him, had fostered a strength of limb beyond the common. A thrust of his knee prostrated one of his captors, a blow in the eye from his elbow staggered the other ; the next instant he had snatched away the cutlass which a third was drawing, and with it he cleared, for a moment, a space around him.

But as he would have bounded into freedom, a felling blow descended on his head from behind, a sheet of flame spread before his eyes, and behind this blaze disappeared the last that Adrian Landale was to see of England for another spell of years.

When he came back to his senses he was once more on board ship—a slave, legally kidnapped ; degraded by full and proper warrant from his legitimate status for no crime that could even be invented against him ; a slave to be retained for work or war at his master's pleasure, liable like a slave to be flogged to death for daring to assert his right of independence.

The memory of that night's doing and of the odious bondage to which it was a prelude, rarely failed to stir the gall of resentment in Sir Adrian ; men of peaceable instincts are perhaps the most prone to the feeling of indignation.

But, to-night, a change had come over the spirit of his dreams ; he could think of that past simply as the past—the period of time which would have had to be spent until the advent of the wonder-working present : these decrees of Fate had had a purpose. Had the past, by one jot, been different, the events of this admirable day might never have been.

The glowing edifice on the hearth collapsed with a darting of sudden flame and a rolling of red cinders. Sir Adrian rose to rebuild his fire for the night ; and, being once roused, was tempted by the ruddiness of the wine, glinting under the quiet rays of the lamp, to advance to the table and partake of his forgotten supper.

The calm atmosphere, the warmth and quiet of the room, in which he broke his bread and sipped his wine, whilst old Jem stretched by the hearth gazed at him with yellow up-turned eyes full of lazy inquiry concerning this departure from the usual nightly regularity ; the serene placidity of the scene indoors as contrasting with the angry voices of elements without, answered to the peace—the strange peace—that filled the man's soul, even in the midst of such uncongenial memories as now rose up before him in vivid concatenation.

She was then five years old. Where was she, when he began that seemingly endless cruise with the frigate *Porcupine ?* He tried to fancy a Cécile five years old—a chubby, curly-headed mite, nursing dolls and teasing kittens, whilst he was bullied and browbeaten by coarse petty officers, shunned and hated by his messmates, and flogged at length by a tyrannizing captain for obduracy—but he could only see a Cécile in the spring of womanhood, nestling in the arm-chair yonder by the fire and looking up at him from the folds of a fur cloak.

She was seven years old when he was flogged. Ah, God ! those had been days ! And yet, in the lofty soul of him he had counted it no disgrace ; and he had been flogged again, ay, and a third time for that obstinate head that would not bend, that obstinate tongue that would persist in demanding restitution of liberty. The life on board the privateer had been a matter of bargain ;

he had bartered also labour and obedience with the merchantman for the passage home, but the king had no right to compel the service of a free man !

She was but twelve years old when he was finally released from thraldom—it had only lasted four years after all ; yet what a cycle for one of his temper ! Four years with scarce a moment of solitude—for no shore-leave was ever allowed to one who openly repudiated any service contract : four years of a life, where the sole prospect of change was in these engagements, orgies of carnage, so eagerly anticipated by officers and men alike, including himself, though for a reason little suspected by his companions. But even the historic sea-fights of the *Porcupine*, so far as they affected Adrian Landale, formed in themselves a chain of monotony. It was ever the same hurling of shot from ship to ship, the same fierce exchange of cutlass-throws and pike-pushes between men who had never seen each other before ; the same yelling and execrations, sights, sounds, and smells ever the same in horror ; the same cheers when the enemy's colours were lowered, followed by the same transient depression ; the cleansing of decks from stains of powder and mire of human blood, the casting overboard of human bodies that had done their life's work, broken waste and other rubbish. For weeks Adrian after would taste blood, smell blood, dream blood, till it seemed in his nausea that all the waters of the wide clean seas could never wash the taint from him again. And before the first horrid impressions had time to fade, the next occasion would have come round again : it was not the fate of Adrian Landale that either steel or shot, or splintered timber or falling tackles should put an end to his dreary life, welcome as such an end would have been to him then.

Then . . . but not now. Remembering now his unaccountable escape from the destruction which had swept from his side many another whose eagerness for the fray had certes not sprung, like his own, from a desire to court destruction, he shuddered. And there arose in his mind the trite old adage :

" Man proposeth . . . . "

God had disposed otherwise.

It was not destined that Adrian Landale should be shot on the high seas any more than he should be drowned in the rolling mud of the Vilaine—he was reserved for this day as a set-off to all the bitterness that had been meted out to him ; he was to see the image of his dead love rise from the sea once more. And, meanwhile, his very despair and sullenness had been turned to his good. It would not be said, if history should take count of the fact, that while the Lord of Pulwick had served four years before the mast, he had ever disgraced his name by cowardice. . . . .

Whether such reasonings were in accordance even with the most optimistic philosophy, Sir Adrian himself at other times might have doubted. But he was tender in thought this stormy night, with the grateful relaxation that a happy break brings in the midst of long-drawn melancholy.

Everything had been working towards this end—that he should be the light-keeper of Scarthey on the day when out of the raging waters Cécile would rise and knock and ask for succour at his chamber.

Cécile ! pshaw !—raving again.

Well, the child ! Where was she on the aay or the last engagement of that pugnacious *Porcupine*, in the year 1805, when England was freed from her long incubus of invasion ? She was then twelve.

It had seemed if nothing short of a wholesale disaster could terminate that incongruous existence of his.

The last action of the frigate was a fruitless struggle against fearful odds. After a prolonged fight with an enemy as dauntless as herself, with two-thirds of her ship's company laid low, and commanded at length by the youngest lieutenant, she was tackled as the sun went low over the scene of a drawn battle, by a fresh sail errant ; and, had it not been for a timely dismasting on board the new-comer, would have been captured or finally sunk then and there. But that fate was only held in reserve for her. Bleeding and disabled, she had drawn away under cover of night from her two hard-hit adversaries, to encounter a squall that further dismantled her, and, in such forlorn conditions, was met and finally conquered by the French privateer *Espoir de Brest*, that pounced upon her in her agony as the vulture upon his prey.

Among the remainder of the once formidable crew, now seized and battened down under French hatches, was of course Adrian Landale—he bore a charmed life.   And for a short while the only change probable in his prospects was a return to French prisons, until such time as it pleased Heaven to restore peace between the two nations.

But the fortune of war, especially at sea, is fickle and fitful.

The daring brig, lettre de marque, *L'Espoir de Brest*, soon after her unwonted haul of English prisoners, was overtaken herself by one of her own species, the *St. Nicholas* of Liverpool, from whose swiftness nothing over the sea, that had not wings, could hope to escape if she chose to give the chase.

Again did Adrian, from the darkness among his fellow-captives, hear the familiar roar and crash of cannon fight, the hustling and the thud of leaping feet, the screams and oaths of battle, and, finally, the triumphant shouts of English throats, and he knew that the Frenchman was boarded.   A last ringing British cheer told of the Frenchman's surrender, and when he and his comrades were once more free to breathe a draught of living air, after the deathly atmosphere under hatches, Adrian learned that the victor was not a man-of-war, but a free-lance, and conceived again a faint hope that deliverance might be at hand.

It was soon after this action, last of the fights that Adrian the peace-lover had to pass through, and as the two swift vessels, now sailing in consort, and under the same colours cleaved the waters, bound for the Mersey, that a singular little drama took place on board the *Espoir de Brest*.

Among the younger officers of the English privateer, who were left in charge of the prize, was a lad upon whom Adrian's jaded eyes rested with a feeling of mournful sympathy, so handsome was he, and so young ; so full of hope and spirits and joy of life, of all, in fact, of which he himself had been left coldly bare.   Moreover, the ring of the merry voice, the glint of the clear eye awakened in his memory some fitful chord, the key of which he vainly sought to trace.

One day, as the trim young lieutenant stood looking across the waters, with his brave eager gaze that seemed

6

to have absorbed some of the blue-green shimmer of the element he loved, all unnoting the haggard sailor at his elbow, a sudden flourish of the spy-glass which he, with an eager movement, swung up to bear on some distant speck, sent his watch and seals flying out of his fob upon the deck at Adrian's feet.

Adrian picked them up, and as he waited to restore them to their owner, who tarried some time intent on his distant peering, he had time to notice the coat and crest engraved upon one of the massive trinkets hanging from their black ribbons.

When at last the officer lowered his telescope, Adrian came forward and saluted him with a slight bow, all unconsciously as unlike the average Jack Tar's scrape to his superior as can be well imagined :

"Am I not," he asked, "addressing in you, sir, one of the Cochranes of the Shaws?"

The question and the tone from a common sailor were, of course, enough to astonish the young man. But there must be more than this, as Adrian surmised, to cause him to blush, wax angry, and stammer like a very school-boy found at fault. Speaking with much sharpness :

"My name is Smith, my man," cried he, seizing his belongings, "and you—just carry on with that coiling !"

"And my name, sir, is Adrian Landale, of Pulwick Priory. I would like a moment's talk with you, if you will spare me the time. The Cochranes of the Shaws have been friends of our family for generations."

A guffaw burst from a group of Adrian's mates working hard by, at this recurrence of what had become with them a standing joke ; but the officer, who had turned on his heels, veered round immediately, and stood eyeing the speaker in profound astonishment.

"Great God, is it possible ! Did you say you were a Landale of Pulwick ? How the devil came you here then, and thus ? "

"Press-gang," was Adrian's laconic answer.

The lad gave a prolonged whistle, and was lost for a moment in cogitation.

"If you are really Mr. Landale," he began, adding hastily, as if to cover an implied admission—"of course I have heard the name : it is well known in Lancashire—you had better see the skipper. It must have been some damnable mistake that has caused a man of your standing to be pressed."

The speaker ended with almost a deferential air and the smile that had already warmed Adrian's heart. At the door of the Captain's quarters he said, with the suspicion of a twinkle in his eye :

"A curious error it was you made, I assure you my name is Smith—Jack Smith, of Liverpool."

"An excusable error," quoth Adrian, smiling back, "for one of your seals bear unmistakably the arms of Cochrane of the Shaws, doubtless some heirloom, some inter-marriage."

"No, sir, hang it !" retorted Mr. Jack Smith of Liverpool, his boyish face flushing again, and as he spoke he disengaged the trinket from its neighbours, and jerked it pettishly overboard, "I know nothing of your Shaws or your Cochranes."

And then he rapped loudly at the cabin-door, as if anxious to avoid further discussion or comment on the subject.

The result of the interview which followed—interview during which Adrian in a few words overcame the skipper's scepticism, and was bidden with all the curiosity men feel at sea for any novelty, to relate, over a bottle of wine, the chain of his adventures—was his passing from the forecastle to the officers' quarters, as an honoured guest on board the *St. Nicholas*, during the rest of her cruise.

Thinking back now upon the last few weeks of his seagoing life, Sir Adrian realised with something of wonder that he had always dwelt on them without dislike. They were gilded in his memory by the rays of his new friendship.

And yet that this young Jack Smith (to keep for him the nondescript name he had for unknown reasons chosen to assume) should be the first man to awaken in the misanthropic Adrian the charm of human intercourse, was singular indeed ; one who followed from choice the odious trade of legally chartered corsair, who was ever ready to barter the chance of life and limb against what fortune might bring in his path, to sacrifice human life to secure his own end of enrichment.

Well, the springs of friendship are to be no more dis-

cerned than those of love ; there was none of high or low
degree, with the exception of René, whose appearance at
any time was so welcome to the recluse upon his rock, as
that of the privateersman.

And so, turning to his friend in to-night's softened
mood, Sir Adrian thought gratefully that to him it was
that he owed deliverance from the slavery of the King's
service, that it was Jack Smith who had made it possible
for Adrian Landale to live to this great day and await its
coming in peace.

The old clock struck two ; and Jem shivered on the
rug as the light-keeper rose at length from the table and
sank in his armchair once more.

Visions of the past had been ever his companions ;
now for the first time came visions of the future to com-
mingle with them. As if caught up in the tide of his
visitor's bright young life, it seemed as though he were
passing at length out of the valley of the shadow of
death.

René, coming with noiseless bare feet, in the angry
yellow dawn of the second day of the storm, to keep an
eye on his master's comfort, found him sleeping in his
chair with a new look of rest upon his face and a smile
upon his lips.

CHAPTER IX

A GENEALOGICAL EPISTLE

> . . . . and braided thereupon
> All the devices blazoned on the shield,
> In their own tinct, and added, of her wit,
> A border fantasy of branch and flower.
>
> *Idylls of the King.*

PULWICK PRIORY, the ancestral home of the Cumbrian Landales, a dignified if not overpoweringly lordly mansion, rises almost on the ridge of the green slope which connects the high land with the sandy strand of Morecambe ; overlooking to the west the great brown breezy bight, whilst on all other sides it is sheltered by its wooded park.

When the air is clear, from the east window of Scarthey keep, the tall garden front of greystone is visible, in the extreme distance, against the darker screen of foliage ; whitely glinting if the sun is high ; golden or rosy at the end of day.

As its name implies, Pulwick Priory stands on the site of an extinct religious house; its oldest walls, in fact, were built from the spoils of once sacred masonry. It is a house of solid if not regular proportions, full of unexpected quaintness ; showing a medley of distinct styles, in and out ; it has a wide portico in the best approved neo-classic taste, leading to romantic oaken stairs ; here wide cheerful rooms and airy corridors, there sombre vaulted basements and mysterious unforeseen nooks.

On the whole, however, it is a harmonious pile of buildings, though gathering its character from many different centuries, for it has been mellowed by time, under a hard climate. And it was, in the days of the pride of the Landales, a most meet dwelling-place for that ancient race, insomuch as the history of so many of their ancestors was written successively upon stone and mortar,

85

brick and tile, as well as upon carved oak, canvas-decked walls, and emblazoned windows.

Exactly one week before the disaster, which was supposed to have befallen Mademoiselle Molly de Savenaye on Scarthey sands, the acting Lord of Pulwick, if one may so term Mr. Rupert Landale, had received a letter, the first reading of which caused him a vivid annoyance, followed by profound reflection.

A slightly-built, dark-visaged man, this younger brother of Sir Adrian, and vicarious master of his house and lands ; like to the recluse in his exquisite neatness of attire, somewhat like also in the mould of his features, which were, however, more notably handsome than Sir Adrian's ; but most unlike him, in an emphasised artificiality of manner, in a restless and wary eye, and in the curious twist of a thin lip which seemed to give hidden sarcastic meaning even to the most ordinary remark.

As now he sat by his desk, his straight brows drawn over his amber-coloured eyes, perusing the closely written sheets of this troublesome missive, there entered to him the long plaintive figure of his maiden sister, who had held house for him, under his own minute directions, ever since the death in premature child-birth of his young year-wed wife.

Miss Landale, the eldest of the family, had had a disappointment in her youth, as a result of which she now played the ungrateful *rôle* of old maid of the family. She suffered from chronic toothache, as well as from repressed romantic aspirations, and was the *âme damnée* of Rupert. One of the most melancholy of human beings, she was tersely characterised by the village folk as a "*wummicky* poor thing."

At the sight of Mr. Landale's weighted brow she propped up her own long sallow face, upon its aching side, with a trembling hand, and, full of agonised prescience, ventured to ask if anything had happened.

"Sit down," said her brother, with a sort of snarl—He possessed an extremely irritable temper under his cool sarcastic exterior, a temper which his peculiar anomalous circumstances, whilst they combined to excite it, forced him to conceal rigidly from most, and it was a relief to him to let it out occasionally upon Sophia's meek, ringleted head.

Sophia collapsed with hasty obedience into a chair, and then Mr. Landale handed to her the thin fluttering sheets, voluminously crossed and re-crossed with fine Italian handwriting:

"From Tanty," ejaculated Miss Sophia, "Oh my dear Rupert!"

"Read it," said Rupert peremptorily. "Read it aloud."

And throwing himself back upon his chair, he shaded his mouth with one flexible thin hand, and prepared himself to listen.

"CAMDEN PLACE, BATH, October 29th," read the maiden lady in those plaintive tones, which seemed to send out all speech upon the breath of a sigh. "MY DEAR RUPERT, —You will doubtless be astonished, but your *invariably* affectionate Behaviour towards myself inclines me to believe that you will also be *pleased* to hear, from these few lines, that very shortly after their receipt—if indeed not before—you may expect to see me arrive at Pulwick Priory."

Miss Landale put down the letter, and gazed at her brother through vacant mists of astonishment.

"Why, I thought Tanty said she would not put foot in Pulwick again till Adrian returned home."

Rupert measured the innocent elderly countenance with a dark look. He had sundry excellent reasons, other than mere family affection, for remaining on good terms with his rich Irish aunt, but he had likewise reasons, these less obvious, for wishing to pay his devoirs to her anywhere but under the roof of which he was nominal master.

"She has found it convenient to change her mind," he said, with his twisting lip. "Constancy in your sex, my dear, is merely a matter of convenience—or opportunity."

"Oh Rupert!" moaned Sophia, clasping the locket which contained her dead lover's hair with a gesture with which all who knew her were very familiar. Mr. Landale never could resist a thrust at the faithful foolish bosom always ready to bleed under his stabs, yet never resenting them. Inexplicable vagary of the feminine heart!

Miss Sophia worshipped before the shrine of her younger brother, to the absolute exclusion of any sentiment for the elder, whose generosity and kindness to her were yet as great as was Rupert's tyranny.

"Go on," said the latter, alternately smiling at his nails and biting them, " Tanty O'Donoghue observes that I shall be surprised to hear that she will arrive very shortly after this letter, if not before it. Poor old Tanty, there can be no mistake about her nationality. Have the kindness to read straight on, Sophia. I don't want to hear any more of your interesting comments. And don't stop till you have finished, no matter how amazed you are."

Again he composed himself to listen, while his sister plunged at the letter, and, after several false starts, found her place and proceeded :

"Since, owing to his most *unfortunate* peculiarity of Temperament and consequent strange choice of abode, I cannot apply to my nephew Adrian, *à qui de droit* (as Head of the House) I must needs address myself to you, my dear Rupert, to request hospitality for myself and the two young Ladies now under my Charge."

The letter wavered in Miss Sophia's hand and an exclamation hung upon her lip, but a sudden movement of Rupert's exquisite crossed legs recalled her to her task.

"'These young ladies are *Mesdemoiselles de Savenaye*, and the daughters of Madame la Comtesse de Savenaye, who was my sister Mary's child. She and I, and Alice your mother, were sister co-heiresses as you know, and therefore these young ladies are *my* grand-nieces and your *own* cousins once removed. Of Cécile de Savenaye, her *strange* adventures and ultimate *sad* Fate in which your own brother was implicated, you cannot but have heard, but you may probably have forgotten even to the *very existence* of these charming young women, who were nevertheless born at Pulwick, and whom you must at some time or other have beheld as infants during your *excellent* and *lamented* father's lifetime. They are, as you are doubtless also unaware—for I have remarked a *growing* Tendency in the younger generations to neglect the study of Genealogy, even as it affects their own Families—as well born on the father's side as upon the maternal. M. de Savenaye bore *argent à la fasce-canton d'hermine*, with an *augmentation of the fleurs de lis d'or, cleft in twain* for his ancestor's *memorable* deed at the siege of Dinan."

"'There is Tante O'Donoghue fully displayed, *haut volante* as she might say herself," here interrupted Mr. Landale with a laugh. "Always the same, evidently. The first thing I remember about her is her lecturing me on genealogy and heraldry, when I wanted to go fishing, till, school-boy rampant as I was, I heartily wished her impaled and debruised on her own Donoghue herse proper. For God's sake, Sophia, do not expect me to explain ! Go on."

" He was entitled to eighteen quarters, and related to such as Coucy and Armagnac and Tavannes," proceeded Miss Sophia, controlling her bewilderment as best she might, "also to Gwynne of Llanadoc in this kingdom— Honours to which Mesdemoiselles de Savenaye, being sole heiresses both of Kermelégan and Savenaye, not to speak of their own mother's share of O'Donoghue, which now-a-days is of greater substance—are personally entitled.

" If I am the *sole* Relative they have left in these Realms, Adrian and you are the next. I have had the charge of my two young Kinswomen during the last six months, that is since they left the Couvent des Dames Anglaises in Jersey.

" Now, I think it is time that your Branch of the Family should incur the share of the *responsibility* your relationship to them entails.

" If Adrian were *as* and *where* he should be, I feel sure he would embrace this opportunity of doing his duty as the Head of the House without the smallest hesitation, and I have no doubt that he would offer the *hospitality* of Pulwick Priory and his *Protection* to these amiable young persons for as long as they *remain unmarried.*

" From you, my dear Nephew, who have undertaken under these melancholy family circumstances to fill your Brother's place, I do not, however, *expect* so much ; all I ask is that you and my niece Sophia be kind enough to *shelter* and *entertain* your cousins for the space of two months, while I remain at Bath for the benefit of my Health.

" At my age (for it is of no use, nephew, for us to deny our years when any Peerage guide must reveal them

pretty closely to the curious), and I am this month passing sixty-nine, at my *age* the charge of two high-spirited
young Females, in whom conventual education has failed
to subdue Aspirations for worldly happiness whilst it has
left them somewhat inexperienced in the Conventions of
Society, I find a *little trying*. It does not harmonise with
the retired, peaceful existence to which I am accustomed
(and at my time of life, I think, entitled), in which it is
my humble endeavour to wean myself from this earth
which is so full of Emptiness and to prepare myself for
that other and *better* Home into which we must all resign
ouselves to enter. And happy, indeed, my dear Rupert,
such of us as will be found worthy ; for come to it we all
must, and the longer we live, the sooner we may expect
to do so.

"The necessity of producing them in Society, is, however, rendered a matter of greater responsibility by the
fact of the *handsome* Fortunes which these young
creatures possess already, not to speak of their expectations."

Rupert, who had been listening to his aunt's letter,
through the intermediary of Miss Sophia's depressing
sing-song, with an abstracted air, here lifted up his head,
and commanded the reader to repeat this last passage.
She did so, and paused, awaiting his further pleasure,
while he threw his handsome head back upon his chair,
and closed his eyes as if lost in calculations.

At length he waved his hand, and Miss Sophia proceeded after the usual floundering :

"A neighbour of mine at Bunratty, Mrs. Hambledon of
Brianstown, a *lively* widow (herself one of the Macnamaras
of the Reeks, and thus a distant connection of the
Ballinasloe branch of O'Donoghues), and whom I had
reason to believe I could trust—but I will not anticipate
—took a prodigious fancy to Miss Molly and proposed,
towards the beginning of the Autumn, carrying her away
to Dublin. At the same time the wet summer, producing
in me an acute recurrence of that Affection from which,
as you know, I suffer, and about which you *never fail* to
make such kind Enquiries at Christmas and Easter, com-
pelled me to call in Mr. O'Mally, the apothecary, who
has been my very *obliging* medical adviser for so many
years, and who strenuously advocated an immediate

course of waters at Bath.   In short, my dear Nephew, thus the matter was settled, your cousin Molly departed *radiant* with *good* spirits, and *good* looks for a spell of gayety in Dublin, while your cousin Madeleine, prepared (with *equal* content) to accompany her old aunt to Bath. It being arranged with Mrs. Hambledon that she should herself conduct Molly to us later on.

" We have been here about three weeks.   Though persuaded by good Mr. O'Mally that the waters would benefit my old bones, I was actuated, I must confess, by another motive in seeking this Fashionable Resort.   In such a place as this, thronged as it is by all the Rank and Family of England, one can at least know *who is who*, and I was not without hopes that my nieces, with their faces, their name, and their fortunes, would have the opportunity of contracting suitable Alliances, and thus relieve me of a charge for which I am, I fear, little fitted.

"But, alas! my dear Rupert, I was most woefully mistaken.   Bath is *distinctly not* the place for two beautiful and unsophisticated Heiresses, and I am certainly neither possessed of the Spirits, nor of the Health to guard them from fortune-hunters and *needy nameless* Adventurers. While it is my desire to impress upon you, and my niece Sophia, that the conduct of these young ladies has been *quite* beyond reproach, I will not conceal from you that the attentions of a certain person, of the name of *Smith*, known here, and a favorite in the circles of frivolity and fashion as *Captain Jack*, have already made Madeleine *conspicuous*, and although the dear girl conducts herself with the utmost propriety, there is an air of *Romance* and *mystery* about the Young Man, not to speak of his unmistakable good looks, which have determined me to remove her from his vicinity before her Affections be *irreparably* engaged.   As for Molly, who is a thorough O'Donoghue and the image of her grandmother, that celebrated Murthering Moll (herself the toast of Bath in our young days), whose elopement with the Marquis de Kermelégran, after he had killed an English rival in a duel, was once a nine-days' wonder in this very town, and of whom you must have heard, Mrs. Hambledon restored her to my care only three days ago, and she has already twenty Beaux to her String, though favouring *nobody*, I am bound to say, but her own amuse-

ment. Yesterday she departed under Mrs. Hambledon's
chaperonage, in the Company of a dozen of the highest
in rank here, on an expedition to Clifton ; the while my
demure Madeleine spends the day at the house of her
dear friend Lady Maria Harewood, whither, I only learnt
upon her return at ten o'clock under his escort, *Captain
Jack*—in my days that sort of *captain* would have been
strongly suspected, of having a shade too much of the
Heath or the *London Road* about him—had likewise been
convened. It was long after midnight when, with a
great *low-row*, a coach full of very merry company
(amongst whom the widow Hambledon struck me as
over-merry, perhaps) landed my other Miss *sur le perron*.
   "This has decided me. We shall decamp *sans tam-
bour ni trompette*. To-morrow, without allowing discussion from the girls (in which I should probably be
worsted), we pack ourselves into my travelling coach,
and find our Way to you. But, until we are fairly on
the Road, I shall not even let these ladies know *whither*
we are bound.
   "With your kind permission, then, I shall remain a
few days at Pulwick, to recruit from the *fatigues* of
such a long Journey, before leaving your fair cousins
in your charge, and in that of the gentle Sophia (whom
I trust to entertain them with something besides her
usual melancholy), till the time comes for me to bring
them back with me to Bunratty.
   "Unless, therefore, you should hear to the contrary,
you will know that on Tuesday your three *unprotected*
female relatives will be hoping to see your travelling
carriage arrive to fetch them at the Crown in Lancaster.
               "Your Affectionate Aunt,
                         "ROSE O'DONOGHUE."

   As Miss Landale sighed forth the concluding words,
she dropped the little folio on her lap, and looked at her
brother with a world of apprehension in her faded eyes.
   "Oh, Rupert, what shall we do?"
   "Do," said Mr. Landale, quickly turning on her, out
of his absorption, "you will kindly see that suitable rooms
are prepared for your aunt and cousins, and you will endeavour, if you please, to show these ladies a cheerful
countenance, as your aunt requests."

"The oak and the chintz rooms, I suppose," Sophia timidly suggested. "Tanty used to say she liked the aspect, and I daresay the young ladies will find it pleasant to look out on the garden."

"Ay," returned Rupert, absently. He had risen from his seat, and fallen to pacing the room. Presently a short laugh broke from him. "Tolerably cool, I must say," he remarked, "tolerably cool. It seems to be a tradition with that Savenaye family, when in difficulties, to go to Pulwick."

Miss Landale looked up with relief. Perhaps Rupert would think better of it, and make up his mind to elude receiving the unwelcome visitors after all. But his next speech dashed her budding hopes.

"Ay, as in the days of their mother before them, when she came here to lay her eggs, like a cuckoo in another bird's nest—I wish they had been addled, I do indeed—we may expect to have the whole place turned topsy-turvy, I suppose. It is a pretty assortment, *faith* (as Tanty says herself) ; an old papist, and two young ones, fresh from a convent school—and of these, one a hoyden, and the other lovesick ! Faugh ! Sophia you will have to keep your eyes open when the old lady is gone. I'll have no unseemly pranks in this house."

"Oh, Rupert," with a moan of maidenly horror, and conscious incompetence.

"Stop that," cried the brother, with a contained intensity of exasperation, at which the poor lady jumped and trembled as if she had been struck. "All your whining won't improve matters. Now listen to me," sitting down beside her, and speaking slowly and impressively, "you are to make our relatives feel welcome, do you understand? Everything is to be of the best. Get out the embroidered sheets, and see that there are flowers in the rooms. Tell the cook to keep back that haunch of venison, the girls won't like it, but the old lady knows a good thing when she gets it—let there be lots of sweet things for the young ones too. I shall be giving some silver out this afternoon. I leave it to you to see that it is properly cleaned. What are you mumbling about to yourself? Write it down if you can't remember, and now go, go—I am busy."

PART II

"MURTHERING MOLL THE SECOND"

Then did the blood awaken in the veins
Of the young maiden wandering in the fields.

LUTEPLAYER'S SONG.

CHAPTER X

THE THRESHOLD OF WOMANHOOD

Onward floweth the water, onward through meadows broad,
" How happy," the meadows say, " art thou to be rippling onward."
" And my heart is beating, beating beneath my girdle here ; "
" O Heart," the girdle saith, " how happy art thou that thou beatest."
Luteplayer's Song.

DUBLIN, *October* 15*th*, 1814.—This day do I, Molly de Savenaye, begin my diary.

Madeleine writes to me from Bath that she has purchased a very fine book, in which she intends to set forth each evening all that has happened her since the morning ; she advises me to do so too. She says that since *real life* has begun for us ; life, of which every succeeding day is not, as in the convent, the repetition of the previous day, but brings some new discovery, pleasure, or pain, we ought to write down and preserve their remembrance.

It will be so interesting for us to read when a new life once more begins for us, and we are *married.* Besides it is the *fashion*, and all the young ladies she knows do it. And she has, she says, already plenty to write down. Now I *should* like to know what about.

When ought one to start such a record ? Surely not on a day like this.

"Why *demme*" (as Mrs. Hambledon's nephew says), " *what the deyvil* have I got to say ? "

Item : I went out shopping this morning with Mrs. Hambledon, and, bearing Madeleine's advice in mind, purchased at Kelly's, in Sackville Street, an album book, bound in green morocco, with clasp and lock, which Mr. Kelly protests is quite secure.

Item : We met Captain Segrave of the Royal Dragoons (who was so attentive to me at Lady Rigtoun's rout, two days ago). He looked very well on his charger, but how conceited ! When he saw me, he rolled his eyes and

grew quite red; and then he stuck his spurs into his
horse, that we might admire how he could sit it; which
he did, indeed, to perfection.

Mrs. Hambledon looked vastly knowing, and I laughed.
If ever I try to fancy myself married to such a man I cannot help laughing.

This, however, is not diary.—*Item :* We returned home
because it began to rain, and to pass the time, here am I
at my book.

But is *this* the sort of thing that will be of interest to
read hereafter? I have begun too late; I should have
written in those days when I saw the dull walls of our
convent prison for the last time. It seems so far back
now (though, by the calendar it is hardly six months),
that I cannot quite recall how it felt to live in prison.
And yet it was not unhappy, and there was no horror in
the thought we both had sometimes then, that we should
pass and end our lives in the cage. It did not strike us
as hard. It seemed, indeed, in the nature of things. But
the bare thought of returning to that existence now, to
resume the placid daily task, to fold up again like a plant
that has once expanded to sun and breeze, to have never
a change of scene, of impression, to look forward to nothing but *submission,* sleep, and *death ;* oh, it makes me
turn cold all over!

And yet there are women who, of their own will, give
up the *freedom of the world* to enter a convent *after* they
have tasted life! Oh, I would rather be the poorest, the
ugliest peasant hag, toiling for daily bread, than one of
these cold cloistered souls, so that the free air of heaven,
be it with the winds or the rain, might beat upon me, so
that I might live and love *as I like,* do right *as I like ;* ay,
and do wrong *if* I liked, with the free will which is my
own.

We were told that the outer world, with all its sorrows
and trials, and dangers—how I remember the Reverend
Mother's words and face, and how they impressed me
then, and how I should laugh at them, *now !*—that the
world was but a valley of tears. We were warned that
all that awaited us, if we left the fold, was *misery ;* that
the joys of this world were *bitter* to the taste, its pleasures
hollow, and its griefs *lasting.*

We believed it. And yet, when the choice was actually

ours to make, we chose all we had been taught to dread and despise. Why? I wonder. For the same reason as Eve ate the apple, I suppose. I would, if I had been Eve. I almost wish I could go back now, for a day, to the cool white rooms, to see the nuns flitting about like black and white ghosts, with only a jingle of beads to warn one of their coming, see the blue sky through the great bare windows, and the shadows of the trees lengthening on the cold flagged floors, hear the bells going ding-dong, ding-dong, and the murmur of the sea in the distance, and the drone of the school, and the drone of the chapel, to go back, and feel once more the dull sort of content, the calmness, the rest!

But no, no! I should be trembling all the while lest the blessed doors leading back to that *horrible* world should never open to me again.

The sorrows and trials of the world! I suppose the Reverend Mother really meant it; and if I had gone on living there till my face was wrinkled like hers, poor woman, I might have thought so too, in the end, and talked the same nonsense.

Was it really I that endured such a life for seventeen years? O God! I wonder that the sight of the swallows coming and going, the sound of the free waves, did not drive me mad. Twist as I will my memory, I cannot recall *that* Molly of six months ago, whose hours and days passed and dropped all alike, all lifeless, just like the slow tac, tac, tac of our great horloge in the Refectory, and were to go on as slow and as alike, for ever and ever, till she was old, dried, wrinkled, and then died. The real Molly de Savenaye's life began on the April morning when that dear old turbaned fairy godmother of ours carried us, poor little Cinderellas, away in her coach. Well do I remember my birthday.

I have read since in one of those musty books of Bunratty, that *moths* and *butterflies* come to life by shaking themselves out, one fine day, from a dull-looking, shapeless, ugly thing they call a *grub*, in which they have been buried for a long time. They unfold their wings and fly out in the sunshine, and flit from flower to flower, and they look beautiful and happy—the world, the wicked world, is open to them.

There were pictures in the book; the ugly grub below,

dreary and brown, and the lovely *butterfly* in all its colours above. I showed them to Madeleine, and said: "Look, Madeleine, as we were, and as we are."

And she said: "Yes, those brown gowns they made us wear were ugly; but I should not like to put on anything so bright as red and yellow. Would you?"

That is the worst of Madeleine; she never realises in the least what I mean. And she *does* love her clothes; that is the difference between her and me, she loves fine things because they are fine and dainty and all that—I like them because they make *me* fine.

And yet, how she did weep when she left the convent. Madeleine would have made a good nun after all; she does so hate anything ugly or coarse. She grows quite white if she hears people fighting; if there is a "row" or a "shindy," as they say here. Whereas Tanty and I think it all the fun in the world, and would enjoy joining in the fray ourselves, I believe, if we dared. I know *I* should; it sets my blood tingling. But Madeleine is a real princess, a sort of Ermine; and yet she enjoys her new life, too, the beauty of it, the refinement, being waited upon and delicately fed and clothed. But although she has ceased to weep for the convent, if it had not been for me she would be there still. The only thing, I believe, that could make me weep now would be to find one fine morning that this had only been a dream, and that I was once more *the grub!* To find that I could not open my window and look into the wide, wide world over to the long, green hills in the distance, and know that I could wander or gallop up to them, as I did at Bunratty, and see for myself *what lies beyond*—surely that was a taste of heaven that day when Tanty Rose first allowed me to mount her old pony, and I flew over the turf with the wind whistling in my ears—to find that I could not go out when I pleased and hear new voices and see new faces, and men and women who *live each their own life*, and not the *same* life as mine.

When I think of what I am now, and what I might have remained, I breathe deep and feel like singing; I stretch my arms out and feel like flying.

Our aunt told us she thought Bunratty would be dull for us, and so it was in comparison with this place. Perhaps *this* is dull in comparison with what *may* come.

For good Tanty, as she likes us to call her, is intent on doing great things for us.

"Je vous marierai," she tells us in her funny old French, "Je vous marierai bien, mes filles, si vous êtes sages," and she winks both eyes.

Marriage! That, it is quite evident, is the goal of every properly constituted young female; and every respectable person who has the care of said young female is consequently bent upon her reaching that goal.

So marriage is *another* good thing to look forward to. And *love,* that love all the verses, all the books one reads are so full of ; *that* will come to us.

They say that *love is life.* Well, all I want is to live. But with a grey past such as we have had, the present is good enough to ponder upon. We now can lie abed if we have sweet dreams and pursue them waking, and be lazy, yet not be troubled with the self-indulgence as with an enormity ; or we can rise and breathe the sunshine at our own time. We can be frivolous, and yet meet with smiles in response, dress our hair and persons, and be pleased with ourselves, and with being admired or envied, yet not be told horrid things about death and corruption and skeletons. And, above all—oh, above *all,* we can think of the future as different from the past, as *changing,* be it even for the worse ; as unknown and fascinating, not as a repetition, until death, of the same dreary round.

In Mrs. Hambledon's parlour here are huge glasses at either end ; whenever you look into them you see a never-ending chain of rooms with yourself standing in the middle, vanishing in the distance, every one the same, with the same person in the middle, only a little smaller, a little more insignificant, a little darker, till it all becomes *nothing.* It always reminds me of life's prospects in the convent.

I dislike that room. When I told Mrs. Hambledon the reason why, she laughed, and promised me that, with my looks and disposition, my life would be eventful enough. I have every mind that it shall.

October 18*th.*—Yesterday, I woke up in an amazing state of happiness, though for no particular reason that I can think of. It could not be simply because we were to go

out for a visit to the country and see new people and
places, for I have already learned to find that most new
people are cut out on the same pattern as those one
already knows.   It must have been rather because I
awoke under the impression of one of my lovely dreams
—such dreams as I have only had since I left my *grub*
state ; dreams of space, air, long, long views of beautiful
scenery, always changing, always wider, such as swallows
flying between sky and earth might see, under an exquisite and brilliant light, till for very joy I wake up, my
cheeks covered with tears.

This time, I was sitting on the prow of some vessel
with lofty white sails, and it was cutting through the
water, blue as the sky, with wreaths of snow-like foam,
towards some unknown shores, ever faster and faster, and
I was singing to some one next to me on the prow—some
one I did not know, but who felt with me—singing a song
so perfect, so sweet (though it had no human words) that
I thought *it explained all :* the blue of the heaven, the
freshness of the breeze, the fragrance of the earth, and
why we were so eagerly pressing onwards.   I thought
the melody was such that when once heard it could never
be forgotten.   When I woke it still rang in my ears, but
now I can no more recall it.   How is it we never know
such delight in waking hours ?   Is that some of the joy we
are to feel in Heaven, the music we are to hear ?   And yet
it can be heard in this life if one only knew where to go
and listen.   And this life is beautiful which lies in front
of us, though they would speak of it as a sorrowful span
not to be reckoned.   It is good to be young and think of
the life still to come.   Every moment is precious for its
enjoyment, and yet sometimes I find that one only knows
of a pleasure when it is just gone.   One ought to try and
be more awake at each hour to the happiness it may
bring.   I shall try, and you, my diary, shall help me.

This is really *no* diary-keeping.   It is not a bit like
those one reads in books.   It ought to tell of other people
and the events of each day.   But other people are really
very uninteresting ; as for events, well, so far, they are
uninteresting too ; it is only what they cause to spring
up in our hearts that is worth thinking upon ; and that is
so difficult to put in words that mostly I spend my time
merely pondering and not writing.

Last night Mrs. Hambledon took me to the *play*. It was for the first time in my life, and I was full of curiosity. It was a long drama, pretty enough and sometimes very exciting. But I could see that though the actress was very handsome and mostly so unhappy as to draw tears from the spectators, there were people, especially some gentlemen, who were more interested in looking at the box where I sat with Mrs. Hambledon. Indeed, I could not pretend, when I found myself before my glass that night, that I was not amazingly prettier than that Mrs. Colebrook, about whose beauty the whole town goes mad.

When I recalled the hero's ravings about his Matilda's eyes and cheeks, and her foot and her sylph-like waist, and her raven hair, I wondered what *that* young man would say of me if he were my lover and I his persecuted mistress. The Matilda was a pleasing person enough; but if I take her point by point, it would be absurd to speak of her charms in the same breath with mine. Oh, my dear Molly, how beautiful I thought you last night! How happy I should be, were I a dashing young lover and eyes like *yours* smiled on me. I never before thought myself prettier than Madeleine, but now I do.

Lovers, love, mistress, bride; they talked of nothing else in the play. And it was all ecstasy in their words, and nothing but *misery* in fact (just as the Reverend Mother would have had it).

The young man who played the hero was a very fine fellow; and yet when I conceive *him* making love to me as he did last night to Mrs. Colebrook, the notion seems really *too* ludicrous!

What sort of man then is it I would allow to love me? I do not mind the thought of lovers sighing and burning for me (as some do now indeed, or pretend to) I like to feel that I can crush them with a frown and revive them with a smile; I like to see them fighting for my favour. But to give a man the right to love me, the right to my smiles, the *right to me!* Indeed, I have yet seen *none* who could make me bear the thought.

And yet I think that I could love, and I know that the man that I am to love must be living somewhere till fate brings him to me. He does not think of me. He does not know of me. And neither of us, I suppose, will taste life as life is till the day when we meet.

CAMDEN PLACE, BATH, *November 1st.*—Bath at last, which must please poor Mrs. Hambledon exceedingly, for she certainly did *not* enjoy the transit. I cannot conceive how people can allow themselves to be so utterly distraught by illness. I feel I can never have any respect for her again; she moaned and lamented in such cowardly fashion, was so peevish all the time on board the vessel, and looked so very begrimed and untidy and *plain* when she was carried out on Bristol quay. The captain called it *dirty* weather, but I thought it *lovely*, and I don't think I ever enjoyed myself more—except when Captain Segrave's Black Douglas ran away with me in Phœnix Park.

It was beautiful to see our brave boat plough the sea and quiver with anger, as if it were a living thing, when it was checked by some great green wave, then gather itself again under the wind and dash on to the fight, until it conquered. And when we came into the river and the sun shone once more it glided on swiftly, though looking just a little tired for a while until its decks and sails were dry and clean again, and I thought it was just like a bird that has shaken and plumed itself. I was sorry to leave it. The captain and the mate and the sailors, who had wrapped me up in their great, stiff tarpaulin coats and placed me in a safe corner where I could sit out and look, were also sorry that I should go.

But it was good to be with Madeleine again and Tanty Donoghue, who always has such a kind smile on her old wrinkled face when she looks at me.

Madeleine was astonished when I told her I had loved the storm at sea and when I mimicked poor Mrs. Hambledon. She says she also thought she was dying, so ill was she on her crossing, and that she was quite a week before she got over the impression.

It seems odd to think that we are sisters, and twin sisters too; in so many things she is different from me. She has changed in manner since I left her. She seems so absorbed in some great thought that all her words and smiles have little meaning in them. I told her I had tried to keep my diary, but had not done much work, and when I asked to see hers (for a model) Madeleine blushed, and said I should see it this day year.

Madeleine is in love ; that is the only way I can account

for that blush. I fear she is a sly puss, but there is such a bustle around us, and so much to do and see, I have no time to make her confess. So I said I would keep mine from her for that period also.

It seems a long span to look ahead. What a number of things will happen before this day year!

BATH, *November 3rd.*—Bath is delightful! I have only been here two days, and already I am what Tanty, in her old-fashioned way, calls *the belle.* Already there are a dozen sparks who declare that my eyes have *shot death* to them. This afternoon comes my Lord of Manningham, nicknamed *King of Bath,* to "drink a dish of tea," as he has it, with his "dear old friend Miss O'Donoghue."

Tanty has been here three weeks, and he has only just discovered her existence, and remembered their tender friendship. Of course, I know very well what has really brought him. He is Lord Dereham's grandfather on the mother's side, and Lord Dereham, who is the son of the Duke of Wells, is "the catch," as Mrs. Hambledon vows, of the fashionable world this year. And Lord Dereham has seen me twice, and *is in love with me.*

But as Lord Dereham is more like a little white rat than a man, and swears more than he converses—which would be very shocking if it were not for his lisp, which makes it very funny—needless to say, my diary dear, your Molly is not in love with him—He has no chance.

And so Lord Manningham comes to tea, and Tanty orders me to remain and see her "old friend" instead of going to ride with the widow Hambledon. The widow Hambledon and I are everywhere together, and she knows all the most entertaining people in Bath, whereas Madeleine, whom I have hardly seen at all except at night, when I am so dead tired that I go to sleep as soon as my head touches the pillow (I vow Tanty's manner of speech is catching), Miss Madeleine keeps to her own select circle, and turns up her haughty little nose at *my* friends.

So now Madeleine is punished, for Tanty and I have had the honour of receiving the *King of Bath,* and I have been vouchsafed the stamp of his august approval.

"My dear Miss O'Donoghue," he cried, as I curtsied, "do my senses deceive me, or do I not once more behold *Murthering Moll ?*"

"I thought you could not fail to notice the likeness; my niece is, indeed, a complete O'Donoghue," says Tanty, amazingly pleased.

"Likeness, ma'am," cried the old wretch, bowing again, and scattering his snuff all over the place, while I sweep him another splendid curtsey, "likeness, ma'am, why this is no feeble copy, no humble imitation, 'tis *Murdering Moll herself*, and glad I am to see her again." And then he catches me under the chin, and peers into my face with his dim, wicked old eyes. "And so you are Murdering Moll's daughter," says he, chuckling to himself. "Ay, she and I were very good friends, my pretty child, very good friends, and that not so long ago, either. Ay, *Mater pulchra, filia pulchrior*."

"But I happen to be her grand-daughter, please my lord," said I, and then I ran to fetch him a chair (for I was dreadfully afraid he was going to kiss me). But though no one has ever accused me of speaking too modestly to be heard, my lord had a sudden fit of deafness, and I saw Tanty give me a little frown, while the old thing—he must be much older than Tanty even—tottered into a chair, and went on mumbling.

"I was only a boy in those days, my dear, only a boy, as your good aunt will tell you. I can remember how the bells rang the three beautiful Irish sisters into Bath, and I and the other dandies stood to watch them drive by. The bells rang in the *belles* in those days, my dear, he, he, he! only we used to call them 'toasts' then, and your mother was the most beautiful of 'the three Graces' —we christened them 'the three Graces'—and by gad she led us all a pretty dance!"

"Ah, my lord," says Tanty, and I could see her old eyes gleam though her tone was so pious, "I fear we were three wild Irish girls indeed!"

Lord Manningham was too busy ogling me to attend to her.

"Your mother was just such another as you, and she had just such a pair of dimples," said he.

"You mean my grandmother," shouted I in his ear, just for fun, though Tanty looked as if she were on pins and needles. But he only pinched my cheek again and went on:

"Before she had been here a fortnight all the bucks in the

town were at her feet. And so was I, so was I. Only, by
gad, I was too young, you know, as Miss O'Donoghue here
will tell you. But she liked me ; she used to call me her
'little manny.' I declare I might have married her, only
there were family reasons, and I was such a lad, you know.
And then Jack Waterpark, some of us thought she would
have had *him* in the end—being an Irishman, and a rich
man, and a marquis to boot—he gave her the name of
Murthering Moll, because of her killing eyes, young lady—
he ! he ! he !—and there was Ned Cuffe ready to hang
himself for her, and Jim Denham, and old Beau Vernon,
ay, and a score of others. And then one night at the
Assembly Rooms, after the dancing was over and we
gay fellows were all together, up gets Waterpark, he was
a little tipsy, my dear, and by gad I can hear him speak
now, with that brogue of his. 'Boys, he says, 'it's no
use your trying for her any more, for by God *I've won her.*'
And out of his breast-pocket he pulls a little knot of blue
ribbon. Your mother, my dear, had worn a very fine
gown that evening, with little knots of blue ribbon all
over the bodice of it. The words were not out of his
mouth when Ned Cuffe starts to his feet as white as a
sheet : ' It's a damned lie,' he cries, and out of his pocket
he pulls another little knot. 'She gave it to me with her
own hands,' he cried and glares round at us all. And
then Vernon bursts out laughing and flourishes a third
little bow in our eyes, and I had one too, I need not tell
you, and so had all the rest, all save a French fellow—I
forget his name—and it was he she had danced with the
most of all. Ah, Miss O'Donoghue, how the little jade's
eyes sparkle ! I warrant you have never told her the story
for fear she would want to copy her mother in other ways
besides looks—Hey ? Well, my pretty, give me your little
hand, and then I shall go on—pretty little hand, um—um
—um !" and then he kissed my hand, the horrid, snuffy
thing ! but I allowed it, for I did so want to hear how it
all ended.

"And then, and then," I said.

"And then, my dear, this French fellow, your papa he
must have been—so I suppose I must not abuse him, and
he was a very fine young man after all, and a man of
honour as well—he stood and cursed us all."

"'You English fools,' he said, 'you braggards—

cowards.' And he seized a glass of wine from the table
and with a sweep he dashed it at us and ended by flinging the empty glass in Lord Waterpark's face. It was the
neatest thing you ever saw, for we all got a drop except
Waterpark, and he got the glass. 'I challenge you all,'
said the Frenchman, 'I'll fight you one by one, and I shall
have her into the bargain.' And so he did, my dear, he
fought us all, one after the other ; there were five of us ;
he was a devil with the sword, but Ned Cuffe ran him
through for all that—and he was a month getting over it,
but as soon as he could crawl again he vowed himself
ready for Waterpark, and weak as he was he ran poor
Waterpark through the lungs. Some said Jack spitted
himself on his sword—but dead he was anyhow, and monsieur your father—what was his name ? Kerme-some-
thing—was off with your mother before the rest of us were
well out of bed."

"Fie, fie, my lord," said Tanty, " you should not recall
old stories in this manner !"

"Gad, ma'am, I warrant this young lady is quite ready
to provide you with a few new ones," chuckled my lord ;
and as there was no more to be extracted from him but
foolish old jokes and dreadful smiles, I contrived to free
my "pretty little hand," and sit down demurely by
Tanty's side like the modest retiring young female I
should be.

But my blood was dancing in my veins—the blood of
Murthering Moll—doddering old idiot as he is, Lord
Manningham is right for once, I mean to take quite as
much out of life as she did. That indeed is worth being
young and beautiful for ! We know nothing of our family,
save that both father and mother were killed in Vendée.
Tanty never will tell us anything about them (except their
coats of arms), and I am afraid even to start the subject,
for she always branches off upon heraldry and then we
are in for hours of it. But after Lord Manningham
was gone I asked her when and how my grandmother
died.

"She died when your mother was born, my dear," said
Tanty, "she was not as old as you are now, and your
grandfather never smiled again, or so they said."

That sobered me a little. Yet she lived her life so well,
while she did live, that I who have wasted twenty pre-

cious years can find in my heart rather to envy than to pity my beautiful grandmother.

November 5th. —It is *three o'clock in the morning*, but I do not feel at all inclined to go to bed. Madeleine is sleeping, poor pretty pale Madeleine! with the tears hardly dry upon her cheeks and I can hear her sighing in her sleep.

I was right, she is in love, and the gentleman she loves is not approved of by Tanty and the upshot of it all is we are to leave dear Bath, delightful Bath, to-morrow—to-day rather—for some unknown penitential region which our stern relative as yet declines to name. I am longing to hear more about it; but Tanty, who, though she talks so much, can keep her own counsel better than any woman I know, will not give me any further information beyond the facts that the delinquent who has dared to aspire to my sister is a person of *the name of Smith*, and that it would not do at all.

I have not the heart to wake Madeleine to make her tell me more, though I really ought to pinch her well for being so secretive—besides, my head is so full of my own day that I want to get it all written down, and I shall never have done so unless I begin at the beginning.

Yesterday, then, at 3 o'clock in the afternoon Lord Dereham's coach and four came clattering up to our door to call for me. Mrs. Hambledon was already installed and Lady Soames and a dozen other of the *fashionables* of Bath. My little Lord Marquis had kept the box seat for me, at which the other ladies, even my dear friend and chaperon, looked rather green. The weather was glorious, and off we went with a flourish of trumpets and whips, and I knew I should enjoy myself monstrously.

And so I did. But it was the drive back that was the *best* of all. We never started till near nine o'clock, and Lord Dereham insisted on my sitting beside him again— at which all the ladies looked daggers *at me* and all the gentlemen daggers *at him*. And then we sang songs and tore along uphill and down dale, under the beautiful moonlight, through the still air, till all at once we found we had lost our way. We had to drive on till we came to an inn and we could make inquiries. There the gentlemen opened another hamper of wine, and when we set off again I promise you they were all pretty *lively* (and most of the ladies too, for the matter of that). As for me, who never drank anything but milk or water till six months ago, I have not learnt to like wine yet, so, though I sipped out of the glass to keep the fun going, I contrived to dispose of the contents, quietly over the side of the coach, when no one was looking.

It was a drive to remember. We came to a big hill, and as we were going down it at a smart pace the coach began to sway, then the ladies began to screech, and even the men looked so scared that I laughed outright. Lord Dereham was perfectly tipsy and he did not know the road a bit, but he drove in beautiful style and was extraordinarily amusing ; as soon as the coach took to swaying, instead of slackening speed as they all begged him, he *lashed* the horses into a tearing gallop, looking over his shoulder at the rest and cursing them with the greatest energy, grinning with rage, and looking more like a little white rat than *ever*.

"Give me the whip," said I, "and I shall whip the team while you drive."

"*Cuth me*," cried he, "if you are not worth the whole coach-load a dozen times over."

On we went ; the coach rocked, the horses galloped, and I knew at any moment the whole thing might upset, and I flourished my whip and lashed at the steaming flanks and I never felt what it was to really enjoy myself before.

Presently, although we were tearing along so fast, the coach steadied itself and went as straight as an arrow ; and this, it seems, it would never have done had not Lord Dereham kept up the pace.

And all the rest of the drive his lordship wanted to kiss me. I was not a bit frightened, though he was drunk, but every time he grew too forward I just flicked at the horses with the whip, and I think he saw that I would have cracked him across the face quite as readily if he dared to presume.

No doubt a dozen times during the day I could have secured a coronet for myself, not to speak of future 'strawberry leaves,' as my aunt says, if I had cared to ; but who could think of loving a man like *that* ? He can manage four horses, and he has shot two men in a duel, and he can drink three bottles of wine at a sitting, and when one tries to find something more to say for him, lo ! that is all !

When we at length arrived at Camden Place, for I vowed they must leave me home the first, there was the rarest sport. My lord's grooms must set to blow the horns, for they were as drunk as their master, while one of the gentlemen played upon the knocker till the whole crescent was aroused.

Then the doors opened suddenly, *and Tanty appears* on the threshold, holding a candle. Her turban was quite crooked, with the birds of Paradise over one eye, and I never saw her old nose look so hooked. All the gentlemen set up a shout, and Sir Thomas Wrexham began to crow like a cock for no reason on earth that I can think of. The servants were holding up lanterns, but the moon was nigh as bright as day.

Tanty just looked round upon them one after another, and in spite of her crooked turban I think they all grew frightened. Then she caught hold of me, and just whisked me behind her. Next she spied out Mrs. Hambledon, who had been asleep inside the coach, and now tumbled forth, yawning and gaping.

"And so, madam," cries Tanty to her, not very loud, but in a voice that made even me tremble ; "so, madam, this is how you fulfil the confidence I placed in you. A pretty chaperon you are to have the charge of a young lady ; though, indeed, considering your years, madam, I might have been justified in trusting you."

Mrs. Hambledon, cut short in the middle of a loud yawn by this attack, was a sight to see.

"Hoighty-toighty, ma'am !" she cried, indignantly, as soon as she could get her voice ; "here's a fine to-do. It is my fault, of course, that Lord Dereham should mistake the road. And my fault too, no doubt, that your miss should make an exhibition of herself riding on the box with the gentlemen at this hour of night, when I implored her to come inside with me, were it only for the sake of common female propriety."

"Common female indeed !" echoed Tanty, with a snort ; "the poor child knew better."

"Cuth the old cats ! they'll have each other'th eyeth out," here cried my lord marquis, interposing his little

tipsy person between them.   He had scrambled down the
box after me, and was listening with an air of profound
wisdom that made me feel fit to die laughing.   "Don't
you mind her, old lady," he went on, addressing Tanty ;
" Mith Molly ith quite able to take care of herself—damme
if she'th not."

Aunt Donoghue turned upon him majestically.

"And then that is more than can be said for you, my
poor young man," she exclaimed ; and I vow he looked
as sobered as if she had flung a bucket of cold water over
him.   Upon this she retired and shut the door, and marched
me upstairs before her without a word.

Before my room door she stopped.

"Mrs. Dempsey has already packed your sister's
trunks," she said, in a very dry way ; "and she will
begin to pack yours early—I was going to say to-morrow
—but you keep such hours, my dear—it will be *to-day*."

I stared at her as if she had gone mad.

"You and your sister," she went on, "have got beyond me.   I have taken my resolution and given my
orders, and there is not the least use making a scene."

And then it came out about Madeleine.   At first I
thought I would go into a great passion and refuse to
obey, but after a minute or two I saw it was, as she said,
no use.   Tanty was as cool as a cucumber.   Then I
thought perhaps I might mollify her if I could cry, but
I couldn't pump up a tear ; I never can ; and at last when
I went into my room and saw poor Madeleine, who has
cried herself to sleep, evidently, I understood that there
was nothing for us but to do as we were told.

And now I can hear Tanty fussing about her room still
—she has been writing, too—cra, cra, cra—this last hour.
I wonder who to ?   After all there is some fun in being
taken off mysteriously we don't know where.   I should
like to go and kiss her, but she thinks I am abed.

CHAPTER XI

A MASTERFUL OLD MAID

No contrary advice having reached Pulwick since Miss O'Donoghue's *letter of invoice*, as Mr. Landale facetiously described it, he drove over to Lancaster on the day appointed to meet the party.

And thus it came to pass that through the irresistible management of Miss O'Donoghue, who put into the promotion of her scheme all the energy belonging to her branch of the family, together with the long habit of authority of the *Tante à héritage*, the daughters of Cécile de Savenaye returned to that first home of theirs, of which they had forgotten even the name.

Mr. Landale had not set eyes on his valuable relative for many years, but her greeting, at the first renewal of intercourse which took place in the principal parlour of the Lancaster Inn, was as easily detached in manner as though they had just met again after a trifling absence and she was bringing her charges to his house in accordance with a mutual agreement.

"My dear Rupert," cried she, "I am glad to see you again. I need not ask you how you are, you look so extremely sleek and prosperous. Adrian's wide acres are succulent, hey? I should have known you anywhere; though to be sure, you are hardly large enough for the breed, you have the true Landale stamp on you, the unmistakable Landale style of feature. *Semper eadem.* In that sense, at least, one can apply your ancient and once worthy motto to you; and you know, nephew, since you have conveniently changed your faith, both to God and king, this sentiment strikes one as a sarcasm amidst the achievements of Landale, you backsliders! Ah, we O'Donoghues have better maintained our device, *sans changier.*"

8   113

Rupert, to whom the well-known volubility of his aunt was most particularly disagreeable, but who had nevertheless saluted the stalwart old lady's cheek with much affection, here bent his supple back with a sort of mocking gallantry.

"You maintain your *device*, permit me to say, my dear aunt, as ostentatiously in your person as we renegade Landales ourselves."

"Pooh, pooh! I am too old a bird to be caught by such chaff, nephew; it is pearls before .... I mean it is too late in the day, my dear. Keep it for the young things. And indeed I see the sheep's eyes you have been casting in their direction. Come nearer, young ladies, and make your cousin's acquaintance," beckoning to her nieces, who, arrayed in warm travelling pelisses and beaver bonnets of fashionable appearance, stood in the background near the fireplace.

"They are very like, are they not?" she continued. "Twins always are; as like as two peas. And yet these are as different as day and night when you come to know them. Madeleine is the eldest; that is she in the beaver fur; Molly prefers bear. Without their bonnets you will distinguish them by their complexion. Molly has raven hair (she is the truest O'Donoghue), whilst Madeleine is fair, *blonde*, like her Breton father."

The sisters greeted their new-found guardian, each in her own way. And, in spite of the disguising bonnets and their surprising similarity of voice, height, and build, the difference was more marked than that of beaver and bear.

Madeleine acknowledged her kinsman's greeting with a dainty curtsey and little half-shy smile, marked by that air of distinction and breeding which was her peculiar characteristic. Molly, however, who thought she had reasonable cause for feeling generally exasperated, and who did not see in Mr. Rupert Landale, despite his good looks and his good manner, a very promising substitute for her Bath admirers (nor in the prospect of Pulwick a profitable exchange for Bath), came forward with her bolder grace to flounce him a saucy "reverence," measuring him the while with a certain air of mockery which his thin-skinned susceptibility was quick to seize.

He looked back at her down the long tunnel of her

bonnet, appraising the bloom and beauty within with cold
and curious gaze, and then he turned to Madeleine and
made to her his courteous speech of welcome.

This was sufficient for Miss Molly, who, for six months
already accustomed to compel admiration at first sight
from all specimens of the male sex that came across her
path, instantly vowed a deadly hatred to her cousin, and
followed the party into the Landale family coach—Rupert
preceding, with a lady on each arm—in a temper as black
as her own locks.

It fell to her lot to sit beside the objectionable relative
on the back seat, while, by the right of her minute's
seniority, Madeleine sat beside Tanty in the front.   The
projecting wings of her headgear effectively prevented
her from watching his demeanour, unless, indeed, she had
turned to him, which was, of course, out of the question ;
but certain fugitive conscious blushes upon the young
face in front of her, certain castings down of long lashes
and timid upward glances, made Molly shrewdly conjecture that Mr. Landale, through all the apparent devotion with which he listened to Tanty's continuous flow
of observations, was able to bestow a certain amount of
attention upon her pretty neighbour.

Tanty herself conducted the conversation with her
usual high hand, feigning utter oblivion of the thunder-
cloud on Molly's countenance ; and, if somewhat rambling
in her discourse, nevertheless contriving to plant her
points where she chose.

Thus the long drive wore to its end.   The sun was
golden upon Pulwick when the carriage at length drew
up before the portico.   Miss Sophia received them in the
hall, in a state of painful flutter and timidity.   She had a
constitutional terror of her aunt's sharp eyes, and, though
she examined her young cousins wistfully, Madeleine's
unconscious air of dignity repelled her as much as Molly's
deliberate pertness.

Rupert conducted his aunt upstairs, and down the long
echoing corridor towards her apartment.

"Ha, my old quarters," quoth Tanty, disengaging
herself briskly from her escort to enter the room and look
round approvingly, "and very comfortable they are.
And my two nieces are next door, I see, as gay as chintz
can make them.   Thank you, nephew, I shall keep you

no longer. We shall dine shortly, I feel sure. Well, well, I do not pretend I am not quite ready to do justice to your excellent fare—beyond doubt, it will be excellent! Go to your room, girls, your baggage is coming up, you see; I shall send Dempsey to assist you presently. No, not you, Sophia, I was speaking to the young ones. I should like to have a little chat with you, my dear, if you have no objection."

One door closed upon Rupert as he smiled and bowed himself out, the other upon Molly hustling her sister before her.

Tanty in the highest good humour, having accomplished her desire, and successfully "established a lodgment" (to use a military term not inappropriate to such a martial spirit) for her troublesome nieces in the stronghold of Pulwick, once more surveyed her surroundings: the dim old walls, the great four-post bed, consecrated, of course, by tradition to the memory of some royal slumberer, the damask hangings, and the uncomfortable chairs, with the utmost favour, ending up with a humorous examination of the elongated figure hesitating on the hearthrug.

" Be seated, Sophia. I am glad to stretch my old limbs after that terrible drive. So here we are together again. What are you sighing for? Upon my soul, you are the same as ever, I see, the same tombstone on your chest, and blowing yourself out with sighs, just as you used. That will never give you a figure, my poor girl; it is no wonder you are but skin and bones. Ah, can't you let the poor fellow rest in his grave Sophia? it is flying in the face of Providence, I call it, to go on perpetually stirring up his ashes like that. I hope you mean to try and be a little more cheerful with those poor girls. But, there, I believe you are never so happy as when you are miserable. And it's a poor creature you would be at any time," added the old lady to herself, after a second thoughtful investigation of Miss Landale's countenance, which had assumed an expression of mulishness in addition to an increase of dolefulness during this homily.

Here, to Miss Landale's great relief, the dying sunset, wavering into crimson and purple, from its first glory of liquid gold, attracted her aunt's attention, and Miss O'Donoghue went over to the window.

Beneath her spread the quaint garden, with its clipped box edges, and beyond the now leafless belt of trees, upon the glimmer of the bay, the outline of Scarthey, a dark silhouette rose fantastically against the vivid sky. Even as she gazed, there leapt upon its fairy turret a minute point of white.

The jovial old countenance changed and darkened.

"And Adrian is still at his fool's game over there, I suppose," she said irately turning upon Sophia. "When have you seen him last? How often does he come here? I gather Master Rupert is nothing if not the master. Why don't you answer me, Sophia?"

The dinner was as well cooked and served a meal as any under Rupert's rule, which is saying a good deal, and if the young ladies failed to appreciate the "floating island," the "golden nests," and "silver web," so thoughtfully provided for them, Tanty did ample justice to the venison.

Indeed the cloud which had been visible upon her countenance at the beginning of dinner, and which according to that downright habit of mind, which rendered her so terrible or so delightful a companion, she made no attempt to conceal, began to lift towards the first remove, and altogether vanished over her final glass of port.

After dinner she peremptorily ordered her grandnieces into the retirement of their bedchambers, unblushingly alleging their exhausted condition in front of the perfect bloom of their beautiful young vigour.

She then, over a cup of tea, luxuriously stretching her thin frame in the best armchair the drawing-room could afford, gave Rupert a brief code of directions as to the special attentions and care she desired to be bestowed upon her wards, during their residence at Pulwick, descanting generously upon their various perfections, gliding dexterously over her reasons for wishing to be rid of them herself, and concluding with the hint—either pregnant or barren of meaning as he chose to take it—that if he made their stay pleasant to them, she would not forget the service.

Then, as Mr. Landale began, with apparent guilelessness, to put a few little telling questions to her anent the episodes which had made Bath undesirable as a residence for these young paragons, the old lady suddenly became overwhelmed with fatigue and sleepiness, and professed herself ready to be conducted to her bower immediately.

Meanwhile, despite the *moue de circonstance* which Molly thought it incumbent on her to assume, neither she nor Madeleine regretted their compulsory withdrawal from the social circle downstairs.

Madeleine had her own thoughts to follow up, and that these were both engrossing and pleasant was easily evident; and Molly, bursting with a sense of injury arising from many causes, desired a special explanation with her sister, which the presence in and out upon them of Tanty's woman had prevented her from indulging in before dinner.

"So here we are at last," cried she, indignantly, after she had walked round and severely inspected her quarters, pausing to "pull a lip" of extreme disfavour at the handsome portrait of Mr. Landale that hung between the windows, "we are, Madeleine, at last, kidnapped, imprisoned, successfully disposed of, in fact."

"Yes, here we are at last," echoed Madeleine, abstractedly, warming her slender ankles by the fire.

"Have you made out yet what particular kind of new frenzy it was that seized chère Tante?" asked Miss Molly, with great emphasis, as she sat down at her toilet-table. "You are the cause of it all, my dear, and so you ought to know. It is all very well for Tanty to pretend that I have brought it on myself by not coming home till three o'clock (as if that was *my* fault). She cannot blink the fact that her Dempsey creature had orders to pack my boxes before bedtime. Your Smith must be a desperately dangerous individual. Well," she continued, looking round over her shoulder, "why don't you say something, you lackadaisical thing?"

But Madeleine answered nought and continued gazing, while only the little smile, tilting the corners of her lips, betrayed that she had heard the petulant speech.

The smile put the finishing touch to Molly's righteous anger. Brandishing a hairbrush threateningly, she marched over to her sister and looked down upon the slender figure, in its clinging white dress, with blazing eyes.

"Look here," she cried, "there must be an end of this. I can put up with your slyness no longer. How *dare* you have secrets from me, miss?—your own twin sister! You and I, who used never to have a thought we did not share. How dare you have a lover, and not tell me all about him? What was the meaning of your weeping like a fountain all the way from Bath to Shrewsbury, and then, without rhyme or reason apparently, smiling to yourself all the way from there to Lancaster. You have had a letter, don't attempt to deny it, it is of no use. . . . . Oh, it is base of you, it is indeed! And to think that it is all through you that I am forced into this exile, through your *airs penchés*, and your sighing and dreaming, and your mysterous *Smith*. . . . . To think that to-night, this very night, is the ball of the season, and we are going to bed! Oh, and to-morrow and to-morrow, and to-morrow, with nothing but a knave and a fool to keep us company—for I don't think much of your female cousin, Madeleine, and, as for your male cousin, I perfectly detest him—and all the tabbies of the country-side for diversion, with perhaps a country buck on high days and holidays for a relish! Pah!"

Molly had almost talked her ill-humour away. Her energetic nature could throw off most unpleasant emotions easily enough so long as it might have an outlet for them; she now laid down the threatening brush, and, kneeling beside her, flung both her arms round Madeleine's shoulders.

"Ma petite Madeleine," she coaxed, in the mother tongue, " tell thy little sister thy secrets."

A faint flush crept to Madeleine's usually creamy cheeks, a light into her eyes. She turned impulsively to the face near hers, then, as if bethinking herself, pursed her lips together and shook her head slightly.

" Do you remember, ma chèrie," she said, at last, "that French tale Mrs. Hambledon lent us in which it is said ' *Qui fuit l'amour, l'amour suit.*'"

" Well?" asked Molly, eagerly, her lips parted as if to drink in the expected confidence.

"Well," replied the other, " well, perhaps things may not be so bad after all. Perhaps," rising from her seat, and looking at her sister with a little gentle malice, while she, too, began to disrobe her fairer beauty for the night,

" some of your many lovers may come after you from
Bath ! Oh, Molly ! " with a little scream, for Molly,
with eyes flashing once more, had sprung up from her
knees to inflict a vicious pinch upon the equivocator's
arm.

" Yes, miss, you shall be pinched till you confess."
Then flouting her with a sudden change of mood, " I am
sure I don't want to know your wonderful secret,"—
seizing her comb and passing it crackling through her
hair with quite unnecessary energy—" Mademoiselle la
Cachotière. Any how, it cannot be very interesting. . . . .
Mrs. Smith ! Fancy caring for a man called Smith ! If
you smile again like that, Madeleine, I shall beat you."

The two sisters looked at each other for a second as
if hesitating on the brink of anger, and then both
laughed.

" Never mind, I shall pay you out yet," quoth Molly,
tugging at her black mane.   " So our lovers are to come
after us, is *that* it ? Do you know, Madeleine," she went
on, calming down, " I almost regret now that I would
not listen to young Lord Dereham, simpleton though he
be.   He looked such a dreadful little fright that I only
laughed at him. . . . . I should have laughed at him all
my life.   But it would perhaps have been better than this
dependence on Tanty, with her sudden whims and scam-
pers and whisking of us away into the wilderness.   Then
I should have had my own way always.   Now it's too
late.   Tanty told me yesterday that she sees he is a dis-
solute young man, and that his dukedom is only a Charles
II. creation, and ' We know what that means,' she added,
and shook her head.   I am sure I had not a notion, but
I shook my head too, and said, ' Of course, that made it
impossible.'   I was really afraid she would want me to
marry him.   She was dreadfully pleased and said I was
a true O'Donoghue.   Oh, dear ! I don't know *anything*
about love.   I can't imagine being in love ; but one thing
is certain, I could never, never, never allow a horrid little
rat like Lord Dereham to make love to me, to kiss me,
nor, indeed, any man—oh, horror ! How you are blushing, my dear ! Come here into the light.   It would be
good for your soul, indeed it would, to confess ! "

But Madeleine, burying her hot cheeks in her sister's
neck and clasping her with gentle caresses, was not to be

drawn from her reticence.   Molly pushed her off at last,
and gave a hard little good-night kiss like a bird-peck.

"Very well; but you might as well have confessed, for
I shall find out in the long run.   And who knows, perhaps
you may be sorry one day that you did not tell me of
your own accord."

CHAPTER XII

A RECORD AND A PRESENTMENT.

THE gallery of family portraits at Pulwick is one of the
most remarkable features of that ancient house.

It was a custom firmly established at the Priory—ever
since the first heralds' visitation in Lancashire, when
some mooted point of claims to certain quarterings had
been cleared in an unexpected way by the testimony of a
well-authenticated ancestral portrait—for each successive
representative to add to the collection. One of the first
cares of every Landale, therefore, on succeeding to the
title was to be painted, with his proper armorial and
otherwise distinguishing honours jealously delineated, and
thus hung in the place of honour over the high mantelshelf of the gallery—displacing on the occasion his own
immediate and revered predecessor.

The chain was consequently unbroken from the Eliza-
bethan descendants of the first acquirers of ecclesiastical
property at Pulwick, down to the present Light-keeper of
Scarthey.

But whilst the late Sir Thomas appeared in all the majesty of deputy-lieutenant, colonel of Militia, magistrate,
and sundry other honourable offices, in his due place on
the right of the present baronet, the latter figured in a
character so strange and so incongruous that it seemed
as if one day the dignified array of Landales—old, young,
middle-aged, but fine gentlemen, all of them—must turn
their backs upon their degenerate kinsman.

Over the chimney-piece, in the huge carved-oak frame
(now already two centuries old), a common sailor, in the
striped loose trousers, the blue jacket with red piping of
a man-of-war's man, with pigtail and coarse open shirt—
stood boldly forth as the representative of the present
owner of Pulwick.

Proud of their long line of progenitors, it was a not unusual thing for the Landales to entertain their guests at breakfast in a certain sunny bow-window in the portrait gallery rather than in the breakfast parlour proper, which in winter, unmistakably harboured more damp than was pleasant.

It was, therefore, with no surprise that Miss Landale received an early order from her brother to have a fire lighted in the apartment sacred to the family honours, and the matutinal repast served there in due course.

Whether Mr. Landale was actuated by a regard for the rheumatism of his worthy relative, or merely a natural family pride, or by some other and less simple motive, he saw no necessity for informing his docile housewife on the matter.

As Sophia was accustomed to no such condescension on his part even in circumstances more extraordinary, she merely bundled out of bed unquestioningly in the darkness and cold of the morning to see his orders executed in the proper manner ; which, indeed, to her credit was so successfully accomplished that Tanty and her charges, when they made their entry upon the scene, could not fail to be impressed with the comfortable aspect of the majestic old room.

Mr. Landale examined his two young uninvited guests with new keenness in the morning light. Molly was demure enough, though there was a lurking gleam in her dark eye which suggested rather armed truce than accepted peace. As for Madeleine, though to be serene was an actual necessity of her delicate nature, there was more than resignation in the blushing radiance of her look and smile.

" Portraits of their mother," said Rupert, bringing his critical survey to a close, and stepping forward with a nice action of the legs to present his arm to his aunt. " Portraits of their mother both of them—I trust to that miniature which used to grace our collection in the drawing-room rather than to the treacherous memory of a school-boy for the impression—but portraits by different masters and in different moods."

There was something patronising in the tone from so young a man, which Molly resented on the spot.

" Oh, we should be as like as two peas, only that we

are as different as day and night, as Tanty says," she
retorted, tossing her white chin at her host, while Miss
O'Donoghue laughed aloud at her favourite's sauciness.

"And after all," said Rupert, as he bestowed his venerable relative on her chair, with an ineffable air of
politeness, contradicted, though only for an instant, by
the look which he shot at Molly from the light hazel
eyes, "Tanty is not so far wrong—the only difference
between night and day is the difference between the
brunette and the *blonde*," with a little bow to each of the
sisters, "an Irish bull, if one comes to analyse it, is but
the expression of the too rapid working of quick wits."

"Faith, nephew," said Tanty, sitting down in high
good humour to the innumerable good things in which her
Epicurean old soul delighted, "that is about as true a
thing as ever you said. Our Irish tongues are apt to
get behind a thing before it is there, and they call that
making a bull."

Rupert's sense of humour was as keen as most of his
other faculties, and at the unconscious humour of this sally
his laugh rang out frankly, while Molly and Madeleine
giggled in their plates, and Miss O'Donoghue chuckled
quietly to herself in the intervals of eating and drinking,
content to have been witty, without troubling to discover
how.

Sophia alone remained unmoved by mirth; indeed, as
she raised her drooping head, amazed at the clamour, an
unwary tear trickled down her long nose into her tea.
She was given to revelling in anniversaries of dead and
gone joys or sorrows; the one as melancholy to her to
look back upon as the other; and upon this November
day, now very many years ago, had the ardent, con-
sumptive rector first hinted at his love.

"And now," said Miss O'Donoghue, who, having disposed of the most serious part of the breakfast, pushed
away her plate with one hand while she stirred her second
cup of well-creamed tea lazily with the other, "Now,
Rupert, will you tell me the arrangements you propose to
make to enable me to see your good brother?"

Rupert had anticipated being attacked upon this subject,
and had fully prepared himself to defend the peculiar
position it was his interest to maintain. To encourage a
meeting between his brother and the old lady (to whom

the present position of affairs was a grievous offence) did not, certainly, enter into his plan of action ; but Tanty had put the question in an unexpected and slightly awkward shape, and for a second or two he hesitated before replying.

"I fear," said he then, gliding into the subject with his usual easy fluency, "that you will be disappointed if you have been reckoning upon an interview with Adrian, my dear aunt. The hermit will not be drawn from his shell on any pretext."

"What," cried Tanty, while her withered cheek flushed, "do you mean to tell me that my nephew, Sir Adrian Landale, will decline to come a few hundred yards to see his old aunt—his mother's own sister—who has come three hundred miles, at seventy years of age, to see him in his own house—*in his own house ?*" repeated the irate old lady, rattling the spoon with much emphasis against her cup. "If you *mean* this, Rupert, it is an insult to me which I shall never forget—*never.*"

She rose from her seat as she concluded, shaking with the tremulous anger of age.

"For God's sake, Tanty," cried Rupert, throwing into his voice all the generous warmth he was capable of simulating, "do not hold me responsible for Adrian in this matter. His strange vagaries are not of my suggesting, heaven knows."

"Well, nephew," said Miss O'Donoghue, loftily, "if you will kindly send the letter I am about to write to your brother, by a safe messenger, immediately. I shall believe that it is *your* wish to treat me with proper respect, whatever may be Adrian's subsequent behaviour."

Mr. Landale's countenance assumed an expression of very genuine distress ; this was just the one proof of dutiful attachment that he was loth to bestow upon his cherished aunt.

"I see how it is." he exclaimed earnestly, coming up to the old lady, and laying his hand gently upon her arm, "you entirely misunderstand the situation. I am not a free agent in this matter. I cannot do what you ask ; I am bound by pledge. Adrian is, undoubtedly, more than—peculiar on certain points, and, really, I dare not, if I would, thwart him."

"Oh !" cried Tanty, shooting off the ejaculation as

from a pop-gun. Then, shaking herself free of Rupert's touch, she sat down abruptly in her chair again, and began fanning herself with her handkerchief. Not even in her interchange of amenities with Mrs. Hambledon, had Molly seen her display so much indignation.

"You want me to believe he is mad, I suppose?" she snapped, at last.

"Dear me! No, no, no!" responded the other, in his airy way. "I did not mean to go so far as that; but—well, there are very painful matters, and hitherto I have avoided all discussion upon them, even with Sophia. My affection for Adrian——"

"Fiddlesticks!" interrupted Tanty. "You meant something, I suppose; either the man's mad, or he is not. And I, for one, don't believe a word of it. The worst sign about him, that I can see, is the blind confidence the poor fellow seems to put in you."

Here Molly, who had been listening to the discussion "with all her ears"—anything connected with the mysterious personality of the absent head of the house was beginning to have a special fascination for her—gave an irrepressible little note of laughter.

Rupert looked up at her quickly, and their eyes met.

"Hold your tongue, Miss," cried Miss O'Donoghue, sharply; aware that she had gone too far in her last remark, and glad to relieve her oppression in another direction, "how dare you laugh? Sophia, this is a terrible thing your brother wants me to believe—may I ask what *your* opinion is? Though I'll not deny I don't think that will be worth much."

Sophia glanced helplessly at Rupert, but he was far too carefully possessed of himself to affect to perceive her embarrassment.

"Come, come," cried Miss O'Donoghue, whose eyes nothing escaped, "you need not look at Rupert, you can answer for yourself. I suppose—you are not absolutely a drivelling idiot—*all* the Landales are not ripening for lunatic asylums—collect your wits, Sophia, I know you have not got any, but you have *enough* to be able to give a plain answer to a plain question, I suppose. Do you think your brother mad, child?"

"God forbid," murmured Sophia, at the very extremity of those wits of which Miss O'Donoghue had so poor an opinion. "Oh, no, dear aunt, not *mad*, of course, not in the least *mad*."

Then, gathering from a restless movement of Rupert's that she was not upon the right tack she faltered, floundered wildly, and finally drew forth the inevitable pocket-handkerchief, to add feelingly if irrelevantly from its folds, "And indeed if I thought such a calamity had really fallen upon us—and of course there *are* symptoms, no doubt there are symptoms . . . ."

"What are his symptoms—has he tried to murder any of you, hey?"

"Oh, my dear aunt! No, indeed, dear Adrian is gentleness itself."

"Does he bite? Does he gibber? Oh, away with you, Sophia! I am sure I cannot wonder at the poor fellow wanting to live on a rock, between you and Rupert. I am sure the periwinkles and the gulls must be pleasant company compared to you. That alone would show, I should think, that he knows right well what he is about. Mad indeed! There never was any madness among the O'Donoghues except your poor uncle Michael, who got a box on the ear from a windmill—and *he* wasn't an O'Donoghue at all! You will be kind enough, nephew, to have delivered to Sir Adrian, no later than to-day, the letter which I shall this moment indite to him."

"Perhaps," said Rupert, "if you will only favour me with your attention for a few minutes first, aunt, and allow me to narrate to you the circumstances of my brother's return here, and of his subsequent self-exile, you will see fit to change your opinion, both as regards him and myself."

A self-controlled nature will in the long run, rightly or wrongly, always assume the ascendency over an excitable one. The moderateness of Rupert's words, the coolness of his manner, here brought Tanty rapidly down from her pinnacle of passion.

Certainly, she said, she was not only ready, but anxious to hear all that Rupert could have to say for himself; and, smoothing down her black satin apron with a shaking hand, the old lady prepared to listen with as much judicial dignity as her flustered state allowed her to assume. Rupert drew his chair opposite to hers and leant his elbow on the table, and fixed his bright, hard eyes upon her.

"You remember, of course," he began after a moment's pause, "how at the time of my poor father's death, Adrian was reported to have lost his life in the Vendée war—though without authoritative confirmation—at the same time as the fair and unhappy Countesse de Savenaye, to whose fortune he had so chivalrously devoted himself."

Tanty bowed her head in solemn assent ; but Molly, watching with the most acute attention, felt her face blaze at the indefinable shade of mockery she thought to catch upon the speaker's curling lip.

"It was," continued he, "the constant strain, the long months of watching in vain for tidings, that told upon my father, rather than the actual grief of loss.   When he died, the responsibilities of the headship of the house devolved naturally upon me, the only male representative left, seemingly, to undertake them.   The months went by ; to the most sanguine the belief in Adrian's death became inevitable.   Our hopes died slowly, but they died at last ; we mourned for him," here Rupert cast down his eyes till the thick black lashes which were one of his beauties swept his cheek ; his tone was perfect in its simple gravity. "At length, urged thereto by all the family, if I remember rightly by yourself as well, dear aunt, I assumed the title as well as the position which seemed mine by right.   I was very young at the time, but I do not think that either then, or during the ten years that followed, I unworthily filled my brother's place."

There was a proud ring of sincerity in the last words, and the old lady knew that they were true ; that during the years of his absolute power as well as of his present more restricted mastership, Rupert's management of the estate was unimpeachable.

"Certainly not, my dear Rupert," she said in softer tones than she had hitherto used to him, "no one would dream of suggesting such a thing—pray go on."

"And so," pursued the nephew, with a short laugh, relapsing into that light tone of banter which was his most natural mode of expression ; "when, one fine day, a hired coach clattered up Sir Rupert Landale's avenue and deposited upon his porch a tattered mariner who an-

nounced himself, in melancholy tones that would have
befitted the ghost no doubt many took him for, as the
rightful Sir Adrian, erroneously supposed defunct, I confess that it required a little persuasion to make me recognise my long-lost brother—and yet there could be no
doubt of it. The missing heir had come to his own
again ; the dead had come back to life. Well, we killed
the fatted calf, and all the rest of it—but I need not
inflict upon you the narrative of our rejoicing."

"Faith, no," said Tanty, drily, "I can see it with
half an eye."

"You know, too, I believe, the series of extraordinary
adventures, or misadventures, which had kept him roaming on the high seas while we at home set up tablets to
his memory and 'wore our blacks' as people here call
it, and cultivated a chastened resignation.   There was a
good deal of correspondence going on at the time between
Pulwick and Bunratty, if I remember aright, and you
heard all about Adrian's divers attempts to land in England, about his fight with the King's men, his crack on
the head and final impressment.   At least you heard as
much as we could gather ourselves.   Adrian is not what
one would call a garrulous person at the best of times.
It was really with the greatest difficulty that we managed
to extract enough out of him to piece together a coherent
tale."

"Well, well," quoth Tanty, with impatience, "you
are glib enough for two anyhow, my dear !   All this does
not tell me how Adrian came to live on a lighthouse, and
why you put him down as a lunatic."

"Not as a lunatic," corrected Rupert, gently, "merely
as slightly eccentric on certain points.   Though, indeed, if
you had seen him during those first months after his return, I think even you with your optimistic spirit would
have feared, as we did, that he was falling into melan-
cholia.   Thank heaven he is better now.   But, dear me,
what we went through !   I declare I expected every
morning to be informed that Sir Adrian's corpse had been
found hanging from his bedpost or discovered in a jelly
at the bottom of the bluffs.   And, indeed, when at length
he disappeared for three days, after he had been last observed mooning along the coast, there was a terrible
panic lest he should have sought a congenial and sooth-

ing end in the embraces of the quicksands. . . . . It
turned out, however, that he had merely strolled over to
Scarthey—where, as you know, my father established a
beacon and installed a keeper to warn boats off our
shoals—and, finding the place to his liking, had remained
there, regardless of our feelings."

"Tut, tut!" said Tanty; but whether in reproof of
Rupert's flippant language or of her elder nephew's
erratic behaviour, it would have been difficult to determine.

"Of course," went on Rupert, smoothly, "I had resolved, after a decent period, to remove my lares and
penates from a house where I was no longer master and
to establish myself, with my small patrimony (I believe
I ought to call it *matrimony*, as we younger children
benefit by our O'Donoghue mother) in an independent
establishment.   But when I first broached the subject,
Adrian was so vastly distressed, expressed himself so well
satisfied with my management of the estate and begged
me so earnestly to consider Pulwick as my home, vowing
that he himself would never marry, and that all he looked
forward to in life was to see me wedded and with future
heirs to the name springing around me, that it would
have been actual unkindness to resist.   Moreover, as you
can imagine, Adrian is not exactly a man of business,
and his spasmodic interferences in the control of the
property being already then of a very injudicious nature,
I confess that, having nursed it myself for eleven years
with some success, I dreaded to think what it would become under his auspices.   And so I agreed to remain.   But
the position increased in difficulty.   Adrian's moroseness
seemed to grow upon him; he showed an exaggerated
horror of company; either flying from visitors as from
the pest, and shutting himself up in his own apartments,
or (on the few disastrous occasions when my persuasions
induced him to show himself to some old family friends)
entertaining them with such unusual sentiments concerning social laws, the magistracy, the government, his
Majesty the King himself, that the most extraordinary
reports about him soon spread over the whole county.
This was about the time—as you may remember—of my
own marriage."

Here an alteration crept into Mr. Landale's voice, and

Molly looked at him curiously, while Miss Sophia gave vent to an audible sniff.

"To be sure," said Tanty, hastily. Comfortably egotistic old ladies have an instinctive dislike to painful topics. And that Rupert's sorrow for his young wife had been, if self-centred and reserved, of an intense and prolonged nature was known to all the family.

The widower himself had no intention of dilating upon it. His wife's name he never mentioned, and no one could guess, heavily as the blow was known to have fallen upon him, the seething bitterness that her loss had left in his soul, nor imagine how different a man he might have been if that one strong affection of his life had been spared to soften it.

"Adrian fled from the wedding festivities, as you may remember, for you were our honoured guest at the time, and greatly displeased at his absence," he resumed, after a few seconds of darkling reflection. "None of us knew where he had flown to, for he did not evidently consider his owl's nest sufficiently remote ; but we had his fraternal blessing to sustain us. And after that he continued to make periodical disappearances to his retreat, stopping away each time longer and longer. One fine day he sent workmen to the island with directions to repair certain rooms in the keep, and he began to transfer thereto furniture, his books and his organ. A dilapidated little French prisoner next appeared on the scene (whom my brother had extracted from the Tower of Liverpool, which was then crammed with such gentry), and finally we were informed that, with this worthy companion, Sir Adrian Landale was determined to take up his abode altogether at Scarthey, undertaking the duties of the recently defunct light-keeper. So off he went, and there he is still. He has extracted from us a solemn promise that his privacy is to be absolutely respected, and that no communications, or, above all, visits are to be made to him. Occasionally, when we least expect it, he descends upon us from his tower, upsets all my accounts, makes the most absurd concessions to the tenants, rides round the estate with his eyes on the ground and disappears again. *Et voilà*, my dear aunt, how we stand."

"Well, nephew," said Miss O'Donoghue, "I am much obliged to you, I am sure, for putting me *au courant* of

the family affairs. It is all very sad—very sad and very
deplorable ; but——"

But Mr. Landale was quite aware that Tanty was not
yet convinced to the desired extent. He therefore here
interrupted her to play his last card—that ace he had up
his sleeve, in careful preparation for this trial of skill with
his keen-witted relative, and to the suitable production
of which he had been all along leading.

Rising from his chair with slow, deliberate movement,
he proceeded, as if following his own train of thought,
without noticing that Miss O'Donoghue was intent on
speech herself :

"You have not seen him, I believe, since he was quite
a lad. You would have some difficulty in recognising
him, though he bears, like the rest of us, what you call
the unmistakable Landale stamp. His portrait is here,
by the way—duly installed in its correct position. That,"
with a laugh, "was one of his freaks. It was his duty to
keep up the family traditions, he said—and there you will
approve of him, no doubt; but hardly, perhaps, of the
manner in which he has had that laudable intention carried
out. My own portrait was, of course, deposed (like the
original)," added Mr. Landale, with something of a sneer ;
"and now hangs meekly in some bedroom or other—in
that, if I mistake not, at present hallowed by my fair
cousins' presence. Well, it is good for the soul of man
to be humbled, as we are taught to believe from our
earliest years ! "

Tanty was fumbling for her eye-glasses. She was glad
to hear that Adrian had remembered some of his obligations (she observed, sententiously, as she hauled herself
stiffly out of her chair to approach the chimney-piece): it
was certainly a sign that he was more mindful of his
duties as head of the house than one would expect from
a person hardly responsible, such as Rupert had represented him to be, and . . . .

Here, the glasses being adjusted and focussed upon the
portrait, Miss O'Donoghue halted abruptly with a dropping jaw.

"There is a curious inscription underneath the escutch-
eon," said Mr. Landale composedly, "which latter, by
the way, you may notice is the only one in the line which
has no room for an impaled coat (Adrian's way of indicat-

ing not only that he is single, but means to remain such);
Adrian composed it himself and indeed attached a marked
importance to it.   Let me read it for you, dear Tanty,
the picture hangs a little high and those curveting letters
are hard to decipher.   It runs thus :

*Sir Adrian William Hugh Landale, Lord of Pulwick
and Scarthey in the County Palatine of Lancaster, eighth
Baronet, born March 12th, 1775.   Succeeded to the title and
estate on the 10th February 1799, whilst abroad.   Iniqui-
tously pressed into the King's service on the day of his return
home, January 2nd, 1801.   Twice flogged for alleged insub-
ordination, and only released at last by the help of a friend
after five years of slavery.   Died*   [Here a space
for the date.]   It is a record with a vengeance, is it not ?
Notice my brother's determination to die unmarried and
to retire, once for all, from all or any of the possible
honours connected with his position !"

They had all clustered in front of the picture ; even
Madeleine roused from her sweet day-dreams to some
show of curiosity ; Miss Landale's bosom, heaving with
such sighs as to make the tombstone rise and fall like a
ship upon a stormy sea ; Molly with an eagerness she
did not attempt to hide ; and Miss O'Donoghue still
speechless with horror and indignation.

Mr. Landale had gauged his aunt's temperament cor-
rectly enough.   To one whose ruling passion was pride
of family, this mockery of a consecrated family custom,
this heirloom destined to carry down a record of degradation into future generations, was an insult to the name
only to be explained to her first indignation by deliberate
malice—or insanity.

And from the breezy background of blue sky and sea,
contrasting as strangely with the dark solemnity of the
other portraits as did the figure itself in its incongruous
sailor dress, the face of the eighth baronet looked down
in melancholy gravity upon the group gathered in judgment upon him.

"Disgraceful !   Positively disgraceful !" at length cried
the last representative of the O'Donoghues of Bunratty, in
scandalised tones.   "My dear Rupert, you should have
a curtain put up, that this exhibition of folly—of madness,
I hardly know what to call it—be not exposed to every
casual visitor.   Dear me, dear me, that I should live to

see any of my kin deliberately throw discredit on his
family, if indeed the poor fellow is responsible !   Rupert,
my good soul, can you ascribe any reason for this terrible
state of affairs . . . . that blow on the head ?"

"In part perhaps," said Mr. Landale.   "And yet there
have been other causes at work.   If I could have a private
word in your ear," glancing meaningly over his shoulder
at the two young girls who were both listening, though
with very different expressions of interest and favou, "I
could give you my opinion more fully."

"Go away now, my dear creatures," hereupon said
Miss O'Donoghue, promptly addressing her nieces.   "It
is a fine morning, and you will lose your roses if you
don't get the air.   I don't care if it has begun to rain,
miss !   Go and have a game of battledore and shuttlecock then.   Young people *must* have exercise.   Well, my
dear Rupert, well !"—when Molly, with a pettish "battledore and shuttlecock indeed !" had taken her sister by the
arm and left the room.

"Well, my dear aunt, the fact is, I believe my unhappy
brother has never recovered from—from his passion for
Cécile de Savenaye, that early love affair, so suddenly and
tragically terminated—well, it seems to have turned his
brain !"

"Pooh, pooh ! why that was twenty years ago.   Don't
tell me it is in a man to be so constant."

"In no *sane* man perhaps ; but then, you know, Tanty,
that is just the point . . . . Remember the circumstances.   He loved her madly ; he followed her, lived
near her for months and she was drowned before his eyes,
I believe.   I never heard, of course, any details of that
strange period of his life, but we can imagine." This
was a difficult, vague, subject to deal with, and Mr. Landale wisely passed on.   "Moreover, his behaviour when
in this house on his return at first has left me no doubt.
I watched him closely.   He was for ever haunting those
rooms which she had inhabited.   When he found her
miniature in the drawing-room he went first as white as
death, then he took it in his hand and stood gazing at it
(I am not exaggerating) for a whole hour without moving ; and, finally, he carried it off, and I know he used to
talk to it in his room.   And now, even if I had not given
my poor brother my word of honour never to disturb his

chosen solitude, I should have felt it a heavy responsibility to promote a meeting which would inevitably bring back past memories in a troublous manner upon him. In fact, were he to come across the children of his dead love—above all Molly, who must be startlingly like her mother—what might the result be? I hardly like to contemplate it. The human brain is a very delicately balanced organ, my dear aunt, and once it gets ever so slightly out of order one cannot be too careful to avoid risk."

He finished his say with an expressive gesture of the hand. Miss O'Donoghue remained for a moment plunged in reflection, during which the cloud upon her countenance gradually lifted.

"It is a strange thing," she said at last, "but constancy seems to run in the family. There is no denying that. Here is Sophia, a ridiculous spectacle—and you yourself, my dear Rupert. . . . . And now poor Adrian, too, and his case of mere calf-love, as one would have thought."

"A calf may grow into a fine bull, you know," returned Mr. Landale, who had winced at his aunt's allusion to himself and now spoke in the most unemotional tone he could assume, "especially if it is well fostered in its youth."

"And I suppose," said Miss O'Donoghue, with a faint smile, "you think I ought to know all about bulls." She again put up her glasses to survey the portrait with critical deliberation ; after which, recommending him once more strenuously to have a curtain erected, she observed, that it would break her heart to look at it one moment longer and requested to be conducted from the room.

Mr. Landale could not draw any positive conclusion from his aunt's manner of receiving his confidence, nor determine whether she had altogether grasped the whole meaning of what he had intended delicately to convey to her concerning his brother's past as well as present position ; but he had said as much as prudence counselled.

CHAPTER XIII

THE DISTANT LIGHT

In spite of their first petulant or dolorous anticipation, and of the contrast between the even tenor of country life and the constant stream of amusement which young people of fashion can find in a place like Bath, the two girls discovered that time glided pleasantly enough over them at Pulwick.

Instead of the gloomy northern stronghold their novel-fed imagination had pictured (the more dismally as their sudden removal from town gaieties savoured distantly of punishment at the hand of their irate aunt), they found themselves delivered over into a bright, admirably-ordered house, replete with things of beauty, comfortable to the extremity of luxury ; and allowed in this place of safety to enjoy almost unrestricted liberty.

The latter privilege was especially precious, as the sisters at that time had engrossing thoughts of their own they wished to pursue, and found more interest in solitary roamings through the wide estate than in the company of the hosts.

On the fifth day Miss O'Donoghue took her departure. Her own travelling coach had rumbled down the avenue, bearing her and her woman away, in its polished yellow embrace, her flat trunk strapped behind, and the good-natured old face nodding out of the window, till Molly and Madeleine, standing (a little disconsolate) upon the porch to watch her departure, could distinguish even the hooked nose no longer. Mr. Landale, upon his mettled grey, a gallant figure, as Molly herself was forced to admit, in his boots and buckskins, had cantered in the dust alongside, intent upon escorting his aged relative to the second stage of her journey.

That night, almost for the first time since their arrival, there was no company at dinner, and the young guests understood that the household would now fall back into its ordinary routine.

But without the small flutter of seeing strangers, or Tanty's lively conversation, the social intercourse soon waned into exceeding dulness, and at an early hour Miss Molly rose and withdrew to her room, pretexting a headache, for which Mr. Landale, with his usual high courtesy, affected deep concern.

As she was slowly ascending the great oaken staircase, she crossed Moggie, the gatekeeper's daughter, who in her character of foster-sister to one of the guests had been specially allotted to them as attendant, during the remainder of their visit to Pulwick.

Molly thought that the girl eyed her hesitatingly, as if she wished to speak :

"Well, Moggie?" she asked, stopping on her way.

"Oh, please, miss," said the buxom lass, blushing and dropping a curtsey, "Renny Potter, please, miss, is up at our lodge to-night, he don't care to come to the 'ouse so much, miss. But when he heard about you, miss, you could have knocked him down with a feather he was so surprised and that excited, miss, we have never seen him so. And he's so set on being allowed to see ye both !"

Molly as yet failed to connect any memories of interest with the possessor of the patronymic mentioned, but the next phrase mentioned aroused her attention.

"He is Sir Adrian's servant, now, miss, and goes back yonder to the island, that is where the master lives, to-morrow morning. But he would be so happy to see the young ladies before he goes, if the liberty were forgiven, he says. He was servant to the Madam your mother, miss."

"Well, Moggie," answered Miss Molly, smiling, "if that is all that is required to make Renny Potter happy, it is very easily done. Tell Renny Potter : to-morrow morning." And she proceeded on her way pondering, while the successful emissary pattered down to the lodge in high glee to gather her reward in her sweetheart's company.

When later on Madeleine joined her sister, she found her standing by the deep recessed window, the curtains of which were drawn back, resting her head on her hand against the wainscot, and gazing abroad into the night.

She approached, and passing her hand round Molly's waist looked out also.

"Again at your window?"

"It is a beautiful night, and the view very lovely," said Molly. And indeed the moon was riding high in a deep blue starry heaven, and shimmered on the strip of distant sea visible from the windows.

"Yes, but yesterday the night was not fine, and nothing was to be seen but blackness; and it was the same the day before, and yet you stared out of this window, as you have every night since our coming. It is strange to see *you* so. What is it, why don't you tell me?"

"Madeleine," said Molly, suddenly, after a lengthy pause, "I am simply *haunted* by that light over yonder, the Light of Scarthey. There is a mystery about those ruins, on which I keep meditating all day long. I want to know more. It draws me. I would give anything to be able, now, to set sail and land there all unknown to any one, and see what manner of life is led where that light is burning."

But Madeleine merely gave a pout of little interest. "What do you think you would find? A half-witted middle-aged man, mooning among a litter of books, with an old woman, and a little Frenchman to look after him. Why, Mr. Landale himself takes no trouble to conceal that his poor brother is an almost hopeless lunatic."

"Mr. Landale—" Molly began, with much contempt; but she interrupted herself, and went on simply, "Mr. Landale is a very fine gentleman, with very superior manners. He speaks like a printed book—but for all that I *would* like to know."

Madeleine laughed. "The demon of curiosity has a hold of you, Molly; remember the fable they made us repeat: *De loin c'est quelque chose, et de près ce n'est rien.* Now you shall go straight into your bed, and not take cold."

And Miss Madeleine, after authoritatively closing the curtains, kissed her sister, and was about to commence immediate disrobing, when she caught sight of the shagreen-covered book, lying open on the table.

"So your headache was your diary—how I should like to have a peep."

"I daresay!" said Molly, sarcastically, and then sat
down and, pen in hand, began to re-read her night's entry,
now and then casting a tantalising glance over her shoulder at her sister.   The lines, in the flowing convent hand,
ran thus :

"Aunt O'Donoghue left us this morning, and so here
we are, planted in Pulwick ; and she has achieved her plan,
fully.   But what is odd is that neither Madeleine nor I
seem to mind it, now.   What has come over Madeleine
is her secret, and she keeps it close ; but that *I* should
like being here is strange indeed.

"And yet, every day something happens to make me
feel connected with Pulwick—something more, I mean,
than the mere fact that we were born here.   So many
of the older people greet me, at first, as if they knew me
—they all say I am so like 'the Madam ;' they don't see
the same likeness in Madeleine for all her *grand air*.
There was Mrs. Mearson, the gatekeeper, was struck
in amazement.   And the old housekeeper, whenever she
has an opportunity tries to entertain me about the beautiful foreign lady and the grand times they had at Pulwick
when she was here, and 'Sir Tummas' was still alive.

"But, though we are made to feel that we are more
than ordinary guests, it is not on account of Mr. Landale,
but *on account of Sir Adrian*—the Master, as they call him,
whom we never see, and whom his brother would make
out to be mad.   Why is he so anxious that Sir Adrian
should not know that Aunt Rose has brought us here?
He seemed willing enough to please her, and yet nothing
that she could say of her wish could induce him even to
send a messenger over to the rock.   And now we may be
here all these two months and never even have caught a
sight of the *Master.*   I wonder if he is still like that portrait—whether he bears that face still as he now sits, all
alone, brooding as his brother says, up in those ruined
chambers, while the light burns calm and bright in the
tower !   What can this man of his have to say to me?"

Molly dotted her last forgotten "i," blotted it, closed
and carefully locked the book.   Then, rising, she danced
over to her sister, and forced her into a pirouette.

"And now," she cried gaily, "our dear old Tanty is
pulling on her nightcap and weeping over her posset in
the stuffy room at Lancaster regretting *me ;* and I should

be detesting her with all my energies for leaving me behind her, were it not that, just at present, I actually find Pulwick more interesting than Bath."

Madeleine lifted her heavy-lidded eyes a little wonderingly to her sister's face, as she paused in her gyration.

"What fly stings thee now?" she inquired in French.

"You do not tell me about *your* wounds, my dear, those wounds which little Dan Cupid has made upon your tender heart, with his naughty little arrow, and which give you such sweet pain, apparently, that you revel in the throes all day long. And yet, I am a good child; you shall guess. If you guess aright, I shall tell you. So now begin."

They stood before the fire, and the leaping tongues of light played upon their white garments, Madeleine's nightgear scarcely more treacherously tell-tale of her slender woman's loveliness than the evening robe that clung so closely to the vigorous grace of Molly's lithe young figure.

The elder, whose face bore a blush distinct from the reflected glow of the embers, fell to guessing, as commanded, a little wildly:

"You begin to find the *beau cousin* Rupert a little more interesting than you anticipated."

"Bah," cried Molly, with a stamp of her sandalled foot, "it is not possible to guess worse! He is more insufferable to me, hour by hour."

"I think him kind and pleasant," returned Madeleine simply.

"Ah, because he makes sweet eyes at you, I suppose—yet no—I express myself badly—he could not make anything sweet out of those hard, hard eyes of his, but he is very—what they call here in England—attentive to you. And he looks at you and ponders you over when you little think it—you poor innocent—lost in your dream of . . . . *Smith!* There, I will not tease you. Guess again."

"You are pleased to remain here because you are a true weather-cock—because you like one thing one day another the next—because the country peace and quiet is soothing to you after the folly and noise of the great world of Bath and Dublin, and reminds you refreshingly, as it does me, of our happy convent days." The glimmer of a dainty malice lurked in the apparent candour of Madeleine's grave blue eyes, and from thence spread into her pretty smile at the sight of Molly's disdainful lip, "Well then, I give it up. You have some mischief on foot, of that at least I am sure."

"No mischief—a work of righteousness rather. Sister Madeleine, you heard all that that gallant gentleman you think so highly of—your cousin Rupert, my dear" (it was a little way of Molly's to throw the responsibility of anything she did not like, even to an obnoxious relationship, upon another person's shoulders), "narrated of his brother Sir Adrian, and how he persuaded Tanty that he was, as you said just now, a hopeless madman—"

"But yes—he does mad things," said the elder twin, a little wonderingly.

"Well, Madeleine, it is a vile lie. I am convinced of it."

"But, my darling——"

"Look here, Madeleine, there is something behind it all. I attacked that creature, that rag, you cannot call her a woman, that female cousin of yours, Sophia, and I pressed her hard too, but she could not give me a single instance about Sir Adrian that is really the least like insanity; and last night, when the young fool who escorted me to dinner, Coventry his name was, told me that every one says Sir Adrian is shut up on the island and that his French servant is really his keeper, and that it was a shame Rupert was not the eldest brother, I quite saw the sort of story Master Rupert likes to spread—don't interrupt, please! When you were wool-gathering over the fire last night (in the lively and companionable way, permit me to remark in parenthesis, that you have adopted of late), and you thought I was with Tanty, I had marched off with my flat candlestick to the picture gallery to have a good look at the so-called lunatic. I dragged over a chair and lit the candles in the candelabra each side of the chimney-piece, and then standing on my perch still, I held up my own torch and I saw the sailor really well. I think he has a beautiful face and that he is no more mad than I am. But he looks so sad, so sad! I longed to make those closed lips part and tell me their secret. And, as I was looking and dreaming, my dear, just as you might, I heard a little noise, and there was Rupert, only

a few yards off, surveying me with such an angry gaze—
Ugh!" (with a shiver) "I hate such ways. He came in
upon me with soft steps like some animal. Look at his
portrait there, Madeleine!—Stay! I shall hold up the
light as I did last night to Sir Adrian—see, it flickers and
glimmers and makes him seem as if he were alive—oh,
I wish he were not hanging in front of our beds, staring
out at us with those eyes! You think them very fine, I
daresay, that is because his lashes are as thick and dark
as a woman's—but the look in them, my dear—do you
know what it reminds me of? Of the beautiful, cruel
greyhound we saw at the coursing at that place near
Bunratty (you remember, just before they started the
hare), when he stood for a moment motionless, looking
out across the plain. I can never forget the expression
of those yellow-circled eyes. And, when I see Rupert
look at you as if he were fixing something in the far distance, it gives me just the feeling of horror and sickness
I had then. (You remember how dreadful it was?)
Rupert makes me think of a greyhound, altogether he is
so lithe and so clean-cut, and so full of eagerness, a sort
of trembling eagerness underneath his seeming quiet, and
I think he could be cruel."

Molly paused with an unusually grave and reflective
look; Madeleine yawned a little, not at all impressed.

"How you exaggerate!" she said. "Well what happened when he came in and caught you? The poor
man! I suppose, he thought you were setting the house
on fire."

"My dear, I turned as red as a poppy and began blowing out all my illumination, feeling dreadfully guilty, and
then he helped me off my chair with such an air of politeness that I could have struck him with pleasure, but I
soon gathered my wits again. And, vexed with myself
for being a ninny, I just dropped him a little curtsey and
said, 'I've been examining my mad cousin.' 'Well, and
what do you think of him?' he asked me, smiling (his
abominable smile!). But I can keep my thoughts to myself as well as other people. 'I think he is very handsome,' I answered, and then I wagged my head and
added, 'Poor fellow,' just as if I thought he was really
mad. 'Poor fellow!' said cousin Rupert, still with his
smile. Whereupon we interchanged good-nights, and he

ceremoniously reconducted me to my door. What was he spying after me for, like that? My dear, your cousin has a bad conscience.—But I can spy too—I have been questioning the servants to-day, and some of the people on the estate."

"Oh, Molly!"

"Come, don't be so shocked. It was diplomatically, of course, but I am determined to find out the truth. Well, so far from looking upon Sir Adrian as a lunatic, they all adore him, it seems to me. He comes here periodically—once every three months or so—and it is like the King's Justices, you know—St. Louis of France —he redresses all wrongs, and listens to grievances and gives alms and counsel, and every one can come with his story, down to the poorest wretch on the estate, and they certainly gave me to understand that they would fare pretty hardly under Mr. Landale if it were not for that mild beneficent restraining influence in his tower yonder. It is very romantic, do you know (you like romance, Madeleine). I wonder if Sir Adrian will come over while we are here. Oh, I hope, I hope he will. I shall never rest till I have seen him."

"Silly child," said Madeleine, "and so that is the reason you are glad to remain here?"

"Even so, my dear," answered the other, skipped into the big four-post bed, carefully ascertained and selected the softest pillow, and then, smiling sweetly at her sister from under a frame of dark curls, let her white lids drop over the lustre of her eyes and so intimated she desired to sleep.

CHAPTER XIV

THE TOWER OF LIVERPOOL: MASTER AND MAN

A prison is a house of care,
A place where none can thrive,
A Touchstone True to try a friend,
A Grave for man alive.
Sometimes a place of right,
Sometimes a place of wrong,
Sometimes a place of rogues and thieves,
And honest men among.

Old Inscription.

It was soon after sunrise—at that time of year an hour not exorbitantly early—when Molly awoke from a tangle of fantastic dreams in which the haunting figure of her waking thoughts, the hermit of Scarthey, appeared to her in varied shapes; as an awe-inspiring, saintly ascetic with long, white hair; as a young, beautiful, imprisoned prince; even as a ragged imbecile staring vacantly at a lantern, somewhere in a dismal sea-cave.

The last vision was uppermost in her mind when she opened her eyes; and the girl, under the impression of so disgusting a disillusion, remained for a while pondering and yawning, before making up her mind to exchange warmth and featherbed for her appointment without.

But the shafts of light growing through the chinks in the shutters ever brighter and more full of dancing motes, decided her.

"A beautiful morning, Madeleine," she said, leaning over and pulling one of the long fair strands upon her neighbour's pillow with sisterly authority. "Get up, lazy-bones, and come and have a walk with me before breakfast."

The sleeping sister awoke, smiled with her usual exquisite serenity of temper, and politely refused. Molly insisted, threatened, coaxed, but to no avail. Madeleine was luxuriously comfortable, and was not to be disturbed either mentally or bodily ; and Molly, aware of the resisting power of will hidden under that soft exterior, at length petulantly desisted ; and wrapped up in furs, with hands plunged deep into the recesses of a gigantic muff, soon sallied forth herself alone into the park.

Half-way down the avenue she met blue-eyed Moggie with round face shining out of the sharp, exhilarating atmosphere like a small sun. The damsel was overcome with blushes and rapture at her young mistress's unexpected promptitude in carrying out her promise, and ran back to warn her sweetheart of that lady's approach.

As Molly drew near the keeper's lodge—a sort of Doric temple, quaintly standing in the middle of a hedge-enclosed garden, and half-buried under thickly-clustering, interlacing creepers—from the side of the enormous nest of evergreen foliage there emerged, in a state of high excitement strenuously subdued, a short, square-built man (none other than René L'Apôtre), whilst between the boughs of the garden-hedge peeped forth the bashful, ruddy face of the lady of his fancy, eager to watch the interview.

René ran forward, then stopped a few paces away, hat in hand, scraping and bowing in the throes of an overwhelming emotion that strove hard with humility.

"Ah, Mademoiselle, Mademoiselle !" he ejaculated between spells of amazed staring, and seemed unable to bring forth another word.

"And so you have known my mother, René," said Miss Molly (in her native tongue) with a smile.

At the sound of the voice and of the French words, René's face grew pale under its bronze, and the tears he had so strongly combated, glistened in his eyes.

"If I had not heard last night," he said at length, "that these ladies had come back—it was Moggie Mearson who told me, who was foster sister to you, or was it Mademoiselle your sister ? and proud she is of it—if I had not known that the young ladies were here again, when I saw Mademoiselle I would have thought that my lady herself had returned to us (may the good God have her soul !). Ah, to think that I should ever see her again in the light of the sun !"

10

He stopped, suffocated with the sob that his respect would not allow him to utter.

But Molly, who had had other objects in view when she rose from her couch this cold, windy morning, than to present an objective to a serving-man's emotion, now thought the situation had lasted long enough for her enjoyment and determined to put an end to it.

"Eh bien, René," she said gaily, "or should I call you Monsieur Potter? which, by the way, is a droll name for a Frenchman, I am very glad to see that you are pleased to see me. If you would care to have some talk with me you may attend me if you like. But I freeze standing here," stamping her feet one after the other on the hard ground. "I must absolutely walk; and you may put on your hat again, please: for it is very cold for you too," she added, snuggling into her muff and under her fur tippet.

The man obeyed after another of his quaint salutes, and as Molly started forward, followed her respectfully, a pace in rear.

"I daresay you will not be sorry to have a little talk with a compatriot in your own tongue, all English as you may have grown," said the young lady presently; "and as Moggie has told me that you were in my mother's service, there is a whole volume of things which, I believe, you alone can relate to me. You shall tell me all that, one day. But what seems to me the most curious, first of all, is your presence here. We ourselves are only at Pulwick by chance."

"Mademoiselle," said René in an earnest voice, "if you knew the whole story, you would soon understand that, since it was not to be, that I should remain the humble servitor of Monseigneur le Comte de Savenaye, Mademoiselle's father, or of Madame, who followed him to heaven, notwithstanding all our efforts to preserve her, it is but natural that I should attach myself (since he would allow it) to my present master."

"Mr. Landale?" asked Molly, affecting ignorance.

"No, Mademoiselle," cried the Frenchman, hotly. "My master is Sir Adrian. Had Mr. Landale remained the lord of this place, I should have been left to die in my prison—or at least have remained there until this spring, for it seems there is peace again, and the Tower of Liverpool is empty now."

" *Voyons, voyons, conte moi cela*, René," said Molly, turning her face, beautifully glowing from the caress of the keen air, eagerly to her companion. And he, nothing loth to let loose a naturally garrulous tongue in such company, and on such a theme, started off upon a long story illustrated by rapid gesticulation.

" I will tell you," cried he, and plunged into explanation with more energy than coherence, "it was like this :

" I had been already two years in that prison ; we were some hundreds of prisoners, and it was a cruel place. A cruel place, Mademoiselle, almost as bad as that where we were shut up, my master and I together, years before, at La Rochelle—and that I will tell you, if you wish, afterwards.

" I had been taken by the marine conscription, when their Republic became the French Empire. And a sailor I was then (just, as I heard later, as Sir Adrian also was at the time ; but that I did not know, you understand), for they took all those that lived on the coast. Now I had only served with the ship six months, when she was taken by the English, and, as I say, we were sent to the prison in Liverpool, where we found so many others, who had been already there for years. When I heard it was Liverpool, I knew it was a place near Pulwick, and I at once thought of Mr. Landale, not him, of course, they *now* call Mr. Landale, but him who had followed my mistress, Madame your mother, to help to fight the Republicans in the old time. And I thought I was saved : I knew he would get me out if it was possible to get any one out. For, you see, I thought his honour was home again, after we had been beaten, and there was no more to be done for my lady. We had contrived to find an English ship to take him home, and he had gone back, as I thought, Mademoiselle. Well, a prisoner becomes cunning, and besides, I had been in prison before ; I managed to make up a letter, and as I knew already some English, I ended by persuading a man to carry it to Pulwick for me. It was a long way, and I had no money, but I made bold to assure him that Mr. Landale—oh, no ! not *this* one," René interrupted himself again with a gesture eloquent of resentful scorn, " but my master ; I assured the man that he would receive recompence from him. You see, Mademoiselle, I knew his heart was so good, that he

would not allow your mother's servant to rot in the
tower. . . . . But days afterwards the man came back.
Oh, he was angry ! terribly angry with me, and said he
should pay me out—And so he did, but it is useless to
tell you how.   He had been to Pulwick, he said, and had
seen Mr. Landale.   Mr. Landale never knew anything
of any French prisoner, and refused to give any money to
the messenger.   Ah, Mademoiselle, it was very sad !   I
had not signed my letter for fear of its getting into wrong
hands, but I spoke of many things which I knew he could
not have forgotten, and now I thought that he would not
trouble his mind about such a wretch as René—triple
brute that I was to conceive such thoughts, I should have
deserved to remain there for ever ! . . . . I did remain,
Mademoiselle, more than three years ; many and many
died.   As for me, I am hard, but I thought I should never
never walk free again ; nor would I, Mademoiselle, these
seven years, but for him."

"He came, then ?" said the girl with sympathetic
enthusiasm.   She was listening with attention, carried
away by the speaker's earnestness, and knew instinctively
to whom the " him," and the " he " referred.

" He came," said René with much emphasis.   " Of
course he came—the moment he knew."   And after a
moment of half-smiling meditation he pursued :

" It was one May-day, and there was some sun ; and
there was a smell of spring in the air which we felt even in
that dirty place.   Ah, how I remember me of it all !   I was
sitting against the wall in the courtyard with two others
who were Bretons, like you and me, Mademoiselle, shifting
with the sun now and then, for you must know a prisoner
loves the sun above all ; and there, we only had it a few
hours in the day, even when it did shine.   I was carving
some stick-heads, and bread-plates in wood—the only thing
I could do to put a little more than bread, into our own
platters," with a grin, " and whistling, whistling, for if you
can't be gay, it is best to play at it. . . . . Well, that day
into our courtyard there was shown a tall man—and I knew
him at once, though he was different enough in his fine
coat, and hat and boots, from the time when I had last
seen him, when he was like me, in rags and with a woollen
cap on his head, and no stockings under his shoes—I knew
him at once !   And when I saw him I stood still, with my

mouth round, but not whistling more. My blood went phizz, phizz, all over my body, and suddenly something said in my head : 'René, he has come to look for you." He was searching for some one, for he went round with the guardian looking into each man's face, and giving money to all who begged—and seeing that, they all got up, and surrounded him, and he gave them each a piece. But I could not get up ; it was as if some one had cut out my knees and my elbows. And that was how he saw me the sooner. He noticed I remained there, looking at him like a dog, saying nothing. When he saw me, he stood a moment quite quiet ; and without pretending anything he came to me and looked down smiling.—'But if I am not mistaken I know this man,' he said to the guardian, pretending to be astonished.   'Why, this is René L'Apôtre? Who would have thought of seeing you here, René L'Apôtre?'says he. And then he smiled again, as much as to say, 'You see I have come at last, René.' And once more, as if to explain : 'I have only lately come back to England,' in a gentle way, all full of meaning. . . . . I don't know what took me, but I cried like an infant, in my cap. And the guardian and some of the others laughed, but when I looked up again, his eyes shone also. He looked so good, so kind, Mademoiselle, that it was as if I understood in words all he meant, but thought better not to say at the time. Then he spoke to the guardian, who shook his head doubtfully. And after saying, 'Have good courage, René L'Apôtre,' and giving me the rest of his money, he went away—but I knew I was not forgotten, and I was so happy that the black, black walls were no more black. And I sang, not for pretence this time, ah no ! and I spent all my money in buying a dinner for those at our end of the prison, and we even had wine ! You may be sure we drank to his happiness."

Here the man, carried away by his feelings, seized his hat and waved it in the air. Then, ashamed of his ebullition, halted and glanced diffidently at the young lady. But Molly only smiled in encouragement.

"Well, and then ?" she asked.

"Well, Mademoiselle," he resumed, "it was long before I saw him again ; but I kept good courage, as I was told. One day, at last, the guardian came to fetch me and took me to the governor's cabinet ; and my master was there—I was told that my release had been obtained, though not without trouble, and that Sir Adrian Landale, of Pulwick Priory, had gone warranty for me that I should not use my liberty to the prejudice of His Majesty, the King of England, and that I was to be grateful to Sir Adrian. I almost laughed at him, Mademoiselle. Oh ! he took care to advise me to be grateful !" And here René paused ironically, but there was a quiver on his lips. "Ah, he little knew, Monsieur the Governor, that when my master had taken me to an inn, and the door was closed over the private room, he who had looked so grand and careless before the governor, took me by both hands and then, in his fine clothes, embraced me—me the dirty prisoner—just as he did when he left me in the old days, and was as poor and ragged as I was ! And let me weep there on his breast, for I had to weep or my heart would have broken. But I wander, Mademoiselle, you only wanted to know how I came to be in his service still. That is how it was : as I tell you."

Molly was moved by this artless account of fidelity and gratitude, and as she walked on in attentive silence, René went on :

"It was then his honour made me know how, only by accident, and months after his own return, he chanced to hear of the letter that some one had sent to Mr. Landale from the Tower of Liverpool, and that Mr. Landale had said he knew nothing of any French prisoner and had thought it great impudence indeed. And how he—my master—had suddenly thought (though my letter had been destroyed) that it might be from me, the servant of my lady your mother, and his old companion in arms (for his honour will always call me so). He could not sleep, he told me, till he had found out. He started for Liverpool that very night. And, having discovered that it was me, Mademoiselle, he never rested till he had obtained my liberty."

Walking slowly in the winter sunshine, the one talking volubly, the other intently listening, the odd pair had reached a rising knoll in the park where, under the shelter of a cluster of firs, stood a row of carved stone seats that had once been sedillas in the dismantled Priory Church.

From this secluded spot could be obtained the most
superb view of the whole country-side. At the end of the
green, gently-sloping stretch of pasture-land, which extended, broken only by irregular clusters of trees, down
to the low cliffs forming the boundary of the strand, lay
the wide expanse of brown sand, with its streamlets and
salt pools scintillating under the morning sun.

Further in the western horizon, a crescent of deep blue
sea, sharply defined under a lighter blue sky and fringed
landwards with a straggling border of foam, advanced
slowly to the daily conquest of the golden bay. In the
midst of that frame the eye was irresistibly drawn, as to
the chief object in the picture, to the distant rock of
Scarthey—a green patch, with the jagged red outline of
the ruins clear cut against the sky.

Since this point of view in the park had been made
known to her, on the first day when she was piloted
through the grounds, Molly had more than once found
her way to the sedillas, yielding to the fascination of the
mysterious island, and in order to indulge in the fancies
suggested by its ever-changing aspect.

At the fall of day the red glow of the sinking sun would
glint through the dismantled windows ; and against the
flaming sky the ruins would stand out black and grim,
suggesting nought but abandonment and desolation until
suddenly, as the gloom gathered upon the bay, the light
of the lamp springing to the beacon tower, would reverse
the impression and bring to mind a picture of faithful
and patient watching.

When the sun was still in the ascendant, the island
would be green and fresh to the gaze, evoking no dismal
impression ; and as the rays glanced back from the two
or three glazed windows, and from the roofed beacon-
tower, the little estate wore a look of solid security and
privacy in spite of its crumbling walls, which was almost
as tantalising to her romantic curiosity.

It was with ulterior motives, therefore, that she had again
wended her way to the knoll this sunny, breezy morning.
She now sat down and let her eyes wander over the wide
panorama, whilst René stood at a humble distance, looking with eyes of delight from her to the distant abode of
his master.

"And now you live with Sir Adrian, in that little isle

yonder," said she, at length. "How came it that you never sought to go back to your country?"

"There was the war then, Mademoiselle, and it was difficult to return."

"But there has been peace these six months," insisted Molly.

"Yes, Mademoiselle, though I only learned it yesterday. But then, bah! What is that? His honour needs me. I have stopped with him seven years, and my faith, I shall stop with him for ever."

There was a long silence.

"Does any one know," asked Molly, at length, with a vague air of addressing the trees, mindful, as she spoke, of the manner in which Mr. Landale had practically dismissed her and her sister at a certain point of his version of his brother's history, "*why* Sir Adrian has shut himself up in that place instead of living at the Hall all this time?"

A certain dignity seemed to come over the servant's squat figure. He hesitated for a moment, and then said very simply, his honest eyes fixed upon the girl's face: "I am only his humble servant, Mademoiselle, and it is enough for me that it is his pleasure to live alone."

"You are indeed faithful," said Molly, with a little generous flush of shame at this peasant's delicacy compared to her own curiosity. And, after another pause, she added, pensively: "But tell me, does Sir Adrian never leave his solitude? I confess I should like to meet one who had known my mother, who could talk of her to me."

René looked at the young girl with a wistful countenance, as though the question had embarked him on a new train of thought. But he answered evasively: "His honour comes rarely to Pulwick—rarely."

Molly, with a little movement of pique, rose abruptly from her seat. But quickly changing her mood again she turned round as she was about to depart, and smiling: "Thank you, René," she said, and held out her dainty hand, which he, blushing, engulfed in his great paw, "I am going in, I am dreadfully hungry. We shall be here two months or more, and I shall want to see you again . . . . if you come back to Pulwick."

She walked quickly away towards the house. René

followed the retreating figure with a meditative look, so long as he could keep her in sight, then turned his gaze to the island and there stood lost in a deep muse, regardless of the fact that his sweetheart, Moggie, was awaiting a parting interview at the lodge, and that the tide that would wait for no man was swelling under his boat upon the beach.

A sudden resolution was formed in Molly's mind as the immediate result of this conversation, and she framed her behaviour that morning solely with a view to its furtherance.

Breakfast was over when, glowing from her morning walk, she entered the dining-room ; but, regardless of Mr. Landale's pointedly elaborate courtesy in insisting upon a fresh repast being brought to her, his sarcastically overacted solicitude, intended to point out what a deal of avoidable trouble she gave to the household, Molly remained perfectly gracious, and ate the good things, plaintively set before her by Miss Landale, with the most perfect appetite and good humour.

She expatiated in terms of enthusiasm on the beauty of the estate and the delight of her morning exploration, and concluded this condescending account of her doings (in which the meeting with René did not figure) with a request that Mr. Landale should put horses at the disposal of herself and her sister for a riding excursion that very afternoon. And with determined energy she carried the point, declaring, despite his prognostications of coming bad weather, that the sunshine would last the day.

In this wise was brought about the eventful ride which cost the life of Lucifer, and introduced such heart-stirring phantasmagories into the even tenor of Sir Adrian Landale's seclusion.

That evening the news rapidly spread throughout Pulwick that the cruel sands of the bay had secured yet another victim.

In an almost fainting condition, speechless with horror, and hardly able yet to realise to the full her own anguish,

Madeleine was conducted by the terrified groom, through the howling wind and drenching rain, back to the Priory.

And there, between the fearful outcries of Miss Landale, and the deep frowning gravity of her brother, the man stammered out his tale.—How the young lady when the rain first began, had insisted, notwithstanding his remonstrances, upon taking the causeway to the island, and how it was actually by force that he prevented the other lady from following so soon as she understood the danger into which her sister was running.

There was no use, he had thought (explained the man, half apologetically), for two more to throw away their lives, just for no good, that way. And so they had sat on their horses and watched in terror, as well as they could through the torrents of rain. They had seen in the distance Lucifer break from the young lady's control, and swerve from the advancing sea. And then had come the great gust that blew the rain and the sand in their faces and set their horses dancing ; and, when they could see again, all traces of horse and rider had disappeared, and there lay nothing before them but the advancing tide, though the island and its tower were still just visible through the storm.

No amount of cross-examination could elicit any further information. The girl's impulse seemed to have been quite sudden, and she had only laughed back at the groom over her shoulder upon his earnest shout of warning, though she had probably expected them to follow her. And as there could be no doubt about the calamity which had ensued, and no possible rescue even of the body, he had returned home at once to bring the disastrous news.

Madeleine had been carried completely unconscious to her bed, but presently Miss Sophia was summoned to her side as the girl showed signs of returning animation, and Rupert was left alone.

He fell to pacing the room, lost in a labyrinth of complicated and far-reaching reflections.

Beyond doubt he was shocked and distressed by the sudden and horrible disaster ; and yet as an undercurrent to these first natural thoughts, there ran presently a distinct notion that he would have felt the grievousness of it more keenly had Madeleine perished in that cruel manner and her sister survived to bring the tale home.

The antagonism which his cousin, in all the insolence of her young beauty and vigorous self-esteem, had shown for him had been mutual. He had instinctively felt that she was an enemy, and more than that—a danger to him. This danger was now removed from his path, and by no intervention or even desire of his own.

The calamity which had struck the remaining sister into such prostration would make her rich indeed ; by anticipation one of the great heiresses in England.

"Sorrow," thought Mr. Landale, and his lip curled disdainfully, " a girl's sorrow, at least, is a passing thing. Wealth is an everlasting benefit."

Madeleine was a desirable woman upon all counts, even pecuniary considerations apart, or would be to one who had a heart to give—and even if the heart was dead. . . . ?

Altogether the sum of his meditations was assuming a not unpleasing aspect ; and the undercurrent in time assumed almost the nature of self-congratulation. Even the ordeal which was yet to come when he would have to face Miss O'Donoghue and render an account of his short trust, could not weigh the balance down on the wrong side.

And yet a terrible ordeal it would be ; women are so unreasonable, and Aunt Rose so much more so even than the average woman. Still it had to be done ; the sooner the better ; if possible while the storm lasted and while roaring waters kept all ill news upon land and the interloping heir on his island.

And thus that very evening, whilst Madeleine sobbed on her pillow and Molly was snugly enjoying the warm hospitality of Scarthey, a mounted messenger departed from the Priory to overtake Miss O'Donoghue on the road to Bath and acquaint her with the terrible fatality that had befallen her darling and favourite.

CHAPTER XV

UNDER THE LIGHT

DECEMBER 16TH.—Again I separate your green boards, my diary. No one has opened you; for your key, now a little rusty, still hangs upon my watch—my poor watch whose heart has ceased to beat, who, unlike its mistress, has *not* survived the ordeal by sand and water! What is better, no one has attempted to force your secrets from you; which, since it appears that it had been agreed that Molly de Savenaye was dead and buried in Scarthey sands, speaks well for all concerned. But she is not dead. She is very much alive; and very happy to be so.

This will indeed be an adventure worth reading, in the days to come; and it must be recounted—though were I to live to a hundred years I do not think I could ever forget it. Tanty Rose (she has not yet stopped scolding everybody for the fright she has had) is in the next room with Madeleine, who, poor dear, has been made quite ill by this prank of mine; but since after the distress caused by her Molly's death she has had the joy of finding her Molly alive again, things are balanced, I take it; and all being well that ends well, the whole affair is pleasant to remember. It has been actually as interesting as I expected—now that I think it over—even more.

Of all the many pictures that I fancied, not one was at all like the reality—and this reality I could not have rested till I had found. It was René's account decided me. I laid my plans very neatly to pay the recluse a little visit, and plead necessity for the intrusion. My machinations would have been perfect if they had not caused Madeleine and poor old Tanty unnecessary grief.

But now that I know the truth, I cannot distinctly remember what it was that I *did* expect to find on that island.

If it had not been that I had already gone through more excitement than I bargained for to reach that mysterious rock, how exciting I should have found it to wander up to unknown ruins, to knock at the closed doors of an enchanted castle, ascend unknown stairs and engage in devious unknown passages—all the while on the tip-toe of expectation!

But when I dragged myself giddy and faint from the boiling breakers and scrambled upon the desolate island under the rain that beat me like the lashes of a whip, pushing against a wind that bellowed and rushed as though determined to thrust me back to the waters I had cheated of their prey, my only thoughts were for succour and shelter.

Such warm shelter, such loving welcome, it was of course impossible that I could for a moment have anticipated!

Conceive, my dear diary, the feelings of a poor, semi-drowned wanderer, shivering with cold, with feet torn by cruel stones, who suddenly emerges from howl and turmoil into a warm, quiet room to be received as a long and eagerly expected guest, whose advent brings happiness, whose presence is a highly prized favour; in fact not as one who has to explain her intrusion, but as one who in the situation holds the upper hand herself.

And *this* was my welcome from him whose absence from Pulwick was more haunting than any presence I can think of!

Of course I knew him at once. Even had I not expected to see him—had I not come to seek him in fact—I should have known him at once from the portrait whose melancholy, wide-open eyes had followed me about the gallery. But I had not dreamed to see him so little altered. Now, apart from the dress, if he is in any way changed from the picture, it is in a look of greater youth and less sombreness. The portrait is handsome, but the original is better.

Had it not been so, I imagine I might have felt vastly different when I was seized and enfolded and—kissed! As it was I cannot remember that, even at the moment of this extraordinary proceeding, I was otherwise than pleased, nor that the dark hints of Mr. Landale concerning Sir Adrian's madness returned to disturb my mind in the least.

And yet I found myself enveloped in great strong arms

out of which I could not have extricated myself by the
most frantic efforts—although the folding was soft and
tender—and I loved that impression. Why? I cannot
say.

His words of love were not addressed to me : from his
exclamation I knew that the real and present Molly was
not the true object of his sudden ecstasy.

And yet I am glad that this is the first man who has
been able to kiss Molly de Savenaye. It is quite incomprehensible ; I ought to be indignant.

Now the whole secret of my reception is plain to see,
and it is pathetic ; Sir Adrian Landale was in love with
my mother ; when she was an unprotected widow he
followed her to our own country ; if she had not died
soon after, he would have married her.

What a true knight must this Sir Adrian be, to keep so
fresh for twenty years the remembrance of his boyish
love that when I came in upon him to look at him with
her eyes, it was to find him pondering upon her, and to
fill his soul with the rapturous thought that his love had
come back to him. Though I was aware that all this
fervour was not addressed to me, there was something
very gratifying in being so like one who could inspire
such long-lived passion.—Yes, it was unexpectedly
pleasant and comforting to be so received. And the
tender care, the thoughtful solicitude next bestowed on
the limp and dishevelled waif of the sea by my *beau
ténébreux were* unmistakably meant for Molly and no one
else, whatever his first imaginings may have been, and
they were quite as interesting to receive.

The half-hour I spent, cosily ensconced by his hands,
and waited upon by his queer household, was perhaps the
best I have ever known. He stood by the fireplace,
looking down from his great height, with a wondering
smile upon me. I declare that the loving kindness of his
eyes, which he has wide, grey, and beautiful, warmed
me as much as the pyramid of logs he had set burning on
the hearth !

I took a good reckoning of the man, from under the
gigantic collar, in which, I felt, my head rested like a
little egg at the bottom of a warm nest. "And so," I
thought, "here is the Light-keeper of Scarthey Island ! "
And I was obliged to confess that he was a more romantic-

looking person than even in my wildest dreams I had
pictured to myself—that in fact I had found out for the
first time *the man* really approved of.

And I congratulated myself on my own cleverness—
for it was evident that, just as I had suspected from René's
reticent manner, even by him our existence at Pulwick
had not been mentioned to "the master."

And as Mr. Landale was quite determined to avail
himself of his brother's *sauvagerie* not to let him know
anything about us, on his side, but for me we might have
remained at and departed from Pulwick unknown to the
head of the house ! And what a pity that would have been !

Now, *why* did not Mr. Landale wish his brother to
know ? Did he think (as indeed has happened) that the
Light-keeper would take too kindly to the Savenaye
children ? Or to one of them ? If so, he will be *bien
attrappé*, for there is no doubt that my sudden and dramatic
arrival upon his especial domain has made an impression
on him that no meeting prepared and discussed beforehand could have produced.

Adrian Landale may have been in love with our beautiful
mamma in his boyish days, but now, Sir Adrian, the *man*
is in love with the beautiful Molly !

That is positive.

I was a long time before I could go to sleep in the
tower ; it was too perfect to be in bed in such a place,
safe and happy in the midst of the rage I could hear
outside ; to have seen the unknown, to have found him
such as he is—to be under *the Light!*

What would have happened if my cousin had really
been mad (and René his keeper, as that stupid country-
side wit suggested in my ear the other night at dinner)?
It would have been still more of an adventure of course,
but not one which even "Murthering Moll the Second"
can regret. Or if he had been a dirty, untidy hermit, as
Madeleine thought? That would have spoilt all.

Thus in the owl's nest, as Mr. Landale (spiteful creature !) called it to Tanty, there lives not owl any more
than lunatic. A polished gentleman, with white, exquisite hands, who, when he is discovered by the most
unexpected of visitors, is shaven as smooth as Rupert
himself ; has the most unexceptionable of snowy linen
and old-fashioned, it is true, but most well-fitting clothes.

As for the entertainment for the said casual visitor, not
even Pulwick with all its resources (where housekeeping,
between the fussy brother and the docile sister is a
complicated science) could have produced more real
comfort.

In the morning, when I woke late (it was broad daylight), feeling as if I had been beaten and passed through
a mangle, for there was not an inch of my poor body
that was not sore, I had not turned round and so given
sign of life, before I heard a whisper outside my door ;
then comes a sturdy knock and in walks old Margery,
still dignified as a queen's housekeeper, bearing a bowl
of warm frothy milk.

And this being gratefully drunk by me, she gravely
inquires, in her queer provincial accent, how I am this
morn ; and then goes to report to some anxious inquirer
(whom ?—I can easily guess) that with the exception of
my cut foot I am very well.

Presently she returns and lights a blazing fire. Then in
come my dress and linen and my one shoe, all cleaned,
dried and mended, only my poor habit is so torn and so
stiff that I have to put up with Margery's best striped
skirt in lieu of it, till she has time to mend and wash it.
As it is she must have been at work all night upon these
repairs for me.

Again she goes out—for another consultation, I suppose—and comes back to find me half clad, hopping
about the room ; this time she has got nice white linen
bandages and with them ties up my little foot, partly for
the cuts, partly for want of a sandal, till it is twice the
size of its companion. But I can walk on it.

Then my strange handmaid—who by the way is a droll,
grumbling old soul, and orders me about as if she were
still my nurse—dresses me and combs my hair, which
will not yet awhile be rid of all its sand. And so, in due
course, Molly emerges from her bower, as well tended
almost as she might have been at Bath, except that Margery's striped skirt is a deal too short for her and she dis-
plays a little more of one very nice ankle and one gouty
foot than fashion warrants.

And in this manner the guest goes to meet her host in
the great room.

He was walking up and down as if impatiently expecting me, and when I hobbled in, he came forward with a smile on his face which, once more, I thought beautiful.

"God be praised!" he said, taking both my hands and kissing one of them, with his fine air of gallantry which was all the more delightful on account of his evident earnestness, "you seem none the worse for this terrible adventure. I dreaded this morning to hear that you were in a fever. You know," he added so seriously that I had to smile, "you might easily have had a fever from this yesterday's work; and what should we have done without doctor and medicines!"

"You have a good surgeon, at least," said I laughing and pointing at my swaddled extremity. He laughed too at the *enmitouflage*. "I tried to explain how it was to be done," he said, "but I think I could have managed it more neatly myself."

Then he helped me to the armchair, and René came in, and, after a profound bow (which did not preclude much staring and smiling at me afterwards), laid, on a dazzling tablecloth, a most tempting breakfast, explaining the while, in his odd English, "The bread is stale, for we bake only twice a month. But there are some cakes hot from the fire, some eggs, new laid last evening, some fresh milk, some tea. It was a happy thing I arrived yesterday for there was no more tea. The butter wants, but Mistress Margery will have some made to-morrow, so that the demoiselle will not leave without having tasted our Scarthey butter."

All the while Sir Adrian looked on with a sort of dreamy smile—a happy smile!

"Poor René!" he said, when the man had left the room, "one would think that you have brought to him almost as much joy as to me."

I wondered what Mr. Landale would have said had he through some magic glass been able to see this little feast. I never enjoyed a meal more. As for my host, he hardly touched anything, but, I could see, was all absorbed in the delight of looking at me; and this he showed quite openly in the most child-like manner.

Not one of the many fine gentlemen it has been my fate to meet in my six months' apprenticeship to the "great world." not cousin Rupert himself with all his elaborate politeness (and Rupert has *de grandes manières*,

I

as Tanty says), could have played the host with a more
exquisite courtesy, and more true hospitality. So I
thought, at least. Now and again, it is true, while his
eyes were fixed on me, I would see how the soul behind
them was away, far in the past, and then at a word, even
at a movement, back it would come to me, with the tenderest softening I have ever seen upon a human face.

It was only at the end of breakfast that he suddenly
adverted to the previous day.

"Of course," he said, hesitatingly, but keeping a frank
gaze on mine, "you must have thought me demented
when—when you first entered, yesterday."

Now, I had anticipated this apology as inevitable, and
I was prepared to put him at his ease.

"I—? Not at all," I said quite gravely; and, seeing
the puzzled expression that came upon his face, I hastened
to add in lower tones : "I know I am very like my mother,
and it was her name you called out upon seeing me."
And then I stopped, as if that had explained everything.

He looked at me with a wondering air, and fell again
into a muse. After a while he said, with his great simplicity which seems somehow in him the last touch of the
most perfect breeding : "Yes, such an apparition was
enough to unhinge any one's mind for the moment. You
never knew her, child, and therefore never mourned her
death. But we—that is, René and I, who tried so hard
to save her—though it is so long ago, we have not forgotten."

It was then I asked him to tell me about the mother I
had never known. At first it was as if he could not; he
fell into a great silence, through which I could feel the
working of his old sorrow. So then I said to him quickly,
for I feared he thought me an indiscreet trespasser upon
sacred ground, that he must remember my right to know
more than the vague accounts I had been given of my
mother's history.

"No one will tell me of her," I said. "It is hard, for
I am her own daughter."

"It is wrong," he said very gently; "you ought to
know, for you are indeed, most verily, her own daughter."

And then by fragments he tried to tell me a little of her
beauty, her loving heart, her faithfulness and bravery.

At first it was with great tripping sighs as if the words hurt him, but by and by it came easier, and with his eyes fixed wistfully on me he took me, as it were, by his side through all their marvellous adventures.

And thus I heard the stirring story of the "Savenaye band," and I felt prouder of my race than I had ever been before. Hitherto, being a Savenaye only meant the pride our aunt tried to instil into us of being undeniably *bien-nées* and connected with numbers of great families. But the tale of the deeds mine had done for the King's cause, and especially the achievements of my own mother in starting such an expedition after my father's death, and following its fortunes to the bitter end, made my blood tingle with a new emotion.

Little wonder that Sir Adrian should have devoted his life to her service. How madly enthralled I should have been, being a man, and free and strong, by the presence of a woman such as my mother. I, too, would have prostrated myself to worship her image returning to life— and I am that living, living portrait!

When he came to the story of her death, he hesitated and finally stopped. It must have been horrible. I could see it in his eyes, and I dared not press him.

Now, I suppose I am the only one in the world, besides René, who knows this man as he is. And I am proud of it.

And it is for this constancy, which no vulgar soul of them can understand, that Rupert and his class have dubbed the gallant gentleman a madman. It fills me with scorn of them. I do not yet know what love is, therefore of course I cannot fathom its grief; but this much I know—that if I loved and yet could not reach as high as ever love may reach both in joy and sorrow, I should despise myself. I, too, would draw the utmost from life that life can give.

He never even hinted at his love for my mother; speaking of himself throughout as René might, as of her humble devoted servant merely. And then the question began to gnaw at me. "Did she love him?" and somehow, I felt as if I could not rest till I knew; and I had it on my lips twenty times to cry out to him: "I know you loved her: oh! tell me, did she love you?" And yet I dared no more have done so, and overstepped the barrier of his gentle, reticent dignity, than I could have thrust the lighthouse tower down; and I could not think, either, whether I should be glad to hear that she had loved him, or that she had not. Not even here, alone with myself, can I answer that question.

But though I respect him because he is as I have found him, and understand how rare a personality it takes to achieve such refinement of faithfulness, it seems to me, that to teach this constant lover to forget the past in the present, would be something worth living for—something worthy of *me!*

Molly!—What is the meaning of this? You have never before put that thought in words, even to yourself! But let me be frank, or else what is the use of this diary?

Looking back to those delightful three days, did not the *thought* come to me, if not the words? Well, well, it is better, sometimes, I believe, to let oneself drift, than to try and guide the boat; and I must hurry back to Scarthey or I shall never have told my story. . . .

How swiftly time had flown by us! I sitting in the armchair, with the old dog's muzzle on my lap, and Sir Adrian standing by his great chimney; the clock struck twelve, in the midst of the long silence, and I had thought that barely an hour had passed.

I got up, and, seeing me limp in my attempt to walk, Sir Adrian gave me his arm; and so we went round the great room *bras dessus, bras dessous,* and it already seemed quite natural to feel like an intimate friend in that queer dwelling.

We paused a long time in silence by the window, the tempest wind was still raging, but the sky was clear, and all round us was a wonderful sight; the sea, as far as eyes could reach, white with foam, lashed and tossing in frenzy round the rock on which we stood so safely, and rising in long jets of spray, which now and then dashed as far as our window; and when I looked down nearer, I could see the little stunted trees, bending backwards and forwards under the blast, and an odd idea came to my mind:—they looked to me when they caught my sight, as though they were bowing deep, hurriedly and frantically greeting me among them.

I glanced up at my silent companion, the true knight, and found his wide grey eyes fixed upon me with the same expression that was already familiar to me, which I had especially noted as he told me his long tale of olden times.

This time I felt the look go to my heart. *And then the thought first came to my mind, all unformed, but still sweet.*

I don't know exactly why, but in answer to his sad look, I smiled at him, without a word, upon which he suddenly grew pale. After a while he gave a sigh, and, as he drew my arm again through his, I fancy his hand trembled a little.

When he had taken me back to my chair, he walked to and fro in silence, looking at me ever and anon.

A long time we passed thus, without speaking ; but it seemed as if our thoughts were intermixing in harmony in the midst of our silence. And then the spell was broken by René, who never came in without making me his great scrape, trying hard not to beam too obtrusively in the delight that evidently overtakes him whenever he sets eyes on me.

It was after a prolonged talk between him and the master, I fancy, concerning the means of attending fitly upon my noble and delicate person, that Sir Adrian, brought back, evidently, to the consideration of present affairs, began to be exercised about the best means of whiling away my time. When he hinted at the difficulty, I very soon disposed of it.

I told him I had never been so happy in my life before —that the hours went all too quickly—I told him there was so much he and René had yet to tell me of their wonderful adventures, that I thought I should have to carry them back to Pulwick with me. At the mention of Pulwick his brow darkened, and René turned away to cough into his hand, and I saw that I had gone too fast. (N. B.—Pulwick is evidently a sore subject ; I am sure I am not surprised. I can conceive how Rupert and Sophia would drive a man of Sir Adrian's sensitiveness nearly to desperation. Yet I *have* brought Sir Adrian back to Pulwick, in spite of all. Is not that a feather in my cap ?)

But to return ; I next made René laugh aloud and Sir Arian give his indulgent smile—such as a father might give to his child—by adding that when I was bored I would soon let them know. "I always do," I said, "for I consider that a duty to myself."

"God knows," said this strange man then, half smiling, " I would we could keep you here for ever."

It was almost a declaration, but his eyes were far off—it was not addressed to me.

I soon found that the recollection of all the extraordinary incidents Sir Adrian had lived through, is one neither of pride nor pleasure to him, but, all the same, never has anything in books seemed to me so stirring, as the tale of relentless fate, of ever-recurring battles and struggles and misfortunes told by the man who, still in the strength of life, has now chosen to forego everything that might for the remainder of his days have compensated him.

Willing as he was to humour me, however, and disproportionately anxious to amuse me, it was little more than the dry bones of his history, I was able to obtain from him.

With René's help, however, and my own lively imagination I have been able to piece together a very wonderful skeleton, from these same dry bones, and, moreover, endow it with flesh and blood and life.

Rene was very willing to descant upon his master's exploits, as far as he knew them : " Whew, Mademoiselle should have seen him fight !" he would say, "a lion, Mademoiselle, a real lion !"

And then I would contrast the reposeful, somewhat immobile countenance, the dreaming eye, the almost womanly softness of his smile, with the picture, and find the contrast piquant in the extreme.

Concerning his present home Sir Adrian was more willing to speak—I had told him how the light on the little island had fascinated me from the distance, and all the surmises I had made about it.

"And so, it was in order to see what sort of dungeon they kept the madman in," he said, laughing quietly, "that you pushed the reconnaissance, which nearly sent you into the jaws of death !"

I was so struck, at first, by his speaking of himself as the reputed "madman" that I could not answer. To think of him as serenely contemptuous of the world's imputation—and an imputation so galling as this one of being irresponsible for his actions—and deliberately continuing his even way without taking the trouble to refute

it, has given me an insight into his nature, that fills me
with admiration, and yet, at the same time, with a sort
of longing to see him reinstated in his proper place, and
casting out those slandering interlopers.

But, as he was waiting to be answered, I had to collect
my thoughts and admit, not without a little bashfulness,
that my first account of my exploit had contained a slight
prevarication.

In all he has to say about his little Scarthey domain,
about the existence he has made for himself there, I cannot help noticing with what affection he speaks of René.
René, according to Sir Adrian, is everything and everywhere ; a perfect familiar genius ; he is counsellor as well
as valet, plays his master's game of chess as well as
shaves him, can tune his organ, and manage his boat,
and cast his nets, for he is fisherman as well as gardener ;
he is the steward of this wonderful little estate, and its
stock of one pony, one cow, and twelve hens ; he tends
the light, and can cook a dinner a great deal better than
his great rival, old Margery.

Of this last accomplishment we had good proof in the
shape of various dainties that appeared at our dinner.
For when I exclaimed in astonishment, the master said,
well pleased, and pointing to the attentive major-domo :
" This is René's way of spoiling me. But now he has
surpassed himself to celebrate so unique an occasion.

And René's face was all one grin of rapture. I observe
that on occasions his eyes wander quite tenderly from
me to his master.

Shall I ever enjoy dinners again like those in that old
ruined tower ! Or hours like those during which I listened to tales of peril and adventure, or to the music that
pealed forth from the distant corner, when Sir Adrian sat
down to his organ and made it speak the wordless language of the soul : that language that made me at times
shiver with a mad yearning for life, more life ; at times
soothed my heart with a caress of infinite softness.

How is it that our organ-songs at the convent *never*
moved me in this fashion ?

Ah ! those will be days to remember ; all the more for
being certain that they will not be forgotten by him.
Yes, those days have brought some light into his melancholy life.

Even René knows that. "Oh, my lady," said he to me as he was leaving the island yesterday. "You have come like the good fairy, you have brought back the joy of life to his honour : I have not heard him really laugh —before this year passed I did not believe he knew any more how to laugh—what you can call laugh !"

It is quite true. I had made some droll remark about Tanty and Cousin Sophia, and when he laughed he looked like a young man.

He was quick enough in grasping at a pretext for keeping me yet another day. Yesterday the wind having suddenly abated in the night, there was quite a bevy of little fishing-boats sailing merrily away. And the causeway at low water was quite visible. As we looked out I know the same idea came to both our minds, though there was no word between us. At last it was I who spoke. "The crossing is quite safe," said I. And I added, as he answered nothing, "I almost wish now it was not. How quick the time has gone by, here !"

His countenance when I looked up was darker. He kept his eyes fixed in the distance. At last he said in a low voice :

"Yes, I suppose it is high time you should go back."

"I am sure I don't wish it," I said quite frankly—he is not the sort of man with whom one would ever think of *minauderie*, "but Madeleine will be miserable about me."

"And so you would really care to stop here," said he, with a smile of wonder on his face, "if it were not for that reason ?"

"Naturally I would," said I. "I feel already as cosy as a tame cat here. And if it were not for Madeleine, poor little Madeleine, who must be breaking her heart !— But then how can I go back ?—I have no wraps and only one shoe ?"

His face had cleared again. He was walking up and down in his usual way, whilst I hopped back, with more limping than was at all necessary, to my favourite arm-chair.

"True, true," he said, as if speaking to himself, "you cannot walk, with one shoe and a bandaged foot. And your clothes are too thin for the roundabout sea journey in this cold wind. This is what we shall do, child," he went on, coming up to me with a sage expression that struggled with his evident eager desire. "René shall go off, as soon as the tide permits, carrying the good news of your safety to your sister, and bring back some warm things for you to wear to-morrow morning, and I shall write to Rupert to send a carriage, to wait for you on the strand."

And so, pleased like two children who have found a means of securing a further holiday, we wrote both our letters. I wonder whether it occurred to Sir Adrian, as it did to me, that, if we had been so very anxious that I should be restored to the care of Pulwick with the briefest delay, I might have gone with René that same day, wrapped up in a certain cloak which had done good warming service already ; and that, as René had constructed with his cunning hands a sufficient if not very pretty sandal for my damaged foot out of some old piece of felt, I might have walked from the beach to the fishing village ; and that there, no doubt, a cart or a donkey might have conveyed me home in triumph.

Perhaps it did *not* occur to him ; and certainly I had no desire to suggest it on my side.

Thus, soon after mid-day, Master René departed alone. And Sir Adrian and I, both very glad of our reprieve, watched, leaning side by side upon the window-sill, the brave little craft glide away on the still ruffled waters, until, when it had grown very small in the distance, we saw the sail lowered and knew René had reached mainland.

And that was perhaps the best day of the three. René having been unexpectedly despatched, we had to help to do everything ourselves with old Margery, who is rather feeble. The sky was clear and beautiful : and, followed gravely by Jem the dog, we went round the little outer domain. I fed the hens, and Sir Adrian carried the pail when Margery had milked the cow ; we paid a visit in his wide paddock to the pony, who trotted up to his master whinnying with pleasure. We looked at the waters rushing past like a mill race on the further side of the island, as the tide was rising, and he explained to me that it was this rush which makes the neighbourhood of Scarthey so dangerous to unwary crafts ; we went down into the sea-caves which penetrate deep under the ruins.—They say that in olden days there was a passage under the rocky causeway that led as far as the old Priory, but all traces of it have been effaced.

Then, later on, Sir Adrian showed me in detail his library.

"I was made to be a man of books," he said, when I wondered at the number he had accumulated around him —there must be thousands, "a man of study, not of action. And you know how fate has treated me. These have been my one consolation of late years."

And it marvelled me to think that one who had achieved so many manly deeds, should love musty old tiresome things so much. He really turned them over quite reverentially. I myself do not think much of books as companions.

When I made that little confession he smiled rather sadly, and said that one like me never would lack the suitable companions of youth and happiness ; but that a creature of his unfortunate disposition could find, in these long rows of folded leaves, the society of the best and the loftiest minds, not of our age, but of all ages, and, what was more, could find them ready for intercourse and at their best humour, just in those hours when he himself was fit and disposed for such intercourse—and this without dread of inflicting his own misery and dulness upon them.

But I could not agree with his appreciation. I felt my nose curl with disdain at the breath of dust and must and age these old tomes gave forth, and I said again it was, to my mind, but a poor and tame sort of fellowship.

He was perched on his ladder and had some odd volume in his hand, from which he was about to give an example in point ; on hearing, however, this uncongenial sentiment he pushed back the book and came down quickly enough to talk to me. And this was the last of our excursions among the bookshelves.

Of this I was glad, for I confess it was there I liked Sir Adrian the least.

When the end of the short day drew near it was time to go and attend to the beacon. We ascended the ladder-like wooden stairs leading to the platform. Then I had the *reverse* of that view that for so many days had engrossed my interest.

Pulwick from Scarthey! . . . . What a long time it seemed then since I had left those rooms the windows of which now sent us back the rays of the setting sun ! and I had no desire to return, though return I must on the morrow.

René, of course, had left everything in his usual trim order, so all we had to do was to see to the lamp. It pleased my fantasy to light the beacon of Scarthey myself, and I struck the steel and kindled the brimstone and set fire to the huge, ill-smelling wicks until they gave a flame as big as my hand ; and " there is the light of Scarthey at close quarters," I thought. And the Lightkeeper was bending over me with his kindly look, humouring me like a child.

As we sat there silently for a while in the twilight, there came from the little room adjoining the turret an odd sound of flapping and uncanny, melancholy cries. Sir Adrian rose, and we remembered the seagull by which he had played the part of good Samaritan.

It had happened on the second day, as the storm was at its height. There had come a great crash at the window, and we saw something white that struggled on the sill outside ; Sir Adrian opened the casement (when we had a little tornado of our own inside, and all his papers began dancing a sarabande in the room), and we gathered in the poor creature that was hurt and battered and more than half stunned, opening alternately its yellow bill and its red eyes in the most absurd manner.

With a solicitude that it amused me to watch, Sir Adrian had tended the helpless, goose-like thing and then handed it to René's further care.

René, it seemed, had thought of trying to tame the wild bird, and had constructed a huge sort of cage with laths and barrel-hoops, and installed it there with various nasty, sea-fishy, weedy things, such as seagulls consider dainty. But the prisoner, now its vigour had returned, yearned for nothing but the free air, and ever and anon almost broke its wings in sudden frenzy to escape.

" I wonder at René," said Sir Adrian, contemplating the animal with his grave look of commiseration ; " René, who, like myself, has been a prisoner ! He will be disappointed, but we shall make one of God's creatures happy this day. There is not overmuch happiness in this world."

And, regardless of the vicious pecks aimed at his hands, he with firmness folded the great strong wings and legs and carried the gull outside on the parapet.

There the bird sat a moment, astonished, turning its head round at its benefactor before taking wing ; and then it rose flying away in great swoops—flap, flap—across the waves till we could see it no longer.   Ugly and awkward as the creature looked in its cage, it was beautiful in its joyful, steady flight, and I was glad to see it go.   I must have been a bird myself in another existence, for I have often that longing to fly upon me, and it makes my heart swell with a great impatience that I cannot.

But I could not help remarking to Sir Adrian that the bird's last look round had been full of anger rather than gratitude, and his answer, as he watched it sweep heavily away, was too gloomy to please me :

"Gratitude," said he, "is as rare as unselfishness.   If it were not so this world would be different indeed.   As it is, we have no more right to expect the one than the other. And, when all is said and done, if doing a so-called kind action gives us pleasure, it is only a special form of self-indulgence."

There is something wrong about a reasoning of this kind, but I could not exactly point out where.

We both stood gazing out from our platform upon the darkening waters.   Then across our vision there crept, round the promontory, a beautiful ship with all sails set, looking like some gigantic white bird ; sailing, sailing, so swiftly yet so surely by, through the dim light ; and I cried out in admiration : for there is something in the sight of a ship silently gliding that always sets my heart beating. But Sir Adrian's face grew stern, and he said : "A ship is a whitened sepulchre."

But for all that he looked at it long and pensively.

Now it had struck me before this that Sir Adrian, with all his kindness of heart, takes but a dismal view of human nature and human destiny ; that to him what spoils the face of this world is that strife of life—which to me is as the breath of my nostrils, the absence of which made my convent days so grey and hateful to look back upon.

I did not like to feel out of harmony with him, and so almost angrily I reproached him.

"Would you have every one live like a limpet on a

rock?" cried I. "Great heavens! I would rather be
dead than not be up and doing."

He looked at me gravely, pityingly.

"May *you* never see what I have seen," said he. "May
you never learn what men have made of the world. God
keep your fair life from such ways as mine has been made
to follow."

The words filled me, I don't know why, with sudden
misgiving. Is this life, I am so eager for, but horror and
misery after all? Would it be better to leave the book
unopened? They said so at the convent. But what can
they know of life at a convent?

He bent his kind face towards mine in the thickening
gloom, as though to read my thoughts, and his lips
moved, but he did not speak aloud. Then, above the
song of the waves as they gathered, rolled in, and fell
upon the shingle all around, there came the beat of oars.

"Hark," said Sir Adrian, "our good René!"

His tone was cheerful again, and, as he hurried me
away down the stairs, I knew he was glad to divert me
from the melancholy into which he had allowed himself
to drift.

And then "good René" came, bringing breezy life and
cheerfulness with him, and a bundle and a letter for me.

Poor Madeleine! It seems she has been quite ill with
weeping for Molly; and, indeed, her dear scrawl was so
illegible that I could hardly read it. René says she was
nearly as much upset by the joy as by the grief. Mr.
Landale was not at home; he had ridden to meet Tanty
at Liverpool, for the dear old lady has been summoned
back in hot haste with the news of my decease!

He for one, I thought to myself, will survive the shock
of relief at learning that Molly has risen from the dead!

Ting, ting, ting . . . . There goes my little clock,
fussily counting the hour to tell me that I have written so
long a time that I ought to be tired. And so I am, though
I have not told you half of all I meant to tell!

CHAPTER XVI

THE RECLUSE AND THE SQUIRE

I THOUGHT I should never get away from supper and be
alone! Rupert's air of cool triumph—it was triumph,
however he may have wished to hide it—and Tanty's flow
of indignation, recrimination, speculation, and amazement were enough to drive me mad. But I held out. I
pretended I did not mind. My cheeks were blazing, and
I talked *à tort et à travers*. I should have *died* rather than
that Rupert should have guessed at the tempest in my
heart. Now I am alone at last, thank God! and it will
be a relief to confide to my faithful diary the feelings that
have been choking me these last two hours.

"Pride must have a fall." Thus Rupert at supper, with
reference, it is true, to some trivial incident, but looking
at me hard and full, and pointing the words with his
meaning smile. The fairies who attended at my birth en-
dowed me with one power, which, however doubtful a
blessing it may prove in the long run, has nevertheless
been an unspeakable comfort to me hitherto. This is the
reverse of what I heard a French gentleman term *l' esprit
de l'escalier*. Thanks to this fairy godmother of mine, the
instant some one annoys or angers me there rises on the
tip of my tongue the most galling rejoinder that can possibly be made in the circumstances. And I need not add:
I make it.

To-night, when Rupert flung his scoff at me, I was
ready for him.

"I trust the old adage has not been brought home to
you, *Sir* Rupert," said I, and then pretending confusion.
"I beg your pardon," I added, "I have been so accustomed to address the head of the house these last days
that the word escaped me unawares." The shot told *well*,
and I was glad—glad of the murderous rage in Rupert's
eyes, for I knew I had hit him on the raw. Even Tanty

174

looked perturbed, but Rupert let me alone for the rest of supper.

He is right nevertheless, that is what stung me.   I am humbled, *and I cannot bear it!*

Sir Adrian has left.

I was so triumphant to bring him back to Pulwick this morning, to have circumvented Rupert's plans, and (let me speak the truth,) so happy to have him with me that I did not attempt to conceal my exultation.   And now he has gone, gone without a word to me; only this miserable letter of determined farewell.   I will copy it—for in my first anger I have so crumpled the paper that it is scarcely readable.

"My child, I must go back to my island.   The world is not for me, nor am I for the world, nor would I cast the shadow of my gloomy life further upon your bright one.   Let me tell you, however, that you have left me the better for your coming; that it will be a good thought to me in my loneliness to know of your mother's daughters so close to me.   When you look across at the beacon of Scarthey, child, through the darkness, think that though I may not see you again I shall ever follow and keep guard upon your life and upon your sister's, and that, even when you are far from Pulwick, the light will burn and the heart of Adrian Landale watch so long as it may beat."

I have shed more tears—hot tears of anger—since I received this than I have wept in all my life before. Madeleine came in to me just now, too full of the happiness of having me back, poor darling, to be able to bear me out of sight again; but I have driven her from me with such cross words that she too is in tears.   I must be alone and I must collect myself and my thoughts, for I want to state exactly all that has happened and then perhaps I shall be able to see my way more clearly.

This morning then, early after breakfast, I started across the waters between René and Sir Adrian, regretting to leave the dear hospitable island, yet with my heart dancing within me, as gaily as did our little boat upon the chopping waves, to be carrying the hermit back with me.   I had been deadly afraid lest he should at the last moment have sent me alone with the servant; but when he put on his big cloak, when I saw René place a

bag at the bottom of the boat, I knew he meant to come
—perhaps remain some days at Pulwick, and my spirits
went up, up !

It was a lovely day, too ; the air had a crisp, cold
sparkle, and the waters looked so blue under the clear,
frosty sky. I could have sung as we rowed along, and
every time I met Sir Adrian's eye I smiled at him out of
the happiness of my heart. His look hung on me—we
French have a word for that which is not translatable, *Il
me couvait des yeux*—and, as every day of the three we
had spent together I had thought him younger and hand-
somer, so this morning out in the bright sunlight I said to
myself, I could never wish to see a more noble man.

When we landed—and it was but a little way, for the
tide was low—there was the carriage waiting, and René,
all grins, handed over our parcels to the footman. Then
we got in, the wheels began slowly dragging across the
sand to the road, the poor horses pulling and straining,
for it was heavy work. And René stood watching us by
his boat, his hand over his eyes, a black figure against
the dazzling sunshine on the bay ; but I could see his
white teeth gleam in that broad smile of his from out of
his shadowy face. As, at length, we reached the high
road and bowled swiftly along, I would not let Sir Adrian
have peace to think, for something at my heart told me
he hated the going back to Pulwick, and I so chattered
and fixed his attention that as the carriage drew up he
was actually laughing.

When we stopped another carriage in front moved off,
and there on the porch stood—Rupert and Tanty !

Poor Tanty, her old face all disfigured with tears and
a great black bonnet and veil towering on her head. I
popped *my* head out of the window and called to them.

When they caught sight of me, both seemed to grow
rigid with amazement. And then across Rupert's face
came such a look of fury, and such a deathly pallor ! I
had thought, certainly, he would not weep the eyes out
of his head for me ; but that he should be stricken with
anger to see me alive I had hardly expected, and for the
instant it frightened me.

But then I had no time to observe anything else, for
Tanty collapsed upon the steps and went off into as fine
a fit of hysterics as I have ever seen. But fortunately it

did not last long. Suddenly in the middle of her screams and rockings to and fro she perceived Sir Adrian as he leant anxiously over her. With the utmost energy she clutched his arm and scrambled to her feet.

"Is it you, me poor child?" she cried, "Is it you?"

And then she turned from him, as he stood with his gentle, earnest face looking down upon her, and gave Rupert a glare that might have slain him. I knew at once what she was thinking: I had experienced myself that it was impossible to see Sir Adrian and connect his dignified presence for one second with the scandalous impression Rupert would have conveyed.

As for Rupert, he looked for the first time since I knew him thoroughly unnerved.

Then Tanty caught me by the arm and shook me:

"How *dare* you, miss, how dare you?" she cried, her face was flaming.

"How dare I what?" asked I, as I hugged her.

"How dare you be walking about when it is dead you are, and give us all such a fright—there—there, you know what I mean.—Adrian," she whimpered, "give me your arm, my nephew, and conduct me into your house. All this has upset me very much. But, oh, am I not glad to see you both, my children!"

In they went together. And my courage having risen again to its usual height, I waited purposely on the porch to tease Rupert a little. I had a real pleasure in noticing how he trembled with agitation beneath his mask.

"Well, are you glad to see me, Cousin Rupert?" said I.

He took my hand; his fingers were damp and cold.

"Can you ask, my fair cousin?" he sneered. "Do you not see me overcome with joy? Am I not indeed especially favoured by Providence, for is not this the second time that a beloved being has been restored into my arms like Lazarus from the grave?"

I was indignant at the heartlessness of his cynicism, and so the answer that leaped to my lips was out before I had time to reflect upon its unladylikeness.

"Ay," said I, "and each time you have cried in your soul, like Martha, 'Behold, he stinketh.'"

My cousin laughed aloud.

"You have a sharp tongue," he said, "take care you are not cut with it yourself some day."

12

Just then the footmen who had been unpacking Tanty's
trunks from the first carriage laid a great wooden box
upon the porch, and one of them asked Rupert which
room they should bring it to.

Rupert looked at it strangely, and then at me.

"Take it where you will," he exclaimed at last. "There
lies good money-value wasted—though, after all, one
never knows."

"What is it?" said I, struck by a sinister meaning in
his accents.

"Mourning, beautiful Molly—mourning for you—crape
—gowns—weepers—wherewith to have dried your sister's
tears—but not needed yet, you see."

He bared his teeth at me over his shoulder—I could not
call it a smile—and then paused, as he was about to brush
past into the hall, to give me the *pas*, with a mocking bow.

He does not even attempt now to hide his dislike of
me, nor to draw for me that cloak of suave composure
over the fierce temper that is always gnawing at his vitals
as surely as fox ever gnawed little Spartan. He sees
that it is useless, I suppose. As I went upstairs to greet
Madeleine, I laughed to myself to think how Fate had
circumvented the plotter.

Alas, how foolish I was to laugh! Rupert is a dangerous enemy, and I have made him mine ; and in a few
hours he has shuffled the cards, and now he holds the
trumps again. For that there is *du Rupert* in this sudden
departure of my knight, I am convinced. Of course, *his*
reasons are plain to see. It is the vulgarest ambition
that prompts him to oust his brother for as long as possible—for ever, if he can.

And now, *I* am outwitted. *Je rage.*

I have never been so unhappy. My heart feels all
crushed. I see no help anywhere. I cannot in common
decency go and seek Sir Adrian upon his island again,
and so I sit and cry.

Immediately upon his arrival Tanty was closeted with
Sir Adrian in the chamber allotted to her for so long a
space of time that Rupert, watching below in an inward
fever, now flung back in his chair biting his nails, now
restlessly pacing the room from end to end, his mind

working on the new problem, his ears strained to catch the least sound the while, was fain at last to ring and give orders for the immediate sounding of the dinner bell (a good hour before that meal might be expected) as the only chance of interrupting a conference which boded so ill to his plans. Meanwhile Madeleine sobbed out the story of her grief and joy on Molly's heart ; and Miss Sophia, who thus inconsiderately arrested in the full congenial flow of a new grief, was thrown back upon her old sorrows for consolation, had felt impelled to pay a visit to the rector's grave with the watering-can, and an extra pocket-handkerchief.

Never perhaps since that worthy clergyman had gasped out his last struggling breath upon her bosom had she known more unmixed satisfaction than during those days when she hovered round poor prostrate Madeleine's bed and poured into her deaf ear the tale of her own woes and the assurances of her thoroughly understanding sympathy. She had been looking forward, with a chastened eagerness, to the arrival of the mourning, and had already derived a good deal of pleasure from the donning of certain aged weeds treasured in her wardrobe ; it was therefore a distinct though quite unconscious disappointment when the news came which put an untimely end to all these funereal revels.

At the shrill clamour of the bell, as Rupert anticipated, Adrian emerged instantly from his aunt's room, and a simultaneous jingle of minor bells announced that the ladies' attention was in all haste being turned to toilet matters.

Whatever had passed between his good old relative and his sensitive brother, Rupert's quick appraising glance at the latter's face, as he went slowly down the corridor to his own specially reserved apartment, was sufficient to confirm the watcher in his misgiving that matters were not progressing as he might wish.

Sir Adrian seemed absorbed, it is true, in grave thought, but his countenance was neither distressed nor gloomy. With a spasm of fierce annoyance, and a bitter curse on the meddling of old females and young, Rupert had to admit that never had he seen his brother look more handsome, more master of the house and of himself, more *sane*.

A few minutes later the guests of Pulwick assembled in the library one by one, with the exception of Sophia, still watering the last resting-place of the Rev. Herbert Lee.

Adrian came first, closely followed by Tanty, who turned a marked shoulder upon her younger nephew and devoted all her attention to the elder—in which strained condition of affairs the conversation between the three was not likely to be lively. Next the sisters, attired alike in white, entered together, bringing a bright vision of youth and loveliness into the old room.

At sight of them Adrian sprang to his feet with a sudden sharp ejaculation, upon which the two girls halted on the threshold, half shy, half smiling. For the moment, in the shadow of the doorway, they were surprisingly like each other, the difference of colouring being lost in their curious similarity of contour.

My God, were there then two Céciles?

Beautiful, miraculous, consoling had been to the mourner in his loneliness the apparition of his dead love restored to life, every time his eyes had fallen upon Molly during these last few blessed days; but this new development was only like a troublous mocking dream.

Tanty turned in startled amazement. She could feel the shudder that shook his frame, through the hand with which he still unconsciously grasped at the back of her chair. An irrepressible smile crept to Rupert's lips.

The little interlude could not have lasted more than a few seconds when Molly, recovering her usual self-possession, came boldly forward, leading her sister by the tips of her fingers.

"Cousin Adrian," she said, "my sister Madeleine has many things to say to you in thanks for your care of my valuable person, but just now she is too bashful to be able to utter one quarter of them."

As the girls emerged into the room, and the light from the great windows struck upon Madeleine's fair curls and the delicate pallor of her cheek; as she extended her hand, and raised to Adrian's face, while she dropped her pretty curtsey, the gaze of two unconsciously plaintive blue eyes, the man dashed the sweat from his brow with a gesture of relief.

Nothing could be more unlike the dark beauty of the

ghost of his dreams or its dashing presentment now smiling confidently upon him from Tanty's side.

He took the little hand with tender pressure: Cécile's daughter must be precious to him in any case. Madeleine, moreover, had a certain appealing grace that was apt to steal the favour that Molly won by storm.

"But, indeed, I could never tell Sir Adrian how grateful I am," said she, with a timidity that became her as thoroughly as Molly's fearlessness suited her own stronger personality.

At the sound of her voice, again the distressful nightmare-like feeling seized Sir Adrian's soul.

Of all characteristics that, as the phrase is, "go in families," voices are generally the most peculiarly generic. When Molly first addressed Sir Adrian, it had been to him as a voice from the grave; now Madeleine's gentle speech tripped forth upon that self-same note—Cécile's own voice!"

And next Molly caught up the sound, and then Madeleine answered again. What they said, he could not tell; these ghosts—these speaking ghosts—brought back the old memories too painfully. It was thus Cécile had spoken in the first arrogance of her dainty youth and loveliness; and in those softer tones when sorrow and work and failure had subdued her proud spirit. And now she laughs; and hark, the laugh is echoed! Sir Adrian turns as if to seek some escape from this strange form of torture, meets Rupert's eye and instinctively braces himself into self-control.

"Come, come," cried Miss O'Donoghue, in her comfortable, commonplace, cheerful tone: "'This dinner bell of yours, Adrian, has raised false hopes, which seem to tarry in their fulfilment. What are we waiting for, may I ask?"

Adrian looked at his brother.

"Rupert, you know, my dear aunt," he said, "has the ordering of these matters."

"Sophia is yet absent," quoth Rupert drily, "but we can proceed without her, if my aunt wishes."

"Pooh, yes. Sophia!" snorted Miss O'Donoghue, grasping Sir Adrian's arm to show herself quite ready for the march, "Sophia! We all know what she is. Why, my dear Adrian, she'll never hear the bell till it has stopped this half hour."

"Dinner," cried Rupert sharply to the butler, whom his pull of the bell-rope had summoned. And dinner being served, the guests trooped into that dining-room which was full of such associations to Sir Adrian. It was a little thing, but, nevertheless, intensely galling to Rupert to have to play second gentleman, and give up his privileges as host to his brother. Usually indeed Adrian cared too little to stand upon his rights, and insisted upon Rupert's continuing to act in his presence as he did in his absence ; but this afternoon Tanty had left him no choice.

Nevertheless, as Mr. Landale sat down between the sisters, and turned smiling to address first one and then the other, it would have taken a very practised eye to discern under the extra urbanity of his demeanour the intensity of his inward mortification. He talked a great deal and exerted himself to make the sisters talk likewise, bantering Molly into scornful and eager retorts, and preventing Madeleine from relapsing into that state of dreaminess out of which the rapid succession of her recent sorrow and joy had somewhat shaken her.

The girls were both excited, both ready to laugh and jest. Tanty, satisfied to see Adrian preside at the head of the table with a grave, courteous, and self-contained manner that completely fulfilled her notions of what family dignity required of him, cracked her jokes, ate her dinner, and quaffed her cup with full enjoyment, laughing indulgently at her grand-nieces' sallies, and showing as marked a disfavour to Rupert as she deemed consistent with good manners.

The poor old lady little guessed how the workings in each brother's mind were all the while, silently but inevitably, tending towards the destruction of her newly awakened hopes.

There was silence between Sir Adrian and Rupert when at last they were left alone together. The elder's gaze wandering in space, his absent hand softly beating the table, his relaxed frame—all showed that his mind was far away from thought of the younger's presence. The relief to be delivered from the twin echoes of a haunting voice—once the dearest on earth to him—was immense. But his whole being was still quivering under the first acuteness of so disturbing an impression.

His years of solitude, moreover, had ill prepared him for social intercourse; the laughter, the clash of conversation, the noise on every side, the length of the meal, the strain to maintain a fit and proper attitude as host, had tried to the utmost nerves by nature hypersensitive.

Rupert, who had leisure to study the suddenly lined and tired lineaments of the abstracted countenance before him, noted with self-congratulation the change that a few hours seemed to have wrought upon it, and decided that the moment had come to strike.

"So, Adrian," he said, looking down demurely as he spoke into the glass of wine he had been toying with— Rupert was an abstemious man. "So, Adrian, you have been playing the chivalrous rôle of rescuer of distressed damsels—squire of dames and what not. The last one would have ascribed to you at least at this end of your life. Ha," throwing up his head with a mirthless laugh; "how little any of us would have thought what a blessing in disguise your freak of self-exile was destined to become to us!"

At the sound of the incisive voice Adrian had returned with a slight shiver from distant musing to the consciousness of the other's presence.

"And did you not always look upon my exile as a blessing undisguised, Rupert?" answered he, fixing his brother with his large grave gaze.

Rupert's eyelids wavered a little beneath it, but his tone was coolly insolent as he made reply:

"If it pleases you to make no count of our fraternal affection for you, my dear fellow; if by insisting upon *our* unnatural depravity you contrive a more decent excuse for your own vagaries, you have my full permission to dub me Cain at once and have done with it."

A light sigh escaped the elder man, and then he resolutely closed his lips. It was by behaviour such as this, by his almost diabolical ingenuity in the art of being uncongenial, that Rupert had so largely contributed to make his own house impossible to him. But where was the use of either argument or expostulation with one so incapable of even understanding the mainsprings of his actions? Moreover (*he*, above all, must not forget it) Rupert had suffered through him in pride and self-

esteem.   And yet, despite Sir Adrian's philosophic mind,
despite his vast, pessimistic though benevolent tolerance
for erring human nature, his was a very human heart ;
and it added not a little to the sadness of his lot at
every return to Pulwick (dating from that first most
bitter home-coming) to feel in every fibre of his being
how little welcome he was where the ties of flesh and
blood alone, not to speak of his most ceaseless yet delicate generosity, should have ensured him a very different reception.

Again he sighed, this time more deeply, and the corners of Rupert's lips, the arch of his eyebrows, moved
upwards in smiling interrogation.

"It must have given you a shock," said Mr. Landale,
carelessly, "to see the resemblance between Molly and
poor Cécile ; not, of course, that *I* can remember her ;
but Tanty says it is something startling."

Adrian assented briefly.

"I daresay it seems quite painful to you at first," proceeded Rupert, much in the same deliberate manner as a
surgeon may lay bare a wound, despite the knowledge of
the suffering he is inflicting, "I noticed that you seemed
upset during dinner.   But probably the feeling will wear
off."

" Probably."

"Madeleine resembles her father, I am told : but then
you never saw the *feu Comte*, did you ?   Well, they are
both fine handsome girls, full of life and spirits.   It is
our revered relative's intention to leave them here—as
perhaps she has told you—for two months or so."

"I have begged her," said Sir Adrian gravely, "to make
them understand that I wish them to look upon Pulwick
as their home."

"Very right, very proper," cried the other ; "in fact I
knew that was what you would wish—and your wishes,
of course, are my law in the matter.   By the way, I
hope you quite understand, Adrian, how it happened that
I did *not* notify to you the arrival of these guests extraordinary—knowing that you have never got over their
mother's death, and all that—it was entirely from a wish
to spare you.   Besides, there was your general prohibition about my visitors ; I did not dare to take the responsibility in fact.   And so I told Tanty."

I do not wish to doubt the purity of your motives, though it would have grieved me had *these* visitors (no ordinary ones as you yourself admit) come and gone without my knowledge. As it fell out, however, even without that child's dangerous expedition, I should have been informed in any case—René knew."

"René knew?" cried Rupert, surprised; and "damn René" to himself with heart-felt energy.

That the infernal little spy, as he deemed his brother's servant, should have made a visit to Pulwick without his knowledge was unpleasant news, and it touched him on his tenderest point.

But now, replenishing his half-emptied glass to give Adrian no excuse for putting an end to the conference before he himself desired it, he plunged into the heart of the task he had set himself without further delay:

"And what would you wish me to do, Adrian," he asked, with a pretty air of deference, "in the matter of entertaining these ladies? I have thought of several things likely to afford them amusement, but, since you are here, you will readily understand that I should like your authorisation first. I am anxious to consult you when I can," he added, apologetically. "So forgive my attacking you upon business to-night when you seem really so little fitted for it—but you know one cannot count upon you from one minute to another! What would you say if I were to issue invitations for a ball? Pulwick was noted for its hospitality in the days of our fathers, and the gloom that has hung over the old home these last eight years has been (I suppose) unavoidable in the circumstances—but none the less a pity. No fear but that our fair cousins would enjoy such a festivity, and I think I can promise you that the sound of our revels should not reach as far as your hermitage."

A slow colour had mounted to Adrian's cheeks; he drew his brows together with an air of displeasure; Rupert, quick to read these symptoms, hastened to pursue the attack before response should be made:

"The idea does not seem to please you," he cried, as if in hurt surprise. "'Tis true I have now no legal right to think of reviving the old hospitable traditions of the family; but you must remember, Adrian, you yourself have insisted on giving me a moral right to act host here in your absence—you have over and over again laid stress upon the freedom you wished me to feel in the matter.   Hitherto I have not made use of these privileges; have not cared to do so, beyond an occasional duty dinner to our nearest neighbours.   A lonely widower like myself, why should I?   But now, with these gay young things in the house—so near to us in blood—I had thought it so much our duty to provide fitting entertainment for them that your attitude is incomprehensible to me.   Come! does it not strike you as savouring a little of the unamiable dog in the fable?   I know you hate company yourself, and all the rest of it; but how can these things here affect you upon your island?   As for the budget, it will stand it, I assure you.   I speak hotly; pray excuse me.   I own I have looked forward to the thought of seeing once more young and happy faces around me."

"You mistake me," said Sir Adrian with an effort; "while you are acting as my representative you have, as you know, all liberty to entertain what guests you choose, and as you see fit.   It is natural, perhaps, that you should now believe me anxious to hurry back to the lighthouse, and I should have told you before that it is my intention this time to remain longer than my wont, in which circumstance the arrangements for the entertaining of our relatives will devolve upon myself."

Rupert broke into a loud laugh.

"Forgive me, but the idea is too ludicrous!   What sort of funeral festivities do you propose to provide to the neighbourhood, with you and Sophia presiding, the living images of mourning and desolation?   There, my dear fellow, I *must* laugh.   It will be the skeleton at the feast with a vengeance.   Why, even to-night, in the bosom of your family, as it were, your presence lay so like a wet blanket upon us all that, 'pon my soul, I nearly cracked my voice trying to keep those girls from noticing it!   Seriously, I am delighted, of course, that you should feel so sportive, and it is high time indeed that the neighbourhood should see something of you, but I fear you are reckoning beyond your strength.   Anyhow, command me.   I shall be anxious to help you all I can in this novel departure.   What are your plans?"

"I have laid no plans," answered Sir Adrian coldly,

after a slight pause, "but you do not need me to tell you, Rupert, that to surround myself with such gaiety as you suggest is impossible."

"You mean to make our poor little cousins lead as melancholy an existence as you do yourself then," cried Rupert with an angry laugh. Matters were not progressing as he could have wished. "I fear this will cause a good deal of disappointment, not only to them but to our revered aunt—for she is very naturally anxious to see her charges married and settled, and she told me that she more or less counted upon my aid in the matter. Now as you are here of course I have, thank Heaven, nothing more to say one way or another. But you will surely think of asking a few likely young fellows over to the house, occasionally? We are not badly off for eldest sons in the neighbourhood ; Molly, who is as arrant a little flirt, they tell me, as she is pretty, will be grateful to you for the attention, on the score of amusement at least."

Mr. Landale, speaking somewhat at random out of his annoyance to have failed in immediately disgusting the hermit of the responsibilities his return home might entail, here succeeded by chance in producing the desired impression.

The idea of Molly—Cécile's double—marrying—worse still, making love, coquetting before his eyes, was intolerable to Adrian. To have to look on, and see *Cécile's* eyes lavish glances of love ; *her* lips, soft words and lingering smiles, upon some country fool ; to have himself to give this duplicate of his love's sweet body to one unworthy perhaps—it stung him with a pain as keen as it was unreasonable. It was terrible to be so made, that the past was ever as living as the present ! But he must face the situation, he must grapple with his own weakness. Tender memories had lured him from his retreat and made him for a short time almost believe that he could live with them, happy a little while, in his own home again ; but now it was these very memories that were rising like avengers to drive him hence.

Of course the child must marry if there her happiness lay. Ay, and both Cécile's children must be amused, made joyful, while they still could enjoy life—Rupert was right—right in all he said—but he, Adrian, could not be there to see. That was beyond his endurance.

It was impossible of course, for one so single-minded himself, to follow altogether the doublings of such a mind as Rupert's ; but through the melancholy relief of this sudden resolution, Adrian was distinctly conscious of the underlying duplicity, the unworthy motives which had prompted his brother's arguments.

He rose from the table, and looked down with sad gaze at the younger's beautiful mask of a face.

"God knows," he said, "God knows, Rupert, I do not so often inflict my presence upon you that you should be so anxious to show me how much better I should do to keep away. I admit nevertheless the justice of all you say. It is but right that Mesdemoiselles de Savenaye should be surrounded with young and cheerful society ; and even were I in a state to act as master of the revels (here he smiled a little dreamily), my very presence, as you say, would cast a gloom upon their merrymaking—I will go. I will go back to the island to-night—I can rely upon you to assist me to do so quietly without unnecessary scenes or explanations—yes—yes—I know you will be ready to facilitate matters ! Strange ! It is only a few hours ago since Tanty almost persuaded me that it was my duty to remain here ; now you have made me see that I have no choice but to leave. Have no fear, Rupert—I go. I shall write to Tanty. But remember only, that as you treat Cécile's children, so shall I shape my actions towards you in future."

Slowly he moved away, leaving Rupert motionless in his seat ; and long did the younger brother remain moodily fixing the purple bloom of the grapes with unseeing eyes.

PART III

"CAPTAIN JACK," THE GOLD SMUGGLER

CHAPTER XVII

THE GOLD SMUGGLER AND THE PHILOSOPHER

On the evening of the day which had seen Miss Molly's departure for the main land, René, after the usual brisk post-prandial altercation with old Margery by her kitchen fire, was cheerfully finding his way, lantern in hand, to his turret, when in the silence of the night he heard the door of the keep open and close, and presently recognised Sir Adrian's tread echoing on the flagged steps beneath him.

Astonished at this premature return and full of vague dismay, he hurried down to receive his master.

There was a cloud on Sir Adrian's face, plainly discernible in spite of the unaltered composure of his manner.

"I did not expect your honour back so soon," said René, tentatively.

"I myself did not anticipate to return. I had thought I might perhaps stay some days at Pulwick. But I find there is no home like this one for me, René."

There was a long silence. But when René had re-kindled a blaze upon the hearth and set the lamp upon the table, he stood a moment before withdrawing, almost begging by his look some further crumb of information.

"My room is ready, I suppose?" inquired Sir Adrian.

"Yes, your honour," quoth the man ruefully, "Margery and I put it back exactly as—as before."

"Good-night then, good-night!" said the master after a pause, warming his hands as the flames began to leap through the network of twigs. "I shall go to bed, I am tired; I had to row myself across. You will take the boat back to-morrow morning."

René opened his mouth to speak; caught the sound of a sigh coming from the hearthside, and, shaking his head, in silence obeyed the implied dismissal. And bitterly did he meditate in his bunk, that night, upon the swift crum-

191

bling of those air-castles he had built himself so gaily erstwhile, in the rose and blue atmosphere that *La Demoiselle* had seemed to bring with her to Scarthey.

From the morrow the old regular mode of life began again in the keep.

Sir Adrian read a good deal, or at least appeared so to do ; but René, who kept him more than ever under his glances of wistful sympathy, noted that far from being absorbed, as of old, in the pages of his book, the recluse's eyes wandered much off its edges into space ; that when writing, or at least intent on writing, his pen would linger long in the bottle and hover listlessly over the paper ; that he was more abstracted, even than his wont, when looking out of the eastern window ; and that on the platform of the beacon it was the landward view which most drew his gaze.

There was also more music in the keep than was the custom in evener days. Seated at his organ the light-keeper seemed to find a voice for such thoughts as were not to be spoken or written, and relief for the nameless pity of them. But never a word passed between the two men on the subject that filled both their hearts.

It was Sir Adrian's pleasure that things at Scarthey should seem to be exactly the same as before, and that was enough for René.

"And yet," mused the faithful fellow, within his disturbed mind, "the ruins now look like a house the day after an interment. If we were lonely before, my faith, now we are desolate?" and, trying to find something or somebody to charge with the curse of it, he invariably fell to upon Mr. Landale's sleek head, why, he could hardly have explained.

Three new days had thus passed in the regularity, if not the serenity of the old—they seemed old already, buried far back in the past, those days that had lapsed so evenly before the brightness of youthful and beautiful life had entered the keep for one brief moment, and departing, again left it a ruin indeed—when the retirement of Scarthey was once more invaded by an unexpected visitor. It was about sundown of the shortest day. Sir Adrian was at his organ, almost unconsciously interpreting his own sadness into music. In time the yearning of his soul had had expression, the echo of the last sighing chord died away in the tranquil air, yet the musician, with head bent upon his breast, remained lost in far-away thoughts.

A slight shuffling noise disturbed him; turning round to greet René as he supposed, he was astonished to see a man's figure lolling in his own arm-chair.

As he peered inquiringly into the twilight, the intruder rose to his feet, and cried with a voice loud and clear, pleasant withal to the ear :

"Sir Adrian, I am sorry you have stopped so soon ; I never heard anything more beautiful! The door was ajar, and I crept in like a cat, not to disturb you."

Still in doubt, but with his fine air of courtesy, the light-keeper advanced towards the uninvited guest.

"Am I mistaken," he said, with some hesitation, "surely this is Hubert Cochrane's voice?"

"Jack Smith's voice, my dear fellow ; Jack Smith, at your service, please to remember," answered the visitor, with a genial ring of laughter in his words. "Not that it matters much here, I suppose! Had I not heard the peal of your organ I should have thought Scarthey deserted indeed. I could find no groom of the chambers to announce me in due form."

As he spoke, the two had drawn near each other and clasped hands heartily.

"Now, to think of your knowing my voice in this manner! You have a devilish knack of spotting your man, Sir Adrian. It is almost four years since I was here last, is it not?"

"Four years?—so it is ; and four years that have done well by you, it would appear. What a picture of strength and lustiness! It really seems to regenerate one, and put heart of grace in one, only to take you by the hand. —Welcome, Captain Smith!"

Nothing could have more succinctly described the outer man of him who chose to be known by that most nondescript of patronymics. Sir Adrian stood for a moment, contemplating, with glances of approval such as he seldom bestowed on his fellow-man, the symmetrical, slender, yet vigorous figure of his friend, and responding with an unwonted cheerfulness to the smile that lit up the steel-blue eyes, and parted the shapely,

13

strong, and good-humoured mouth of the privateers-man.

"Dear me, and what a buck we have become!" continued the baronet, "what splendid plumage! It is good to see you so prosperous. And so this is the latest fashion? No doubt it sets forth the frame of a goodly man, though no one could guess at the 'sea dog' beneath such a set of garments. I used to consider my brother Rupert the most especial dandy I had ever seen; but that, evidently, was my limited experience: even Rupert cannot display so perfect a fit in bottle-green coats, so faultless a silken stock, buckskins of such matchless drab!"

Captain Jack laughed, blushed slightly under the friendly banter, and allowed himself to be thrust back into the seat he had just vacated.

"Welcome again, on my lonely estate. I hope this is not to be a mere flying visit? You know my misanthropy vanishes when I have your company. How did you come? Not by the causeway, I should say," smiling again, and glancing at the unblemished top-boots.

"I have two men waiting for me in the gig below; my schooner, the *Peregrine*, lies in the offing."

The elder man turned to the window, and through the grey curtain of crepuscule recognised the rakish topsail schooner that had excited Molly's admiration some days before. He gazed forth upon it a few meditative moments.

"Not knowing whether I would find you ready to receive me," pursued the captain, "I arranged that the *Peregrine* was to wait for me if I had to return to-night."

"Which, of course, is not to be heard of," said Sir Adrian. "Here is Renny; he will carry word that with me you remain to-night . . . . Come, Renny, do you recognise an old acquaintance?"

Already well disposed towards any one who could call this note of pleasure into the loved voice, the Breton, who had just entered, turned to give a broad stare at the handsome stranger, then burst into a guffaw of pure delight. "By my faith, it is Mr. the Lieutenant!" he ejaculated; adding, as ingeniously as Tanty herself might have done, that he would never have known him again.

"It is Mr. the Captain now, Renny," said that person, and held out a strong hand to grip that of the little Frenchman, which the latter, after the preliminary rubbing upon his trousers that his code of manners enjoined, readily extended.

"Ah, it is a good wind that sent you here this day," said he, with a sigh of satisfaction when this ceremony had been duly gone through.

"You say well," acquiesced his master, "it has ever been a good wind that has brought Captain Jack across my path."

And then receiving directions to refresh the gig's crew and dismiss them back to their ship with instructions to return for orders on the morrow, the servant hurried forth, leaving the two friends once more alone.

"Thanks," said Captain Jack, when the door had closed upon the messenger. "That will exactly suit my purpose. I have a good many things to talk over with you, since you so kindly give me the opportunity. In the first place, let me unburden myself of a debt which is now of old standing—and let me say at the same time," added the young man, rising to deposit upon the table a letter-case which he had taken from his breast-pocket, "that though my actual debt is now met, my obligation to you remains the same and will always be so. You said just now that I looked prosperous, and so I am—owing somewhat to good luck, it is true, but owing above all to you. No luck would have availed me much without *that* to start upon." And he pointed to the contents of the case, a thick bundle of notes which his host was now smilingly turning over with the tip of his fingers.

"I might have sent you a draft, but there is no letter-post that I know of to Scarthey, and, besides, it struck me that just as these four thousand pounds had privately passed between you and me, you might prefer them to be returned in the same manner."

"I prefer it, since it has brought you in person," said Sir Adrian, thrusting the parcel into a drawer and pulling his chair closer towards his guest. "Dealings with a man like you give one a taste of an ideal world. Would that more human transactions could be carried out in so simple and frank a manner as this little business of ours!"

Captain Jack laughed outright.

"Upon my word, you are a greater marvel to me every time I see you—which is not by any means often enough!"

The other raised his eyebrows in interrogation, and the sailor went on :

"Is it really possible that it is to *my* mode of dealing that you attribute the delightful simplicity of a transaction involving a little fortune from hand to hand ? And where pray, in this terraqueous sublunary sphere—I heard that good phrase from a literary exquisite at Bath, and it seems to me comprehensive—where, then, on this terraqueous sublunary globe of ours, Sir Adrian Landale, could one expect to find another person ready to lend a privateers-man, trading under an irresponsible name, the sum of four thousand pounds, without any other security than his volunteered promise to return it—if possible ?"

Sir Adrian, ignoring the tribute to his own merits, arose and placed his friendly hand on the speaker's shoulder : "And now, my dear Jack," he said gravely, "that the war is over, you will have to turn your energies in an-other direction. I am glad you are out of that unworthy trade."

Captain Jack bounded up : "No, no, Sir Adrian, I value your opinion too much to allow such a statement to pass unchallenged. Unworthy trade ! We have not given back those French devils one half of the harm they have done to our own merchant service ; it was war, you know, and you know also, or perhaps you don't—in which case let me tell you—that my *Cormorant* has made her goodly name, ay, and brought her commander a fair share of his credit, by her energy in bringing to an incredible number of those d——d French sharks—beg pardon, but you know the pestilent breed. Well, we shall never agree upon the subject I fear. As for me, the smart of the salt air, the sting of the salt breeze, the fighting, the danger, they have got into my blood ; and even now it sometimes comes over me that life will not be perfect life to me without the dancing boards under my feet and the free waves around me, and my jolly boys to lead to death or glory. Yet, could you but know it, this is the veriest treason, and I revoke the words a thou-sand times. You look amazed, and well you may : ah, I have much to tell you ! But I take it you will not care to hear all I have been able to achieve on the basis of your munificent help at my—ahem, unworthy trade."

"Well, no," said Sir Adrian smiling, "I can quite

imagine it, and imagine it without enthusiasm, though, perhaps, as you say, such things have to be. But I should like to know of these present circumstances, these prospects which make you look so happy. No doubt the fruits of peace?"

"Yes, I suppose in one way they may be called so. Yet without the war and your helping hand they would even now hang as far from me as the grapes from the fox. —When I arrived in England three months after the peace had been signed, I had accumulated in the books of certain banks a tolerably respectable account, to the credit of a certain person, whose name, oddly enough, you on one or two occasions have applied, absently, to Captain Jack Smith. I was, I will own, already feeling inclined to discuss with myself the propriety of assuming the name in question, when, there came something in my way of which I shall tell you presently ; which something has made me resolve to remain Captain Smith for some time longer. The old *Cormorant* lay at Bristol, and being too big for this new purpose, I sold her. It was like cutting off a limb. I loved every plank of her ; knew every frisk of her ! She served me well to the end, for she fetched her value—almost. Next, having time on my hands, I bethought myself of seeing again a little of the world ; and when I tell you that I drove over to Bath, you may perhaps begin to see what I am coming to."

Sir Adrian suddenly turned in his chair to face his friend again, with a look of singular attention.

"Well, no, not exactly, and yet—unless—? Pshaw ! impossible——!" upon which lucid commentary he stopped, gazing with anxious inquiry into Captain Jack's smiling eyes. "Ah, I believe you have just a glimmer of the truth with that confounded perspicacity of yours," saying which the sailor laughed and blushed not unbecomingly. "This is how it came about : I had transactions with old John Harewood, the banker, in Bristol, transactions advantageous to both sides, but perhaps most to him—sly old dog. At any rate, the old fellow took a monstrous fancy to me, over his claret, and when I mentioned Bath, recommended me to call upon his wife (a very fine dame, who prefers the fashion of the Spa to the business of Bristol, and consequently lives as much in the former place as good John Harewood will allow).

Well, you wonder at my looking prosperous and happy.
Listen, for here is the *hic* : At Lady Maria Harewood's
I met one who, if I mistake not, is of your kin.   Already,
then, somewhere at the back of my memory dwelt the
name of Savenaye——Halloa, bless me ! I have surely
said nothing to——!"

The young man broke off, disconcerted.   Sir Adrian's
face had become unwontedly clouded, but he waved the
speaker on impatiently : "No, no, I am surprised, of
course, only surprised ; never mind me, my thoughts
wandered—please go on.   So you have met her ?"

"Ay, that I have ! Now it is no use beating about
the bush. You who know her—you do know her of
course—will jump at once to the only possible conclusion. Ah, Adrian !" Captain Jack pursued, pacing
enthusiastically about, "I have been no saint, and no
doubt I have fancied myself as a lover once or twice ere
this ; but to see that girl, sir, means a change in a man's
life : to have met the light of those sweet eyes is to love,
to *love* in reality. It is to feel ashamed of the idiotic
make-believes of former loves. To love her, even in vague
hope, is to be glorious already ; and, by George, to have
her troth, is to be—I cannot say what . . . . to be what
I am now !"

The lover's face was illumined ; he walked the room
like one treading on air as the joy within him found its
voice in words.

Sir Adrian listened with an extraordinary tightness at
his heart. He had loved one woman even so ; that love
was still with him, as the scent clings to the phial ; but
the sight of this young, joyful love made him feel old in
that hour—old as he had never realised before. There
was no room in his being for such love again. And yet
. . . . ? There was a tremulous anxiety in the question
he put, after a short pause. "There are *two* Demoiselles
de Savenaye, Jack ; which is it ?"

Captain Jack halted, turned on his heels, and exclaimed
enthusiastically : "To me there is but one—one woman
in the world—Madeleine !" His look met that of Sir
Adrian in full, and even in the midst of his own self-
centred mood he could not fail to notice the transient
gleam that shot in the elder's eyes, and the sudden relaxation of his features. He pondered for a moment or

two, scanning the while the countenance of the recluse;
then a smile lighted up his own bronzed face in a very
sweet and winning way. "As her kinsman, have I your
approval?" he asked and proceeded earnestly: "To tell
the truth at once, I was looking to even more than your
approval—to your support."

Sir Adrian's mood had undergone a change: as a
breeze sweeping from a new quarter clears in a moment
a darkening mist from the face of the earth, Captain Jack's
answer had blown away for the nonce the atmosphere of
misgiving that enveloped him. He answered promptly,
and with warmth: "Being your friend, I am glad to
know of this; being her kinsman, I may add, my dear
Hubert"—there was just a tinge of hesitation, followed
by a certain emphasis, on the change of name—"I promise to support you in your hopes, in so far as I have any
influence; for power or right over my cousin I have
none."

The sailor threw himself down once more in his arm-
chair; and, tapping his shining hessians with the stem
of his long clay in smiling abstraction, began, with all a
lover's egotism, to expatiate on the theme that filled his
heart.

"It is a singular, an admirable, a never sufficiently-to-
be-praised conjunction of affairs which has ultimately
brought me near you when I was pursuing the Light o'
my Heart, ruthlessly snatched away by a cunning and
implacable dragon, known to you as Miss O'Donoghue.
I say *dragon* in courtesy; I called her by better names
before I realised what a service she was unconsciously
rendering us by this sudden removal."

"Known to me!" laughed Sir Adrian. "My own
mother's sister!"

"Then I still further retract. Moreover, seeing how
things have turned out, I must now regard her as an
angel in disguise. Don't look so surprised! Has she
not brought my love under your protection? I thought
I was tolerably proof against the little god, but then he
had never shot his arrows at me from between the long
lashes of Madeleine de Savenaye. Oh, those eyes,
Adrian! So unlike those southern eyes I have known
so well, too well in other days, brilliant, hard, challeng-
ing battle from the first glance, and yet from the first

promising that surrender which is ever so speedy.   Pah!
no more of such memories.   Before *her* blue eyes, on my
first introduction, I felt—well, I felt as the novice does
under the first broadside."

The speaker looked dreamily into space, as if the delicious moment rose again panoramically before him.

"Well," he pursued, "that did me no harm, after all.
Lady Maria Harewood, who, I have learned since, deals
strongly in sentiment, and, being unfortunately debarred
by circumstances from indulgence in the soothing luxury
on her own behalf, loves to promote matches more
poetical—she calls it more 'harmonious'—than her own
very prosaic one, she, dear lady, was delighted with
such a rarity as a bashful privateersman—her 'tame
corsair,' as I heard her call your humble servant.—I
was a hero, sir, a perfect hero of romance in the course
of a few days!   On the strength of this renown thrust
upon me I found grace before the most adorable blue
eyes; had words of sympathy from the sweetest lips,
and smiles from the most bewitching little mouth in all
the world.   So you see I owe poor Lady Maria a good
thought. . . . . You laugh?"

Sir Adrian was smiling, but all in benevolence, at the
artlessness of this eager youth, who in all the unconscious glory of his looks and strength, ascribed the credit
of his entrance into a maiden's heart to the virtue of a
few irresponsible words of recommendation.

"Ah! those were days!   Everything went on smoothly,
and I was debating with myself whether I would not, at
once, boldly ask her to be the wife of Hubert Cochrane;
though the casting of Jack Smith's skin would have neces-
sitated the giving up of several of his free-trading engagements."

"Free trading!   You do not mean to say, man alive,
that you have turned smuggler now!" interrupted Sir
Adrian aghast.

"Smuggler," cried Jack with his frank laugh, "peace,
I beg, friend!   Miscall not a gentleman thus.   Smuggler—pirate?   I cut a pretty figure evidently in your
worship's eyes.   Lucky for me you never would be
sworn as a magistrate, or where should I be . . . . and
you too, between duty and friendship?—But to proceed:
I was about, as I have said, to give that up for the

reasons I mentioned, when, upon a certain fine evening, I crossed the path of one of the most masterful old maids I have ever seen, or even heard of ; and, would you believe it ? "—this with a quizzical look at his host's grave face— "this misguided old lady took such a violent dislike to me at first sight, and expressed it so thoroughly well, that, hang me if I was not completely brought to.   And all for escorting my dear one from Lady Maria's house to her own !   Well, the walk was worth it—though the old crocodile was on the watch for us, ready to snap ; had got wind of the secret, somehow, a secret unspoken even between us two.   This first and last interview took place on the flags, in front of No. 17 Camden Place, Bath.   Oh !   It was a very one-sided affair from the beginning, and ended abruptly in a door being banged in my face.   Then I heard about Miss O'Donoghue's peculiarities in the direction of exclusiveness.   And then, also, oddly enough, for the first time, of the great fortune going with my Madeleine's hand.   Of course I saw it all, and, I may say, forgave the old lady.   In short, I realised that, in Miss O'Donoghue's mind, I am nothing but an unprincipled fortune-seeker and adventurer.   Now you, Adrian, can vouch that, whatever my faults, I am none such."

Sir Adrian threw a quiet glance at his friend, whose eyes sparkled as they met it.

"God knows," continued the latter, "that all I care for, concerning the money, is that *she* may have it.   This last venture, the biggest and most difficult of all, I then decided to undertake, that I might be the fitter mate for the heiress—bless her !   Oh, Adrian, man, could you have seen her sweet tearful face that night, you would understand that I could not rest upon such a parting.   In the dawn of the next morning I was in the street—not so much upon the chance of meeting, though I knew that such sweetness would have now to be all stolen—but to watch her door, her window ; a lover's trick, rewarded by lover's luck !   Leaning on the railings, through the cold mist (cold it was, though I never felt it, but I mind me now how the icicles broke under my hand), what should I see, before even the church-bells had set to chiming, or the yawning sluts to pull the kitchen curtains, but a bloated monster of a coach, dragging and sliding

up the street to halt at her very door. Then out came
the beldam herself, and two muffled-up slender things—
my Madeleine one of course ; but I had a regular turn at
sight of them, for I swear I could not tell which was
which ! Off rattled the chariot at a smart pace ; and
there I stood, friend, feeling as if my heart was tied behind with the trunks."

The sailor laughed, ran his fingers through his curls and
stamped in lively recollection.

"Nothing to be drawn from their landlady. But I am
not the man to allow a prize to be snatched from under
my very nose. So, anathematising Miss O'Donoghue's
family-tree, root, stem, and branch—except that most
lovely off-shoot I mean to transplant (you will forgive
this heat of blood ; it was clearing for action so to speak)
—I ran out and overtook the ostler whom I had seen putting the finishing touch to the lashing of boxes behind !
'Gloucester !' says he. The word was worth the guinea
it cost me, a hundred times over.—In less than an hour
I was in the saddle, ready for pursuit, cantering boot to
boot with my man—a trusty fellow who knows how to
hold his tongue, and can sit a horse in the bargain.
Neither at Gloucester, nor the next day, up to Worcester,
could we succeed in doing more than keep our fugitives in
view. When they had alighted at one inn, as ascertained
by my squire, we patronised the opposition hostelry, and
the ensuing morning cantered steadily in pursuit, on *our*
new post-horses half an hour after they had rumbled
away with *their* relays. But the evening of our arrival at
Worcester, my fellow found out, at last, what the next
stage was to be, and—clever chap, he lost nothing for
his sharpness—that the 'Three Kings' Heads' had been
recommended to the old lady as the best house in Shrewsbury. This time we took the lead, and on to Shrewsbury,
and were at the glorious old Kings' Heads (I in a private
room, tight as wax) a good couple of hours before the
chariot made its appearance. And there, man, there !
my pretty one and I met again !"

"That was, no doubt," put in Sir Adrian, in his gentle,
indulgent way, "what made the Kings' Heads so glorious ?"

"Ay. Right ! And yet it was but a few seconds,
on the stair, under a smoky lamp, but her beauty filled

the landing with radiance as her kindness did my soul.
—It was but for a moment, all blessed moment, too
brief, alas! Ah, Adrian, friend—old hermit in your
cell—*you* have never known life, you who have never
tasted a moment such as that! Then we started
apart: there was a noise below, and she had only time
to whisper that she was on her way to Pulwick to some
relatives—had only heard it that very day—when steps
came up the stairs, creaking. With a last promise, a last
word of love, I leaped back into my own chamber, there
to see (through the chink between door and post) the untimely old mischief-maker herself pass slowly, sour and
solemn, towards her apartments, leaning upon her other
niece's arm. How could I have thought *that* baggage
like my princess? Handsome, if you will; but, with
her saucy eye, her raven head, her brown cheek, no
more to be compared to my stately lily than brass to
gold!"

The host listening wonderingly, his eyes fixed with
kindly gravity upon the speaker as he rattled on, here
gave a slight start, all unnoticed of his friend.

"The next morning, when I had seen the coach and its
precious freight move on once more northward, I began
the retreat south, hugging myself upon luck and success.
I had business in Salcombe—perhaps you may have heard
of the Salcombe schooners—in connection with the fitting
out of that sailing wonder, the *Peregrine*. And so," concluded Captain Jack, laughing again in exuberance of
joy, "you may possibly guess one of the reasons that
has brought her and me round by your island."

There ensued a long silence, filled with thoughts,
equally pressing though of widely different complexion,
on either side of the hearth.

During the meal, which was presently set forth and
proclaimed ready by René, the talk, as was natural in
that watchful attendant's presence, ran only on general
topics, and was in consequence fitful and unspontaneous.
But when the two men, for all their difference of age,
temper, and pursuits so strongly, yet so oddly united in
sympathy, were once more alone, they naturally fell
back under the influence of the more engrossing strain of
reflection. Again there was silence, while each mused,

gazing into space and vaguely listening to the plash of high water under the window.

"It must have been a strong motive," said Sir Adrian, after his dreamy fashion, like one thinking aloud, "to induce a man like you to abandon his honourable name."

Captain Jack flushed at these words, drew his elbows from the table, and shot a keen, inquiring glance at his friend, which, however, fell promptly before the latter's unconscious gaze and was succeeded by one of reflective melancholy. Then, with a slight sigh, he raised his glass to the lamp, and while peering abstractedly through the ruby, "The story of turning my back upon my house," he said musingly, "shaking its very dust off my feet, so to speak, and starting life afresh unbeholden to my father (even for what he could not take away from me — my own name), — is a simple affair, although pitiful enough perhaps. But memories of family wrongs and family quarrels are of their nature painful; and, as I am a mirth-loving fellow, I hate to bring them upon me. But perhaps it has occurred to you that I may have brought some disgrace upon the name I have forsaken."

"I never allowed myself to think so," said Sir Adrian, surprised. "Your very presence by my fireside is proof of it."

Again the captain scrutinised his host; then with a little laugh: "Pardon me," he cried, "with another man one might accept that likely proof and be flattered. But with you? why, I believe I know you too well not to feel sure that you would have received me as kindly and unreservedly, no matter what my past if only you thought that I had repented; that you would forgive even a *crime* regretted; and having forgiven, forget. . . . . But, to resume, you will believe me when I say that there was nothing of the sort. No," he went on, with a musing air, "but I could tell you of a boy, disliked at home for his stubborn spirit, and one day thrashed, thrashed mercilessly — at a time when he had thought he had reached to the pride of man's estate, thrashed by his own father, and for no just cause. . . . . Oh, Adrian, it is a terrible thing to have put such resentment into a lad's heart." He rose as he spoke, and placed himself before the hearth.

"If ever I have sons," he added after a pause, and at

the words his whole handsome face relaxed, and became
suffused with a tender glow, "I would rather cut my
right hand off than raise such a spirit in them. Well, I
daresay you can guess the rest ; I will even tell you in a
few words, and then dismiss the subject.—I have always
had a certain shrewdness at the bottom of my recklessness. Now there was a cousin of the family, who had
taken to commerce in Liverpool, and who was therefore
despised, ignored and insulted by us gentry of the Shaws.
So when I packed my bundle, and walked out of the park
gate, I thought of him ; and two days later I presented
myself at his mansion in Rodney Street, Liverpool. I
told him my name, whereat he scowled ; but he was
promptly brought round upon hearing of my firm determination to renounce it and all relations with my father's
house for ever, and of my reasons for this resolve, which
he found excellent. I could not have lighted upon a
better man. He hated my family as heartily as even I
could wish, and readily, out of spite to them, undertook
to aid me. He was a most enterprising scoundrel, had
a share in half a dozen floating ventures. I expressed a
desire for life on the ocean wave, and he started me
merrily as his nephew, Jack Smith, to learn the business
on a slaver of his. The 'ebony trade,' you know, was
all the go then, Adrian. Many great gentlemen in Lancashire had shares in it. Now it is considered low. To
say true, a year of it was more than enough for me—too
much ! It sickened me. My uncle laughed when I demurred at a second journey, but to humour me, as I had
learned something of the sailing trade, he found me another berth, on board a privateer, the *St. Nicholas*. My
fortune was made from the moment I set foot on that
lucky ship, as you know."

"And you have never seen your father since ?"

"Neither father, nor brothers, nor any of my kin, save
the cousin in question. All I know is that my father is
dead—that he disinherited me expressly in the event of
my being still in the flesh ; my eldest brother reigns ;
many of us are scattered, God knows where. And my
mother"—the sailor's voice changed slightly—"my
mother lives in her own house, with some of the younger
ones. So much I have ascertained quite recently. She
believes me dead, of course. Oh, it will be a good day,

Adrian, when I can come back to her, independent, prosperous, bringing my beautiful bride with me! . . . . But until I can resume my name in all freedom, this cannot be."

"But why, my dear fellow, these further risks and adventures? Surely, even at your showing you have enough of this world's goods; why not come forward, now, at once, openly? I will introduce you, as soon as may be, in your real character, for the sake of your mother—of Madeleine herself."

The sailor shook his head, tempted yet determined.

"I am not free to do so. I have given my word; my honour is engaged," he said. Then abruptly asked: "Have you ever heard of guinea smuggling?"

"Guinea smuggling! No," said Sir Adrian, his amazement giving way to anxiety.

"No? You surprise me. You who are, or were, I understand, a student of philosophical matters, freedom of exchange, and international intercourse and the rest of it—things we never shall have so long as governments want money, I am thinking.—However, this guinea smuggling is a comparatively new business. Now, *I* don't know anything about the theory; but I know this much of the practice that, while our preventive service won't let guineas pass the Channel (as goods) this year, somebody on the other side is devilish anxious to have them at almost any cost. And the cost, you know, is heavy, for the risk of confiscation is great. Well, your banker or your rich man will not trust his bullion to your common free trader—he is not quite such a fool."

"No," put in Sir Adrian, as the other paused on this mocking proposition. "In the old days, when I was busy in promoting the Savenaye expedition, I came across many of that gentry, and I cannot mind a case where they could have been trusted with such a freight. But perhaps," he added with a small smile, "the standard may be higher now."

Captain Jack grinned appreciatively. "That is where the 'likes of me' comes in. I will confess this not to be my first attempt. It is known that I am one of the few whose word is warranty. What is more, as I have said, it is known that I have the luck. Thus, even if I could bring my own name into such a trade, I would not; it would be the height of folly to change now."

For all his disapproval Sir Adrian could not repress a look of amusement. "I verily believe, Jack," he said, shaking his head, "that you are as superstitious yourself as the best of them!"

"I ought to make a good thing out of it," said Jack, evasively. "And even with all that is lovely to keep me on shore, I would hardly give it up, if I could. As things stand I could not if I would. Do not condemn me, Adrian,—that would be fatal to my hopes—nay, I actually want your help."

"I would you were out of it," reiterated Sir Adrian; "it takes so little to turn the current of a man's life when he seems to be making straight for happiness. As to the morals of it, I fail, I must admit, to perceive any wrong in smuggling, at least in the abstract, except that a certain kind of moral teaches that all is wrong that is against the law. And yet so many of our laws are so ferocious and inept, and as such the very cause of so much going wrong that might otherwise go well; so many of those who administer them are themselves so ferocious and inept, that the mere fact of a pursuit being unlawful is no real condemnation in my eyes. But, as you know, Jack, those who place themselves above some laws almost invariably renounce all. If you are hanged for stealing a horse, or breaking some fiscal law and hanged for killing a man, the tendency, under stress of circumstances is obvious. Aye, have we not a proverb about it : as well be hanged for a sheep as for a lamb? . . . . There are gruesome stories about your free traders—and gruesome endings to them. I well remember, in my young days, the clanking gibbet on the sands near Preston and the three tarred and iron-riveted carcases hanging, each in its chains, with the perpetual guard of carrion crows. . . . Hanging in chains is still on the statute book, I believe. But I'll stop my croaking now. You are not one to be drawn into brutal ways; nor one, I fear, to be frightened into prudence. Nevertheless," laughing quietly, "I am curious to know in what way you expect help from me, in practice. Do you, seriously, want me to embark actually on a smuggling expedition?—I demur, my dear fellow."

Obviously relieved of some anxiety, the other burst out laughing. "Never fear! I know your dislike to bilge water too well. I appreciate too well also your comfortable surroundings," he returned, seating himself once more complacently in his arm-chair, "much as I should love your company on board my pleasure ship—for, if you please, the *Peregrine* is no smuggling lugger, but professes to be a yacht. Still, you can be of help for all that, and without lifting even a finger to promote this illicit trade. You may ignore it completely, and yet you will render me incalculable service, provided you do not debar me from paying you a few more visits in your solitude, and give me the range of your caves and cellars."

"You are welcome enough," said the recluse. "I trust it may end as well as it promises." And, after a pause, "Madeleine does not know the nature of your present pursuit?"

"Oddly enough, and happily (for our moments of interview are short, as you may imagine) she is not curious on the subject. I don't know what notions the old Lady Maria may have put into her head about me. I think she believes that I am engaged on some secret political intrigue and approves of such. At least I gathered as much from her sympathetic reticence ; and, between ourselves, I am beginning to believe it myself."

"How is that?" asked the listener, moved to fresh astonishment by this new departure.

"Well, I may tell you, who not only can be as silent as the tomb, but really have a right to know, since you are tacitly of the conspiracy. This time the transaction is to be with some official of the French Court. They want the metal, and yet wish to have it secretly. What their motive may be is food for reflection if you like, but it is no business of mine. And, besides the fact that one journey will suffice for a sum which at the previous rate would have required half a score, all the trouble and uncertainty of landing are disposed of ; at any rate, I am, when all is ready, to be met by a government vessel, get my *quid pro quo* as will be settled, and there the matter is to end."

"A curious expedition," mused Sir Adrian.

"Yes," said the sailor, "my last will be the best. By the way, will you embark a few bags with me? I will take no commission."

Sir Adrian could not help laughing.

"No, thank you ; I have no wish to launch any more of my patrimony on ventures—since it would be of no service to you. I had almost as lief you had made use of my old crow's nest without letting me into the ins and outs of your projects. But, be it as it may, it is yours, night and day. Your visits I shall take as being for me."

"What a man you are, upon my soul, Sir Adrian !" cried Captain Jack, enthusiastically.

Later on, when the "shaking down" hour, in Captain Jack's phraseology, had sounded, and the two friends separated to rest, the young man refused the offer, dictated by hospitality, of his host's own bedroom. Sir Adrian did not press the point, and, leaving his guest at liberty to enjoy the couch arranged by René in a corner under the bookshelves, even as when Mademoiselle de Savenaye had been the guest of the peel, himself retired to that now hallowed apartment.

"Odd fellow, that," soliloquised Captain Jack, as, slowly divesting himself, he paced about the long room and, in the midst of roseate reflections, examined his curious abode. "Withal, as good as ever stepped. It was a fine day's work our old *St. Nicholas* did, about this time eight years ago. Rather unlike a crowded battery deck, this," looking from the solemn books to the glinting organ pipes, and conscious of the great silence. "As for me, I should go crazy by myself here. But it suits him. Queer fish !" again ruminated the young sailor. "He hates no one and yet dislikes almost everybody, except that funny little Frenchy and me. Whereas *I* like every man I meet—unless I detest him ! . . . . My beautiful plumage !" this whilst carefully folding the superfine coat and thereon the endless silken stock. "Now there's a fellow who does not care a hang for any woman under the sun, and yet enters into another chap's love affairs as if he understood it all. I believe it will make him happy to win my cause with Madeleine. I wish one could do something for *his* happiness. It is absurd, you know," as though apostrophising an objector, "a man can't be happy without a woman. And yet again, my good Jack, you never thought that before you met Madeleine. He has not met his Madeleine, that's what it means. Where

14

ignorance is bliss . . . . Friend Adrian ! Let us console ourselves and call you ignorantly happy, in your old crow's nest. You have not stocked it so badly either.— For all your ignorance in love, you have a pretty taste in liquor."

So thinking, he poured himself a last glass of his host's wine, which he held for a moment in smiling cogitation, looking, with the mind's eye, through the thick walls of the keep, across the cold mist-covered sands of Scarthey and again through the warm and scented air of a certain room (imagination pictured) where Madeleine must at that hour lie in her slumber. After a moment of silent adoration he sent a rapturous kiss landwards and tossed his glass with a last toast :

"Madeleine, my sweet ! To your softly closed lids."

And again Captain Jack fell to telling over the precious tale of that morning's interview, furtively secured, by that lover's luck he so dutifully blessed, under the cluster of Scotch firs near the grey and crumbling boundary walls of Pulwick Park.

CHAPTER XVIII

"LOVE GILDS THE SCENE AND WOMAN GUIDES THE PLOT"

TANTY's wrath upon discovering Sir Adrian's departure was all the greater because she could extort no real explanation from Rupert, and because her attacks rebounded, as it were, from the polished surface he exposed to them on every side. Madeleine's indifference, and Molly's apparently reckless spirits, further discomposed her during supper; and upon the latter young lady's disappearance after the meal, it was as much as she could do to finish her nightly game of patience before mounting to seek her with the purpose of relieving her overcharged feelings, and procuring what enlightenment she might.

The unwonted spectacle of the saucy damsel in tears made Miss O'Donoghue halt upon the threshold, the hot wind of anger upon which she seemed to be propelled into the room falling into sudden nothingness.

There could be no mistake about it. Molly was weeping; so energetically indeed, with such a passion of tears and sobs, that the noise of Tanty's tumultuous entrance fell unheeded upon her ears.

All her sympathies stirred within her, the old lady advanced to the girl with the intention of gathering her to her bosom. But as she drew near, the black and white of the open diary attracted her eye under the circle of lamplight, and being possessed of excellent long sight, she thought it no shame to utilise the same across her grand-niece's prostrate, heaving form, before making known her presence.

"*And so I sit and cry.*"

Miss Molly was carrying out her programme with much precision, if indeed her attitude, prone along the table, could be described as sitting.

Miss O'Donoghue's eyes and mouth grew round, as with the expression of an outraged cockatoo she read and re-read the tell-tale phrases. Here was a complication she had not calculated upon.

"Dear, dear," she cried, clacking her tongue in disconsolate fashion, so soon as she could get her breath. "What is the meaning of this, my poor girl?"

Molly leaped to her feet, and turning a blazing, disfigured countenance upon her relative, exclaimed with more energy than politeness: "Good gracious, aunt, what *do* you want?"

Then catching sight of the open diary, she looked suspiciously from it to her visitor, and closed it with a hasty hand. But Miss O'Donoghue's next words settled the doubt.

"Well, to be sure, what a state you have put yourself into," she pursued in genuine distress. "What has happened then between you and that fellow, whom I declare I begin to believe as crazy as Rupert says, that you should be crying your eyes out over his going back to his island?—you that I thought could not shed a tear if you tried. Nothing left but to sit and cry, indeed."

"So you have been reading my diary, you mean thing," cried Miss Molly, stamping her foot. "How dare you come creeping in here, spying at my private concerns! Oh! oh! oh!" with unpremeditated artfulness, relapsing into a paroxysm of sobs just in time to avert the volley of rebuke with which the hot-tempered old lady was about to greet this disrespectful outburst. "I am the most miserable girl in all the world. I wish I were dead, I do."

Again Tanty opened her arms, and this time she did draw the stormy creature to a bosom, as warm and motherly as if all the joys of womanhood had not been withheld from it.

"Tell me all about it, my poor child." There was a distinct feeling of comfort in the grasp of the old arms, comfort in the very ring of the deep voice. Molly was not a secretive person by nature, and moreover she retained quite enough shrewdness, even in her unwonted break-down, to conjecture that with Tanty lay her sole hope of help. So rolling her dark head distractedly on the old maid's shoulder, the young maid narrated her tale of woe. Pressed by a pointed question here and there, Tanty soon collected a series of impressions of Molly's visit to Scarthey, that set her busy mind working upon a startlingly new line. It was her nature to jump at conclusions, and it was not strange that the girl's passionate display of grief should seem to be the unmistakable outcome of tenderer feelings than the wounded pride and disappointment which were in reality its sole motors.

"I am convinced it is Rupert that is at the bottom of it," cried Molly at last, springing into uprightness again, and clenching her hands. "His one idea is to drive his brother permanently from his own home—and he *hates me.*"

Tanty sat rigid with thought.

So Molly was in love with Sir Adrian Landale, and he —who knows—was in love with her too ; or if not with her, with her likeness to her mother, and that was much the same thing when all was said and done. Could anything be more suitable, more fortunate ? Could ever two birds be killed with one stone with more complete felicity than in this settling of the two people she most loved upon earth ? Poor pretty Molly ! The old lady's heart grew very tender over the girl who now stood half sullenly, half bashfully averting her swollen face ; five days ago she had not known her handsome cousin, and now she was breaking her heart for him.

It might be, indeed, as she said, that they had to thank Rupert for this—and off flew Tanty's mind upon another tangent. Rupert was very deep, there could be no doubt of that ; he was anxious enough to keep Adrian away from them all ; what would it be then when it came to a question of his marriage ?

Tanty, with the delightful optimism that seventy years' experience had failed to damp, here became confident of the approach of her younger nephew's complete discomfiture, and in the cheering contemplation of that event chuckled so unctuously that Molly looked at her amazed.

"It is well for you, my dear," said the old lady, rising and wagging her head with an air of enigmatic resolution, "that you have got an aunt."

Some two days later, René, sitting upon a ledge of the

old Scarthey wall, in the spare sunshine which this still, winter's noon shone pearl-like through a universal mist, busy mending a net, to the tune of a melancholy, inward whistle, heard up above the licking of the waves all around him and the whimper of the seagulls overhead, the beat of steady oars approaching from land side.

Starting to his feet, the little man, in vague expectation, ran to a point of vantage from which to scan the tideway; after a few seconds' investigation he turned tail, dashed into the ruins, up the steps, and burst open the door of the sitting-room, calling upon his master with a scared expression of astonishment.

Captain Jack, poring over a map, his pipe sticking rakishly out of one side of his mouth, looked up amused at the Frenchman's evident excitement, while Adrian, who had been busy with the uppermost row of books upon his west wall, looked down from his ladder perch, with the pessimist's constitutional expectation of evil growing upon his face.

"One comes in a boat," ejaculated René, "and I thought I ought to warn his honour, if his honour will give himself the trouble to look out."

"It must be the devil to frighten Renny in this fashion," muttered Captain Jack as distinctly as the clench of his teeth upon the pipe would allow him. Sir Adrian paled a little, he began to descend his ladder, mechanically flicking the dust from his cuffs.

"Your honour," said René, drawing to the window and looking out cautiously, "I have not yet seen her, but I believe it is old miss—the aunt of your honour and these ladies."

Captain Jack's pipe fell from his dropping jaw and was broken into many fragments as he leaped to his feet with an elasticity of limb and a richness of expletive which of themselves would have betrayed his calling.

Flinging his arm across one of Adrian's shoulders he peeped across the other out of the window, with an alarm half mocking, half genuine.

"The devil it is, friend Renny," he cried, drawing back and running his hands with an exaggerated gesture of despair through his brown curls; "Adrian, all is lost unless you hide me."

"My aunt here, and alone," exclaimed Adrian, retreating from the window perturbed enough himself, "I must go down to meet her. Pray God it is no ill news! Hurry, Renny, clear these glasses away."

"In the name of all that's sacred, clear me away first!" interposed Captain Jack, this time with a real urgency; through the open lattice came the sound of the grating of the boat's keel upon the sand and a vigorous hail from a masculine throat—"Ahoy, Renny Potter, ahoy!" "Adrian, this is a matter of life and death to my hopes, hide me in your lowest dungeon for goodness' sake; I do not know my way about your ruins, and I am convinced the old lady will nose me out like a badger."

There was no time for explanation; Sir Adrian made a sign to René, who highly enjoying the situation and grinning from ear to ear, was already volunteering to "well hide Mr. the Captain," and the pair disappeared with much celerity into the inner room, while Adrian, unable to afford himself further preparation, hurried down the great stairs to meet this unexpected guest.

He emerged bareheaded into the curious mist which hung pall-like upon the outer world, and seemed to combine the opposite elements of glare and dulness, just as Tanty, aided by the stalwart arm of the boatman, who had rowed her across, succeeded in dragging her rheumatic limbs up the last bit of ascent to the door of the keep.

She halted, disengaged herself, and puffing and blowing surveyed her nephew with a stony gaze.

"My dear aunt," cried Adrian, "nothing has happened, I trust?"

"Sufficient has already happened, nephew, I should *hope*," retorted the old lady with extreme dignity. "sufficient to make me desire to confer with you most seriously. I thank you, young man," turning to William Shearman who stood on one side, his eager gaze upon "the master," ready to pull his forelock so soon as he could catch his eye, "be here again in an hour, if you please."

"But you will allow me to escort you myself," exclaimed Adrian, rising to the situation, "and I hope there need be no hurry so long as daylight lasts—Good-morning, Will, I am glad the new craft is a success—you need not wait. "Tanty, take my arm, I beg, the steps are steep and rough."

Gripping her nephew's arm with her bony old woman's hand, Miss O'Donoghue began a laborious ascent, pausing every five steps to breathe stertorously and reproachfully, and look round upon the sandstone walls with supreme disdain ; but this was nothing to the air with which, when at last installed upon a high hard chair, in the sitting-room (having sternly refused the easy one Sir Adrian humbly proffered), she deliberately proceeded to survey the scene. In truth, the neatness that usually characterised Adrian's surroundings was conspicuously absent from them, just then.

Two or three maps lay overlapping each other upon the table beside the tray with its flagon of amber ale, which had formed the captain's morning draught ; and the soiled glass, the fragments of his pipe, and its half-burnt contents lay strewn about the prostrate chair which that lively individual had upset in his agitation. Adrian's ladder, the books he had been handling and had not replaced, the white ash of the dying fire, all contributed to the unwonted aspect of somewhat melancholy disorder ; worse than all, the fumes of the strong tobacco which the sailor liked to smoke in his secluded moments hung rank, despite the open window, upon the absolute motionlessness of the atmosphere.

Tanty snorted and sniffed, while Adrian, after picking up the chair, began to almost unconsciously refold the maps, his eyes fixed wonderingly upon his visitor's face.

This latter delivered herself at length of some of the indignation that was choking her, in abrupt disjointed sentences, as if she were uncorking so many bottles.

"Well I'm sure, nephew, I am not surprised at your *extraordinary* behaviour, and if this is the style you prefer to live in—style, did I say?—sty would be more appropriate. Of course it is only what I have been led to expect, but I must say I was ill prepared to be treated by you with actual disrespect. My sister's child and I your guest, not to speak of your aunt, and you your mother's son, and her host besides ! It is a slap in the face, Adrian, a slap in the face which has been a very bitter pill to have to swallow, I assure you—I may say without exaggeration, in fact, that it has cut me to the quick."

" But surely," cried the nephew, laughing with gentle indulgence at this complicated indictment, " surely you cannot suppose I would have been willingly guilty of the smallest disrespect to you. I am a most unfortunate man, most unfortunately situated, and if I have offended, it is, you must believe, unwittingly and unavoidably. But you got my letter—I made my motives clear to you."

"Oh yes, I got your letter yesterday," responded Tanty, not at all softened, "and a more idiotic production from a man of your attainments, allow me to remark, I never read. Adrian, you are making a perfect fool of yourself, and *you cannot afford it !*"

"I fear you will never really understand my position," murmured Adrian hopelessly.

Tanty rattled her large green umbrella upon the floor with a violence that made her nephew start, then turned upon him a countenance inflamed with righteous anger.

"It is only three days ago since I gave you fully my view of the situation," she remarked, "you were good enough at the time to admit that it was a remarkably well-balanced one. I should be glad if you will explain in what manner your position could have changed in the space of just three hours after, to lead you to rush back to your island, really as if you were a mole or a wild Indian, or some other strange animal that could not bear civilised society, without even so much as a good-bye to me, or to your cousins either? What is that?—you say you wrote—oh, ay—you wrote—to Molly as well as to me ; rigmaroles, my dear nephew, mere absurd statements that have not a grain of truth in them, that do not hold water for an instant. You are not made for the world forsooth, nor the world for you ! and if that is not flying in the face of your Creator, and wanting to know better than Providence !—And then you say, ' you cast a gloom by your mere presence.' Fiddle-de-dee ! It was not much in the way of gloom that Molly brought back with her from her three days' visit to you—or if that is gloom—well, the more your presence casts of it the better—that is all I can say. Ah, but you should have seen her, poor child, after you went away in that heartless manner and you had removed yourself and your shadow, and your precious gloom—if you could have seen how unhappy she has been ! "

"Good God ! " exclaimed the man with a paling face, " what are you saying? "

"Only the truth, sir—Molly is breaking her heart because of your base desertion of her."

"Good God," muttered Adrian again, rose up stiffly in a sort of horrified astonishment and then sat down again and passed his hand over his forehead like a man striving to awaken from a painful dream.

"Oh, Adrian, don't be more of a fool than you can possibly help!" cried his relative, exasperated beyond all expression by his inarticulate distress. "You are so busy contemplating all sorts of absurdities miles away that I verily believe you cannot see an inch beyond your nose. My gracious! what is there to be so astonished at? How did you behave to the poor innocent from the very instant she crossed your threshold? Fact is, you have been a regular gay Lothario. Did you not"—cried Tanty, starting again upon her fine vein of metaphor—"did you not deliberately hold the cup of love to those young lips only to nip it in the bud? The girl is not a stock or a stone. You are a handsome man, Adrian, and the long and the short of it is, those who play with fire must reap as they have sown."

Tanty, who had been holding forth with the rapidity of a loose windmill in a hurricane, here found herself forced to pause and take breath; which she did, fanning herself with much energy, a triumphant consciousness of the unimpeachability of her logic written upon her heated countenance. But Adrian still stared at her with the same incredulous dismay; looking indeed as little like a gay Lothario as it was possible, even for him.

"Do you mean," he said at last, in slow broken sentences, as his mind wrestled with the strange tidings; "am I to understand that Molly, that bright beautiful creature, has been made unhappy through me? Oh, my dear Tanty," striving with a laugh, "the idea is too absurd, I am old enough to be her father, you know—what evidence can you have for a statement so distressing, so extraordinary."

"I am not quite in my dotage yet," quoth Tanty, drily; "neither am I in the habit of making unfounded assertions, nephew. I have heard what the girl has said with her own lips, I have read what she has written in her diary; she has sobbed and cried over your cruelty in these very arms—I don't know what further evidence——"

But Sir Adrian had started up again—" Molly crying, Molly crying for me—God help us all—Cécile's child, whom I would give my life to keep from trouble ! Tanty, if this is true—it must be true since you say so, I hardly know myself what I am saying—then I am to blame, deeply to blame—and yet—I have not said one word to the child—did nothing . . . ." here he paused and a deep flush overspread his face to the roots of his hair ; "except indeed in the first moment of her arrival—when she came in upon me as I was lost in memories of the past—like the spirit of Cécile."

" Humph," said Tanty, pointedly, " but then you see what you took for Cécile's spirit happened to be Molly in the flesh." She fixed her sharp eyes upon her nephew, who, struck into confusion by her words, seemed for the moment unable to answer. Then, as if satisfied with the impression produced, she folded her hands over the umbrella handle and observed in more placid tones than she had yet used :

" And now we must see what is to be done."

Adrian began to pace the room in greater perturbation.

" What is to be done ? " he repeated, " alas ! what can be done ? Tanty, you will believe me when I tell you that I should have cut off my right hand rather than brought this thing upon the child—but she is very young —the impression, thank heaven, cannot in the nature of things endure. She will meet some one worthy of her— with you, Tanty, kindest of hearts, I can safely trust her future. But that she should suffer now, and through me, that bright creature who flitted in upon my dark life, like some heaven-sent messenger—these are evil tidings. Tanty, you must take her away, you must distract her mind, you must tell her what a poor broken-down being I am, how little worthy of her sweet thoughts, and she will learn, soon learn, to forget me, to laugh at herself."

Although addressing the old lady, he spoke like a man reasoning with himself, and the words dropped from his lips as if drawn from a very well of bitterness. Tanty listened to him in silence, but the tension of her whole frame betrayed that she was only gathering her forces for another explosion.

When Adrian's voice ceased there was a moment's silence and then the storm burst ; whisking herself out of her chair, the umbrella came into play once more. But though it was only to thump the table, it was evident Miss O'Donoghue would more willingly have laid it about the delinquent's shoulders.

" Adrian, are you a man at all ? " she ejaculated fiercely. Then with sudden deadly composure : " So *this* is the reparation you propose to make for the mischief you have wrought ? "

" In God's name ! " cried he, goaded at length into some sort of despairing anger himself, " what would you have me do ? "

The answer came with the promptitude of a return shot :

" Do? why marry her, of course ! "

" *Marry her !* "

There was a breathless pause. Tanty, leaning forward across the table, crimson, agitated, yet triumphant ; Adrian's white face blasted with astonishment. " Marry her," he echoed at length once more, in a whisper this time. Then with a groan : " This is madness ! "

Miss O'Donoghue caught him up briskly. " Madness? My good fellow, not a bit of it ; on the contrary, sanity, happiness, prosperity.—Adrian, don't stand staring at me like a stuck pig ! Why, in the name of conscience, should not you marry? You are a young man still—pooh, pooh, what is forty !--you are a very fine-looking man, clever, romantic—hear me out, sir, please—*and you have made the child love you.* There you are again, as if you had a pain in your stomach ; you would try the patience of Job ! Why, I don't believe there is another man on earth that would not be wild with joy at the mere thought of having gained such a prize. A beautiful creature, with a heart of gold and a purse of gold to boot."

" Oh, heavens, aunt ! " interrupted the man, passionately, " leave that question out of the reckoning. The one thing, the only thing, to consider is *her* happiness. You cannot make me believe it can be for her happiness that she should marry such as me."

" And why shouldn't it be for her happiness ? " answered the dauntless old lady. " Was not she happy enough with you here in this God-forsaken hole, with nothing but the tempest besides for company ? Why should not she be happy, then, when you come back to your own good place ? Would not you be *kind* to her ?—would not you cherish her if she were your wife ?"

" Would I not be kind to her ?—would I not cherish her ?—would I not—— ? My God !"

" Why, Adrian," cried Tanty, charmed at this unexpected disclosure of feeling and the accent with which it was delivered, " I declare you are as much in love with the girl as she is with you. Why, now you shall just come back with me to Pulwick this moment, and she shall tell you herself if she can find happiness with you or not. Oh—I will hear no more—your own heart, your feelings as a gentleman, as a man of honour, all point, my dear nephew, in the same direction. And if you neglect this warning voice you will be blind indeed to the call of duty. Come now, come back to your home, where the sweetest wife ever a man had awaits you. And when I shall see the children spring up around you, Adrian, then God will have granted my last wish, and I shall die in peace . . . . . There, there, I am an old fool, but when the heart is over full, then the tears fall. Come, Adrian, come, I'll say no more ; but the sight of the poor child who loves you shall plead for her happiness and yours. And hark, a word in your ear : let Rupert bark and snarl as he will ! And what sort of a devil is it your generosity has made of *him* ? You have done a bad day's work there all these years, but, please God, there are better times dawning for us all.—What are you doing, Adrian ? Oh ! writing a few orders to your servant to explain your departure with me —quite right, quite right, I won't speak a word then to interrupt you. Dear me ! I really feel quite in spirits. Once dear Molly and you settled, there will be a happy home for Madeleine : with you, we can look out a suitable husband for her. Well, well, I must not go too fast yet, I suppose : but I have not told you in what deep anxiety I have been on *her* account by reason of a most deplorable affair—a foolish girl's fancy only, of course, with a most undesirable and objectionable creature called *Smith*. . . . Oh ! you are ready, are you ?—My dear Adrian, give me your arm then, and let us proceed."

Silence had reigned for but a few seconds in the great room of the keep when Captain Jack re-entered, bearing on his face an expression at once boyishly jubilant and

mockingly astonished. He planted himself in front of
the landward window, and gazed forth a while.

"There goes my old Adrian, as dutifully escorting that
walking sack of bones, that tar-barrel ornament—never
mind, old lady, from this moment I shall love you for
your brave deeds of this morning—escorting his worthy
aunt as dutifully as though he were a penniless nephew....
Gently over the gunnel, madam! That's done! So you
are going to take my gig? Right, Adrian. Dear me,
how she holds forth! I fancy I hear her from here.—
Give way, my lads! That's all right. Gad! Old Adrian's
carried off on a regular journey to Cythera, under a proper
escort!"

With this odd reminiscence of early mythological reading, the sailor burst into a loud laugh and walked about
slapping his leg.

"Would ever any one have guessed anything approaching this? Star-gazing, book-grubbing Sir Adrian . . . .
in love! Adrian the solitary, the pessimist, the I-don't-
know-what superior man, in love! Neither more nor less!
In love, like an every-day inhabitant of these realms, and
with that black-eyed sister of mine that is to be! My
word, it's too perfect! Adrian my brother-in-law—for if
I gauge that fine creature properly—splendid old lady—
she won't let him slide back this time. No, my dear
Adrian, you are hooked for matrimony and a return to the
living world. That black-eyed jade too, that Molly sister
of my Madeleine, will wake up and lead you a life, by
George! . . . . Row on, my lads," once more looking
at the diminishing black spot upon the grey waters.
"Row on—you have never done a better day's work!"

René, entering a few moments later, with an open note
in his hand, found his master's friend still chuckling, and
looked at him inquisitively.

"His honour has returned to Pulwick," said he, in
puzzled tones, handing the missive.

"Ay, lad," answered the sailor, cheerily. "The fact
is, my good Renny, that in that room of Sir Adrian's where
you ensconced me for safety from that most wonderful
specimen of her sex (I refer to your master's worthy
aunt), it was impossible to avoid overhearing many of
her remarks—magnificent voice for a storm at sea, eh?
Never mind what it was all about, my good man; what

I heard was good news. Ah!" directing his attention to the note; "his honour does not say when he will return, but will send back the gig immediately; and you, M. Potter, are to look after me for as long as I choose to stop here."

René required no reflection to realise that anything in the shape of good news which took his master back to his estate must be good news indeed; and his broad face promptly mirrored, in the broadest of grins, the captain's own satisfaction.

"For sure, we will try to take care of M. the captain, as well as if his honour himself was present. He told me you were to be master here."

"Make it so. I should like some dinner as soon as possible, and one of my bro—— of Sir Adrian's best bottles. It's a poor heart that never rejoices. Meanwhile, I want to inspect your ruins and your caves in detail, if you will pilot me, Renny. This is a handy sort of an old Robinson Crusoe place for hiding and storing, is it not?"

CHAPTER XIX

A JUNIOR'S OPINION

A RARELY failing characteristic of very warm-hearted and strongly impulsive people is their inability of graduating their likes and dislikes ; a state of mind which cannot fail to lead to frequent alterations of temper.

On more than one occasion, since the domineering old lady had started upon her peregrinations, had her favour for the two brothers undergone reversal ; but the ground Rupert gained by Adrian's offences was never of safe tenure. At the present hour, under the elation of her victorious sally upon the hermit's pessimistic entrenchments—the only thing in him of which she disapproved—he at once resumed the warm place she liked to keep for him in her heart. And as a consequence "Master Rupert," as she contemptuously called the "locum tenens Squire," who, in the genealogical order of things, should have been a person of small importance, fell promptly into his original state of disgrace.

During the drive from the village (where she had ordered the carriage to await her return) to the gates of Pulwick, Miss O'Donoghue entertained her companion with an indignant account of his brother's ingratitude, of his hypocritical insinuating method of disparagement of Sir Adrian himself, winding up each indictment with a shrewd, "but he could not impose upon *me*," which, indeed, she firmly believed.

Her object was, of course, to strengthen the baronet in his resolve to return to the headship of his family—little guessing what a strong incentive to seclusion these very tales of a state of things he suspected but too well would have proved, had it not been for the new unforeseen motive that the morning's revelation had brought.

"Does Molly know of your visit to me?" he asked, as the carriage halted before the gate, and the enormous, red-headed Cumbrian gatekeeper with his rosy Moggie, proudly swung it open to stand on either side, the one bowing with jubilant greeting and the other curtseying with bashful smiles at the real master. "Does she expect my visit?" relapsing into gravity after returning the salutation in kindliness.

"I have told no one of my purpose this day. Rupert walked off to the stables immediately after breakfast— going a-hunting he said he was, and offered to bear the girls to the meet. And then, feeling lonely without his company," added Tanty, with a wink, "I ordered the carriage and thought I would go and have a peep at the place where poor Molly was drowned, just for a little diversion. Whether the little rogue expects you or not, after your note of the other day, I am sure I could not take upon myself to say. She sits watching that crazy old tower of yours by day and your light by night. Well, well, I must not tell tales out of school, you may find out for yourself. But mind you, Adrian," she impressed on him, sagely, "it is not I who bring you back: you return of your own accord. The child would murder me, if she knew—with that proud heart of hers."

"My dear Tanty, trust me. This incomprehensible discovery of yours, which I cannot yet believe in, really is, so far as my discretion is concerned, as if I had never heard of it. Heavens! I have been a blundering fool, but I could not insult her with a hint of it for the world. I have come to see Rupert to-day, as usual, of course— and, as you say . . . . I shall see for myself. You have opened my eyes."

Miss O'Donoghue looked at her nephew with admiration. "*Voyez un peu*," she said, "*comme l'amour vous dégourdit* even a doleful Sir Adrian! Faith, here we are. This has been a pleasant ride, but my old bones are so tired, and you and yours have set them jogging so much of late, that I think I'll never want to stir a foot again once I get back to Bunratty . . . . except indeed to come and be godmother to the heir."

Having lent a dutiful arm up the stairs to his now beaming relative, Sir Adrian came down pensively and entered the library.

There, booted and spurred, but quietly installed at a

15

writing table, sat Mr. Landale, who rose in his nonchalant manner and with cold looks met his brother.

There was no greeting between them, but simply thus :

"I understood from Aunt Rose you were out hunting."

"Such was my intention, but when I found out that she had gone to see you—don't look so astonished, Adrian—a man must know what is going on in his household—I suspected you would escort her back ; so I desisted and waited for you. It is an unexpected pleasure to see you, for I thought we had sufficiently discussed all business, recently. But doubtless you will profit of the opportunity to go into a few matters which want your attention. Do you mean to remain?"

Speaking these words in a detached manner, Mr. Landale kept a keenly observant look upon his brother's countenance. In a most unwonted way the tone and the look irritated Sir Adrian.

"I came back, Rupert, because there were some things I wished to see for myself here," he answered frigidly. And going to the bell, rang it vigorously.

On the servant's appearance, without reference to his brother, he himself, and very shortly, gave orders :

"I shall dine here to-day. Have the tapestry-room made ready for me."

Then turning to Rupert, whose face betrayed some of the astonishment aroused by this most unusual assumption of authority, and resuming as it were the thread of his speech, he went on :

"No, Rupert, I have no desire to talk business with you. It is a pity you should have given up your day. Is it yet too late?"

"Upon my word, Adrian," said Mr. Landale, clenching his hand nervously round his fine cambric handkerchief, "there must be something of importance in the wind to have altered your bearing towards me to this extent. I have no wish to interfere. I came back and gave up good company for the reason I have stated. I will now only point out that, with your sudden whims, you render my position excessively false in a house where, at your own wish, I am ostensibly established as master."

And without waiting for another word, the younger

brother, having shot the arrow which hitherto never failed to reach the bull's-eye of the situation, left the room with much dignity.

Once more alone, Sir Adrian, standing motionless in the great room, darkened yet more in the winter light by the heavy festoons of curtains that hung over the numerous empty bookshelves, the souls of which had migrated to the peel to keep the master company, cogitated upon this first unpleasant step in his new departure, and wondered within himself why he had felt so extraordinarily moved by anger to-day at the cold inquisitiveness of his brother. No doubt the sense of being watched thus, held away at arm's-length as it were, was cause sufficient. And yet that was not it ; ingratitude alone, even to enmity, in return for benefits forgot could not rouse this bitterness. But had it not been for Tanty's interference he would be now exiled from his home until the departure of Cécile's child, just as, but for chance, he would have been kept in actual ignorance of her arrival. It was his brother's doing that he had blindly withdrawn himself when his presence would have caused happiness to her. Yes, that was it. Rupert had a scheme. That was what dwelt in his eyes,—a scheme which would bring, indeed did bring, unhappiness to that dear guest. . . . No wonder, now, that the unconscious realisation of it awoke all the man's blood in him.

"No, Rupert," Sir Adrian found himself saying aloud, "I let you reign at Pulwick so long as you crossed not one jot of such pleasure and happiness that might belong to Cécile's child. But here our wills clash ; and now, since there cannot be two masters in a house as you say, *I* am the master here."

As Sir Adrian's mind was seething in this unusual mood, Miss O'Donoghue, entering her nieces' room, found Molly perched, in riding dress, on the window-sill, looking forth upon the outer world with dissatisfied countenance.

Mr. Landale had sent word at the last moment that, to his intense regret, he could not escort the ladies to the meet, some important business having retained him at Pulwick.

So much did Miss Molly pettishly explain in answer

to the affectionate inquiry concerning the cloud on her brow, slashing her whip the while and pouting, and generally out of harmony with the special radiance of the old lady's eye and the more than usual expansiveness of the embrace which was bestowed upon her.

"Tut, tut, tut, now," observed the artful person in tones of deep commiseration. "Ah well, Rupert's a poor creature which ever side he turns up. Will you go now, my child, and fetch me the letters I left on the drawing-room table? Isn't it like me to spend half the morning writing them and leave them down there after all!"

Molly rose unwillingly, threw her whip on the bed, her hat on the floor; and mistily concerned over Tanty's air of irrepressible and pleasurable excitement, walked out of the room, bestowing as she passed her long pier glass a moody glance at her own glowering beauty.

"What's the use of *you* ?" she muttered to herself, "Anybody can fetch and carry for old aunts and look out of windows on leafless trees!"

The way to the drawing-room was through the library. As Molly, immersed in her reflections, passed along this room, she stopped with a violent start on perceiving the figure of Sir Adrian, a tall silhouette against the cold light of the window. As she came upon him, her face was fully illumined, and there was a glorious tale-telling in the widening of her eyes and the warm flush that mounted to her cheek that on the instant scattered in the man's mind all wondering doubts. A rush of tenderness filled him at one sweep, head and heart, to the core.

"Molly!" he cried, panting; and then with halting voice as she advanced a pace and stood with mouth parted and brilliant expectant eyes : "You took away all light and warmth with you when you left my lonely dwelling. I tried to take up my life there, but——"

"But you have come back—for me?" And drawn by his extended hands she advanced, her burning gaze fixed upon his.

"I dared not think of seeing you again," he murmured, clasping her hands; "yet my return .... pleases you?"

"Yes."

Thus was crowned this strange wooing, was clenched a life's union, based upon either side on fascinating un-realities.

She was drawn into his arms ; and against his heart she lay, shaking with little shivers of delight, looking into the noble face bent so lovingly over hers, her mind floating between unconscious exultation and languorous joy.

For a long while without a word he held her thus on his strong arm, gazing with a rending conflict of rapture and anguish on the beautiful image of his life's love, until his eyes were dimmed with rising tears. Then he slowly stooped over the upturned face, and as she dropped her lids with a faint smile, kissed her lips.

There came a warning rattle at the door handle, and Molly, disengaging herself softly from her betrothed's embrace, but still retaining his arm, turned to witness the entrance of Miss O'Donoghue and Mr. Landale.

On the former's face, under a feigned expression of surprise, now expanded itself in effulgence the plenitude of that satisfaction which had been dawning there ever since her return from the island.

Rupert held himself well in hand. He halted, it is true, for an instant at the first sight of Sir Adrian and Molly, and put his handkerchief furtively to his forehead to wipe the sudden cold sweat which broke out upon it. But the hesitation was so momentary as to pass unperceived ; and if his countenance, as he advanced again, bore an expression of disapproval, it was at once dignified and restrained.

"So you are there, Molly," exclaimed the old lady with inimitable airiness. "Just imagine, my dear, I had those letters in my pocket all the while, after all. You did not find them, did you?"

But Adrian, still retaining the little hand on his arm, came forward slowly and broke through the incipient flow.

"Aunt Rose," said he in a voice still veiled by emotion, "I know your kind heart will rejoice with me, although you may not be so surprised, as no doubt Rupert will be, at the news we have for you, Molly and I."

"You are right, Adrian," interrupted Rupert gravely, "to any who know your life and *your past* as I do, the news you seem to have for us must seem strange indeed. So strange that you will excuse me if I withhold congratulations. For, if I mistake not," he added, with a delicately shaded change of tone to sympathetic courtesy, and slightly turning his handsome face towards Molly,

" I assume that my fair cousin de Savenaye has even but now promised to be my sister, Lady Landale."

Sir Adrian who, softened by the emotion of this wonderful hour, had made a movement to grasp his brother's hand, but had checked himself with a passionate movement of anger, instantly restrained, as the overt impertinence of the first words fell on his ears, here looked with a shadowing anxiety at the girl's face.

But Molly, who could never withhold the lash of her tongue when Rupert gave the slightest opening, immediately acknowledged her enemy's courtly bow with sauciness.

"What! No congratulations from the model brother? Not even a word of thanks to Molly de Savenaye for bringing the truant to his home at last? But you malign yourself, my dear Rupert. I believe 'tis but excess of joy that ties your tongue."

With gleaming smile Mr. Landale would have opposed this direct thrust by some parry of polished insult; but he met his elder's commanding glance, remembered his parting words on two previous occasions, and wisely abstained, contenting himself with another slight bow and a contemptuous shrug of the shoulders.

At the same time Miss O'Donoghue, with an odd mixture of farcically pretended astonishment and genuine triumph, fell on the girl's neck.

"It is possible, soul of my heart, my sweet child—I can't believe it—though I vow I knew it all along! So I am to see my two favourites made one by holy matrimony!" punctuating her exclamation with kisses on the fair young face, and wildly seeking in space with her dried-up old fingers to meet Adrian's hand. "I, the one barren stock of the O'Donoghues, shall see my sister's children re-united. Ah, Adrian, what a beautiful coat this will make for you to hand to your children! O'Donoghue, Landale, Kermelégan, Savenaye—eighteen quarters with this heiress alone, Adrian child, for the descendants of Landale of Pulwick!" And Miss O'Donoghue, overcome by this culminating vision of happiness and perfection, fairly burst into tears.

In the midst of this scene, Mr. Landale, after listening mockingly for a few instants, retired with ostentatious discretion.

Later in the day, as Madeleine bent her pretty ears,
dutifully yet with wandering attention, to Molly's gay
prognostications concerning Pulwick under her sway ;
whilst the servants in the hall, pantry and kitchen discussed the great news which, by some incomprehensible
agency, spread with torrent-like swiftness through the
whole estate ; while Miss O'Donoghue was feverishly
busy with the correspondence which was to disseminate
far and wide the world's knowledge of the happy betrothal, Sir Adrian met his brother walking meditatively
along the winding path of the garden, flicking with the
loop of his crop the border of evergreens as he went.
From their room, Molly and Madeleine, ensconced in the
deep window-seat, could see the meeting.

"How I should like to hear," said Molly.   "I know
this supple wretch will be full of Adrian's folly in marrying me—first, because, from the Rupertian point of view,
it is a disastrous thing that his elder should marry at all ;
and secondly, because Molly, mistress at Pulwick Priory,
means a very queer position indeed for Mr. Rupert
Landale.   How I wish my spirit could fly into Adrian's
head just for a moment !   Adrian is too indulgent.   It
requires a Molly to deal with such impertinence."

"Indeed you are unjust with our cousin," said Madeleine, gently.   "Why this hatred ?   I cannot understand."

"No, of course not, Madeleine.   Rupert is charming
—with you.   I am not blind.   But take care he does not
find out *your* secret, miss.   Oh, I don't ask you any more
about it.   But if he ever does—*gare, ma chère.*"

But at the present juncture, Molly's estimate of Sir
Adrian's mood was mistaken.   His love of peace, which
amounted to a well-known weakness where he alone was
concerned, weighed not a feather in the balance when
such an interest as that now engaged was at stake.

As a matter of fact, Rupert Landale was to be taken
by surprise again, that day, and again not pleasantly.
On noticing his brother's approach, he stopped his angry
flickings, and slowly moved to meet him.   At first they
walked side by side in silence.   Presently Sir Adrian
began :

"Rupert," he said gravely, "after our first interview
to-day, it was my intention to have begged your pardon
for a certain roughness in my manner which I should

have controlled and which you resented. I would have done so, had you allowed me, at that moment when I announced my forthcoming marriage and my heart was full of good-will to all, especially to you. Now, on the contrary, to re-establish at least that outward harmony without which life in common would be impossible, I expect from you some expression of regret for your behaviour."

The first part of his brother's say was so well in accordance with his more habitual mood, that Mr. Landale had already sketched his equally habitual deprecating smile ; but the conclusion changed the entire standpoint of their relations.

"An expression of regret—from *me?*" cried he, exaggerating his astonishment almost to mockery.

"From any one but my brother." said Adrian, with a slight but perceptible hardening in his tone, "I should say an apology for an impertinence."

Mr. Landale, now genuinely taken aback, turned a little pale and halted abruptly.

"Adrian, Adrian !" he retorted, quickly. "This is one of your mad moments. I do not understand."

"No, brother, I am not mad, and never have been, dearly as you would wish me to be so in reality—since Death would have none of me. But though you know this yourself but too well, you have never understood me really. Now listen—once for all. Try and see our positions as they are: perhaps then matters will go more pleasantly in the future for you as well as for me."

Mr. Landale looked keenly at the speaker's face for a second, and then without a word resumed his walk, while Sir Adrian by his side pursued with quiet emphasis :

"When I returned, from the other world so to speak, at least from your point of view (one which I fully understood), I found that this very return was nothing short of a calamity for all that remained of my kin. I had it in my power to reduce that misfortune to a great extent. You loved the position—that worldly estimation, that fortune, all those circumstances which, with perfect moral right, you had hitherto enjoyed. They presented little attraction to me. Moreover, there were many reasons, which I am quite aware you know, that made this very house of mine a dismal dwelling for me. You see I have no wish to give too generous a colour to my motives, too self-denying a character to the benefits I conferred upon you. But, as far as you are concerned, they were benefits. For them I received no gratitude; but as I did not expect gratitude it matters little. I might, however, have expected at least that you should be neutral, not directly hostile to me—— Pray let me finish" (in anticipation of a rising interruption from his companion), "I shall soon have done, and you will see that I am not merely recriminating. Hostile you have been, and are now. So long as the position you assumed towards me only bore on our own relations, I acquiesced: you had so much more to lose than I could gain by resenting your hidden antagonism. I held you, so to speak, in the hollow of my hand; I could afford to pass over it all. Moreover, I had chosen my own path, which was nothing if not peaceful. I say, you always were hostile to me; you have been so, more than ever since the arrival of Cécile de Savenaye's children. You were, however, grievously mistaken if you thought— I verily believe you did—that I did not realise the true motives that prompted you to keep me away from them. —I loved them as their mother's children; I love Molly with a sort of love I myself do not understand, but deep enough for all its strangeness. Yet I submitted to your reasoning, to your plausible representations of the disastrous effects of my presence. I went back to my solitude because it never entered my mind that it could be in my power to help their happiness; you indeed had actually persuaded me of the contrary, as you know, and I myself thought it better to break the unfortunate spell that was cast on me. Unfortunate I thought it, but it has proved far otherwise."

They had reached the end of the alley, and as they turned back, facing each other for a moment, Sir Adrian noticed the evil smile playing upon his brother's lips.

"It has proved otherwise," he repeated. "How I came to change my views, I daresay you have guessed, for you have, of late, kept a good watch on your mad brother, Rupert. At any rate you know what has come to pass. Now I desire you to understand this clearly— interference with me as matters stand means interference with Molly: and as such I must, and shall, resent it."

"Well, Adrian, and what have I done *now* ?" was Mr. Landale's quiet reply. He turned a gravely attentive, innocently injured countenance to the paling light.

"When I said you did not understand me," returned Sir Adrian with undiminished firmness ; "when I said you owed me some expression of regret, it was to warn you never again to assume the tone of insinuation and sarcasm to me, which you permitted yourself to-day in the presence of Molly. You could not restrain this long habit of censuring, of unwarrantable and impertinent criticism, of your elder, and when you referred to my past, Molly could not but be offended by the mockery of your tones. Moreover, you took upon yourself, if I have heard aright, to disapprove openly of our marriage. Upon what ground that would bear announcing I know not, but let this be enough : try and realise that our respective positions are totally changed by this unforeseen event, and that, as Molly is now to be mistress at Pulwick, I must of course revoke my tacit abdication. Nevertheless, if you think you can put up with the new state of things, there need be little alteration in your present mode of life, my dear Rupert ; if you will only make a generous effort to alter your line of conduct."

And here, Sir Adrian, succumbing for a moment to the fault, so common to kindly minds, of discounting the virtue of occasional firmness by a sudden return to geniality, offered his hand in token of peace.

Mr. Landale took it ; his grasp, however, was limp and cold.

"I am quite ready to express regret," he said in a toneless voice, "since that would seem to be gratification to you, and moreover seems to be the tacit condition on which you will refrain from turning me out.   I ought indeed to have abstained from referring, however vaguely, to past events, for the plain reason that anything I could say would already have come too late to prevent the grievous deed you have now pledged yourself to commit."

"Rupert—!" exclaimed Sir Adrian stepping back a pace, too amazed, at the instant, for indignation.

"Now, in your turn, hear me, Adrian," continued Mr. Landale with his blackest look.   "I have listened to your summing up of our respective cases with perfect patience, notwithstanding a certain assumption of superiority which

—allow me to insist on this—is somewhat ridiculous from
you to me.   You complain of my misunderstanding you.
Briefly, this is absurd.   As a matter of fact I understand
you better than you do yourself.   On the other hand it
is you that do not understand me.   I have no wish to
paraphrase your little homily of two minutes ago, but
the heads of my refutation are inevitably suggested by
the points of your indictment.   To use your own manner
of speech, my dear Adrian, I have no wish to assume injured disinterestedness, when speaking of my doings with
regard to you and your belongings and especially to this
old place of yours, of our family.   You have only to look
and see for yourself. . . ."

Mr. Landale made a wide comprehensive gesture which
seemed to embrace the whole of the noble estate, the ad-
mirably kept mansion with walls now flushed in the light
of the sinking sun, the orderly maintenance of the vast
grounds, the prosperousness of its dependencies—all in
fact that the brothers could see with the eyes of the body
from where they stood, and all that they could see with
the eyes of the mind alone :   "Go and verify whether I
fulfilled my duty with respect to the trust which was yours,
but which you have allowed to devolve upon my shoulders,
and ask yourself whether you would have fulfilled it better—if as well.   I claim no more than this recognition ;
for, as you pointed out, the position carried its advantages, if it entailed arduous responsibility too.   It was my
hope that heirs of my body would live to perpetuate this
pride—this work of mine.   It was not to be.   Now that
you step in again and that possibly your flesh will reap
the benefits I have laboured to produce, ask yourself,
Adrian, whether you, who shirked your own natural
duties, would have buckled to the task, under *my* circumstances—distrusted by your brother, disliked and secretly
despised by all your dependants, who reserved all their
love and admiration for the "real master" (oh, I know
the cant phrase), although he chose to abandon his position and yield himself to the stream of his own inertness,
the real master who in the end can find no better description for these years of faithful service than ' hostility ' and
' ingratitude.' "

Sir Adrian halted a pace, a little moved by the specious-
ness of the pleading.   The incidental reference to that

one grief of his brother's life was of a kind which could never fail to arouse generous sympathy in his heart. But Mr. Landale had not come to the critical point of his say, and he did not choose to allow the chapter of emotion to begin just yet.

"But," he continued, pursuing his restless walk, "again to use your own phraseology, I am not merely recriminating. I, too, wish you to understand me. It would be useless to discuss now, what you elect to call my hostility in past days. I had to keep up the position demanded by our ancient name : to keep it up amid a society, against whose every tenet almost—every prejudice, you may call them—you chose to run counter. My antagonism to your mode of acting and thinking was precisely measured by your own against the world in which the Landales, as a family, hold a stake. Let that, therefore, be dismissed ; and let us come at once to the special hostility you complain of in me, since the troublesome arrival of Aunt Rose and her wards. As the very thing which I was most anxious to prevent, if possible, has, after all, come to pass, the present argument may seem useless ; but you have courted it yourself."

"Most anxious to prevent—if possible . . . . !" repeated Sir Adrian, slowly. "This, from a younger brother, is almost cynical, Rupert !"

"Cynical !" retorted Mr. Landale, with a furious laugh. "Why, you have given sound to the very word I would, in anybody else's case, have applied to a behaviour such as yours. Is it possible, Adrian," said Rupert, turning to look his brother in the eyes with a look of profound malice, "that it has not occurred to you yet, that *cynical* will be the verdict the world will pass on the question of your marriage with that young girl ?"

Sir Adrian flushed darkly, and remained silent for a pace or two ; then, with a puzzled look :

"I fail to understand you," he said simply. "I am no longer young, of course ; yet, in years, I am not preposterously old. As for the other points—name and fortune——"

But Rupert interrupted him with a sharp exclamation, which betrayed the utmost nervous exasperation.

"Pshaw ! If I did not know you so well, I would say you were playing at candour. This—this unconventionality of yours would have led you into curious pitfalls, Adrian, had you been obliged to live in the world. My 'hostility' has saved you from some already, I know— more is the pity it could not save you from this—for it passes all bounds that you should meditate such an un- natural act, upon my soul, in the most natural manner in the world. One must be an Adrian Landale, and live on a tower for the best part of one's life, to reach such a pitch of—unconventionality, let us call it."

"For God's sake," exclaimed Sir Adrian, suddenly los- ing patience, "what are you driving at, man? In what way can my marriage with a young lady, who, incon- ceivable as it may be, has found something to love in me ; in what way, I say, can it be accounted cynical? I am not subtle enough to perceive it."

"To any one but you," sneered the other, coming to his climax with a sort of cruel deliberation, "it would hardly require special subtleness to perceive that for the man of mature age to marry the *daughter*, after having, in the days of his youth, been the lover of the *mother*, is a proceeding, the very idea of which is somewhat revolt- ing in the average individual. . . . There are many roués in St. James' who would shrink before it ; yet you, the enlightened philosopher, the moralist——"

But Sir Adrian, breathing quickly, laid his hand heavily on his brother's shoulder.

"When you say the mother's lover, Rupert," he said, in a contained voice, which was as ominous of storm as the first mutters of thunder, "you mean that I loved her— you do not mean to insinuate that that noble woman, widowed but a few weeks, whose whole soul was filled with but one lofty idea, that of duty, was the mistress— the mistress of a boy, barely out of his teens?"

Rupert shrugged his shoulders.

"I insinuate nothing, my dear Adrian ; I think nothing. All this is ancient history which after all has long con- cerned only you. You know best what occurred in the old days, and of course a man of honour is bound to deny all tales affecting a lady's virtue ! Even you, I fancy, would condescend so far. But nevertheless, reflect how this marriage will rake up the old story. It will be re- membered how you, for the sake of remaining by Cécile de Savenaye's side, abandoned your home to fight in a cause that did not concern you ; nay, more, turned your back for the time upon those advanced social theories which even at your present season of life you have not all shaken off. You travelled with her from one end of England to the other, in the closest intimacy, and finally departed over seas, her acknowledged escort. She on her side, under pretext of securing the best help on her political mission that England can afford her, selected a young man notoriously in love with her, at the very age when the passions are hottest, and wisdom the least consideration—as her influential agent, of course. Men are men, Adrian—especially young men—small blame to you, young that you were, if then . . . . but you cannot expect, in sober earnest, the world to believe that you went on such a wild pilgrimage for nothing ! Women are women—especially young women, of the French court —who have never had the reputation of admiring bashfulness in stalwart young lovers. . . . ."

Sir Adrian's hand, pressing upon his brother's shoulder, as if weighted by all his anger, here forced the speaker into silence.

"Shame ! Shame, Rupert !" he cried first, his eyes aflame with a generous passion ; then fiercely : "Silence, fellow, or I will take you by that brazen throat of yours and strangle the venomous lie once for all." And then, with keen reproach, " That you, of my blood, of hers too, should be the one to cast such a stigma on her memory —that you should be unable even to understand the nature of our intercourse . . . . Oh, shame, on you for your baseness, for your vulgar, low suspiciousness ! . . . . But, no, I waste my breath upon you, you do not believe this thing. You have outwitted yourself this time. Hear me now : If anything could have suggested to me this alliance with the child of one I loved so madly and so hopelessly, the thought that such dastardly slander could ever have been current would have done so. The world, having nothing to gain by the belief, will never credit that Sir Adrian Landale would marry the daughter of his paramour—however his own brother may deem to his advantage to seem to think so ! The fact of Molly de Savenaye becoming Lady Landale would alone, had such ill rumours indeed been current in the past, dispel the ungenerous legend for ever."

There were a few moments of silence while Sir Adrian battled, in the tumult of his indignation, for self-control again ; while Rupert, realising that he had outwitted himself indeed, bestowed inward curses upon most of his relations and his own fate.

The elder brother resumed at length, with a faint smile :

"And so, you see, even if you had spoken out in time, it would have been of little avail." Then he added, bitterly. "I have received a wound from an unforeseen quarter. You have dealt it, to no purpose, Rupert, as you see . . . . though it may be some compensation to such a nature as yours to know that you have left in it a subtle venom."

The sun had already sunk away, and its glow behind the waters had faded to the merest tinge. In the cold shadow of rising night the two men advanced silently homewards. Sir Adrian's soul, guided by the invidious words, had flown back to that dead year, the central point of his existence—It was true : men will be men— in that very house, yonder, he had betrayed his love to her ; on board the ship that took them away and by the camp fire on the eve of fight, he had pleaded the cause of his passion, not ignobly indeed, with no thought of the baseness which Rupert assigned to him, yet with a selfish disregard of her position, of his own grave trust. And it was with a glow of pride, in the ever living object of his life's devotion—of gratitude almost—that he recalled the noble simplicity with which the woman, whom he had just heard classed among the every-day sinners of society, had, without one grandiloquent word, without even losing her womanly softness, kept her lover as well as herself in the path of her lofty ideal—till the end. And yet she did love him : at the last awful moment, sinking into the very jaws of death, the secret of her heart had escaped her. And now—now her beauty, and something of her own life and soul was left to him in her child, as the one fit object on which to devote that tenderness which time could not change.

After a while, from the darkness by his side came the voice of his brother again, in altered, hardly recognisable accents.

"Adrian, those last words of yours were severe—unjust. I do not deserve such interpretation of my motives. Is it my fault that you are not as other men? Am I to be blamed for judging you by the ordinary standard? But you have convinced me : you were as chivalrous as Cécile was pure, and if needs be, believe me, Adrian, I will maintain it so in the face of the world. Yes, I misunderstood you—and wounded you, as you say, but such was not my intention. Forgive me."

They had come to the door. Sir Adrian paused. There was a rapid revulsion in his kindly mind at the extraordinary sound of humble words from his brother; and with a new emotion, he replied, taking the hand that with well-acted diffidence seemed to seek his grasp :

"Perhaps we have both something to forgive each other. I fear you did not misjudge me so much as you misjudged her who left me that precious legacy. But believe that, believe it as you have just now said, Rupert, the mother of those children never stooped to human frailty—her course in her short and noble life was as bright and pure as the light of day."

Without another word the two brothers shook hands and re-entered their home.

Sir Adrian sought Miss O'Donoghue whom he now found in converse with Molly, and with a grave eagerness, that put the culminating touch to the old lady's triumph, urged the early celebration of his nuptials.

Mr. Landale repaired to his own study where in solitude he could give loose rein to his fury of disappointment, and consider as carefully as he might in the circumstances how best to work the new situation to his own advantage.

Even on that day that had been filled with so many varied and poignant emotions for him; through the dream in which his whole being seemed to float, Sir Adrian found a moment to think of the humble followers whom he had left so abruptly on the island, and of the pleasure the auspicious news would bring to them.

It was late at night, and just before parting with the guest who was so soon to be mistress under his roof, he paused on the stairs before a window that commanded a view of the bay. Molly drew closer and leant against his shoulder ; and thus both gazed forth silently for some time at the clear distant light, the luminous eye calmly watching over the treacherous sands.

That light of Scarthey—it was the image of the solitary placid life to which he had bidden adieu for ever ; which even now, at this brief interval of half a day, seemed as far distant as the years of despair and vicissitude and disgust to which it had succeeded. A man can feel the suddenly revealed charm of things that have ceased to be, without regretting them.

With the dear young head that he loved, with a love already as old as her very years, pressing his cheek ; with that slender hand in his grasp, the same, for his love was all miracle, that he had held in the hot-pulsed days of old—he yet felt his mind wander back to his nest of dreams. He thought with gratitude of René, the single-minded, faithful familiar ; of old Margery, the nurse who had tended Cécile's children, as well as her young master ; thought of their joy when they should hear of the marvellous knitting together into the web of his fate, of all those far-off ties.

In full harmony with such fleeting thoughts, came Molly's words at length breaking the silence.

"Will you take me back to that strange old place of yours, Adrian, when we are married?"

Sir Adrian kissed her forehead.

"And would you not fear the rough wild place, child," he murmured.

"Not for ever, I mean," laughed the girl, "for then my mission would not be fulfilled—which was to make of Adrian, Sir Adrian, indeed. But now and again, to recall those lovely days, when—when you were so distracted for the love of Murthering Moll and the fear lest she should see it. You will not dismantle those queer rooms that received so hospitably the limping, draggled-tailed guest—they must again shelter her when she comes as proud Lady Landale ! How delicious it would be if the tempest would only rage again, and the sea-mew shriek, and the caverns roar and thunder, and I knew you were as happy as I am sure to be !"

"All shall be kept up even as you left it," answered Sir Adrian moved by tender emotion ; "to be made glorious again by the light of your youth and fairness. And

16

Renny shall be cook again, and maid of all work. My poor Renny, what joy when he hears of his master's happiness, and all through the child of his beloved mistress! But he will have to spend a sobering time of solitude out there, till I can find a substitute for his duties."

"You are very much attached to that funny little retainer, Adrian!" said Molly after a pause.

"To no man alive do I owe so much. With no one have I had, through life, so much in common," came the grave reply.

"Then," returned the girl, "you would thank me for telling you of the means of making the good man's exile less heavy, until you take him back with you."

"No doubt." There was a tone of surprise and inquiry in his voice.

"Why, it is simple enough. Have you never heard of his admiration for Moggie Mearson, our maid? Let them marry. They will make a good pair, though funny. What, you never knew it? Of course not, or you would not have had the heart to keep the patient lovers apart so long. Let them marry, my Lord of Pulwick: it will complete the romance of the persecuted Savenayes of Brittany and their helpful friends of the distant North."

Musing, Sir Adrian fell into silence. The faithful, foolish heart that never even told its secret desire, for very fear of being helped to win it; by whom happiness and love were held to be too dearly bought at the price of separation from the lonely exile!

"*Eh bien*, dreamer?" cried the girl gaily.

"Thank you, Molly," said Sir Adrian, turning to her with shining eyes. "This is a pretty thought, a good thought. Renny will indeed doubly bless the day when Providence sent you to Pulwick."

And so, the following morn, Mr. Renny Potter was summoned to hear the tidings, and informed of the benevolent prospects more privately concerning his own life; was bidden to thank the future Lady Landale for her service; was gently rebuked for his long reticence, and finally dismissed in company of the glowing Moggie with a promise that his nuptials should be celebrated at the same time as those of the lord of the land. The good fellow, however, required first of all an assurance that these very fine plans would not entail any interference

with his duties to his master before he would allow himself to be pleased at his fortunes. Great and complex,
then, was his joy ; but it would have been hard to say,
as Moggie confessed to her inquiring mistress that night,
when he had returned to his post, whether the pride and
delight in his master's own betrothal was not uppermost in his bubbling spirits.

CHAPTER XX

> Neighbour, what doth thy husband when he cometh
>   home from work ?
> He thinks of her he loved before he knew me
>
> *Luteplayer's Song.*

February 18*th.*   Upon the 18th of January, 1815. did I commit that most irreparable of all follies ; then by my own hand I killed fair Molly de Savenaye, who was so happy, so free, so much in love with life, and whom I loved so dearly, and in her stead called into existence Molly Landale, a poor-spirited miserable creature who has not given me one moment's amusement.   How could I have been so stupid ?

Let me examine.

It is only a month ago, only a month, 4 weeks, 31 days, millions of horrible dreary minutes, Oh, Molly, Molly, Molly ! since you stood, that snowy day, in the great drawing-room (*my* drawing-room now, I hate it), and vowed twice over, once before the Jesuit father from Stonyhurst, once before jolly, hunting heretical parson Cochrane to cleave to Adrian Landale till death bid you part !   Brr—what ghastly words and with what a light heart I said them, tripped them out, *ma foi*, as gaily as "good-morning" or "good-night !"   They were to be the *open sesame* to joys untold, to lands flowing with milk and honey. to romance, adventure, splendour—and what have they brought me ?

It is a cold day, sleeting, snowing, blowing, all that is abominable.   My lord and master has ridden off, despite it, to some distant farm where there has been a fire.   The "Good Sir Adrian," as they call him now—he is *that* ; but, oh dear me—there !   I must yawn, and I'll say no more on this head, at present, for I want to think and

work my wretched problem out in earnest, and not go to
sleep.

It is the first time I have taken heart to write since
yonder day of doom, and God knows when I shall have
heart again! Upon such an afternoon there is nothing
better to do, since Sir Adrian would have none of my
company—he is so precious of me that he fears I should
melt like sugar in the wet—he never guessed that it was
just because of the storm I wished the ride! Were we to
live a hundred years together—which, God forfend—he
would never understand me.

Ah, lack-a-day, oh, misery me! (My lady, you are
wandering; come back to business.)

What, then, has marriage brought me? First of all a
husband. That is to say, another person, a man who
has the right to me—to whom I myself have given that
right—to have me, to hold me, as it runs in the terrible
service, the thunders of which were twice rolled out upon
my head, and which have been ringing there ever since.
And I, Molly, gave of my own free will, that best and
most blessed of all gifts, my own free will, away. I am
surrounded, as it were, by barriers; hemmed in, bound
up, kept in leading strings. I mind me of the seagull on
the island. 'Tis all in the most loving care in the world,
of course, but oh! the oppression of it! I must hide my
feelings as well as I can, for in my heart I would not
grieve that good man, that *excellent* man, that pattern of
kind gentleman—oh, oh, oh—it will out—that *dreary* man,
that dull man, that most melancholy of all men! Who
sighs more than he smiles, and, I warrant, of the two, his
sighs are the more cheerful; who looks at his beautiful
wife as if he saw a ghost, and kisses her as if he kissed a
corpse!

There is a mate for Molly! the mate she chose for herself!

So much for the husband. What else has marriage
brought her?

Briefly I will capitulate.

A title—I am *my lady*. For three days it sounded
prettily in my ears. But to the girl who refused a duchess'
coronet, who was born comtesse—to be the baronet's lady
—Tanty may say what she likes of the age of creation,
and all the rest of it—that advantage cannot weigh heavy

in the balance. Again then, I have a splendid house—which is my prison, and in which, like all prisoners, I have not the right to choose my company—else would Sophia and Rupert still be here? They are going, I am told occasionally; but my intimate conviction is, however often they may be going, *they will never go. Item four:* I have money, and nothing to spend it on—but the poor.

What next? What next?—alas, I look and I find nothing! This is all that marriage has brought me; and what has it not taken from me?

My delight in existence, my independence, my hopes, my belief in the future, my belief in *love.* Faith, hope, and charity, in fact, destroyed at one fell sweep. And all, to gratify my curiosity as to a romantic mystery, my vanity as to my own powers of fascination! Well, I have solved the mystery, and behold it was nothing. I have eaten of the fruit of knowledge, and it is tasteless in my mouth.

I have made my capture with my little bow and spear, and I am as embarrassed of my captive as he of me. We pull at the chain that binds us together; nay, such being the law of this world between men and women, the positions are reversed, my captive is now my master, and Molly is the slave.

Tanty, I could curse thee for thy officiousness, from the tip of thy coal black wig to the sole of thy platter shoe—but that I am too good to curse thee at all!

Poor book of my life that I was so eager to fill in, that was to have held a narrative all thrilling, and all varied, now will I set forth in thee, my failure, my hopelessness, and after that close thee for ever.

Of what use indeed to chronicle, when there is nought to tell but flatness, chill monotony, on every side; when even the workings of my soul cannot interest me to follow, since they can now foreshadow nothing, lead to nothing but fruitless struggle or tame resignation!

I discovered my mistake—not the whole of it, but enough to give me a dreadful foreboding of its hideousness, not two hours after the nuptial ceremony.

Adrian had borne himself up to that with the romantic, mysterious dignity of presence that first caught my silly fancy; behind which I had pictured such fascinating depths of passion—of fire—Alas! When he looked at me it was with that air of wondering, almost timid, affection battling with I know not what flame of rapture, with which look I have become so fatally familiar since—without the flame of rapture, be it understood, which seems to have rapidly burnt away to a very ash of grey despondency and self-reproach.   I could have sworn even as he gave me his arm to meet and receive the congratulations of our guests, that the glow upon his cheek, the poise of his head denoted the pride any man, were he not an idiot nor a brute, must feel in presenting his bride—such a bride !—to the world.   Then we went in to the great dining hall where the wedding feast, a very splendid one, was spread. All the gentlemen looked with admiration at me ; many with envy at Adrian.   I knew that I was beautiful in my fine white satin with my veil thrown back, without the flattering whispers that reached me now and again ; but these were sweet to hear nevertheless.   I knew myself the centre of all eyes, and it elated me.   So too did the tingling flavour of the one glass of sparkling wine I drank to my fortunes.   Immediately upon this silent toast of Lady Landale to herself, Rupert rose and in choice words and silver-ringing voice proposed the health of the bride and bridegroom.   There was a merry bustling pause while the glasses were filled ; then rising to their feet as with one man, all the gentlemen stood with brimming goblets one instant extended, the next emptied to the last drop ; and then the cheers rang out, swelling up the rafters, three times three, seeming to carry my soul along with them.   I felt my heart expand and throb with an emotion I never knew in it before, which seemed to promise vast future capacities of pain and delight.   I turned to my husband instinctively ; looking for, expecting, I could not explain why, an answering fire in his eyes.   This was the last moment of my illusions.   From thence they began to shrivel away with a terrifying rapidity.

Adrian sat with a face that looked old and lined and grey ; with haggard unseeing eyes gazing forth into space as though fixing some invisible and spectre show. He seemed as if wrapt in a world of his own, to which none of us had entrance ; least of all, I, his wife.

The shouts around us died away, there were cries upon him for " Speech—speech," then playful queries—" How

is this, Sir Adrian ? So bashful, egad !" next nudges were
exchanged, looks of wonder, and an old voice speaking
broadly :

"*Yes, by George,*" it was saying, "*I remember it well,
by George, in this very room, now twenty years ago, 'Here,
gentlemen,' says old Sir Tummas, "Here's to Madam de
Savenaye,' and gad, ma'am, we all yelled,—she was a lovely
creature—Eh—Eh?*"

"Hush," said some one, and there was a running
circle of frowns and the old voice ceased as abruptly as
if its owner had been seized by the weasand. In the
heavy embarrassed silence, I caught Tanty's red perturbed look and Rupert's smile.

But Adrian sat on—like a ghost among the living, or a
live man among the dead. And this was my gallant bridegroom ! I seized him by the hand—"Are you ill, Adrian ?"

He started and looked round at me—Oh that look ! It
seemed to burn into my soul, I shall never forget the
hopelessness, the dull sadness of it, and then—I don't
know what he read in my answering glance—the mute
agonised question, followed by a terror.

"They want you to speak," I whispered, and shook
the cold hand I held in a fury of impatience.

His lips trembled : he stared at me blankly. "My
God, my God, what have I done?" he muttered to himself, "Cécile's child—Cécile's child !"

I could have burst out sobbing. But seeing Rupert's
face bent down towards his plate, demure and solemn,
yet stamped, for all his cleverness, with an almost devilish
triumph, my pride rose and my courage. Every one else
seemed to be looking towards us : I stood up.

"Good friends," I said, "I see that my husband is so
much touched by the welcome that you are giving his bride,
the welcome that you are giving him after his long exile
from his house, that he is quite unable to answer you as
he would wish. But lest you should misunderstand this
silence of his, I am bold enough to answer you in his name,
and—since it is but a few moments ago that you have seen
us made one, I think I have the right to do so. . . . . We
thank you."

My heart was beating to suffocation—but I carried
bravely on till I was drowned in a storm of acclamations
to which the first cheers were as nothing.

They drank my health again, and again I heard the old gentleman of the indiscreet voice—I have learned since he is stone deaf, and I daresay he flattered himself he spoke in a whisper—proclaim that I was *my mother all over again : begad—so had she spoken to them twenty years ago in this very room !*

Here Tanty came to the rescue and carried me off.

I dared not trust myself to look at Adrian as I left, but I knew that he followed me to the door, from which I presumed that he had recovered his presence of mind in some degree.

Since that day we have been like two who walk along on opposite banks of a widening stream—ever more and more divided.

I have told no one of my despair.   It is curious, but, little wifely as I feel towards him, there is something in me that keeps me back from the disloyalty of discussing my husband with other people.

And it is not even as it might have been—this is what maddens me.   *We are always at cross purposes.*   Some wilful spirit wakes in me, at the very sound of his voice (always gentle and restrained, and echoing of past sadness) ; under his mild, tender look ; at the every fresh sign of his perpetual watchful anxiety—I give him wayward answers, frowning greetings, sighs, pouts ; I feel at times a savage desire to wound, to anger him, and as far as I dare venture I have ventured, yet could not rouse in him one spark, even of proper indignation.

The word of the riddle lay in that broken exclamation of his at our wedding feast.

"Cécile's child ! "

His wife, then, is only Cécile's child to him.   I have failed when I thought to have conquered—and with the consciousness of failure have lost my power, even to the desire of regaining it.   My dead mother is my rival ; her shade rises between me and my husband's love.   Could he have loved me, I might perhaps have loved him—and now—now I, *Molly*, I, shall perhaps go down to my grave without having known *love*.

I thought I had found it on that day when he took me in his arms in that odious library—my heart melted when he so tenderly kissed my lips.   And now the very remembrance of that moment angers me.   Tenderness !   Am I

only a weak, helpless child that I can arouse no more
from the man to whom I have given myself! I thought
the gates of life had been opened to me—behold, they led
me to a warm comfortable prison! And this is Molly's
end!

There is a light in Madeleine's eyes, a ring in her voice,
a smile upon her lip. She has bloomed into a beauty
that I could hardly have imagined, and this is because of
this unknown whom she *loves*. She breathes the fulness
of the flower; and by-and-by, no doubt, she will taste
the fulness of the fruit; she will be complete; she will be
fed and I am to starve. What is coming to me? I do
not know myself. I feel that I could grudge her these
favours, that I *do* grudge them to her. I am sick at heart.

And she—even she has proved false to me. I know
that she meets this man. Adrian too knows it, and more
of him than he will tell me; and he approves. I am
treated like a child. The situation is strange upon every
side; Madeleine loving a plebeian—a sailor, not a king's
officer—stooping to stolen interviews! Adrian the punc-
tilious, in whose charge Tanty solemnly left her, pretending ignorance, virtually condoning my sister's behaviour!
For though he has distinctly refused to enlighten me or
help me to enlighten myself, he could not, upon my tax-
ing him with it, deny that he was in possession of facts
ignored by me.

Then there is Rupert paying now open court to this sly
damsel—for the sake of her beautiful eyes, or for the
beautiful eyes of her casket? And last and strangest, the
incongruous friendship struck up this week between her
and that most irritating of melancholy fools, Sophia. The
latter bursts with suppressed importance, she launches
glances of understanding at my sister; sighs, smiles (when
Rupert's eye is not on her), starts mysteriously. One
would say that Madeleine had made a confidant of her—
only that it would be too silly. What? Make a confidant
of that funereal mute and deny *me* the truth! If I had the
spirit for it I would set myself to discovering this grand
mystery; and then let them beware! They would have
none of Molly as a friend: perhaps she will yet prove one
too many upon the other side.

If I have grown bitter to Madeleine, it is her own fault;
I would have been as true as steel to her if she had but

trusted me.   Now and again, when a hard word and look
escape me, she gives me a great surprised, reproachful
glance, as of a petted child that has been hurt ; but mostly
she scarcely seems to notice the change in me—Moonlike
in dreamy serenity she sails along, wrapt in her own
thoughts, and troubles no more over Molly's breaking her
heart than over Rupert's determined suit.   To me when
she remembers me, she gives the old caresses, the old
loving words ; to him smiles and pretty courtesy.   Oh,
she keeps her secret well !   But I came upon her in the
woods alone, last Friday, fresh, no doubt, from her lover's
arms ; tremulous, smiling, yet tearful, with face dyed rose.
And when to my last effort to attain the right of sister-
hood she would only stammer the tell-tale words : *she
had promised !* and press her hot cheeks against mine, I
thrust her from me, indignant, and from my affections for
ever.   Yet I hold her in my power, I could write to
Tanty, put Rupert on the track. . . . . Nay, I have not
fallen so low as to become Rupert's accomplice yet !

And so the days go on.   Between my husband's increasing melancholy, my own mad regrets, Rupert's
watchfulness, Madeleine's absorption and Sophia's
twaddle, my brain reels.   I feel sometimes as if I could
scream aloud, as we all sit round the table, and I know
that *this* is the life that I am doomed to, and that the days
may go on, go on thus, till I am old.   Poor Murthering
Moll the second !   Why even the convent, where at least
I knew nothing, would have been better !   No, it is not
possible !   Something is still to come to me.   Like a bird,
my heart rises within me.   I have the right to my life,
the right to my happiness, say what they may.

CHAPTER XXI

THE DAWN OF AN EVENTFUL DAY

RUPERT's behaviour at home, since his brother's wedding, had been, as even Molly was bound to admit to herself, beyond reproach in tactfulness, quiet dignity, and seeming cheerfulness.

He abdicated from his position of trust at once and without the smallest reservation ; wooed Madeleine with so great a discretion that her dreamy eyes saw in him only a kind relative ; and he treated his sister-in-law, for all her freaks of bearing to him, with a perfect gentleness and gentility.

At times Sir Adrian would watch him with great eyes. What meant this change? the guileless philosopher would ask himself, and wonder if he had judged his brother too harshly all through life ; or if it was his plain speaking in their last quarrel which had put things in their true light to him, and awakened some innate generosity of feeling ; or yet if—this with misgiving—it was love for pretty Madeleine that was working the marvel. If so, how would this proud rebellious nature bear another failure?

Rupert spoke with unaffected regret about leaving Pulwick, at the same time, in spite of Molly's curling lip, giving it to be understood that his removal was only a matter of time.

For the ostensible purpose, indeed, of finding himself another home he made, in the beginning of March, the second month after his brother's marriage, several absences which lasted a couple of days or more, and from which he would return with an eager sparkle in his eye, almost a brightness on his olive cheek, to sit beside Madeleine's embroidery frame, pulling her silks and snipping with her scissors, and talking gaily, persistently, with such humour and colour as at last to draw that young lady's attention from far off musings to his words with smiles and laughter.

Meanwhile, Molly would sit unoccupied, brooding, watching them, now fiercely, from under her black brows, now scornfully, now abstractedly ; the while she nibbled at her delicate finger-nails, or ruthlessly dragged them along the velvet arms of her chair with the gesture of a charming, yet distracted, cat.

Sir Adrian would first tramp the rooms with unwitting restlessness, halting, it might be, beside his wife to strive to engage her into speech with him ; and, failing, would betake himself at length with a heavy sigh to solitude ; or, yet, he would sit down to his organ—the new one in the great hall which had been put up since his marriage, at Molly's own gay suggestion, during their brief betrothal —and music would peal out upon them till Lady Landale's stormy heart could bear it no longer, and she would rise in her turn, fly to the shelter of her room and roll her head in the pillows to stifle the sound of sobs, crying from the depths of her soul against heaven's injustice ; anon railing in a frenzy of impotent anger against the musician, who had such passion in him and gave it to his music alone.

During Rupert's absences that curious intimacy which Molly had contemptuously noted between her sister and sister-in-law displayed itself in more conspicuous manner.

Miss Landale's long sallow visage sported its airs of mystery and importance, its languishing leers undisguisedly, so long as her brother Rupert's place was empty ; and though her visits to the rector's grave were now almost quotidian, she departed upon them with looks of wrapt importance, and, returning, sought Madeleine's chamber (when that maiden did not herself stroll out to meet her in the woods), her countenance invariably wreathed with suppressed, yet triumphant smiles, instead of the old self-assertive dejection.

The 15th of March of that year was to be a memorable day in the lives of so many of those who then either dwelt in Pulwick, or had dealings on that wide estate.

Miss Landale, who had passed the midnight hour in poring over the delightful wickedness of Lara, and, upon at length retiring to her pillow, had had a sentimental objection to shutting out the romantic light of the moon

by curtain or shutter, was roused into wakefulness soon
after dawn by a glorious white burst of early sunshine.
As a rule, the excellent soul liked to lie abed till the last
available moment; but that morning she was up with the
sun. When dressed she drew a letter from a secret casket
with manifold precautions as though she were surrounded
with prying eyes, and, placing it in her reticule, hastened
forth to seek the little lonely disused churchyard by the
shore. She afterwards remarked that she could never
forget in what agitation of spirits and with what strange
presentiment of evil she was led to this activity at so
unwonted an hour. The truth was, however, that Miss
Landale tripped along through the damp wooded path as
gaily as if she were going to visit her living lover instead
of his granite tomb; and that in lieu of evil omens
a hundred fantastically sentimental thoughts floated
through her brain, as merrily and irresponsibly as the
motes in the long shafts of brilliancy that cleaved, sword-
like through the mists, upon her from out the east.
Visions of Madeleine's face when she would learn before
breakfast that Sophia had actually been to the churchyard
already; visions of whom she might meet there; re-
hearsals of a romantic scene upon that hallowed spot, of
her own blushes, her knowing looks, her playful remonstrances, with touching allusions to one who had loved
and lost, herself, and who thus, &c. &c.

Miss Landale tossed her long faded ringlets quite
coquettishly, turned one slim bony hand with coy gesture
before her approving eyes. Then she patted her reticule
and hurried on with fresh zest, enjoying the tart whisper
of the wind against her well bonneted face, the exquisite
virginal beauty of the earth in the early spring of the day
and of the year.

As she stepped out of the shadow of the trees, her heart
leaped and then almost stood still as she perceived in the
churchyard lying below her, beside the great slab of
granite which lay over the remains of her long-departed
beloved one, the figure of a man, whose back was turned
towards her, and whose erect outline was darkly
silhouetted against the low, dazzling light.

Then a simper of exceeding archness crept upon Miss
Landale's lips; and with as genteel an amble as the somewhat precipitate nature of the small piece of ground that

yet divided her from the graveyard would allow, she proceeded on her way.

At the click of the lych-gate under her hand the man turned sharply round and looked at her without moving further. An open letter fluttered in his hand.

His face was still against the light, and Miss Landale's eyes had wept so many tears by day and night that her sight was none of the best. She dropped a very elegant curtsey, simpered, drew nearer, and threw a fetching glance upwards. Then her shrill scream rang through the still morning air and frightened the birds in the ruined church.

"You are early this morning, Sophia," said Mr. Landale.

Sophia sank upon the tombstone. To say that she was green or yellow would ill describe the ghastliness of the tint that suffused her naturally bilious countenance; still speechless, she made a frantic plunge towards the great urn that adorned the head of the grave. Mr. Landale looked up from his reading again with a quiet smile.

"I shall have done in one minute," he remarked, "It is a fine production, egad! full of noble protestations and really high-sounding words. And then, my dear Sophia, you can take charge of it, and I shall be quite ready for the other, which I presume you have as usual with you—ah, in your bag! Thanks."

"Rupert?" ejaculated the unfortunate lady, first in agonised query, and next in agonised reproach, clasping her hands over the precious reticule—"Rupert!"

Mr. Landale neatly folded the sheet he had been reading, moistened with his tongue a fresh wafer which he drew from his waistcoat pocket, and, deftly placing it upon the exact spot from which the original one had been removed, handed the letter to his sister with a little bow. But, as with a gesture of horror the latter refused to take it, he shrugged his shoulders and tossed it carelessly into the urn.

"Now give me Madeleine's," he said, peremptorily.

Rolling upwards eyes of appeal the unhappy Iris called upon heaven to witness that she would die a thousand deaths rather than betray her solemn trust. But even as she spoke the fictitious flame of courage withered away in her shrinking frame; and at the mere touch of her brother's finger and thumb upon her wrist, the mere sight of his face bending masterfully over her with white teeth just gleaming between his twisting smile and half-veiled eyes of insolent determination, she allowed him, unresisting, to take the bag from her side ; protesting against the breach of faith only by her moans and the inept wringing of her hands.

Mr. Landale opened the bag, tossed with cynical contempt upon the flat tombstone, sundry precious relics of the mouldering bones within, and discovered at length in an inner pocket a dainty flower-scented note. Then he flung down the bag and proceeded with the same deliberation to open the letter and peruse its delicate flowing handwriting.

"Upon my word," he vowed, "I think this is the prettiest she has written yet! What a sweet soul it is! Listen, Sophia : 'You praise me for my trust in you—but, Jack, dear love, my trust is so much a part of my love that the one would not exist without the other. Therefore, do not give me any credit, for you know I could not help loving you.' Poor heart! poor confiding child ! Oh!" ejaculated Mr. Landale as if to himself, carefully proceeding the while with his former manœuvres to end by placing the violated missive, to all appearance intact, beside its fellow, "we have here a rank fellow, a foul traitor to deal with !"

Then, wheeling round to his sister, and fixing her with piercing eyes : "Sophia," he exclaimed, in tones of sternest rebuke, "I am surprised at you. I am, indeed ! "

Miss Landale raised mesmerised, horror-stricken eyes upon him ; his dark utterances had already filled her foolish soul with blind dread. He sat down beside her, and once more enclosed the thin arm in his light but warning grasp.

"Sophia," he said solemnly, "you little guess the magnitude of the harm you have been doing ; the frightful fate you have been preparing for an innocent and trusting girl ; the depth of the villainy you are aiding and abetting. You have been acting, as I say, in ignorance, without realising the awful consequences of your folly and duplicity. But that you should have chosen *this* sacred place for such illicit and reprehensible behaviour ; that by the grave of this worthy man who loved you, by the stones chosen and paid for by my fraternal affection, you should plot and scheme to deceive your family, and help to lead, a confiding and beautiful creature to ruin, I should never have expected from *you*, Sophia—Sophia ! "

Miss Landale collapsed into copious weeping.

" I am sure, brother," she sobbed, " I never meant any harm. I am sure nobody loves the dear girl better than I do. I am sure I never wished to hide anything from you ! —Only—they told me—they trusted me—they made me promise—Oh brother, what terrible things you have been saying ! I cannot believe that so handsome a young gentleman can mean anything wrong—I only wish you could have seen him with her, he is so devoted—it is quite beautiful."

" Alas—the tempter always makes himself beautiful in the eyes of the tempted ! Sophia, we can yet save this unhappy child, but who knows how soon it may be too late !—You can still repair some of the wrong you have done, but you can only do so by the most absolute obedience to me . . . . Believe me, I know the truth about this vile adventurer, this Captain Jack Smith."

" Good Heavens ! " cried Sophia, " Rupert, do not tell me, lest I swoon away, that he is married already ? "

" The man, my dear, whose plots to compromise and entangle a lovely girl you have favoured, is a villain of the deepest dye—a pirate."

" Oh ! " shivered Sophia with fascinated misery—thrilling recollections of last night's reading shooting through her frame.

" A smuggler, a criminal, an outlaw in point of fact," pursued Mr. Landale. " He merely seeks Madeleine for her money—has a wife in every port, no doubt—"

Miss Landale did not swoon ; but her brother's watchful eye was satisfied with the effect produced, and he went on in a well modulated tone of suppressed emotion :

" And after breaking her heart, ruining her body and soul, dragging her to the foulest depths he would have cast her away like a dead weed—perhaps murdered her ! Sophia, what would your feelings be then ? "

A hard red spot had risen to each of Miss Landale's cheek bones ; her tears had dried up under the fevered glow.

" We believed," she said trembling in every limb, " that he was working on a mission to the French court—"

17

"Faugh—" cried Mr. Landale, contemptuously, "smuggling French brandy for our English drunkards and traitorous intelligence for our French enemies!"

"Such a handsome young man, so gentlemanly, such an air!" maundered the miserable woman between her chattering teeth. "It was quite accidental that we met, Rupert, quite accidental, I assure you. Madeleine—poor dear girl—came down with me here, I wanted to show her the g-grave——" here Sophia gurgled convulsively, remembering her brother's cruel reproaches.

"Well?"

"She came here with me, and as I was kneeling down, planting crocuses just here, Rupert, and she was standing *there*, a young man suddenly leaped over the wall, and fell at her feet. He had not seen *me*—Alas, it reminded me of my own happiness! And he was so well-dressed, so courteous—and seemed such a perfect gentleman—and he took off his hat so gracefully I am sure I never could have believed it of him. And they confided in me and I promised by—by—those sacred ashes to keep their secret. I remembered of course what Tanty had said in her letter, and quite understood he was the young gentleman in question—but they explained to me how she was under a wrong impression altogether. He said that the instant he laid eyes upon me, he saw I had a feeling heart, and he knew they could trust me. He spoke so nobly, Rupert, and said: What better place could they have for their meetings than one consecrated to such faithful love as this? It was so beautiful—and oh dear! I can't but think there is some mistake." And Miss Landale again wrung her hands.

"But I have proof!" thundered her brother," convincing proof, of what I have told you. At this very moment the man who would marry Madeleine, forsooth, runs the risk of imprisonment—nay, of the gallows! You may have thought it strange that I should have opened and read letters not addressed to me, but with misfortune hanging over a beloved object I did not pause to consider myself. My only thought was to save her."

Here Mr. Landale looked very magnanimous, and thrust his fingers as he spoke through the upper buttons of his waistcoat with the gesture which traditionally accompanies such sentiments: these cheap effects proved

generally irresistible with Sophia. But his personality
had paled before the tremendous drama into which the
poor romance-loving soul was so suddenly plunged, and
in which in spite of all her woe she found an awful kind
of fascination. Failing to read any depth of admiration
in her roving eye, Rupert promptly abandoned grandilo-
quence, and resuming his usual voice and manner, he
dropped his orders upon her heat of agitation like a cool
relentless stream under which her last protest fizzed,
sputtered, and went out.

"I mean to unmask the gay lover at my own time and
in my own way ; never fear, I shall deal gently with *her*.
You will now take this letter of his and put it in your bag,
leaving hers in that curious post-office of yours."

"Yes, Rupert."

"And you will give his letter to her at once when you
go in without one word of having met me."

"Y . . . . yes, Rupert."

"As you are too great a fool to be trusted if you once
begin to talk, you will have a headache for the rest of the
day and go to bed in a dark room."

"Y . . . . yes, Rupert."

"You will moreover swear to me, now, that you will
not speak of our interview here till I give you leave ; say
I swear I will not."

"I swear I will not."

"So help me God !"

"Oh, Rupert."

"*So help me God*, you fool !"

Sophia's lips murmured an inaudible something ; but
there was such complete submission in every line and
curve of her figure, in the very droop of her ringlets and
the helpless appeal of her gaze that Rupert was satisfied.
He assisted her to arise from her tombstone, bundled the
clerical love-tokens back into the bag, duly placed Captain Jack's letter in the inner pocket, and was about to
present her with his arm to conduct her homewards, when
he caught sight of a little ragged urchin peeping through
the bars of the gate, and seemingly in the very act of
making a mysterious signal in the direction of Miss Landale's unconscious figure.

Rupert stared hard at the ruddy, impudent face, which
instantly assumed an appearance of the most defiant un-

concern, while its owner began to devote his energies to shying stones at an invisible rook upon the old church tower with great nicety of aim.

"Sophia," said her brother in a low tone, "go to the gate : that boy wants to speak to you. Go and see what he wants and return to me."

Miss Landale gasped, gazed at her brother as if she thought him mad, looked round at the little boy, coloured violently, then meeting Rupert's eye again staggered off without a word of protest.

Rupert, shaken with silent laughter, humming a little song to himself, stooped to pick a couple of tender spring flowers from the border beside the grave, and after slipping them into a button-hole of his many caped overcoat, stood looking out over the stretch of land and sea, where Scarthey rose like a dream against the sparkle of the water and the exquisite blue of the sky.

Presently rapid panting breaths and a shuffling rustle of petticoats behind him informed him of his sister's return.

"So you are there, my dear," he said loudly. "One of your little fishing friends from the village, I suppose—a Shearman, unless I am mistaken. Yes, a Shearman ; I thought so. Well, shall we return home now? They will be wondering what has become of us. Pray take my arm." Then beneath his breath, seeing that words were struggling to Sophia's lips, "Hold your tongue."

The small ragged boy watched their departure with a derisive grin, and set off at a brisk canter down to the shore, jingling some silver coin in his pocket with relish as he went.

When Rupert and Sophia had reached the wood the former paused.

"Letter or message ? "

"Oh, Rupert, it was a letter ; had I not better destroy it ? "

"Give it to me."

A hasty scrawl, it seemed, folded anyhow. Only two or three lines, yet Rupert conned them for a curiously long time.

"My darling," it ran, "meet me to-day in the ruins at noon. A misfortune has happened to me, but if you trust me, all will still be well.—Your Jack."

Mr. Landale at length handed it back to Sophia.

"You will give it to Madeleine with the other," he said briefly. "Mention the fact of the messenger having brought it." And then in a terrible bass he added, "And remember your oath!"

She trembled; but as he walked onwards through the wood, his lips were smiling, and his eyes were alight with triumph.

CHAPTER XXII

THE DAY: MORNING

THE appointment of a regular light-keeper at Scarthey, intended to release René and old Margery from their exile, had been delayed so as to suit the arrangement which was to leave for a time the island domain of Sir Adrian at the disposal of Captain Jack. Meanwhile Moggie's presence greatly mitigated the severity of her husband's separation from his master.

On his side the sailor was in radiant spirits. All worked as he could wish, and Sir Adrian's marriage, besides being a source of unselfish satisfaction, was, with regard to his own prospects, an unexpected help; for, his expedition concluded, he would now be able in the most natural manner to make his appearance at Pulwick, an honoured guest of the master, under the pride of his own name. And for the rest, hope unfolded warm-coloured visions indeed.

During the weeks which had elapsed since Sir Adrian's departure, Captain Jack's visits to the island had been fitful and more or less secret—He always came and left at night. But as it was understood that the place was his to be used and enjoyed as he thought best, neither his sudden appearances with the usual heavy travelling-bag, nor his long absences excited any disturbance in the arcadian life led by René between his buxom young wife and the old mother—as the good-humoured husband now termed the scolding dame.

A little sleeping closet had been prepared and allotted to the use of the peripatetic guest in one of the disused rooms when René's own accommodation under the light tower had been enlarged for the new requirements of his matrimonial status. And so Monsieur the Captain (in René's inveterate outlandish phraseology) found his liberty of action complete. Both the women's curiosity was allayed, and all tendency to prying into the young stranger's mysterious purposes amid their seclusion condemned beforehand, by René's statement : that Monsieur the Captain was a trusted friend of the master—one indeed (and here the informant thought fit to stretch a point, if but slightly) to whom the Lord of Pulwick was indebted, in bygone days, for life and freedom.

Except when weather-bound, a state of things which at that time of year occurred not unfrequently, René journeyed daily as far as the Hall, ostensibly to report progress and take possible orders, but really to gratify himself with the knowledge that all was well with the master.

About the breakfast hour, upon this 15th of March, as Sir Adrian was discussing with the bailiff sundry matters of importance to the estate, a tap came to the door, which he recognised at once as the Frenchman's own long accustomed mode of self-announcement.

Since he had assumed the reins of government, the whilom recluse had discovered that the management of such a wide property was indeed no sinecure ; and moreover—as his brother, who certainly understood such matters in a thoroughly practical manner, had warned him— that a person of his own philosophical, over-benevolent and abstracted turn of mind, was singularly ill-fitted for the task. But a strong sense of duty and a determination to act by it will carry a man a long way. He had little time for dreaming and this was perhaps a providential dispensation, for Sir Adrian's musings had now lost much of the grave placidity born of his long, peaceful residence in his Thelema of Scarthey. The task was long and arduous ; on sundry occasions he was forced to consult his predecessor on the arcana of landed estate government, which he did with much simplicity, thereby giving Mr. Landale, not only inwardly mocking satisfaction, but several opportunities for the display of his self-effacing loyalty and superior capacities.

The business of this day was of sufficiently grave moment to make interruption unwelcome—being nothing less than requests from a number of tenants to the " Good Sir Adrian," " the real master come to his own again "— for a substantial reduction of rent ; a step towards which the master's heart inclined, but which his sober reason condemned as preposterous. But Réne's countenance, as he entered, betrayed news of such import that Sir Adrian instantly adjourned the matter on hand, and, when the bailiff had retired, anxiously turned to the new-comer, who stood in the doorway mopping his steaming brow.

"Well, Renny," said he, "what is wrong? Nothing about your wife—?"

"No, your honour," answered the man, "your honour is very good. Nothing wrong with our Moggie. But the captain. . . . . I ran all the way from the Shearmans."

"No accident there, I hope."

"I fear there is, your honour. The captain—he has been attacked this morning."

"Not wounded—!" exclaimed Sir Adrian. "Not dead, Renny?"

"Oh no, your honour, well. But he has, I fear, killed one of the men . . . . the revenue men—"

Then, seeing his master start aghast, he went on rapidly;

"At least he is very bad—but what for did he come to make the spy upon our island? We have left him at the Shearmans—the mother Shearman will nurse him. But the captain, your honour"—the speaker lowered his voice to a whisper and advanced a step, looking round—"that is the worst of all, the captain has turned mad, I believe —Instead of going off with his ship and his crew, (they are safe out to sea, as they should be) he remains at Scarthey. Yes—in your honour's rooms. He is walking up and down and clutching his hair and talking to himself, like a possessed. And when I respectfully begged him to consider that it was of the last folly his having rested instead of saving himself, I might as well have tried to reason a mule. And so, knowing that your honour would never forgive me if misfortune arrived, I never drew breath till I reached here to tell you. If his honour would come himself he might be able to make Mr. his friend hear reason—Your honour will run no risk, for it is only natural that you should go to the peel after what has occurred—but if you cannot get Mr. the captain to depart this night, there will arrive to us misfortune—it is I who tell you so."

"I will go back with you, at once," said Sir Adrian, rising much perturbed. "Wait here while I speak to Lady Landale."

Molly was standing by the great log fire in the hall, yawning fit to dislocate her pretty jaws, and teasing the inert form of old Jim, as he basked before the flame, with the tip of her pretty foot. She allowed her eyes to rest vaguely upon her husband as he approached, but neither interrupted her idle occupation nor endeavoured to suppress the yawn that again distended her rosy lips.

He looked at her for a moment in silence; then laying a hand upon her shoulder, said gently: "My child, I am called back to Scarthey and must leave instantly. You—you will be careful of yourself—amuse yourself during my absence—it may be for two or three days."

Lady Landale raised her black brows with a fine air of interrogation, and then gazed down at the old dog till the lashes swept her cheek, while a mocking dimple just peeped from the corner of her mouth and was gone again. "Oh yes," she answered drily, "I shall take endless care of myself and amuse myself wildly. You need have no fear of that."

Sir Adrian sighed, and his hand fell listless from her shoulder.

"Good-bye, then," he said, and stooped it seemed hesitatingly to lay his lips between the little dark tendrils of hair that danced upon her forehead. But with a sudden movement she twitched her face away. "Despite all the varied delights which bind me to Pulwick," she remarked carelessly, "the charms of Sophia and Rupert's company, and all the other *amusements*—I have a fancy to visit your old owl's nest again—so we need not waste sentiment upon a tender parting, need we?"

Sir Adrian's cheek flushed, and with a sudden light in his eyes he glanced at her quickly; but his countenance faded into instant melancholy again, at sight of her curling lip and cold amused gaze.

"Will you not have me?" she asked.

"If you will come—you will be welcome—as welcome," his voice shook a little, "as my wife must always be wherever I am."

"Ah—oh," yawned Lady Landale, "(excuse me pray —it's becoming quite an infirmity) so that is settled. I hope it will storm to-night, that the wind will blow and howl—and then I snuggle in the feather bed in that queer

old room and try and fancy I am happy Molly de Savenaye again."

Adrian's lip quivered ; yet in a second or two he spoke
lightly. "I do not want to hurry you, but I have to
leave at once." Then struck by a sudden thought, by
that longing to bring pleasure to others which was always
working in him, "Why not let Madeleine come with you
too?" he asked, "she could share your room, and—it
would be a pleasure to her I think." He sighed as he
thought of the trouble in store for the lovers.

Lady Landale grew red to the roots of her hair and
shot a look of withering scorn at her husband's unconscious face. "It would be charming," she said, sarcastically, "but after all I don't know that I care to go
so much—oh, don't stare at me like that, for goodness'
sake ! A woman may change her mind, I suppose—at
least, in a trifle here and there if she can't as regards the
whole comfort of her life.—Well, well, perhaps I shall go
—this afternoon—later—you can start now. I shall
follow—I can always get a boat at the Shearmans. And
I shall bring Madeleine, of course—it is most kind and
thoughtful of you to suggest it. *Mon Dieu*, I have a husband in a thousand !"

She swept him a splendid curtsey, kissed her hand at
him, and then burst out laughing at the pale bewilderment of his face.

When Sir Adrian returned to the morning-room, he
found René, half hidden behind the curtain folds, peering
curiously out of the window which overlooked the
avenue. On his master's entrance, the man turned his
head, placed his finger on his lip, and beckoned him to
approach. "If I may take the liberty," said he with
subdued voice, "will his honour come and look out,
without showing himself ?"

And he pointed to a group, consisting of Mr. Landale
and two men in blue jackets and cockaded hats of semi-
naval appearance, now slowly approaching the house.
Mr. Landale was listening with bent head, slightly
averted, to the smaller of his two companions—a stout
square-looking fellow, who spoke with evident volubility,
whilst the other followed defferentially one pace in
rear. Presently the trio halted, a few yards from the

entrance, and Mr. Landale, cutting designs upon the sand with the end of his stick in a meditative way, appeared to be giving directions at some length, on the conclusion of which the two men, touching their hats with much respect, departed together, while the magistrate pensively proceeded on his way to the house.

"Those, your honour," said René, "were with him that was struck in the fight this morning. It was I rowed them over, together with the wounded. I left them at the Shearmans, and slipped away myself to carry the news. If I might take upon myself to advise, it would be better if your honour would come with me now, at once, for fear Mr. Landale should delay us by questioning me—Mr. Landale being a magistrate, as I heard these men say ; and Moggie has assured me that he always arranges himself for knowing when I arrive from the island —ever since the day when the demoiselles had just come, and I found it out. Ever since then he has not liked me, Mr. Landale. Come away, your honour, before he finds out I have been here to-day."

Following upon this advice, which he found to the point, Sir Adrian left his house by a back passage ; and, through a side garden, found his way to the coast and to the fishing village.

The wounded man who had not recovered consciousness, lay in the brother Shearman's hut, as René had said, surrounded by such uncouth attendance as the rude fisherfolk could dispense. After giving directions for the summoning of medical aid and the removal, if it should prove advisable, of the patient to the Hall, but without a single comment upon the unfortunate occurrence, Sir Adrian then took the road of the peel.

During the transit, walking rapidly by his master's side, across the now bare causeway, René gave his account of events.

The captain (he related) after three days' absence had reappeared the night before the last, and requested him to warn the womankind not to be alarmed if they heard, as no doubt they would, strange noises on the beach at night. He was, said he, storing provisions and water for the forthcoming journey, and the water in the well was so excellent that he had determined to take in his store. Of course his honour understood well that René

did not concern himself in these matters; but that was
the explanation he conveyed to his wife, lest she should
be alarmed and wonder. As for the old mother, she was
too deaf to be awakened out of sleep by anything short
of the trumpet of the last judgment.

As announced, there had been during the night the
noise of a party of men landing, of the hoisting and rolling of barrels — a great *remuc-ménage* altogether — and the
next morning, that was yesterday, the captain had slept
sound in his bunk till late.

During several hours of the following day, he had some
secret work to do in the caves of which René had shown
the ins and outs, and whilst so engaged had requested
that watch should be kept from the light-tower, and message sent by some arranged signal should any one approach the island. But no one had come near. Whilst at
his post, the watcher had heard at different times the sound
of hammering; and when the captain had come to relieve
him, the good gentleman was much begrimed with dust
and hot with work, but appeared in excellent humour.
In the castle, he sang and whistled for joyfulness, and
made jokes with Moggie, all in his kind way, saying that
if he were not to be married himself soon, he would feel
quite indignant and jealous at the happiness of such a
rascal as her husband.

Oh! he was happy — Monsieur the Captain — he had
brought Moggie a beautiful shawl; and to René, he had
given a splendid watch, telling him to keep count of the
hours of his unmerited bliss. Alas, this morning all had
been different indeed! The captain looked another man;
his face was as white as linen. The very look of him
would have told any one that a misfortune had occurred.
René did not quite understand it himself, but this is what
had taken place :

The captain had left Scarthey on foot late in the evening, and when he returned (he was not long away) he
bade René again not to mind what he heard during the
night; and, in faith, once more there had been a real
noise of the devil; men coming to and fro, a deal of rowing on the water, away and back again, in the early night
and then once more before dawn.

"But I was not unquiet," said René, "I knew they had
come for the remainder of what Mr. Smith was pleased

to call his provisions. From our room I could see by the
light on the stairs that the lamp was burning well, and
Moggie slept like a child, so sound, she never moved. Just
before the rising sun, I had got up and put out the lamp,
and was going to bed again, when there came thumps of the
devil at the lower door. Well knowing that the captain
had his own way of entering—for he had spent many days
in finding out all sorts of droll passages in the ruins—I
was quite seized ; and as I hurried down, the thumps came
again and great cries for the lighthouse-keeper. And, your
honour, when I unbarred the door, there was a man in
uniform whom I did not know, and he asked me, grumbling, if I knew of the pretty doings on the beach, whilst
I slept like pig, he said—Of course I made the astonished
as his honour may imagine : I knew nothing, had heard
nothing, though my heart was beating like to burst not
knowing what was coming. Then he ordered me to lend a
hand and bring a ladder to carry away one of his men who
had been murdered by the smugglers, he said. And there,
on the sands, in front of the small cave was another man,
in a blue coat too, watching over the body of one who was
stretched out, quite tranquil, his face covered with blood
and his eyes closed. They are gone, says the gross man.
And I was glad, as your honour may well think, to see the
chaloupe full of the captain's men rowing hard towards
the vessel. She had just come out of the river mouth
and was doubling round the banks. We carried the man
on his ladder to the kitchen and we and the women did
all we could, but he remained like a log. So after a time
the two men (who said they had come along the dyke
soon after midnight, on foot, as they thought it would be
more secret, and had watched all night in the bent)
wanted to eat and drink and rest. They had missed their
game, the big man said ; they had been sent to find out
what sort of devil's tricks were being played on in the
island unbeknown to Sir Adrian ;—but it was the devil's
luck altogether, for the smugglers had slipped away and
would not be seen in this part of the world again. That
is the way the fat man spoke. The other had nothing to
say, but swallowed our bacon and our beer as if he did
not care. And then, your honour, they told me I should
have to lend them the yawl to go on land, and go myself
to help, and take the body with us. And as he was

speaking, I saw Moggie the wife, who had been backwards and forwards serving them, looking at me very
straight but without blowing a word, as if she had fear.
And all at once I felt there was something on foot. So I
drew the men more beer and said I would see after the
yawl. Outside the door the wife whispered : 'Upstairs,
quick ! Renny,' and she herself whisked back into the
kitchen so that she should not cause suspicion to those
others—Ah, your honour, that is a woman !"

"Well, well," interrupted his master, anxiously.

"Well, I went upstairs, four by four ; and there, in
your honour's room, without an attempt to conceal himself (when any moment it might have entered into those
brigands' heads downstairs to search the place), there
was Monsieur the Captain, raging up and down, like a
wolf in cage, as I had the honour to describe before. No
wonder Moggie was afraid for him. A woman is quick
to feel danger ahead. He looked at me as if he did not
know me, his face all unmade. 'You know what has
happened ;' he says. 'Am I not the most unfortunate
. . . . ? All is lost.' 'With respect,' says I ; 'nothing
is lost so long as life is safe, but it is not a good thing
Monsieur the Captain that you are here, like this, when
you should be on your good ship as many miles away as
she can make. Are you mad ?' to him I say, and he to
me, 'I think I am.' 'At least let me hide you,' I beg of
him, 'I know of many beautiful places,' and so for the
matter of that does he. But it was all lost trouble. At
length he sits down at the table and begins to write, and
his look brightens : 'You *can* help me, my good friend,'
he says ; 'I have a hope left—who knows—who knows,'
—and he writes a few lines like an enraged and folds
them and kisses the billet. 'Find means,' says he, 'René,
to get Johnny, the Shearman boy, to take this to the old
churchyard and place it in the place he knows of ; or,
better still, should he chance upon Miss Landale to give
it to her. He is a sharp rogue,' says he, 'and I can trust
his wits ; but should you not find him, dear René, you
must do the commission for me yourself. Now go—go,'
he cries, and pushes me to the stairs. And, as I dared
remain no more, I had to leave him. Of course Monsieur
the Captain has not been here all this time without telling
me of his hopes, and it is clear that it is to bid farewell

to Mademoiselle Madeleine that he is playing with his life. It is as ill reasoning with a lover as a lunatic : they are the same thing, *Ma foi*, but I trust to your honour to bring him to his senses if any one can. And so, to continue, I went down and I told the men in blue the boat was ready, we carried the body ; I left them at the Shearmans, as your honour knows. I found Johnny and gave him the letter ; he knew all about what to do, it seemed. And then I came straight to the Hall."

"It is indeed a miserable business ! " said Sir Adrian.

René heaved a great sigh of sympathy, as he noticed the increasing concern on his master's face.

" You heard them mention my brother's name ? " inquired the latter, after following the train of his misgivings for a few moments. " You have reason to think that Mr. Landale knew of these men's errand ; other reason, I mean, than having seen them with him just now ? "

René's quick mind leaped at the meaning of the question :

" Yes, your honour. ' Mr. Landale will want to know of this,' says the fat one ; ' though it is too late,' he says." And René added ruefully : " I have great fear. The captain is not at the end of his pains, if Mr. Landale is ranged against him ! "

Such was also Sir Adrian's thought. But he walked on for a time in silence ; and, having reached Scarthey, rapidly made his way into the peel.

Captain Jack was still pacing the room much as René had described when Sir Adrian entered upon him. The young man turned with a transient look of surprise to the new-comer, then waved away the proffered hand with a bitter smile.

" You do not know," he said, " who it is you would shake hands with—an outlaw—a criminal. Ah, you have heard ? Then Renny, I suppose, has told you."

" Yes," groaned the other, holding his friend by both shoulders and gazing sorrowfully into the haggard face, " the man may die—oh, Jack, Jack, how could you be so rash ? "

" I can't say how it all happened," answered Captain Jack, falling to his walk to and fro again in the extremity of his distress, and ever and anon mopping his brow. " I felt such security in this place. All was loaded but the last barrel, when, all of a sudden, from God knows where, the man sprang on me and thrust his dark lantern in my face. ' It is Smith,' I heard him say. I do believe now that he only wanted to identify me. No man in his senses could have dared to try and arrest me surrounded by my six men. But I had no time to think then, Adrian. I imagined the fellow was leading a general attack . . . . If that last barrel was seized the whole secret was out ; and that meant ruin. Wholesale failure seemed to menace me suddenly in the midst of my success. I had a hand-spike in my hand with which I had been helping to roll the kegs. I struck with it, on the spur of the moment ; the man went down on the spot, with a groan. As he fell I leaped back, ready for the next. I called out, ' Stretch-ers, lads ; they want to take your captain ? ' My lads gathered round me at once. But there was silence ; not another creature to be seen or heard. They set to work to get that last blessed bit of cargo, the cause of all the misery, on board with the rest ; while I stood in the grow-ing dawn, looking down at the motionless figure and at the blood trickling into the sand, trying to think, to settle what to do, and only conscious of one thing : the intense wish that I could change places with my victim. Can you wonder, Adrian, that my brain was reeling ? You who know all, all this means to me, can you wonder that I could not leave this shore—even though my life depended on it—without seeing her again ! Curwen, my mate, came up to me at last, and I woke up to some sort of rea-son at the idea that they, the crew and the ship, must be removed from the immediate danger. But the orders I gave must have seemed those of a madman : I told him to sail right away but to double back in time to have the schooner round again at twelve noon to-day, and then to send the gig's crew to pick me up on Pulwick sand. ' Life and death,' said I to him, and he, brave fellow, ' Ay, ay, sir,' as if it was the most simple thing in the world, and off with him without another word."

" What imprudence, what imprudence ! " murmured Sir Adrian.

" Who knows ? None will believe that I have not seized the opportunity of making my escape with the others. The height of imprudence may become the height of security. I have as yet no plan—but it will come.

My luck shall not fail me now! who knows: nothing
perhaps is damaged but an excise man's crown. Thank
heaven, the wind cannot fail us to-day."

"But, meanwhile," urged Sir Adrian, quite unconvinced,
highly disturbed, "that treasure on board . . . . I know
what has been your motive, Jack, but indeed it is all nothing short of insanity, positive insanity. Can you trust
your men?"

"I would trust them with my own secrets, willingly
enough; but not with those of other people. So they do
not know what I have in those barrels. Four thousand
golden guineas in each . . . .! No, the temptation would
be too terrible for the poor lads. Not a soul knows that,
beyond you and me. Curwen has charge of the cargo,
such as it is. But I can answer for it none of them will
dream of tampering with the casks. They are picked men,
sober, trusty; who have fought side by side with me. I
am their best friend. They are mine, body and soul, I believe. They do know there is some risk in the business,
but they trust me. They are sure of treble pay, and besides, are not troubled with squeamishness. As for Curwen,
he would go to hell for me, and never ask a question.
No, Adrian, the scheme was perfect, but for this cursed
blow of mine this morning. And now it is a terrible
responsibility," continued the young man, again wiping
his forehead; "every ounce of it weighs on my shoulders.
But it is not that that distracts me. Oh, Adrian . . . .
Madeleine!"

The elder man felt his heart contract at the utter despairing of that cry.

"When my handspike crashed on that damned inter-
ferer's skull," the sailor went on, "I felt as if the blow
had opened an unfathomable chasm between her and me.
Now I am felon—yes, in law, a felon! And yet I am the
same man as yesterday. I shall have to fly to-night, and
may never be able to return openly to England again.
All my golden dreams of happiness, of honour, vanished
at the sound of that cursed blow. But I must see her,
Adrian, I *must* see her before I go. I am going to meet
her at noon, in the ruins of Pulwick."

"Impossible!" ejaculated the other aghast. "Listen,
Jack, unfortunate man! When I heard of the—the misfortune, and of your folly in remaining, I instantly planned

18

a last meeting for you.   As it fell out, my wife has a fancy
to spend the night here : I have asked her to bring her
sister with her.   But this inconceivably desperate plan of
leaving in your ship, in broad light of day, frustrates all I
would have done for you.   For God's sake let us contrive
some way of warning the *Peregrine* off till midnight ; keep
hidden, yourself ; do not wilfully run your head into the
noose ! "

But the young man had stopped short in his tramping,
and stood looking at his friend, with a light of hope flaming in his eye.

"You have done that, Adrian ! You have thought of
that ! " he repeated, as if mechanically.   A new whirlwind of schemes rushed through his mind.   For a while
he remained motionless, with his gaze fixed on Sir Adrian,
putting order in his own thoughts with that genius of precision and swiftness which, in strong natures, rises to
meet a crisis.   Then advancing, and seizing him by both
hands :

"Adrian," he cried, in something more like his own
voice, again, "I shall yet owe my happiness to you, to
this thought, this sublime thought of your heart ! "

And, as Sir Adrian, astounded, unable to understand
this extremity of hopefulness, following upon the previous
depth of misery, stared back at him, speechless, the latter
proceeded in still more surprising fashion.

"Now, you listen to me, this time.   I have been selfish
in running the risk of having you mixed up in my dangerous affairs.   But, God is my witness, I acted under
the belief that all was absolutely secure.   Now, however,
you must do nothing more that might implicate you.
Remember, do nothing to let people suspect that you have
seen me to-day.   Renny, too, must keep close counsel.
You know nothing of my future movements.   Remain
here for a while, do not even look out of the window . . . .
I fear we shall not meet for a long time.   Meanwhile,
God bless you—God bless you ! "

After another wrench of the hands he held in his, the
sailor released them and fairly ran out of the room, without heeding his friend's bewildered expostulations.   At the
door of the keep he met René again.   And after a brief but
earnest colloquy, the man whose life was now forfeit to the
community and upon whose head there would soon be a

price, was quietly walking along the causeway, making for the shore, with the greatest apparent unconcern and deliberation.

And whilst Sir Adrian, alone in his chamber, with his head resting upon his hand, anxiously pondered upon the possible issues of this nefarious day's doings, the sailor advanced, in broad daylight towards the land to keep his appointment.

A solitary speck of life upon the great waste, with the consciousness of the precarious thread of chance upon which it hung! What wonder that, for all his daring, the traveller felt, as he deliberately regulated his pace to the most nonchalant gait, a frantic desire to run forward, or to lie down! How many approach glasses might now be laid, like so many guns, upon him from secret points of the coast until he came within range of recognition; what ambushes those clumps of gorse and juniper, those plantations of alders and young firs on the bluffs yonder, might conceal? The eye could reach far and wide upon the immense stretch of sand, along the desert coast; and his solitary figure, moving upon the yellow strand was a mark for miles around. Steadily, nevertheless did he advance; the very daring, the unpardonable foolhardiness of the deed his safety. And yet the strain was high. Were they watching the island? Among the eager crew, to each of whom the capture might mean a splendid prize and chance of promotion, was there one would have the genius of suddenly suspecting that this foolhardy wayfarer might be the man they wanted and not merely Sir Adrian returning on foot towards his home? . . . . And then came the answer of hopeful youth and hardy courage——.

No. The preventive are a lubberly lot—It will require something better than a water-guard to track and take Lucky Jack Smith!

But for all his assurance Lucky Jack Smith drew a long breath of relief when he felt the shadow of Pulwick woods closing around him at last.

CHAPTER XXIII

THE DAY: NOON

There stood two men and they did point their fingers at
     that house,
And on his finger one had blood; the other's finger shook.
                                                Luteplayer's Song.

BROKEN lengths of wall, a crumbling indication of the
spring of once exquisite arches, windows gaping darkly
like the eye sockets of a skull—this was all that was left
of the old priory of Pulwick, whilom proud seat of clerical power and learning. But the image of decay was
robbed of all melancholy by the luxuriance of climbing
vegetation, by the living screen of noble firs and larches
arranged in serried ranks upon the slopes immediately
behind it, with here and there a rugged sentinel within
the ruinous yards and rooms themselves ; by wild bushes
of juniper and gorse and brambles. And, with the bright
noon sun pouring down upon the worn red sandstone,
and gilding the delicate tassels of the larches' green
needles ; with the light of young love, spreading glamour
upon every leaf and stone, in the eyes of the lovers, the
scene, witness of so many sweet meetings, bore that day
a beautiful and homelike aspect.

Captain Jack was standing upon the grass-grown floor
of what had been the departed monks' refectory, with
ears eagerly bent to listen.

Three ragged walls, a clump of fir trees, and a bank of
brambles screened him from any chance passer-by, and
he now and again peered through a crevice on to a path
through the woods, cautiously, as if fearful to venture
forth. His face was pale beneath its tan, and had none
of its usual brightness ; his attire for him was disordered ;
his whole appearance that of a man under the pressure of
doubt and anxiety. Yet, when the sound of a light footfall struck among the thousand whispering noises of wind

276

and leaf that went to make up the silence of the ruins, the glory of joy that lit up eye and lip left no room for any other impression.

Madeleine stood in the old door-way: a vision of beautiful life amid emblems of decay and death.

"I come alone to-day," she said, with her half-shy smile. And then, before she could utter a further word of explanation, she was gathered into her lover's strong arms with a passion he had never as yet shown in his chivalrous relations with her. But it was not because they met without the sympathetic rapture of Miss Landale's eye upon them; not because there was no other witnesses but the dangling ivy wreath, the stern old walls, the fine dome of spring sky faintly blue; not because of lover's audacious joy. This Madeleine, feeling the stormy throbbing of his heart against hers, knew with sure instinct. She pushed him gently from her as soon as she could, the blushes chased from her cheeks by pale misgivings, and looked at him with eyes full of troubled questioning.

Then he spoke, from his full heart:

"Madeleine, something has happened—a misfortune, as I wrote to you. I must now start upon my venture sooner than I thought—at once. I shall have to *fly* in fact, to-day. There have been spies upon me, and my secret trust is in danger. How they have tracked me, how suspicion has been aroused, I cannot guess. But I have been tracked. A fellow came at dawn. I had to defend my secret—the secret not my own, the charge entrusted to me. The man was hurt. I cannot explain, dear love, there is no time; even now I run the risk of my life by being here, and life is so dear to me now, my Madeleine! Hush! No, do not be afraid! I am afraid of nothing, so long as you trust me. Will you trust me? I cannot leave you here behind; and now, with this cursed stroke of ill-luck, this suspicion upon me, it may be long before I can return to England. I cannot leave you behind, I cannot! Will you trust me, Madeleine, will you come with me? We shall be married in France, my darling. You should be as a queen in the guard of her most humble slave. I am half mad to think I must go. Ah, kiss me, love, and say yes! Listen! I must sail away and make believe that I have gone. My *Peregrine* is a bird that none can overtake, but I shall

come back to-night.   Listen : If you will be on the island
to-night—Sir Adrian is there already, and I hear your
sister is coming—a freak of fancy—and he, God bless him,
has told her to bring you too (it shows my luck has not
deserted me yet).   I shall be there, unknown to all except
Renny.   I cannot meet you nearer home, but you will
be my own brave bride and keep your own counsel.   You
will not be frightened, will you, my beautiful love?   All
you have to do is to follow Renny's instructions.   My
ship will be back, waiting, an hour after dark, ready,
when you set foot on it, to spread its wings with its
treasures—treasures, indeed !   And then we shall have
the world before us—riches, love, such love !   And once
safe, I shall be free to prove to you that it is no common
blood I would mate with that dear and pure stream that
courses in your veins.   You shall soon know all ; will you
trust me ? "

She hung upon his hot words, looking at him with
loving, frightened eyes.   Now he gathered her to his arms
again, again his bursting heart throbbed its stormy passion
to her ear.   She was as one carried away by a torrent
against which resistance is useless.   He bent his head
over her face ; the scent of the bunch of violets in her
breast rose deliciously to his nostrils.   Alas !   Hubert
Cochrane was not to reach that kiss of acquiescence, that
kiss from which it seemed that but so small a fraction of
space and time divided him !   Some one, who had stepped
along in the shadow as silently as a cat coming upon a
bird, clapped here a hand upon his shoulder.

" Who are you, sir, and what do you want ? " exclaimed
Captain Jack, wrenching himself free, falling back a pace
and measuring the new-comer from head to foot with
furious glances, while, with burning blushes Madeleine
faltered :

" Rupert ! "

Nothing awakens anger in hot blood sooner than an
unsanctioned touch.   In certain moods the merest contact
is as infuriating as a blow.   Such an insult, added to the
irreparable injury of interrupting their meeting at the most
exquisite and crucial moment, drove Captain Jack beside
himself with rage.

But Madeleine's hand was still on his arm.   She felt
it suddenly harden and twitch with murderous anger.

But, by an effort that made the veins of his temple swell like whipcord, he refrained from striking the double offender.

Mr. Landale surveyed the pair for a moment in silence with his grave look ; then coldly he answered the sailor's irate speech.

"My name, fellow, is Rupert Landale. I am here to protect my cousin from an unprincipled and criminal adventurer."

"You take a sharp tone sir," cried Captain Jack, the flush on his face deepening yet a shade, his nostrils ominously dilated, yet speaking without further loss of self-control. "You probably count upon the presence of this lady to prevent my resenting it ; but as my time with her is short and I have still much to say, I shall be forced promptly to eject you from the ruins here, unless you will be good enough to immediately remove yourself. I shall hope for another meeting with you to discuss the question as to your right of interference ; but to-day—I cannot spare the time."

Rupert smiled without moving ; then the sailor gently disengaging himself from Madeleine would have put her behind him but that she pressed forward and laid a hand upon an arm of each of the men.

"Stay, Jack," she pleaded, "let me speak. There is some mistake here. Cousin Rupert, you cannot know that I am engaged to this gentleman and that he is a friend of your brother's as well as of other good friends of mine."

"My poor child," answered Rupert, closing a cold hand gently over hers and speaking with a most delicate tenderness of accent, "you have been grossly imposed upon, and so have others. As for my poor brother Adrian, he is, if anything, easier to deceive than you, innocent convent-bred girl ! I would have you to go home, my dear, and leave me to deal with this—gentleman. You have bitter truths to learn ; would it not be better to wait and learn them quietly without further scandal ?"

This was too much for Captain Jack, who fairly ground his teeth. Rupert's honeyed tones, his grasp of Madeleine's hand were more unbearable even than the words. He advanced upon the elder man and seizing him by the collar whirled him away from the girl as easily as a straw puppet.

The fine gentleman of sensitive nerves and unworked sinews had no chance against the iron strength of the man who had passed all the years of virility fighting against sea and storm. The two faced each other; Jack Smith, red and panting with honest rage, only the sense of his lady's proximity keeping him from carrying his high-handed measures a little further. Mr. Landale, livid, with eyes suddenly black in their orbits, moistening his white lips while he quivered from head to foot with a passion so tense that not even his worst enemy could have attributed it to fear.

An unequal match it would seem, yet unequal in a way that the young man, in the conscious glory of his strength could not have conceived. Madeleine neither screamed nor fainted; she had grown white, in natural apprehension, but her eyes fixed upon her lover's face shone with admiration. Mr. Landale turned slowly towards her.

"Madeleine," he said, readjusting his stock and smoothing the folds of his collar with a steadfast striving after coolness, "you have been grossly deceived. The man you would trust with your life and honour is a mere smuggler. He has no doubt told you fine stories, but if he has given himself out for aught else he lied, take my word for it—he lied. He is a common smuggler, and the vessel he would carry you away in is packed with smuggled goods. To-day he has attacked and wounded an officer, who, in the discharge of his duty, endeavoured to find out the nature of his suspicious purpose. Your would-be lover's neck is in danger. A felon, he runs the risk of his life every moment he remains on land—but he would make a last effort to secure the heiress! Look at him," his voice raising in spite of himself to a shriller pitch—"he cannot deny it!"

Madeleine gazed from one to the other. Her mind, never a very quick one at decision, was too bewildered to act with clearness; moreover with her education and ignorance of the world the indictment conveyed no special meaning to her.

But there was an agony of suspense and beseeching in the glance that her lover cast upon her; and to that appeal she smiled proudly. Hers were no true love, she felt, were its confidence shaken by the slandering of anger. Then the thought of his danger, danger admitted by his own lips, flashed upon her with terror. She rushed to him,

"Oh go, Jack, go !—As you love me, go !"

Mr. Landale, who had already once or twice cast impatient looks of expectation through a window of the east wall, taken by surprise at this unforeseen result of his speech, suddenly climbed up upon a broken piece of stone-work, from which there was an abrupt descent towards the shore, and began to signal in eager gesticulation. There was a sound of heavy running footfalls without. Captain Jack raised his head, every nerve on the alert.

"Go, go," again cried Madeleine, dreading she knew not what.—A fat panting red face looked over the wall ; Mr. Landale turned for a second to throw at the lovers a glance of elation.

But it seemed as if the sailor's spirits rose at the breath of danger. He rapidly looked round upon the ruins from which there were no other outlets than the window guarded by Mr. Landale, and the doorway in which the red-faced new-comer now stood, framed in red stone ; then, like a cat he darted on to the ledge of the wall at the opposite end, where some invading boughs of larch dropped over the jagged crest, before the burly figure in the blue coat of the preventive service had recovered from the surprise of finding a lady in his way, or gathered his wits and his breath sufficiently to interfere.

There the nimble climber stood a moment balancing himself lightly, though the ivied stones rocked beneath him.

"I go, love," he cried in ringing voice, "but one word from you and I go———"

"Oh, I trust you ! I will trust you !" screamed the girl in despair, while her fascinated gaze clung to the erect figure silhouetted against the sky and the stout man looked up, open-mouthed. Mr. Landale snarled at him :

"Shoot, fool—shoot !" And straining forward, himself drew a pistol from the man's belt, cocked it and thrust it into his grasp.

Captain Jack kissed his hand to Madeleine with a joyful gesture, then waved his hat defiantly in Rupert's
direction, and with a spring disappeared, just as the
pistol cracked, drawing a shriek of terror from the girl,
and its bullet flattened itself against the upper stone of
the wall—considerably wide of the mark.

"Come, this way——!" screamed Mr. Landale from
his window sill, "you have another!"

But the preventive shook his head, and thrust his
smoking barrel back through his belt, with an air of
philosophical resignation; and slowly approaching the
window, through which the fugitive could now be seen
steadily bowling down the seaward slope, observed in
slow, fat tones:

"Give you a hand, sir?"

Rupert, thrusting his extended arm aside jumped down
beside him as if he would have sprung at his throat.

"Why are you so late?—why have you brought no
one with you? I gave you notice enough. You fool!
You have let him slip through your fingers, now, after
all! Couldn't you even shoot straight? Such a mark as
he made against the sky—Pah! well may the sailors say,
lubberly as a land preventive——!"

"Why, there you are, Mr. Landale!" answered the
man with imperturbable, greasy good-humour. "The
way you shoved that there pistol into my hand was
enough to put off anybody. But you country magistrate
gentlemen, as I have always said, you are the real sort
to make one do illegal actions with your flurry and your
hurry over everything. 'Shoot!' says you, and damme,
sir, if I didn't shoot straight off before I knew if I were on
my head or on my heels. It's a mercy I didn't hit the
sweet young lady—it is indeed. And as for the young
gentleman, though to be sure he did show a clean pair
of heels at the sight of me, I had no proper time for
i-dentification—no time for i-den-ti-fi-cation, Mr. Landale,
sir. So I say, sir, it's a mercy I did not hit him either,
now I can think of it. Ah, slow and sure, that's my
motter! I takes my man on his boat, in the very middle
of his laces and his brandy and his silk—I takes him, sir,
in the very act of illegality, red-handed, so to speak, and
then, if he shows fight, or if he runs away, then I shoots,
sir, and then if I hits, why it's a good job too—but none

of this promiscuous work for Augustus Hobson. Slow and sure, that's my motter."

The speaker who had been rolling a quid of tobacco in his mouth during this exposition of policy, here spat emphatically upon the grass, and catching Madeleine's abstracted eye, begged pardon for the liberty with a gallant air.

"Aye, so slow, man, that you are pretty sure to fail," muttered Mr. Landale.

"I knows my business, sir, meaning no offence," retorted Mr. Hobson serenely. "When I has no orders I acts on regulation. I brought no one with me because I had no one to bring, having sent, as per regulation, my one remaining man to give notice to the water service, seeing that that there schooner has had the impudence to come back, and is at this very moment cruising quite happy-like just the other side of the bank; though if ever their cutter overhauls her—well, I'm a Dutchman! You might have done wiser, perhaps (if I may make so bold as to remark), to leave the management of this business to them as understands such things. As to being late, sir, you told me to be in the ruins at twelve noon, and I beg to insinuate that it's only just past the hour now."

At this point the preventive man drew from his capacious breeches a brass time-piece, of congenial stoutness, the face of which he turned towards the magistrate.

The latter, however, waved the proffered witness impatiently aside. Furtively watching his cousin, who, leaning against the door-post, her pale head thrown out in strong relief by the dark stones, stood as if absolutely detached from her surroundings, communing over troubled thoughts with her own soul, he said with deliberate distinctness:

"But have I been misled, then, in understanding that you were with the unfortunate officer who was so ferociously assaulted this morning? that you and he did come upon this Captain Smith, red-handed as you call it, loading or unloading his vessel on Scarthey Island?"

"Aye, sir," rolled out the other, unctuously, "there you are again, you see. Poor Nat Beavor, he was one of your hot-headed ones, and see what it has brought *him* to—a crack in his skull, sir, so that it will be days before he'll know himself again, the doctor says, if ever he does in this world, which I don't think. Ah, I says to him, when we started in the dawn this morning agreeable to our arrangement with you : 'For peeping and prying on the quiet without any running risks and provoking others to break the law more than they're doing, I'm your man,' says I ; 'but as for attacking desperate individles without proper warrant and authority, not to speak of being one to ten, I tell you fair, Nat Beavor, I'll have nothing to do with it.' But Nat, he went off his head, clean, at the sight of Captain Jack and his men a trundling the little kegs down the sands, as neat and tidy as could be ; and so he cut out from behind the rocks, and I knew there was mischief ahead ! Ah, poor fellow, if he would only have listened to me ! I did my best for him, sir ; started off to call up the other man, who was on the other side of the ruins, as soon as I saw his danger, but when I came back——"

"The birds were flown, of course," interrupted Rupert with a sneer, "and you found the body of your comrade who had been dastardly wounded, and who, I hear, is dead now. So the villain has twice escaped you. Cousin Madeleine," hastily breaking off to advance to the girl, who now awakening from her reflective mood seemed about to leave the ruins, "Cousin Madeleine, are you going ? Let me escort you back."

She slowly turned her blue eyes, burning upon him from her white face. "Cousin Rupert, I do not want your company." Then she added in a whisper, yet with a passion for which Rupert would never have given her credit and which took him vastly by surprise, "I shall never forgive you."

"My God, Madeleine," cried he, with genuine emotion, "have I deserved this ? I have had no thought but to befriend you, I have opened your eyes to your own danger——"

"Hold your tongue, sir," she broke in, with the same repressed anger. "Cease vilifying the man I love. All your aspersions, your wordy accusations will not shake my faith in him. *Mon Dieu*," she cried, with an unsteady attempt at laughter, looking under her lashes and tilting her little white round chin at Mr. Hobson, who, now seated upon a large stone, and with an obtrusive quid of tobacco bulging in an imperfectly shorn cheek, was mop-

ping his forehead with a doubtful handkerchief. "*That*
is the person, I suppose, whose testimony I am to believe
against my Jack!"

"Your Jack was prompt enough in running away
from him, such as he is," retorted her cousin bitterly.
He could not have struck, for his purpose, upon a weaker
joint in her poor woman's armour of pride and trust.

She caught her breath sharply, as if indeed she had
received a blow. "Well, say your say," she exclaimed,
coming to a standstill and facing him; "I will hear all
that you and your—your friend have to say, lest," with a
magnificent toss of her head, "you fancy I am afraid, or
that I believe one word of it all. I know that Jack—
that Captain Smith, as he is called—is engaged upon a
secret and important mission; but it is one, Rupert,
which all English gentlemen should wish to help, not
impede."

"Do you know what the mission is—do you know to
whom? And if, my fair cousin, it is such that all English gentlemen would help, why then this secrecy?"

She bit her lip; but it trembled. "What is it you
accuse him of?" she asked, with a stamp of her foot.

"Listen to me," said Rupert gently, "it is the kinder
thing that you should know the truth, and believe me,
every word I say I can substantiate. This Captain Jack
Smith, whatever his real name may be, was picked up
when a mere boy by an old Liverpool merchant, starving
in the streets of that town. This merchant, by name
Cochrane, an absurd person who gave himself out to be
a relative of Cochrane of Shaws, adopted the boy and
started him upon a slaver, that is a ship which does trade
in negro slaves, my dear—a pretty trade. He next entered a privateer's ship as lieutenant. You know what
these are—ocean freebooters, tolerated by government
for the sake of the harm they wreck upon the ships of
whatever nation we may happen to be at war with—a
sort of pirate ship—hardly a much more reputable business than the slaver's; but Captain Smith made himself a
name in it. Now that the war is over, he has taken to a
lower traffic still—that of smuggling."

"But *what* is smuggling?" cried the girl, tears brimming up at last into her pretty eyes, and all her heat of
valiance suddenly gone. "What does it mean?"

" What is smuggling? Bless your innocence! I beg your pardon, my dear—miss I should say—but if you'll allow *me* I think I'm the man to explain that 'ere to you." The husky mellifluous tones of the preventive-service man, who had crept up unnoticed to listen to the conversation, here murmured insinuatingly in her ear.

Rupert hesitated ; then reading shrinking aversion upon Madeleine's face, shrewdly conjectured that the exposition of her lover's doings might come with more force from Mr. Hobson's lips than from his own, and allowed the latter to proceed unmolested.

" Smuggling, my pretty," wheezed the genial representative of the custom laws, "again asking pardon, but it slipped out, smuggling is, so to say, a kind of stealing, a kind of cheating and that of a most rank and heinous kind. For, mind you, it ain't stealing from a common man, nor from the likes of you and me, nor from a nobleman eithe : it's cheating and stealing from his most gracious Majesty himself. For see you, how 'tis, his Majesty he says, ' Every keg of brandy,' says he, ' and every yard of lace and every pipe o' tobacco as is brought into this here country shall be paid for, so much on, to me, and that's called a tax, miss, and for that there are the custom houses and custom officers—which is me—to see his Majesty paid right and proper his lawful dues. But what does your smuggler do, miss—your rollicking, dare-devil chap of a smuggler? Why he lands his lace and his brandy and his 'baccy unbeknownst and sells 'em on the sly—and pockets the profit ! D'ye see ?—and so he cheats his Majesty, which is a very grievous breaking of the law ; so much so that he might as well murder at once—Kind o' treason, you may say—and that's what makes 'em such desperate chaps. They knows if they're caught at it, with arms about them, and two or three together—it's—clck."

Mr. Hobson grasped his own bull neck with an unpleasantly significant gesture and winked knowingly at the girl, who turned white as death and remained gazing at him with a sort of horrified fascination which he presently noted with an indulgent smile.

" Don't take on now, my lass—no offence, miss—but I can't bear to see a fine young 'oman like you upset-like —I'm a damned, hem, hem, a real soft hearted fellow.

Your sweetheart's heels have saved his gullet this time—
and though he did crack poor Nat upon the skull (as I
can testify for I as good as saw him do it—which makes
it a hanging matter twice over I won't deny), yet there's
a good few such as him escapes the law and settles down
arter, quite respectable-like. A bit o' smuggling now is
a thing many a pretty fellow has taken to in his day, and
has made a pretty penny out of too, and is none the
worse looked to arter, as I said. Aye, and there's many
a gentleman and a magistrate to boot as drinks his glass
of smuggled brandy and smokes his smuggled baccy and
finds them none the worse, oh dear no ! Human nature
it is and human nature is a queer thing. Even the ladies,
miss, are well-known to be soft upon the smuggled lace :
it's twice as cheap you see as t'other, and they can get
double as handsome for the money. Begging your pardon—if I may make so bold—" stretching out a great,
coarse, tobacco-stained finger and thumb to close them
appreciatively upon the hanging lace of Madeleine's neck
handkerchief, "may be your spark brought you that
there, miss, now ? He, he, he—as pretty a bit of French
point it is as has ever been my fate to lay hands on—
Never fear," as the girl drew back with a gesture of loathing from the contact. " I ain't agoing to seize it off you
or take you up, he—he—he—eh, Mr. Landale ? I'm a
man o' my duty, I hope, but our orders don't run as far
as that."

" Rupert !" cried Madeleine, piteously turning a dark
gaze of anguish at him—it seemed as if she were going
to faint.

He hastened up to her, shouldering the clumsy form of
Mr. Augustus Hobson unceremoniously out of the way :
the fellow had done his work for the time being, and this
last piece of it so efficaciously indeed that his present
employer felt, if not remorse, at least a certain pity stir
within him at the stricken hopelessness of the girl's
aspect. He passed his arm round her waist as she
shivered and swayed. " Lean on me," he said, his fine
eyes troubled with an unwonted softness and anxiety.

" Rupert," she whispered, clutching at his sleeve,
eagerly fixing him with a look eloquent of unconscious
pleading, "all these things this—this man talks of are
things which are brought into England—are they not ? I

know that—*he* was bringing nothing into the country, but he was going to another country upon some important trust, the nature of which he had promised not to reveal. Therefore he cannot be cheating the King, if that is smuggling—Oh Rupert, is there not some grievous mistake?"

"My poor child," said Rupert, holding her close and tenderly, and speaking with a gentle gravity in which there was this time less hypocrisy, "there is one thing which is smuggled out of England, and it is as dishonest and illegal work as the other, the most daring and dangerous smuggling of all in fact; one in which none but a desperate man would engage—that of gold."

"Yes, gold," exclaimed the girl sharply, withdrawing herself from her cousin's arms, while a ray of intelligence and hope lit up her face. "Gold for the French King's service."

Rupert betrayed no emotion; he drew from the inner pocket of his coat a crushed news-sheet.

"Deceived there, as well as everywhere else, poor little cousin," he said. "And did the scoundrel say so? Nay, he is a damnable scoundrel who could betray your trustfulness to your own sweet face. Gold indeed—but not for the King—gold for the usurper, for the tyrant who was supplied already, no doubt, by the same or similar traitor hands with enough to enable him to escape from the island where he was so justly imprisoned. See here, Madeleine, Bonaparte is actually landed in France: it has all been managed with the most devilish ingenuity and takes the whole world by surprise. And your lover, doubtless, is engaged upon bringing him fresh supplies to enable him to begin again and rack humanity with hideous wars. Oh, he never told you of the Corsican's escape, yet this news is three days old. See you, my dear, this explains the whole mystery, the necessity for absolute secrecy; all England is friendly to the French monarch; no need to smuggle gold for his aid—but the other. . . . ! It is treason, the blackest treason on every side of it, treason to his King, to his country, to *your* King, to you. And he would have cozened you with tales of his loyalty to the rightful cause!"

"Give me the paper," said Madeleine. A tide of blood had swept into her face; she was no longer white and shaken, but erect and beautiful in strong indignation. Rupert examined her, as if a little doubtful how to take the sudden change; but he handed her the printed sheet in silence. She read with lips and nostrils expanded by her quick breathing; then crumpled up the sheet and cast it at his feet. And after a pause, with her princess air of dignity, "I thank you, cousin Rupert," she said; then, passing him with stately steps, moved towards the house.

He pressed forward to keep up with her; and upon the other side, smiling, irrepressible, jocose, Mr. Hobson did the same.

"You are not fit to go alone," urged the former, while the latter engagingly protruding an elbow, announced that he'd be proud to give her an arm as far as the Hall.

She drew away from this well-meaning squire of dames with such shuddering distaste, and looked once more so white and worn and sickened after her sudden blaze of passion, that Mr. Landale, seeing that the only kindness was to let her have her will, arrested his companion roughly enough, and allowed her to proceed as she wished.

And so, with bent head, Madeleine hurried forth. And the same glorious sun smiled down upon her in her anguish that had greeted her when she hastened an hour before glowing and light-hearted—if, indeed, a heart so full of love could be termed light—to meet her lover; the same brambles caught her dress, the same bird trilled his song. But Madeleine thought neither of ray nor leaf, nor yet of mating songsters: all the spring world, as she went, was to her strewn with the wreck of her broken hopes, and encompassed by the darkness of her lonely future.

Mr. Landale and the preventive service man stood some time watching her retreating figure through the wood, and then walked slowly on for a while, in silent company.

Presently the latter, who during the last part of the interview, had begun to feel a little ruffled by the magistrate's persistently overbearing manner, inquired with something of dudgeon in his voice: "Begging your pardon, sir, what was that I heard the young lady call out just now? 'Gold!' she cries. Is it guineas that

19

nipping young man is a taking over seas, if I may make
so bold? Now you see, sir, we haven't had no orders
about no gold on this station—that sort of thing is mostly
done down south. But what I wants to know is : Why,
if you knew all about the fellow's little games, you sent
us to spy on him? Ah, poor Nat would want a word or
two with you on that score, I fancy! Now it's as plain
as Salisbury . . . . ."

"But I know nothing certain," impatiently interrupted
Mr. Landale. "I know no more than you do yourself.
Only not being a perfect idiot, I can put two and two
together. What in the name of goodness can a man
smuggle *out* of England but gold? But I wanted the
proofs. And your business, it was agreed with the Chief
Officer, was to follow my instructions."

"And so we did," grumbled Mr. Hobson ; "and a pretty
business it's turned out ! Nat's to pocket his bludgeoning,
I suppose, and I am to bear the blame and lose my share.
A cargo of guineas, by God ! I might have nosed it,
down south, but here . . . . Blast it ! But since you was
so clever over it, sir, why in blazes—if I may speak so to
a gentleman and a magistrate," pursued the man with a
rueful explosion of disgust, "didn't you give *me* the hint?
Why, guineas is contraband of war—it's treason, sir—and
guineas is a cargo that's *fought* for, sir ! I shouldn't have
moved with two men in a boat patrol, d'ye think? I
should have had the riding officers, and the water-guard,
and a revenue cruiser in the offing, and all tight and
regular. But you *would* have all the credit, and where are
you? and *where's* my share? and where is Nat?—Bah !"

"You are forgetting yourself, officer," said Mr. Landale,
looking severely into the eyes of the disappointed preventive man, whose rising ebullition became on the instant reduced.

"So I am, sir, so I am—and beg your pardon. But
you must admit, it's almost enough to make . . . . but
never mind, sir, the trick is done. Whatever it may be
that that there schooner carries in her bottom, she is free
now to take it, barring accident, wherever she pleases.
I'll trouble you to look this way, sir."

They had emerged from the wooded part of the park,
and the rising ground on which they stood commanded a
wide sea-view, west of the great bay.

"There she is again, sir," said Mr. Hobson, waving his broad paw, like a showman displaying his goods, with a sort of enraged self-satisfaction. "There is the schooner, ready to hoist sail as soon as he comes alongside. And that there black point which you may see, if your eyes are good enough, is a six-oared galley with as ship-shaped a crew—if it's the same as I saw making off this morning— as ever pulled. Your Captain Smith, you may take your oath, is at the tiller, and making fun of us two to the lads. In five minutes he will be on board, and then the revenue cutter from the station may give chase if she likes ! . . . . And there she is, due to the time—about a mile astern. But bless you, that's all my eye, you may take your oath ! They know well enough that in an open sea they can't run down a Salcombe schooner. But to earn their pay they will hang on till they lose her, and then sail home, all cosy.—I'm thinking," he added slily, with a side glance at the magistrate : "we won't hang him *this* time."

Mr. Landale made no answer ; during the last few minutes his reflections had enabled him to take a new view of the situation. After all the future fate of Captain Jack was of little moment. He had been successfully exposed before Madeleine, whose love for the young man was, as had just been sufficiently proved, chiefly composed of those youthful illusions which dispelled once, never can return.

Rupert fell gradually into a reverie in which he found curious satisfaction. His work had not been unsuccessful, whatever Mr. Hobson's opinion might be. But, as matters stood between Madeleine and her lover, the girl's eyes had been opened in time, and that without scandal. . . . . And even the escape of Captain Jack was, upon reflection, the best thing that could have happened.

And so it was with a return to his usual polite bearing, that he listened to the officer's relapse into expostulation.

"Now if you had only given me the hint first of all," the man was grumblingly saying, "and then let me act —for who would have suspected a boat, yacht-rigged like that?—A friend of Sir Adrian's, too ! If you'd only left it to me ! Why that six-oared galley alone is agin the law unless you can prove good reason for it . . . . as for the vessel herself . . . ."

"Yes, my dear Mr. Hobson," interrupted Mr. Landale,

smiling propitiously. "I have no doubt you would have secured him. I have made a mess of it. But now you understand, least said, soonest mended, both for me and (between ourselves, Mr. Hobson) for the young lady."

The man, in surprise at this sudden alteration of manner, stopped short and gaped; and presently a broad smile, combined with a knowing wink, appeared on his face. He received the guineas that Mr. Landale dropped in his palm with an air of great candour, and, without further parley, acted on the kind advice to repair to the Priory and talk with one Mrs. Puckett the housekeeper, on the subject of corporeal refreshment.

"Well," said Molly, bursting in upon her sister, who sat by her writing-table, pen in hand, and did not even raise her head at the unceremonious entrance. "This is evidently the day for mysterious disappearances. First Rupert and Sophia; then my lord and master who is fetched hurriedly to his island (that isle of misfortune!) God knows for what—though *I* mean to know presently; then you, Mademoiselle, and Rupert again. It is, faith, quite a comedy. But the result has been that I have had my meals alone, which is not so gay. Sophia is in bed, it turns out; Rupert out a-riding, on important business, of course! all he does is desperately important. And there you are—alone in your room, moping. God, child, how pale you are! What ails you then?"

"Molly," cried Madeleine, ignoring Lady Landale's question and feverishly folding the written sheet which lay under her hand, "if you love me, if ever you loved me, will you have this letter conveyed by a safe messenger to Scarthey, and given to René—to none but René, at once? Oh, Molly, it will be a service to me, you little guess of what moment!"

"*Voyez un peu!*" said Lady Landale coolly. "What trust in Molly, all at once! Aha, I thought it would come. If I love you? Hum, I'm not so sure about that. If ever I loved you?—a droll sort of plea, in truth, considering how you have requited my love!"

Madeleine turned a dazed look upon her sister, who stood surveying her, glowing like a jewel of dazzling radiance, from her setting of black mantle and black plumed hat. "So you will not!" she answered hopelessly, and let her forehead fall upon her hand without further protest.

"But I did not say I would not—as it happens I am going to the island myself. How you stare—oh you remember now do you? Who told you I wonder?—of course, such a couple as we are, Adrian and I, could not be divided from each other for over half a day, could we? By the way, I was to convey a gracious invitation to you too. Will you come with me?—No?—strange girl. So even give me the letter, I will take it to—no, not to René, 'tis addressed to Captain Smith, I see. Dear me—you don't mean to say, Madeleine, that you are corresponding with that person; that he is near us? What would Tanty say?"

"Oh, Molly, cease your scoffs," implored poor Madeleine, wearily. "You are angry with me, well, now rejoice, for I am punished—well punished. Oh, I would tell you all but I cannot! my heart is too sick. See, you may read the letter, and then you will understand—but for pity's sake go—Do not fail to go; he will be there on the island at dark—he expects *me*—Oh, Molly! I cannot explain—indeed I cannot, and there is no time, it will soon be dusk; but there is terrible danger in his being there at all."

Molly took the letter, turned it over with scornful fingers and then popped it in her pocket. "If he expects you," she asked, fixing cold, curious eyes on her sister's distress, "and he is in danger, why *don't* you go?"

A flush rose painfully to Madeleine's face, a sob to her throat. "Don't ask me," she murmured, turning away to hide her humiliation. "I have been deceived, he is not what I thought."

Lady Landale gazed at the shrinking figure for a little while in silence. Then remarking contemptuously: "Well you are a poor creature," turned upon her heel to leave her. As she passed the little altar, she paused to whisk a bunch of violets out of a vase and dry the stems upon her sister's quilt.

"Molly," cried Madeleine, in a frenzy, "give me back my letter, or go."

"I go, I go," said Lady Landale with a mocking laugh. "How sweet your violets smell!—There, do not agitate yourself: I'm going to meet your lover, my dear. I vow I am curious to see the famous man, at last."

CHAPTER XXIV

THE NIGHT

So the blood burned within her,
And thus it cried to her:
And there, beside the maize field
The other one was waiting—
He, the mysterious one.

Luteplayer's Song.

THE mantle of night had already fallen upon the land
when Lady Landale, closely wrapped in her warmest
furs, with face well ensconced under her close bonnet,
and arms buried to the elbow in her muff, sallied from
her room on the announcement that the carriage was
waiting. As, with her leisurely daintiness, she tripped it
down the stairs, she crossed Mr. Landale, and paused a
moment, ready for the skirmish, as she noticed the cynical curiosity with which he examined her.

"Whither, my fair sister," said he, ranging himself
with his best courtesy against the bannisters, "so late in
the day?"

"To my lord and master's side, of course," said Molly.

"Why—is not Adrian coming back to-night?"

"Apparently not, since he has graciously permitted me
to join him upon his rock. I trust you will not find it too
unhappy in our absence: that would be the crowning
misfortune of a day when everything seems to have gone
wrong. Sophia invisible with her vapours; Madeleine
with the megrim; and you in and out of the house as
excited and secret as the cat when she has licked all the
cream. I suppose I shall end by knowing what it is all
about. Meanwhile I think I shall enjoy the tranquillity
of the island—although I have actually to tear myself
away from the prospect of a tête-à-tête evening with
you."

But as Rupert's serenity was not to be moved, her

ladyship hereupon allowed herself to be escorted to the carriage without further parley.

As she drove away through the dark night, first down the level, well-metalled avenue, then along the uneven country road, and finally through the sand of the beach in which hoofs and tyres sank noiselessly, inches deep, Molly gave herself up, with almost childish zest to the leaven of imagination. . . . . Here, in this dark carriage, was reclining, not Lady Landale (whose fate deed had already been signed, sealed and delivered to bring her nothing but disappointment), but her happier sister, still confronted with the fascinating unknown, hurrying under cover of night, within sound of the sea, to that enthralling lure, a lover—a real lover, ardent, daring, *young*, ready to risk all, waiting to spread the wings of his boat, and carry her to the undiscovered country.

Glowing were these fleeting images of the "might have been," angry the sudden relapses into the prose of reality.

No, Madeleine, the coward, who thought she had loved her lover, was now in her room, weak and weeping, whilst he, no doubt, paced the deck in mad impatience (as a lover should), now tortured by the throes of anxiety, now hugging himself with the thought of his coming bliss . . . . that bliss that never was to be his. And in the carriage there was only Molly, the strong-hearted but the fettered by tie and vow, the slave for ever of a first girlish fancy but too successfully compassed; only Lady Landale rejoining her husband in his melancholy solitude ; Lady Landale who never—never! awful word! would know the joys which yonder poor fool had had within her grasp and yet had not clutched at.

Molly had read, as permitted, her sister's letter, and to some purpose ; and scorn of the girl who from some paltry quibble could abandon in danger the man she professed to love, filled her soul to the exclusion of any sisterly or ever womanly pity.

At the end of half an hour the carriage was stopped by the black shadow of a man, who seemed to spring up from the earth, and who, after a few rapid words interchanged with the coachman, extinguished both the lights, and then opened the door.

Leaning on the offered elbow Molly jumped down upon the yielding sand.

"Renè?" she asked; for the darkness even on the open beach was too thick to allow of recognition.

"René, your ladyship -or Mademoiselle is it?" answered the man in his unmistakable accent. "I must ask ; for, by the voice no one can tell, as your ladyship, or Mademoiselle knows—and the sky is black like a chimney."

"Lady Landale, René," and as he paused, she added, "My sister would not come."

"Ah, *mon Dieu!* She would not come," repeated the man in tones of dismay ; and the black shadow was struck into a moment of stillness. Then with an audible sigh Mr. Potter roused himself, and saying with melancholy resignation, "The boat is there, I shall be of return in a minute, My Lady," took the traveller's bag on his shoulder and disappeared.

The carriage began to crunch its way back in the darkness and Molly was left alone.

In front of her was a faint white line, where the rollers spread their foam with mournful restless fugue of long drawn roar and hissing sigh.

In the distance, now and then glancing on the crest of the dancing billows, shone the steady light of Scarthey. The rising wind whistled in the prickly star-grass and sea-holly. Beyond these, not a sight, not a sound—the earth was all mystery.

Molly looked at the light—marking the calm spot where her husband waited for her ; its very calm, its familiar placidity, monotony, enraged her ; she hearkened to the splashing, living waves, to the swift flying gusts of the storm wind, and her soul yearned to their life, and their mysteriousness.

What she longed for, she herself could not tell. No words can encompass the desire of pent-up young vitality for the unknown, for the ideal, for the impossible. But one thing was overpoweringly real : that was the dread of leaving just then the wide, the open world whose darkness was filled to her with living scenes of freedom and space, and blood-stirring emotions ; of re-entering the silent room under the light ; of consorting with the shadowy personality, her husband ; of feeling the web of his melancholy, his dreaminess, imprison as it were the

wings of her imagination and the thoughtful kindness of
his gaze, paralyse the course of her hot blood through
her veins.

And yet, thither she was going, must be going! Ah
Madeleine, fool—you may well weep, yonder on your
pillow, for the happiness that was yours and that you
have dropped from your feeble hands!

In a few minutes the black shadow re-appeared close
to her.

"If My Lady will lean on my shoulder, I shall lead her
to the boat." And after a few steps, the voice out of the
darkness proceeded in explanation : " I have not taken
a lantern, I have put out those of the carriage, for I must
tell My Lady, that since what arrived this morning, there
may be *gabelous*—they call them the preventive here—in
every corner, and the light might bring them, as it does
the night papilions, and . . . . as I thought Mademoiselle was to accompany you—they might have frightened
her. These people want to know so much!"

"I know nothing of what has happened this morning,
that you speak of as if the whole world must know,"
retorted Lady Landale coolly. "You are all hatching
plots and sitting on secrets, but nobody confides in me.
It seems then, that you expected Mademoiselle, my sister,
here for some purpose and that you regret she did not
come ; may I ask for an explanation ?"

A few moments elapsed before the man replied, and
then it was with embarrassment and diffidence : "For
sure, I am sorry, My Lady . . . . there have been misfortunes on the island this morning—nothing though to
concern her ladyship—and, as for Mademoiselle, mother
Margery would have liked to see her, no doubt. . . . .
and Maggie the wife also—and—and no doubt also Mademoiselle would have liked to come . . . . What do I
know ?"

"Oh, of course!" said Molly with her little note of
mocking laughter.

Then again they walked a while in silence. As René
lifted his mistress in his arms to carry her over the licking hissing foam, she resumed : "It is well, René, you
are discreet, but I am not such a fool as people seem to
think. As for her, you were right in thinking that she

might easily be frightened. She was afraid even to come out ! "

René shoved his boat off, and falling to his sculls, suddenly relapsed into the old vernacular : *"Ah Madame,"* he sighed, *c'est bien triste—un gentilhomme si beau--si brave !"*

During the crossing no further words passed between them.

"So brave—so handsome ?" The echo of the words came back to the woman in every lap of the water on the sides of the boat, in every strain of the oars.

The keel ground against the beach, and René leaped out to drag the boat free of the surf. As he did so, two blacker outlines segregated themselves from the darkness and a rough voice called out, subdued but distinct: "Savenaye, St. Malo !"

"Savenaye, St. Malo !" repeated René, and helped Lady Landale to alight. Then one of the figures darted forward and whispered a rapid sentence in the Frenchman's ear. René uttered an exclamation, but his mistress intervened with scant patience :

"My good René," said she, "take the bag into the peel, and come back for me. I have a message for these gentlemen."

René hesitated. As he did so a rustle of anger shook the lady in her silks and furs. "Do you hear me ?" she repeated, and he could guess how her little foot stamped the yielding sand.

"Oui, Madame," said he, hesitating no longer. Immediately the other two drew near. Molly could just see that they stood in all deference, cap in hand.

"Madam," began one of these in hurried words, "there is not a moment to be lost : the captain had to remain on board."

"What !" interrupted Lady Landale with much asperity, "not come in person !" She had been straining her eyes to make out something of her interlocutor's form, unable to reconcile her mind's picture with the coarse voice that addressed her—And now all her high expectations fell from her in an angry rush. "Have I come all this way to be met by a messenger ! Who are you ?"

"Madam," entreated the husky voice, "I am the mate of the *Peregrine.* The captain has directed me to beg and pray you not to be afraid, but to have good courage and confidence in us—the schooner is there; in five minutes you can be safe on board. You see, madam," continued the man with an earnestness that spoke well of his devotion, "the captain found he couldn't, he dared not leave the ship—he is the only one who knows the bearings of these waters here—any one of us might run her on the bank, and where would we be then, madam, and you, if we were found in daylight still in these parts?—'For God's sake, Curwen,' says he, 'implore the lady not to be afraid and tell her to trust, as she has promised,' so he says. And for God's sake, say I, madam, trust us. In five minutes you will be with him? Say the word, madam, am I to make the signal? There he is, eating his heart out. There are all the lads ready waiting for your foot on the ladder, to hoist sail. No time to lose, we are already behind. Shall I signal?"

Molly's heart beat violently; under the sudden impulse, the fascination of the black chasm, of the peril, the adventure, the unfathomed, took possession of her, and whirled her on.

"Yes," she said.

On the very utterance of the word the man, who had not yet spoken, uncovered a lantern, held it aloft, as rapidly replaced it under his coat, and moved away.

Almost immediately, against the black pall, behind the dim line of grey that marked the shore, suddenly sprang up three bright points in the form of a triangle.

It was as if all the darkness around had been filled with life; as if the first fulfilment of those promises with which it had been drawing this woman's soul was now held out to her to lure her further still.

"See, madam, how they watch!—By your leave."

And with no further warning, Molly felt herself seized with uncompromising, but deferential, energy, by a pair of powerful arms; lifted like a child, and carried away at a bear-like trot. By the splashing she judged it was through the first line of breakers. Then she was handed into another irresistible grasp. The boat lurched as the mate jumped in. Then:

"Now give way, lads," he said, "and let her have it. Those lights must not be burning longer than we can help. 'Tain't wholesome for any of us."

And under the pulse of four willing pairs of arms the

skiff, like a thing of life, clove the black waters and rose to the billows.

"You see, madam," explained the mate, "we could not do without the lights, to show us where she lay, and give us a straight course. We are all right so long as we keep that top 'un in the middle—but he won't be sorry, I reckon, when he can drop them overboard. They can't be seen from the offing yet, but it's astounding how far a light will reach on a night like this. Cheerily, lads, let her have it!"

But Molly heeded him not. She had abandoned herself to the thrilling delight of the excitement. The die was cast—not by her own hand, no one should be able to hold her responsible—she had been kidnapped. Come what might she must now see the adventure out.

The lights grew larger; presently a black mass, surmounted by a kind of greyish cloud, loomed through the pitch of the night; and next it was evident that the beacon was hanging over the side of a ship, illuminating its jagged leaping water line.

A voice, not too loud, yet, even through the distance, ringing clear in its earnestness sounded from above. "Boat ahoy! what boat is that?"

And promptly the helmsman by Molly's side returned: "Savenaye, St. Malo."

On the instant the lights went out. There was a creaking of block and cordage, and new ghostly clouds rose over the ship—sails loosened to the wind. As the skiff rowers came alongside, boat-hooks leaped into action and gripped the vessel; an arm, strong as steel, was held out for the passenger as she fearlessly put her foot on the ladder; another, a moment later, with masterful tenderness bent round her waist, and she was fairly lifted on board the *Peregrine*. But before her foot touched the deck, she felt upon her lips, laid like a burning seal, a passionate kiss; and her soul leaped up to it, as if called into sudden life from slumber, like the princess of fairy lore. She heard Madeleine's mysterious lover whisper in her ear: "At last! Oh, what I have suffered, thinking you would not come!"

From the warm shelter of her loosened cloak the violets in her bosom sent forth a wave of sweetness.

For a moment these two were in all creation alone to

each other, while in a circle the *Peregrine's* crew stood
apart in respectful silence : a broad grin of sympathy
upon the mouth of every mother's son.

Released at last, Lady Landale took a trembling step
on the deck. Into what strange world had she come
this night?

The schooner, like a mettled steed whose head is
suddenly set free, was already in motion, and with gentle
forward swaying leaps rising to the wave and gathering
speed under her swelling sails.

Captain Jack had seized Molly's hand, and the strong
clasp trembled round the little fingers ; he said no more
to her ; but, in tones vibrating with emotion which all the
men, now silently seeking their posts in the darkness,
could hear :

"My lads," he cried, "the lady is safe with us after
all. Who shall say that your skipper is not still Lucky
Smith? Thank you, my good fellows ! Now we have
yet to bring her safe the other side. Meanwhile—no
cheering, lads, you know why—there is a hundred guineas
more among you the hour we make St. Malo. Stand to,
every man. Up with those topsails !"

Scarcely had the last words been spoken when, from
the offing, on the wings of the wind, came a long-drawn
hail, faint through the distance, but yet fatally distinct :
"Ahoy, what schooner is that?"

Molly, who had not withdrawn her hand, felt a shock
pass over Captain Jack's frame. He turned abruptly, and
she could see him lean and strain in the direction of the
voice.

The call, after an interval, was repeated. But the
outlook was impenetrable, and it was weird indeed to feel
that they were seen yet could not see.

Molly, standing close by his side, knew in every fibre
of her own body that this man, to whom she seemed in
some inexplicable fashion already linked, was strongly
moved. Nevertheless she could hardly guess the extremity of the passion that shook him. It was the frenzy
of the rider who feels his horse about to fail him within a
span of the winning post ; of the leader whose men waver
at the actual point of victory. But the weakness of dismay was only momentary. Calm and clearness of mind
returned with the sense of emergency. He raised his

night-glass, with a steady hand this time, and scanned the depth of blackness in front of him: out of it after a moment, there seemed to shape itself the dim outline of a sail, and he knew that he had waited too long and had fallen in again with the preventive cutter. Then glancing aloft, he understood how it was that the *Peregrine* had been recognised.

The overcast sky had partly cleared to windward during the last minutes, a few stars glinted where hitherto nothing but the most impenetrable pall had hung. In the east, the rays of a yet invisible moon, edging with faint silver the banks of clouds just above the horizon, had made for the schooner a tell-tale background indeed.

On board no sound was heard now save the struggle of rope and canvas, the creaking of timber and the swift plashing rush of water against her rounded sides as she sped her course.

"Madeleine," he said, forcibly controlling his voice, and bringing, as he spoke, his face close to Molly's to peer anxiously at its indistinct white oval, "we are not free yet; but in a short time, with God's help, we shall have left those intermeddling fools yonder who would bar our way, miles out of the running. But I cannot remain with you a moment longer; I must take the helm myself. Oh, forgive me for having brought you to this! And, should you hear firing, for Heaven's sake do not lose courage. See now, I will bring you to your cabin; there you will find warmth and shelter. And in a little while, a very little while, I will return to you to tell you all is well. Come, my dearest love."

Gently he would have drawn her towards the little deck-cabin, guiding her steps, as yet untutored to the motion of the ship, when out of the black chasm, upon the weather bow of the *Peregrine*, leaped forth a yellow tongue of light fringed with red and encircled by a ruddy cloud; and three seconds later the boom of a gun broke with a dull, ominous clangour above the wrangling of sea and wind. Molly straightened herself. "What is that?" she asked.

"The warning gun," he answered, hurriedly, "to say that they mean to see who we are and that if we do not stop the next will be shotted. Time presses, Madeleine, go in—fear nothing! We shall soon be on their other side, out of sight in darkness again."

" I shall stop with you. Let no thought of me hinder you. I am not afraid. I want to see."

At these words the lover was struck with a surprise that melted into a proud and new joy. He had loved Madeleine for her woman's grace and her woman's heart ; now, he told himself, he must worship her also for her brave soul. But this was no time for useless words. It was not more unsafe for her on deck than in the cabin, and at the thought of her beside him during the coming struggle the strength of a god rose within him. " Come," he answered, briefly, and moved with her to the helm which a sailor silently surrendered to him whilst she steadied herself by holding to the binnacle- the only place on board at that time where (from sheer necessity) any light had been allowed to remain. It was faint enough, but the reflection from the compass board, as he bent to examine it, was sufficient to make just visible, with a dim fantastic glow, the strong beauty of his face, and put a flash into each wide dilated eye.

And thus did Molly, for the first time, see Captain Jack.

She sank down at the foot of the binnacle, her hands clasped round her knees, as if hugging the new rapture as closely to her as she could. And looking up at the alert figure before her which she now began to discern more clearly under the lightening sky ; at the face which she divined, although she could only see the watchful gleam of the eyes as now and again they sought her down in the shadow at his feet, she felt herself kindle in answer to the glow of his glorious life-energy. They were going, side by side, this young hero of romance and she, to fight their way through some unknown peril !

" Madeleine, my sweet bride, my brave love, they are about to fire again, and this time you will hear the shot burring ; but be not afraid, it will strike ahead of us."

Another flash sprang out of the night, much nearer this time, and louder, for it belched forth a shot which ploughed its way in the water across the schooner's bow.

" I am not afraid," said Molly again ; and she laughed a little fierce, nervous laugh.

" They are between us and the open sea. Thus far the luck is on their side. Had you come but half an hour sooner, Madeleine, we should be running as free as any king's ship. Now they think, no doubt, they will drive me on to the sand ; but," he tossed back his head with a superb gesture ; "there is no power from heaven or hell that can keep me out of my course to-night."

By this time the preventive cutter was faintly discernible two cables length on the larboard bow. There came another hail—a loud, husky bellow from over the water, "Schooner ahoy! Heave to, or we'll sink you!"

"Madeleine," said Captain Jack; "come closer to me, lie down, behind me, quick—The next shot will be in my rigging. Heave to?—with my treasures, my bride on board and a ten knot breeze. . . . !" And he looked down at Molly, laughing in his contempt. Then he shouted some order which brought the *Peregrine* some points more off the wind, and she bounded forward with renewed zest. "Sink us! Why don't you fire now, you lubbers?" He glanced back over his shoulder to see the beacon of Scarthey straight over the stern. "You have got us in line with the light, and that's your last chance. In another minute I shall be past you. Ah, I can see you now, my fine fellows!—Courage, Madeleine."

To Molly, of course, his words conveyed no meaning, except that the critical moment had come, that the ship which carried her flying upon the water like a living thing, eager, yet obedient in all its motions to the guiding will of the man beside her, was rushing to the fray. The thought fired her soul, and she sprang up to look over the side.

"What," she exclaimed, for the little cutter on close quarters looked insignificant indeed by the side of the noble vessel that so scornfully bore down on her. "Is that all!"

"They have a gun, and we have none," answered Captain Jack. "Down, Madeleine! down behind, in the name of God!"

"Why should I crouch if you stand up?"

The man's heart swelled within him ; but as he looked with proud admiration at the cloaked and hooded figure by his side, the cutter's gun fired for the third time. With roar and hiss the shot came over the bow of the schooner, as she dipped into the trough, and raking the deck, crashed through her side on the quarter. Molly gave a shriek and staggered.

A fearful malediction burst from Captain Jack's lips : he left the tiller and sprang to her.

One of the hands, believing his skipper to have been struck, ran to the helm, and again put the vessel on her proper course which a few moments later was to make her shoot past the revenue cutter.

"Wounded, Madeleine! Wounded through my fault! By the living God, they shall pay for this!"

"Oh," groaned Molly, "something has cut me in the arm and shoulder." Then rapidly gathering composure, "But it's not much, I can move it."

At one glance the sailor saw from the position of the shot hole in the vessel's side that the wound could only have been made by a splinter. But the possibility of exposing his beloved to such another risk was not to be borne—a murderous rush of blood flew to his brain.

The cutter, perceiving the tactics of the swifter schooner, was now tacking about with the intention of bringing the gun to bear upon her once more as she attempted to slip by. But Captain Jack in his new-fanned fury had made up his mind to a desperate cast of the die.

"Starboard, hard a starboard," he called out in a voice that his men had known well in old fighting days and which was heard as far as the cutter itself. "They shall not fire that gun again!"

With a brief, "Starboard it is, sir," the man who had taken the helm brought the ship round, and the silent, active crew in a trice were ready to go about. Majestically the schooner changed her course, and as the meaning of the manœuvre became fearfully apparent, shouts and oaths arose in confusion from the cutter.

"What are you going to do?" eagerly asked Molly, enthralled by the superb motion of the vessel under her foot as it swept round and increased speed upon the new tack.

He held her in his arms. His hand had sought her wounded shoulder and pressed the lacerated spot in his effort to staunch the precious blood that rose warm through the cloth, torturing his cold fingers.

"I am going to clear those men from our way to freedom and to love! I am going to sink that boat: they shall pay with their lives for this! Come to the other side, Madeleine, and watch how my stout *Peregrine* sweeps our course—and then I may see how these scoundrels have mangled you, my love. But, nay, this is no sight

20

for you.   Hold on close to me, sweet, and hide your eyes while they go."

He steadied himself firmly with one hand on the rigging.

Now musket shots flashed on board the cutter in quick succession, and sundry balls whizzed over the poop, intended for the helmsman by their side.   Captain Jack gnashed his teeth, as the menacing drone of one of them came perilously close to the beloved head by his cheek.

"Look out, every man.   We'll run her down !" he called.   His voice was like the blast of bugles.   Cheers broke out from every part of the ship, drowning the yells of execration and the shouts of fear from below.   And now, with irresistible sway, the rushing *Peregrine* heavy and powerful was closing and bearing down upon her frailer enemy.

There was a spell of suspense when all was silence, save the rush and turmoil of the waters, and the flapping of the cutter's sails, helpless for the moment in the teeth of the breeze.   Like a charging steed the schooner seemed to leap at her foe.   Then came the shock.   There was a brief check in her career, she rose by the head ; the rigging strained and sighed, the masts swayed groaning, but stood.   Over the bows, in the darkness was heard a long-drawn crash, was seen a white wall of foaming water rising silently to break the next moment with a great roar.

The cutter, struck obliquely amidships, was thrown straightway on her beam ends : the *Peregrine*, with every sail spread and swollen, held her as the preying bird with outstretched wings holds its quarry, and pressed her down until she began to fill and settle.   It was with wide-open eyes, with eager, throbbing heart that Molly watched it all.

"Lights, my lads," cried Captain Jack, with a shout of exultation, when the anxious instant had passed. "Take in every man you can save but handspike is the word for the first who shows fight !   Curwen, do you get her clear again."

All around upon the deck, sprang rumour and turmoil, came shouts and sounds of scuffling and the rushing of feet ; from the blank waters came piteous calls for help. But paying little heed to aught but Molly, Captain Jack seized a lighted lantern from the hands of a passing sailor and drew her aside.

Fevered with pain and fascinated by the horror of fight and death's doings, yet instinctively remembering to pull her hood over her face, she allowed herself to be taken into the little deck cabin.

He placed the lantern upon the table :

"Rest here," he said quickly, once more striving to see her beneath the jealous shade. "I must find out if anything is amiss on board the ship and attend to these drowning men—even before you, my darling! But I shall be back instantly. You are not faint?"

The light shone full on his features which Molly eagerly scanned from her safe recess. When she met his eyes, full of the triumph of love and hope, her soul broke into fierce revolt—again she felt upon her lips that kiss of young passionate love that had been the first her life had ever known. . . . and might be the last, for the disclosure was approaching apace.

She was glad of the respite.

"Go," she said with as much firmness as she could muster. "Let me not stand between you and your duty. I am strong."

Strong indeed—Captain Jack might have wondered whence had come to this gentle Madeleine this lioness-strength of soul and body, had he had time to wonder, time for aught but his love thoughts and his fury, as he dashed back again panting for the moment when he could have her to himself.

"Any damage, Curwen?"

"Bowsprit broken, and larboard bulwark stove in, otherwise everything has stood."

"Casualties?"

"No, sir. We have three of the cutter's men on board already. They swarmed over the bows. One had his cutlass out and had the devil's impudence to claim the schooner, but a boat-hook soon brought him to reason. There they be, sir," pointing to a darker group huddled round the mast. "I have lowered the gig to see if we can pick up the others, damn them!"

"As soon as they are all on board bring them aft, I will speak to them."

When, with a master's eye, he had rapidly inspected

his vessel from the hold to the rigging, without finding aught to cause anxiety for its safety, Captain Jack returned to the poop, and there found the party of prisoners arranged under the strong guard of his own crew. Molly stood, wrapped up in her cloak, at the door of the cabin, watching.

One of the revenue men came forward and attempted to speak—but the captain impatiently cut him short.

"I have no time to waste in talk, my man," he said commandingly. "How many were you on board the cutter?"

"Nine," answered the man sullenly.

"How many have we got here?"

"Six, sir," interposed Curwen. "Those three," pointing to three disconsolate and dripping figures, "were all we could pick up."

"Hark ye, fellows," said the captain. "You barred my road, I had to clear you away. You tried to sink me, I had to sink you. You have lost three of your shipmates, you have yourselves to blame for it; your shot has drawn blood from one for whom I would have cut down forty times your number. I will send you back to shore. Away with you! No, I will hear nothing. Let them have the gig, Curwen, and four oars."

"And now God speed the *Peregrine*," cried Jack Smith, as the revenue men pushed off in the direction of the light and the wind was again swelling every sail of his gallant ship. "We are well out of our scrape. Shape her course for St. Malo, Curwen. If this wind holds we should be there by the nineteenth in the morning, at latest."

CHAPTER XXV

THE FIGHT FOR THE OPEN

As o'er the grass, beneath the larches there
We gaily stepped, the high noon overhead,
Then Love was born—was born so strong and fair.
Knowest thou! Love is dead.

Gipsy Song.

At last he was free. He had wrested his bride and the treasure trusted to his honour from the snares so unexpectedly laid on his path ; whatever troubles might remain stored against him in the dim distance of time, he would not reck them now. The present and the immediate future were full of splendour and triumph.

All those golden schemes worked out under yonder light of Scarthey—God bless it—now receding in the gloom behind his swift running ship, whether in the long watches of the night, or in the recent fevered resolves of imminent danger, they had come to pass after all! And she, the light of his life, was with him. She had trusted her happiness, her honour, herself, to his love. The thought illumined his brain with glory as he rushed back to the silent muffled figure that still stood awaiting his coming.

"At last!" he said, panting in the excess of his joy ; "At last, Madeleine . . . . I can hardly believe it! But selfish brute that I am, you must be crushed with fatigue. My brave darling, you would make me forget your tender woman's frame, and you are wounded!"

Supporting her—for the ship, reaching the open sea, had begun to roll more wildly—he led her back into the little room now lighted by the fitful rays of a swinging lamp. With head averted, she suffered herself to be seated on a kind of sofa couch.

When he had closed the door, he seized her hand, on which ran streaks of half-dried blood, and covered it with kisses.

309

"Ah, Madeleine! here in the sanctuary I had prepared for you, where I thought you would be so safe, so guarded, tell me that you forgive me for having brought this injury to you. Wounded, torn, bleeding . . . . I who would give all my blood, my life, if life were not so precious to me now that you have come into it, to save you from the slightest pain! At least here you are secure, here you can rest, but—but there is no one to wait on you, Madeleine." He fell on his knees beside her. "Madeleine, my wife, you must let me tend you." Then, as she shivered slightly, but did not turn to him, he went on in tones of the most restrained tenderness mingled with humblest pleading :

"Had it not been for your accident, I had not ventured even to cross the threshold of this room. But your wound must be dressed ; darling, darling, allow me, forgive me ; the risk is too great."

Rising to his feet again he gently pulled at her cloak. Molly spoke not a word, but untied it at the neck and let it fall away from her fair young body ; and keeping her hooded face still rigidly averted, she surrendered her wounded arm.

He muttered words of distress at the sight of the broad blood stains ; stepped hurriedly to a little cupboard where such surgical stores as might be required on board were hoarded, and having selected scissors, lint, and bandages, came back and again knelt down by her side to cut off, with eager, compassionate hands, the torn and maculated sleeve.

The wound was but a surface laceration, and a man would not have given a thought to it in the circumstances. But to see this soft, white woman's skin, bruised black in parts, torn with a horrid red gap in others; to see the beauty of this round arm thus brutally marred, thus twitching with pain—it was monstrous, hideously unnatural in the lover's eyes!

With tenderness, but unflinchingly, he laved the mangled skin with cool, fresh water ; pulled out, with far greater torture to himself than to her, some remaining splinters embedded in the flesh ; covered the wound with lint, and finished the operation by a bandage as neat as his neat sailor's touch, coupled with some knowledge of surgery, gained in the experiences of his privateering days, could

accomplish it.   He spoke little : only a word of encouragement, of admiration for her fortitude now and then ;
and she spoke not at all during the ministration.   She had
raised her other hand to her eyes, with a gesture natural to
one bracing herself to endurance, and had kept it there
until, his task completed, her silence, the manner in which
she hid her face from him awoke in him all that was best
and loftiest in his generous heart.

As he rose to his feet and stood before her, he too dared
not speak for fear of bruising what he deemed an exquisite maidenliness, before which his manhood was
abashed at itself.   For some moments there was no sound
in the cabin save that of the swift rushing waters behind
the wooden walls and of the labour and life of the ship
under full sail ; then he saw the tumultuous rising of her
bosom, and thought she was weeping.

" Madeleine," he cried with passionate anxiety, " speak !
Let me see your face—are you faint ?   Lie upon this
couch.   Let me get you wine—oh that these days were
passed and I could call you wife and never leave you !
Madeleine, my love, speak ! "

Molly rose to her feet, and with a gesture of anger
threw off her hood and turned round upon him.   And
there in the light of the lamp, he glared like one distraught
at the raven locks, the burning eyes of a strange woman.

She was very pale.

" No," said Molly, defiantly, when twice or thrice his
laboured breath had marked the passing of the horrible
moment, " I am not Madeleine."   Then she tried to
smile ; but unconsciously she was frightened, and the
smile died unformed as she pursued at random :

" You know me—perhaps by hearsay—as I know you,
Captain Smith."

But he, shivering under the coldness of his disappointment, answered in a kind of weary whisper :

" Who are you—you who speak with her voice, who
stand at her height and move and walk as she does ?   I
have seen you surely—Ah, I know . . . . Madam, what
a cruel mockery !   And she, where is she ? "

Still staring at her with widely dilated eyes, he seized
his forehead between his hands.   The gesture was one
of utter despair.   Before this weakness Molly promptly
resumed the superiority of self-possession.

"Yes," she said, and this time the smile came back to her face, "I am Lady Landale, and my sister Madeleine —I grieve to have to say so—has not had that courage for which you gave her credit to-night."

Little was required at a moment like this to transmute such thoughts as seethed in the man's head to a burst of fury. Fury is action, and action a relief to the strained heart. There was a half-concealed, unintended mockery in her tones which brought a sudden fire of anger to his eyes. He raised both hands and shook them fiercely above his head :

"But why—why in the name of heaven—has such a trick been played on me . . . . at such a time ? "

He paused, and trembling with the effort, restrained himself to a more decent bearing before the woman, the lady, the friend's wife. His arms fell by his side, and he repeated in lower tones, though the flame of his gaze could not be subdued :

"Why this deception, this playing with the blindness of my love ? Why this comedy, which has already had one act so tragic ?—Yes, think of it, madam, think of the tragedy this is now in my life, since she is left behind and I never now, with these men's lives to account for, may go back and claim her who has given me her troth ! Already I staked the fortune of my trust, on the bare chance that she would come. What though her heart failed her at the eleventh hour ?—God forgive her for it ! —surely she never sanctioned this masquerade ? . . . . Oh no ! she would not stoop to such an act, and human life is not a thing to jest upon. She never played this trick, the thought is too odious. What have you done ! Had I known, had I had word sooner—but half an hour sooner—those corpses now rolling under the wave with their sunken ship would still be live men and warm. . . . . And I—I should not be the hopeless outlaw, the actual murderer that this night's work has made of me ! "

His voice by degrees rose once more to the utmost ring of bitterness and anger. Molly, who had restored her cloak to her shoulders and sat down, ensconced in it as closely as her swaddled arm would allow her, contemplated him with a curious mixture of delight and terror ; delight in his vigour, his beauty, above everything in his mastery and strength ; and delight again at the new thrill of the fear it imposed upon her daring soul. Then she flared into rage at the thought of the coward of her blood who had broken faith with such a man as this, and she melted all into sympathy with his anger—A right proper man most cruelly used and most justifiably wrathful !

And she, being a woman whose face was at most times as a book on which to read the working of her soul, there was something in her look, as in silence she listened and gazed upon him, which struck him suddenly dumb. Such a look on a face so like, yet so unlike, that of his love was startling in the extreme—horrible.

He stepped back, and made as if he would have rushed from the room. Then bethinking himself that he was a madman, he drew a chair near her in a contrary mood, sat down, and fixed his eyes upon her very steadily.

She dropped her long lids, and demurely composed her features by some instinct that women have, rather than from any sense of the impression she had produced.

A little while they sat thus again in silence. In the silence, the rolling of the ship and the manner in which, as she raced on her way, she seemed to breathe and strain, worked in with the mood of each ; in his, with the storm and stress of his soul ; in hers, as the very expression of her new freedom and reckless pleasure.

Then he spoke ; the strong emotion that had warmed her had now left his voice. It was cold and scornful.

" Madam, I await your explanation. So far, I find myself only the victim of a trick as unworthy and cruel as it is purposeless."

She had delayed carrying out her mission with the most definite perverseness. She could not but acknowledge the justice of his reproof, realise the sorry part she must play in his eyes, the inexcusable folly of the whole proceeding, and yet she was strung to a very lively indignation by the tone he had assumed, and suddenly saw herself in the light of a most disinterested and injured virtue.

" Captain Smith," she exclaimed, flashing a hot glance at him, " you assume strangely the right to be angry with me ! Be angry if you will with things as they are ; rail against fate if you will, but be grateful to me.—I have risked much to serve you."

The whole expression of his face changed abruptly to one of eager, almost entreating, inquiry.

"Do me the favour," she continued, "to look into the pocket of my cloak—my arm hurts me if I move—you will find there a letter addressed to you. I was adjured to see that it should reach you in safety. I promised to place it in your own hands. This could hardly have been done sooner, as you know."

The words all at once seemed to alter the whole situation. He sprang up and came to her quickly.

"Oh, forgive me, make allowances for me, Lady Landale, I am quite distracted!" There had returned a tinge of hope into his voice. "Where is it?" he eagerly asked, seeking, as directed, for the pocket. "Ah!" and mechanically repeating, "Forgive me!" he drew out the letter at last and retreated, feverishly opening it under the light of the lamp.

Molly had turned round to watch. Up to this she had felt no regret for his disillusion, only an irritable heat of temper that he should waste so much love upon so poor an object. But now all her heart went to him as she saw the sudden greyness that fell on his face from the reading of the very first line; there was no indignation, no blood-stirring emotion; it was as if a cold pall had fallen upon his generous spirit. The very room looked darker when the fire within the brave soul was thus all of a sudden extinguished.

He read on slowly, with a kind of dull obstinacy, and when he came to the miserable end continued looking at the paper for the moment. Then his hand fell; slowly the letter fluttered to the floor, and he let his eyes rest unseeingly, wonderingly upon the messenger.

After a little while words broke from him, toneless, the mere echo of dazed thoughts: "It is over, all over. She has lost her trust. She does not love me any more."

He picked up the letter again, and sitting down placed it in front of him on the table. "'Tis a cruel letter, madam, that you have brought me," he said then, looking up at Molly with the most extraordinary pain in his eyes. "A cruel letter! Yet I am the same man now that I was this morning when she swore she would trust me to the end—and she could not trust me a few hours longer! Why did you not speak? One word from you as you stepped upon the ship would have saved my soul from

the guilt of these men's death!" Then with a sharper
uplifting of his voice, as a new aspect of his misfortune
struck him: "And you—you, too! What have I to do
with you, Adrian's wife? He does not know?"

She did not reply, and he cried out, clapping his hands
together:

"It only wanted this. My God, it is I—I, his friend,
who owes him so much, who am to cause him such fear,
such misery! Do you know, madam, that it is impossible
that I should restore you to him for days yet. And then
when, and where, and how? God knows! Nothing
must now come between me and my trust. I have
already dishonourably endangered it. To attempt to return with you to-night, as perhaps you fancy I will—as,
of course, I would instantly do had I alone myself and
you to consider, would be little short of madness. It
would mean utter ruin to many whom I have pledged
myself to serve. And yet Adrian—my honour pulls me
two ways—poor Adrian! What dumb devil possessed
you that you did not speak before. Had you no thought
for your woman's good name? Ill-fated venture, ill-fated
venture, indeed! Would God that shot had met me in its
way—had only my task been accomplished!"

He buried his head in his hands.

Lady Landale flushed and paled alternately, parted her
lips to speak, and closed them once more. What could
she say, and how excuse herself? She did not repent
what she had done, though it had been sin all round; she
had little reck of her woman's good name, as he called it;
the death of the excise men weighed but lightly, if at all,
upon her conscience; the thought of Adrian was only
then a distasteful memory to be thrust away; nay—even
this man's grief could not temper the wild joy that was in
her soul to-night. Fevered with fatigue, with excitement,
by her wound, her blood ran burning in her veins, and
beat faster in every pulse.

And as she felt the ship rise and fall, and knew that
each motion was an onward leap that separated her
further and ever further from dull home and dull husband,
and isolated her ever more completely with her sister's
lover, she exulted in her heart.

Presently he lifted his head.

"Forgive me," he said, "I believe that you meant

most kindly, and as you say, I should be grateful. Your
service is ill-requited by my reproaches, and you have
run risk indeed—merciful Heaven, had my old friend's
wife been killed upon my ship through my doings! But
you see I cannot command myself; you see how I am
situated. You must forgive me. All that can be done to
restore you to your home as soon as possible shall be
done, and all, meanwhile, to mitigate the discomfort you
must suffer here—And for your good intention to her and
me, I thank you."

He had risen, and now bowed with a dignity that sat
on his sailor freedom in no wise awkwardly. She, too,
with an effort, stood up as if to arrest his imminent departure. A tall woman, and he but of average height,
their eyes were nearly on a level. For a second or two her
dark gaze sought his with a strange hesitation, and then,
as if the truth in him awoke all the truth in her, the
natural daring of her spirit rose proudly to meet this kindred soul. She would let no falsehood, no craven feminine subterfuge intervene between them.

"Do not thank me," she exclaimed, glowing with a
brilliant scorn in which the greatness of her beauty, all
worn as she was, struck him into surprise, yet evoked no
spark of admiration. "What I did I did, to gratify myself. Oh, aye, if I were as other women I should smile
and take your compliments, and pose as the martyr and
as the self-sacrificing devoted sister. But I will not. It
was nothing to me how Madeleine got in or out of her
love scrapes. I would not have gone one step to help
her break her promise to you, or even to save your life,
but that it pleased me so to do. Madeleine has never
chosen to make me her confidant. I would have let her
manage her own affairs gaily, had I had better things to
occupy my mind—but I had not, Captain Smith. Life at
Pulwick is monotonous. I have roaming blood in my
veins: the adventure tempted, amused me, fascinated
me—and there you have the truth! Of course I could
have given the letter to the men and sent them back to
you with it—it was not because of my promise that I did
not do it. Of course I could have spoken the instant I
got on board, perhaps——" here a flood of colour dyed
her face with a gorgeous conscious crimson, and a dimple faintly came and went at the corner of her mouth,

"perhaps I would have spoken.   But then, you must remember, you closed my lips!"

"My God!" said Captain Jack, and looked at her with
a sort of horror.

But this she could not see for her eyes were downcast.
"And now that I have come," she went on, and would
have added, "I am glad I did," but that all of a sudden a
new bashfulness came upon her, and she stammered instead, incoherently: "As for Adrian—René knew I had
a message for you, and René will tell him—he is not stupid
—you know—René, I mean."

"I am glad," answered the man gravely, after a pause,
"if you have reasonable grounds for believing that your
husband knows you to be on my ship.   He will then be
the less anxious at your disappearance: for he knows too,
madam, that his wife will be as honoured and as guarded
in my charge as she would be in her mother's house."

He bowed again in a stately way and then immediately
left her.

Molly sank back upon her couch, and she could not
have said why, burst into tears.   She felt cold now, and
broken, and her stiffening wound pained her.   But nevertheless, as she lay upon the little velvet pillow, and wept
her rare tears were strangling sobs, the very ache of her
wound had a strange savour that she would not have
exchanged for any past content.

René, having obeyed his mistress's orders, and left her
alone with the sailors on the beach, withdrew within the
shelter of the door, but remained waiting, near enough
to be at hand in case he should be called.

It was still pitch dark and the rollers growled under a
rough wind; he could catch the sound of a man's voice,
now and again, between the clamour of the sea and the
wuthering of the air, but could not distinguish a word.
Presently, however, this ceased, and there came to him the
unmistakable regular beat of oars retreating.   The interview was over, and breathing a sigh of relief at the thought
that, at last, his master's friend would soon be setting
on his way to safety, the servant emerged to seek her
ladyship.

A few minutes later he dashed into Sir Adrian's room
with a livid face, and poured forth a confused tale:

Milady had landed without Mademoiselle ; had stopped
to speak to two of the *Peregrine,* whilst he waited apart.
The men had departed in their boat.

"The *Peregrine* men ! But the ship has been out of
sight these eight hours !" ejaculated Sir Adrian, bewildered. Then, catching fear from his servant's distraught
countenance :

"My wife," he exclaimed, bounding up ; and added,
"you left her, Renny ? "

The man struck his breast : he had searched and called
. . . . My Lady was nowhere to be found. "As God is
my witness," he repeated, "I was within call. My Lady
ordered me to leave her. Your honour knows My Lady
has to be obeyed."

"Get lanterns !" said Sir Adrian, the anguish of a
greater dread driving the blood to his heart. Even to one
who knew the ground well, the isle of Scarthey, on a
black, stormy night, with the tide high, was no safe
wandering ground. For a moment, the two—comrades
of so many miserable hours—faced each other with
white and haggard faces. Then with the same deadly
fear in their hearts, they hurried out into the soughing
wind, down to the beach, baited on all sides by the swift-
darting hissing surf. Running their lanterns close to the
ground, they soon found, by the trampled marks upon
the sand, where the conclave had been held. From thence
a double row of heavy footprints led to the shelving bit
of beach where it was the custom for boats to land from
seawards.

"See, your honour, see," cried René, in deepest agitation, "the print of this little shoe, here—and there, and
here again, right down to the water's edge. Thank God
—thank God ! My Lady has had no accident. She has
gone with the sailors to the boat. Ah ! here the tide has
come—we can see no farther."

"But why should she have gone with them ? " came,
after a moment, Sir Adrian's voice out of the darkness.
"Surely that is strange—and yet. . . . . Yes, that is
indeed her foot-print in the sand."

"And if your honour will look to sea, he will perceive
the ship's lights yonder, upon the water. That is the captain's ship. . . . Your honour, I must avow to you that I
have concealed something from you—it was wrong, in-

deed, and now I am punished—but that poor Monsieur
the Captain, I was so sorry for him, and he so enamoured.
He had made a plan to lift off Mademoiselle Madeleine
with him to-night, marry her in France; and that was
why he came back again, at the risk of his life. He sup-
plicated me not to tell you, for fear you would wish to
prevent it, or think it your duty to. Mademoiselle had
promised, it seemed, and he was mad with her joy, the
poor gentleman! and as sure of her faith as if she had
been a saint in Heaven. But My Lady came alone, your
honour, as I said. The courage had failed to Mademoiselle, I suppose, at the last moment, and Madame bore
a message to the captain. But the captain was not able
to leave his ship, it seems; and, my faith," cried Mr.
Potter; his spirits rising, as the first ghastly dread left
him, "the mystery explains itself! It is quite simple,
your honour will see. As the captain did not come to the
island, according to his promise to Mademoiselle—he had
good reasons, no doubt—Madame went herself to his
ship with her message. She had the spirit for it—Ah! if
Mademoiselle had had but a little of it to-night, we should
not be where we are!"

Sir Adrian caught at the suggestion out of the depths of
his despair. "You are right, Renny, you must be right.
Yet, on this rough sea, in this black night—what madness! The boat, instantly; and let us row for those
lights as we never rowed before!"

Even as the words were uttered the treble glimmer
vanished. In vain they strained their eyes: save for the
luminous streak cast by their own beacon lamp, the
gloom was unbroken.

"His honour will see, a boat will be landing instantly
with My Lady safe and sound," said René at last. But
his voice lacked confidence, and Sir Adrian groaned
aloud.

And so they stood alone in silence, forced into inaction, that most cruel addition to suspense, by the darkness and the waters which hemmed them in upon every
side. The vision of twenty dangerous places where one
impetuous footfall might have hurled his darling into the
cruel beating waves painted themselves—a hideous phan-
tasmagory—upon Sir Adrian's brain. Had the merciless
waters of the earth that had murdered the mother, grasped

at the child's life also? He raised his voice in a wild cry, it seemed as if the wind caught it from him and tore it into shreds.

"Hark!" whispered René, and clasped his master's icy hand. Like an echo of Sir Adrian's cry, the far-off ring of a human voice had risen from the sea.

Again it came.

"*C'est de la mer, Monseigneur!*" panted the man; even as he spoke the darkness began to lift. Above their heads, unnoticed, the clouds had been rifted apart beneath the breath of the north wind; the horizon widened, a misty wing-like shape was suddenly visible against the receding gloom.

The captain's ship! The *Peregrine!*

As master and man peered outward as if awaiting unconsciously some imminent solution from the gliding spectre, it seemed as if the night suddenly opened on the left to shoot forth a burst of red fire. A few seconds later, the hollow boom of cannon shook the air around them. Sir Adrian's nails were driven into René's hands.

The flaming messenger had carried to both minds an instant knowledge of the new danger.

"Great Heavens!" muttered Adrian. "He will surrender; he must surrender! He could not be so base, so wicked, as to fight and endanger *her!*"

But the servant's keener sight, trained by long stormy nights of watching, was following in its dwindling, mysterious course that misty vision in which he thought to recognize the *Peregrine.*

"*Elle file, elle file joliment la goëlette!* Mother of Heaven, there goes the gun again! I never thought my blood would turn to water only to hear the sound of one like this. But your honour must not be discouraged; he can surely trust the captain. Ah, the clouds—I can see no more."

The wild blast gathering fresh droves of vapour from the huddled masses on the horizon was now, in truth, herding them fiercely across the spaces it had cleared a few moments before. Confused shouts, strange clamour seemed to ring out across the waves to the listeners: or it might have been only the triumphant howlings of the rising storm.

"Will not your honour come in? The rain is falling."

"No, Renny, no, give me my lantern again, friend, and let us examine anew."

Both knew it to be of no avail, but physically and mentally to move about was, at least, better than to stand still. Step by step they scanned afresh the sand, the shingle, the rocks, the walls, to return once more to the trace of the slender feet, leading beside the great double track of heavy sea boots to the water's edge.

Sir Adrian knelt down and gazed at the last little imprint that seemed to mock him with the same elusive daintiness as Molly herself, as if he could draw from it the answer to the riddle.

René endeavouring to stand between his master and the driving blast laid down his lantern too, and strove by thumping his breast vigorously to infuse a little warmth into his numbed limbs and at the same time to relieve his overcharged feelings.

As he paused at length, out of breath, the noise of a methodical thud and splash of oars arose, above the tumult of the elements, very near to them, upon their left.

Sir Adrian sprang to his feet.

"She returns, she returns," shouted René, capering, in the excess of the sudden joy, and waving his lantern; then he sent forth a vigorous hail which was instantly answered close by the shore.

"Hold up your light, your honour—ah, your honour, did I not say it?—while I go to help Madame. Now then, you others down there," running to the landing spot, "make for the light!"

The keel ground upon the shingle.

"My Lady first," shouted René.

Some one leaped up in the boat and flung him a rope with a curse.

"The lady, ay, ay, my lad, you'd better go and catch her yourself. There she goes," pointing enigmatically behind him with his thumb.

Sir Adrian, unable to restrain his impatience, ran forward too, and threw the light of his lantern upon the dark figures now rising one by one and pressing forward. Five or six men, drenched from head to foot, swearing and grumbling; with faces pinched with cold, all lowering with the same expression of anger and resentment and

21

shining whitely at him out of the confusion. He saw the emptying seats, the shipped oars, the name *Peregrine* in black letters upon the white paint of the dingey; and she? . . . . she was not there!

The revulsion of feeling was so cruel that for a while he seemed turned to stone, even his mind becoming blank. The waves lashed in up to his knees; he never felt them.

René's strong hands came at last to drag him away, and then René's voice, in a hot whisper close to his ear, aroused him:

"It is good news, your honour, after all, good news. My Lady is on board the *Peregrine*. I made these men speak. They are the revenue men—that God may damn them! and they were after the captain; but he ran down their cutter, that brave captain. And these are all that were saved from her, for she sank like a stone. The *Peregrine* is as sound as a bell, they say—ah, she is a good ship! And the captain, out of his kind heart, sent these villains ashore in his own boat, instead of braining them or throwing them overboard. But they saw a lady beside him the whole time, tall, in a great black cloak. My Lady in her black cloak, just as she landed here. Of course Monsieur the Captain could not have sent her back home with these brigands then—not even a message—that would have compromised his honour. But his honour can see now how it is. And though My Lady has been carried out to sea, he knows now that she is safe."

CHAPTER XXVI

THE THREE COLOURS

THE sun was high above the Welsh hills ; the *Peregrine* had sheered her way through a hundred miles or more of fretted waters before her captain, in his hammock slung for the nonce near the men's quarters, stirred from his profound sleep—nature's kind restorer to healthy brain and limbs—after the ceaseless fatigue and emotions of the last thirty-six hours.

As he leaped to his feet out of the swinging canvas, the usual vigour of life coursing through every fibre of him, he fell to wondering, in half-awake fashion, at the meaning of the unwonted weight lurking in some back recess of consciousness.

Then memory, the ruthless, arose and buffeted his soul.

The one thing had failed him without which all else was as nothing ; fate, and his own hot blood, had conspired to place his heart's desire beyond all reasonable hope. Certain phrases in Madeleine's letter crossed and recrossed his mind, bringing now an unwonted sting of anger, now the old cruel pain of last night. The thought of the hateful complication introduced into his already sufficiently involved affairs by the involuntary kidnapping of his friend's wife filled him with a sense of impotent irritation, very foreign to his temper ; and as certain looks and words of the unwished-for prisoner flashed back upon him, a hot colour rose, even in his solitude, to his wholesome brown cheek.

But in spite of all, in spite of reason and feeling alike his essential buoyancy asserted itself. He could not despair. He had not been given this vigour of soul and body to sit down under misfortune. Resignation was for the poor of heart ; only cravens gave up while it was yet possible to act. His fair ship was speeding with him as

323

he loved to feel her speed ; around him spread the vast
spaces in which his spirit rejoiced—salt sea and vaulted
heavens ; the full air of the open, the brisk dash of the
wind filled him with physical exhilaration at every breath,
and tingled in his veins ; the sporting blood, which had
come to him from generations of hunting squires, found
all its craving satisfied in this coursing across the green
ocean fields, and the added element of danger was as the
sting of the brine to his palate.   What—despair now ?
with his perilous enterprise all but accomplished, the
whole world, save one country, before him, and Madeleine unwed !   Another might, but not Jack Smith ; not
Hubert Cochrane !

He was actually trolling out the stave of a song as
he sprang up the companion ladder after his rough breakfast in the galley, but the sound expired at the sight of
the distant flutter of a woman's scarf in the stern of the
ship.   He halted and ran his fingers through his crisp
hair with an expressive gesture of almost comical perplexity ; all would be plain sailing enough, with hope at
the prow again, but for this—he stamped his foot to
choke down the oath of qualification—this encumbrance.
Adrian's wife and Madeleine's sister, as such entitled to
all honour, all care, and devotion ; and yet, as such again,
hideously, doubly unwelcome to him !

As he stood, biting his lips, while the gorgeous sunshine of the young spring morning beat down upon his
bare head, the brawny figure of the mate, his mahogany-
tinted face wrinkled into as stiff a grin as if it had been
indeed carved out of the wood in question, intervened between his abstracted gaze and the restless amber beyond.

" It's a fine day, sir," by way of opening conversation.

The irrepressible satisfaction conveyed by the wide
display of tobacco-stained teeth, by the twinkle in the
hard, honest eyes called up a queer, rueful grimace to the
other man's face.

" Do you know, Curwen," he said, " that you brought
me the wrong young lady last night ? "

The sailor jumped back in amazement.   " The wrong
young lady, sir," staring with starting, incredulous eyeballs, " the wrong, young lady ! " here he clapped his
thigh, " Well of all—the wrong young lady !   Are you
quite sure, sir ? "

Captain Jack laughed aloud. But it was with a bitter twist at the corners of his lips.

"Well I'm ——," said poor Curwen. All his importance and self-satisfaction had left him as suddenly as the starch a soused collar. He scanned his master's face with almost pathetic anxiety.

"Oh, I don't blame you—you did your part all right. Why, I myself fell into the same mistake, and we had not much time for finding it out, had we? The lady you see—the lady—she is the other lady's sister and she came with a message. And so we carried her off before we knew where we were—or she either," added Captain Jack as a mendacious after thought.

"Well I'm ——," reiterated Curwen who then rubbed his scrubby, bristling chin, scratched his poll and finally broke into another grin—this time of the kind classified as sheepish.

"And what'll be to do now?"

"By the God that made me, I haven't a notion! We must take all the care of her we can, of course. Serve her her meals in her cabin, as was arranged, and see that she is attended to, just as the other young lady would have been you know, only that I think she had better be served alone, and I shall mess downstairs as usual. And then if we can leave her at St. Malo, we shall. But it must be in all safety, Curwen, for it's a terrible responsibility. Happily we have now the time to think. Meanwhile I have slept like a log and she—I see is astir before me."

"Lord bless you, sir, she has been up these two hours! Walking the deck like a sailor, and asking about things and enjoying them like. Ah, she is a rare lady, that she is! And it is the wrong one—well this is a go! And I was remarking to Bill Baxter, just now, that it was just our captain's luck to have found such a regular sailor's young woman, so I said—begging pardon for the word. And not more than he is worth, says he, and so said I also. And she the wrong lady after all! Well, it's a curious thing, sir, nobody could be like to guess it from her. She's a well-plucked one, with her wound and all. She made me look at it this morning, when I brought her a cup of coffee and a bite: 'You're old enough to be my father,' says she, as pretty as can be, 'so you shall be

doctor as well as lady's maid : and, if you've got a girl
of your own, it'll be a story to tell her by the fire at night,
when you're home again,' so she said ; and never winced
when I put my great fingers on her arm.   I was all of a
tremble, I declare, with her a smiling up at me, but the
wound—it's doing finely ; healing as nice as ever I see,
and not a sign of sickness on her.   The very lady as I
was saying, for our captain—but here she comes."

This was an unwontedly long speech for Curwen ; and,
silent again, he effaced himself discreetly, just in time to
avoid the angry ejaculation that had sprung to his captain's lips, but not without a backward glance of admiration at the tall, alert figure now bearing down in their
direction with steps already firmly balanced to the movement of the ship.

At a little distance from Captain Jack, Molly paused as
if to scrutinise the horizon, and enjoy the invigorating
atmosphere.   In reality her heart was beating fast, her
breath came short ; and the gaze she flung from the faint
outline of coast upon one side to the vast monotony of
sparkling sea upon the other conveyed no impression to
her troubled mind.   The next instant he was by her side.
As she smiled at him, he noticed that her face was pale,
and her eyes darkly encircled.

"Ah, madam," said he, as he drew close and lifted his
hand to his head, with a gesture of formal courtesy that
no doubt somewhat astonished a couple of his men who
were watching the group with covert smiles and nudges,
being as yet unaware of the misadventure, "you relieve
my mind of anxiety.   How is the arm?   Does it make
you suffer much?   No !   You must be strong indeed."

"Yes, I am strong," answered she, and flushed, and
looked out across the sea, inhaling the air with dilated
nostrils.

Within her, her soul was crying out to him.   It was as
if there was a tide there, as fierce and passionate as the
waves around her, all bearing, straining to him, and this
with a struggle and flow so resistless, that she could neither remember the past, nor measure the future, but only
feel herself carried on, beaten and tossed upon these great
waters, like a helpless wreck.

"I trust you are well attended to," began the man con-
strainedly again.   "I fear you will have to endure much

discomfort. I had reckoned——." Here he halted galled by the thought of what it was he had reckoned upon, the thought of the watchful love that was to have made of the little ship a very nest for his bride, of the exquisite joy it was to have harboured! And he set his teeth at fate.

She played for a while with her little finger tips upon the rail, then turned her gaze, full and bold, upon him.

" I do not complain," she said.

He bowed gravely. " We will do our best for you, and if you will take patience, the time will pass at last, as all time passes. I have a few books, they shall be brought into your cabin. In three days we shall be in St. Malo— There, if you like——" he hesitated, embarrassed.

" There !" echoed Lady Landale with her eyes still fixed upon his downcast face—" If I like—what ?"

" We could leave you——"

Her bosom rose and fell quickly with stormy breaths. "Alone, moneyless, in a strange town—that is well and kindly thought !" she said.

Whence had come to her this strange power of feeling pain ? She had not known that one could suffer in one's heart like this ; she, whose quarrel with life hitherto had been for its too great comfort, security and peace. She felt a lump rise to her throat, and tears well into her eyes, blurring all the sunlit vision and she turned her head away and beat her sound left hand clenched upon the ledge.

" Before heaven," cried Jack, distressed out of his unnatural stiffness, "you mistake me, Lady Landale ! I am only anxious to do what is best for you, what Adrian would wish. To leave you alone, deserted, helpless at St. Malo, you could not have thought I should mean that ? No, indeed, I would have seen you into safe hands, in some comfortable hotel, with a maid to wait upon you— I know of such a place—Adrian could not have been long in coming to fetch you. I should have had a letter ready to post to him the instant we landed. As to money," flushing boyishly, " that is the least consideration—there is no dearth of that to fear. If you prefer it I can, however, convey you somewhere upon the English coast after we quit St. Malo ; but that will entail a longer residence for you here on board ship ; and it is no fit place for you."

Still looking out across the sea, Molly replied, in a deep shaken voice, unlike her own, "You did not think it unfit for my sister."

"Your sister? But your sister was to have been my wife!"

Burning through the mists of her unshed tears once more her glance returned to his: "And I—" she cried and here was suddenly silent again, gazing at the thin circlet of gold upon her left hand, beneath the flashing diamonds. After a moment then, she broke out fiercely—"Oh do with me what you will, but for God's sake leave me in peace!" And stamping, turned her shoulder on him to stare straight outwards as before.

Captain Jack drew back, paused an instant, clutched his hair with a desperate gesture and slowly walked away.

The voyage of the *Peregrine* was as rapid as her captain had hoped, and the dawn of the fourth day broke upon them from behind the French coast, where Normandy joins old Armorica.

For a little while, Lady Landale, awakened from her uneasy sleep by the unusual stir on deck, lay languidly watching the light as it filtered through the port-hole of her little cabin, the colours growing out of greyness on the walls; listening to the tramp of feet and the mate's husky voice without. Then her heart tightened with a premonition of the coming separation. She sat up and looked out of her window: as the horizon rose and fell giddily to her eye there lay the fatal line of land. The land of her blood but to her now, the land of exile!

She had seen but little of Captain Jack these last two days; interchanged but few and formal words with him, now and then, as they met morning and evening or came across each other during the day. She felt that he avoided her. But she had seen him, she had heard his voice, they had been close to each other upon the great seas, however divided, and this had been something to feed upon. Now what prospect before her hungry heart but—starvation?

At least the last precious moments should not be lost to her. She rose and dressed in haste; a difficult operation in her maimed state. Before leaving her narrow quarters, she peered into the looking-glass with an eagerness she had never displayed in the days of her vain girlhood.

"What a fright!" she said to the anxious face that looked back at her with yearning eyes and dark burning lips. And she thought of Madeleine's placid fairness as Cain might of Abel's modest altar.

When she emerged upon deck, a strange and beautiful scene was spread to her gaze. A golden haze enveloped the water and the coast, but out of it, in brown jagged outline, against the blazing background of glowing sunlight rose the towers, the pointed roofs and spires of that old corsair's hive, St. Malo. The waters were bright green, frothed with oily foam around the ship. The masts cast strange long black shadows, and Molly saw one spring from her own feet as she moved into the morning glow. The *Peregrine*, she noticed, was cruising parallel with the coast, instead of making for the harbour, and just now all was very still on board. Two men, conspicuous against the yellow sky, stood apart, a little forward, with their backs turned to her.

One of these was Captain Jack, gazing steadily at the town through a telescope ; the other the mate. Both were silent. Silently herself and unnoticed Molly went up and stood beside them ; observing her sister's lover as intently as he that unknown distant point, she presently saw the lean hand nearest her tremble ever so slightly as it held the glass ; then he turned and handed it to his companion, saying briefly, "See what you make of it."

The man lifted the glass, set it, looked, dropped his hand and faced his captain. Their eyes met, but neither spoke for a second or two.

"It is so, then?" said the captain at last.

"Aye, sir, no mistake about that. There's the tricolour up again—and be damned to it—as large as life, to be sure!"

The healthy tan of the captain's face had not altered by one shade ; his mouth was set in its usual firm line, but, by the intuition of her fiery soul, the woman beside him knew that he had received a blow.

"A strange thing," went on Curwen in a grumbling guttural bass, "and it's only a year ago since they set up the old white napkin again. You did not look for this, sir?" He too had his intuitions.

"No, Curwen, it is the last thing I looked for.   And
it spells failure to me—failure once more!"

As he spoke he turned his head slightly and perceiving
Molly standing close behind him glanced up sharply and
frowned, then strove to smooth his brow into conventional serenity and greeted her civilly.

Curwen, clenching his hard hands together round the
telescope, retired a step and stood apart, still hanging on
his captain's every gesture like a faithful dog.

"What does it mean?" asked Molly, disregarding the
morning salutation.

"It means strange things to France," responded Captain Jack slowly, with a bitter smile; "and to me, Madam,
it means that I have come on a wild goose chase——"

He stretched out his hand for the glass once more as
he spoke—although even by the naked eye the flag, minute
as it was, could be seen to flash red in the breeze—and
sought the far-off flutter again; and then closing the
instrument with an angry snap, tossed it back.

"But what does it mean?" reiterated Molly, a wild
impatience, a wild hope trembling in her breast.

"It means, Madam, that I have brought my pigs to the
wrong market," cried Captain Jack, still with the smile
that sat so strangely upon his frank lips; "that the goods
I have to deliver, I cannot deliver.   For if there is any
meaning in symbols, by the wave of that tricolour yonder
the country has changed rulers again.   My dealings were
to be with the king's men, and as they are not here, at
least, no longer in power—how could they be under that
rag?—I must even trot the cargo home again.   Not a
word to the men, Curwen, but give the order to sheer off!
We have lowered the blue, white and red too often, have
not we? to risk a good English ship, unarmed, under the
nozzles of those Republican or Imperial guns."

The man grinned.   The two could trust each other.
Molly turned away and moved seawards, for she knew
that the joy upon her face was not to be hidden.   Captain Jack fell to pacing the deck with bent head, and
long, slow steps.

Absorbed in dovetailing the last secret arrangements
of his venture, and more intent still, during his very few
hours of idleness, on the engrossing thought of love, he
had had no knowledge of the extraordinary challenge to

fate cast by Bonaparte, of that challenge which was to end in the last and decisive clash of French and English hosts. He had not even heard of the Corsican's return to France with his handful of grenadiers, for newspapers were scarce at Scarthey. But even had he heard, like the rest of the world, he would no doubt have thought no more of it than as a mad freak born of the vanquished usurper's foolhardy restlessness.

But the conclave of plenipotentiaries assembled at Vienna were not more thunderstruck when, on that very 19th of March, the semaphore brought them news of the legitimate King of France once more fled, and of his country once more abandoned to the hated usurper, than was Captain Jack as he watched the distant flagstaff in the sunrise, and saw, when the morning port gun had vomited forth its white cloud on the ramparts of St. Malo, the fatal stripes run up the slender line in lieu of the white standard.

But Jack Smith's mind, like his body, was quick in action. The sun had travelled but a degree or two over the wide undulating land, the mists were yet rising, when suddenly he halted, and called the mate in those commanding tones that had, from the first time she had heard them, echoed in Molly's heart :

"Bring her alongside one of those smacks yonder, the furthest out to sea."

Thereupon followed Curwen's hoarse bellow, an ordered stampede upon the deck, and gracefully, with no more seeming effort than a swan upon a garden pond, the *Peregrine* veered and glided towards the rough skiff with its single ochre sail and its couple of brown-faced fishermen, who had left their nets to watch her advance. Captain Jack leant over the side, his hands over his mouth, and hailed them in his British-French—correct enough, but stiff to his tongue, as Molly heard and smiled at, and loved him for, in woman's way, when she loves at all.

"Ahoy, the friend ! A golden piece for him who will come on board and tell the news of the town."

A brief consultation between the fisher pair.

"*Un écu d'or*," repeated Captain Jack. Then there was a flash of white teeth on the two weather-beaten faces.

"*On y va, patron*," cried one of the fellows, cheerfully,

and jumped into his dinghey, while his comrade still
stared and grinned, and the stalwart lads of the *Peregrine*
grinned back at the queer foreign figure with the brown
cap and the big gold earrings.

Soon the fisherman's bare feet were thudding on the
deck, and he stood before the English captain, cap in
hand, his little, quick black eyes roaming in all directions, over the wonders of the beautiful white ship, with
innocent curiosity. But before Captain Jack could get
his tongue round another French phrase, Molly, detach-
ing herself from her post of observation, came forward,
smiling.

"Let me speak to him," she said, "he will understand
me better, and it will go quicker. What is it you want
to know?"

Captain Jack hesitated a moment, saw the advantage
of the suggestion, and then accepted the offer with the
queer embarrassment that always came over him in his
relations with her.

"You are very good," he said.

"Oh, I like to talk the father and mother tongue," she
said, gaily and sweetly. Her eyes danced; he had never
seen her in this mood, and, as before, grudgingly had to
admit her beauty.

"And if you will allow it," she went on, "I am glad
to be of use too."

The fisherman, twirling his cap in his knotted fingers,
stared at her open mouthed. *Une si belle dame!* like a
queen and speaking his tongue that it was a music to
listen to. This was in truth a ship of marvels. *Ah, bon
Dieu, oui, Madame*, there were news at St. Malo, but it
depended upon one's feelings whether they were to be
regarded as good or bad—*Dame*, every one has one's
opinions—but for him—*pourvu qu'on lui fiche la paix*—
what did it matter who sat on the throne—His Majesty
the King—His Majesty the Emperor, or Citizen Bonaparte. Oh, a poor fisherman, what was it to him? He
occupied himself with his little fishes, not with great folk.
(Another white-teethed grin.) What had happened? *Par-
bleu*, it began by the military, those accursed military
(this with a cautious look around, and gathering courage
by seeing no signs of disapproval, proceeding with greater
volubility). The poor town was full of them, infantry

and artillery ; regiments of young devils—and a band of
old ones too. The veterans of *celui là* (spitting on the
deck contemptuously) they were the worst ; that went
without saying. A week ago there came a rumour that
he had escaped—was in France—and then the ferment
began—duels every day—rows in the cafés, fights in the
ports. At night one would hear shouts in the streets—
Vive l'Empereur! and it spread, it spread. *Ma foi*—one
regiment mutinied, then another—and then it was known
that the Emperor had reached Paris. Oh, then it was
warm! All those gentlemen, the officers who were for
the King, were arrested. Then there was a grand
parade on the *place d'armes*—Yes, he went there too,
though he did not care much about soldiers. All the
garrison was there. The colonel of the veterans came
out with a flag in its case. *Portez armes!* Good. They
pull out the flag from the case : it's the old tricolour with
the eagle on the top! *Presentez armes!* And this time
it was all over. Ah, one should have seen that, heard
the houras, seen the bonfires! *Monsieur le Maire* and the
rest, appointed by the King, they were in a great fright,
they had to give way—what does Madame say? Traitors? Oh, *bédame* (scratching his head), it was no joke
with the military just now—the whole place was under
military law and, *saperlotte*, when the strong commands
it is best for the weak to obey. As for him, he was only
a poor fisherman. What did he know? he was not a
politician : every one to his trade. So long as they let
one have the peace—He thanked the gentleman, thanked
him much ; thanked the lady, desired to wish her the
good-morning and *Monsieur* too. Did they like no little
fresh soles this morning? He had some leaping then
below in his boat. No? well the good-morning then.

They had heard enough. The fisherman paddled back
to his skiff, and Molly stood watching from a little distance
the motionless figure of the captain of the *Peregrine* as
with one hand clenching the hand-rail he gazed towards
St. Malo with troubled eyes.

After a few minutes Curwen advanced and touched him
lightly on the arm.

Captain Jack turned slowly to look at him : his face
was a little pale and his jaw set. But the mate, who had
served under him since the day he first stepped upon the

old *St. Nicholas*, a gallant, fair-faced lad (and who knew
" every turn of him," as he would have expressed it himself), saw that he had taken his decision ; and he stepped
back satisfied, ready to shape his course for the near
harbour, or for the Pacific Ocean, or back to Scarthey
itself at his master's bidding.

" Call the men up," said the captain, " they have earned
their bounty and they shall have it.   Though their skipper is a poorer man than he thought to be, by this fool's
work yonder, his good lads shall not suffer.   Tush, man,
that's the order—not a word.   And after that, Curwen,
let her make for the sea again, northwards."

CHAPTER XXVII

THE LIGHT AGAIN—THE LADY AND THE CARGO

> Does not all the blood within me
> Leap to meet thee, leap to meet thee,
> As the spring to meet the sunshine !
>
> *Hiawatha.*

"CURWEN," said Captain Jack, suddenly—the two stood together at the helm on the afternoon of the same day, and the *Peregrine* was once more alone, a speck upon the waste of waters, "I have made up my mind to return to Scarthey."

The mate wagged his bushy eyebrows and shifted his hand on the helm. "Ay, ay, sir," he said, after just an instant's pause.

"I would not run you and the men into unnecessary danger, that you may be sure of ; but the fact is, Curwen, I'm in a devil of a fix all round. There's no use hiding it from you. And, all things considered, to land the lady and the cargo at the lighthouse itself, gives me as fair a chance of getting out of it as any plan I can think of. The cargo's not all my own and it's a valuable one, I daresay you have guessed as much ; and it's not the kind we want revenue men to pry into. I could not unload elsewhere that I know of, without creating suspicion. As to storing it elsewhere, it's out of the question. Scarthey's the place, though it's a damned risky one just now ! But we've run many a risk together in our day, have we not ? "

"Ay, sir ; who's afraid ? "

"Then there's the lady," lowering his voice ; "she's Lady Landale, my friend's wife, the wife of the best friend ever man had. Ay, you remember him, I doubt not—the gentleman seaman of the *Porcupine*—I owe him more than I can ever repay, and he owes me something

335

too. That sort of thing binds men together ; and see what I have done to him—carried off his wife !"

Curwen grunted, enigmatically, and disengaged a hand to scratch his chin.

"I must have speech with him. I must, it is enough to drive me mad to think what he may be thinking of me. What I purpose is this : we'll disguise the ship as far as we can (we have the time), paint her a new streak and alter those topsails, change the set of the bowsprit and strike out her name."

"That's unlucky," said the mate.

"Unlucky, is it? Well, she's not been so lucky this run that we need fear to change the luck. Then, Curwen, we'll slip in at night at a high tide, watching for our opportunity and a dark sky ; we'll unship the cargo, and then you shall take command of her and carry her off to the East Coast and wait there, till I am able to send you word or join you. It will only be a few hours danger for the men, after all."

Still keeping his seaman eye upon the compass, Curwen cleared his throat with a gruesome noise. Then in tones which seemed to issue with difficulty from some immense depth :

"Beg pardon, sir," he said, "that ain't a bargain."

"How now?" cried his captain, sharply.

"No, sir," rolling his head portentously ; "that don't run to a bargain, that don't. The lads of the *Peregrine* 'll stick to their skipper through thick and thin. I'll warrant them, every man Jack of them ; and if there was one who grumbled, I'd have my knife in him before another caught the temper from him—I would, or my name's not Curwen. If ye bid us steer to hell we'll do it for you, sir, and welcome. But for to go and leave you there— no, sir, it can't be done."

Captain Jack gave a little laugh that was as tender as a woman's tear. Curwen rolled his head again and mumbled to himself :

"It can't be done."

Then Jack Smith clapped his hand on the sailor's shoulder.

"But it's got to be done !" he cried. "It is the only thing you can do to help me, Curwen. To have our *Peregrine* out in the daylight on that coast would be stark madness—no disguise could avail her, and you can't change your ugly old phiz, can you? As for me, I must have a few days on shore, danger or no danger. Ah, Curwen," with a sudden, passionate outbreak, "there are times when a man's life is the least of his thoughts!"

"Couldn't I stop with you, sir?"

"I would not trust the ship to another, and you would double the risk for me."

"I could double a blow for you too," cried the fellow, hoarsely. "But if it's got to be—it must be. I'll do it, sir."

"I count on it," said the captain, briefly.

As the ring of his retreating steps died away upon his ear the mate shook his head in melancholy fashion :

"Women," he said, "is very well, I've nought to say against them in their way. And the sea's very well—as I ought to know. But women and the sea, it don't agree. They's jealous one of the other and a man gets torn between."

As Molly sat in her cabin, watching the darkening sky outside with dreaming eyes, she started on seeing Captain Jack approach, and instead of passing her with cold salute, halt and look in.

"I would speak a word with you," he said.

"On deck, then," said Molly. She felt somehow as if under the broad heaven they were nearer each other than in that narrow room. The sea was rough, the wind had risen and still blew from the north, it was cold; but her blood ran too fast these days to heed it.

She drew one of the capes of her cloak over her head and staggering a little, for the schooner, sailing close to the wind, pitched and rolled to some purpose, she made for her usual station at the bulwarks.

"Well?" she asked.

He briefly told her his purpose of returning to Scarthey direct.

Her eye dilated; she grew pale.

"Is that not dangerous?"

He made a contemptuous gesture.

"But they must be watching for you on that coast. You have sunk the boat—killed those men. To return there—My God, what folly!"

"I must land my goods, Madam. You forget that I

22

have more contraband on board than, smuggler as I am, even I bargained for."

"If it is for me?—I would rather fling myself into the waves this instant than that you should expose yourself to danger."

"Then I should fling myself after you, and that would be more dangerous still."

He smiled a little mockingly upon her as he spoke; but the words called a transient fire into her face.

"You would risk your life to save me?" she cried.

"To save Adrian's wife, Madam."

"*Bah!*"

He would have gone then, but she held him with her free hand. She was again white to the lips. But her eyes—how they burned!

He would have given all his worth to avoid what he felt was coming. A woman, at such a juncture may forbid speech, or deny her ear: a man, unless he would seem the first of Josephs or the last of coxcombs, dare not even hint at his unwelcome suspicions.

"I will not have you go into this danger, I will not!" stammered Molly incoherently. The dusk was spreading, and her eyes seemed to grow larger and larger in the uncertain light.

"Lady Landale, you misunderstand. It is true that to see you safely restored to your husband's roof is an added reason for my return to Scarthey—but were you not on board, I should go all the same. I will tell you why, it is a secret, but you shall know it. I have treasures on board, vast treasures confided to me, and I must store them in safety till I can give them back to their rightful owners. This I can only do at Scarthey—for to cruise about with such a cargo indefinitely is as impossible as to land it elsewhere. And more than this, had I not that second reason, I have yet a third that urges me to Scarthey still."

"For Madeleine?" she whispered, and her teeth gleamed between her lips.

He remained silent and tried gently to disengage himself from her slender fingers, but the feeling of their frailness, the knowledge of her wound, made her feeble grasp as an iron vice to his manliness.

She came closer to him.

"Do you not remember then—what she has said to you? what she wrote to you in cold blood—the coward—in the very moment when you were staking your life for love of her? I remember, if you do not—'You have deceived me,' she wrote, and her hand never trembled, for the words ran as neatly and primly as ever they did in her convent copy books. 'You are not what you represented yourself to be—You have taken advantage of the inexperience of an ignorant girl, I have been deluded and deceived. I never wish to see you, to hear of you again.'"

"For Heaven's sake, Lady Landale——" cried the man fiercely.

Molly laughed—one of those laughs that have the ring of madness in them.

"Do I not remember? Ah, that is not all! She knows you now for what you are, knows what your 'mission' is—but you must not believe she writes in anger. No, she——"

Captain Jack's patience could bear no further strain.

"Be silent," he commanded fiercely, and wrenched his arm away to face her with menacing eyes.

"Ah, does it rouse so much anger in you even to hear repeated what she did not hesitate to write, did not hesitate to allow me to read? And yet you love her? If you had seen her, if you knew her as I do! I tell you she means it; when she wrote that she was not angry; it was the truth—she did it in cold blood. She loved you, you think, and yet she believed you a liar; she loved you, and she thinks you a traitor to all she holds dear. She believes that of *you*, and you . . . . you love her still!"

"Lady Landale!"

"Listen—she could never love you, as you should be loved. She was not born your kin. Between you and her there is nothing—nothing but your own fancy. Do not risk your life again for her—your life!"

She stopped, drew her breath with a long gasp, the spray from a turbulent wave came dashing across the bows into her face, and as once the blood of Cécile de Savenaye had been roused by the call of the wild waters to leave safety and children and seek her doom, so now the blood she had transmitted to her child, leaped to the same impulse and bore her onwards with irresistible force.

"When," she pursued, "in the darkness you took me in your arms and kissed me ; what did the touch of my lips bring to you? My lips, not Madeleine's. . . . Were you not happy then? Oh, you were, do not deny it, I felt, I knew our souls met! My soul and yours, not yours and Madeleine's. And I knew then that we were made for each other. The sea and the wide free life upon it : it draws me as it draws you ; it was that drew me to you before I had ever seen you. Listen, listen. Do not go to Scarthey—you have your beautiful ship, your faithful crew—there are rich and wonderful worlds, warm seas that beckon. You can have life, money, adventure—and love, love if you will. Take it, take me with you! What should I care if you were an adventurer, a smuggler, a traitor? What does anything matter if we are only together? Let us go, we have but one life, let us go!"

Bereft of the power of movement he stood before her, and the sweat that had gathered upon his brow ran down his face. But, as the meaning of her proposition was borne in upon him, a shudder of fury shook him from head to foot. No man should have offered dishonour to Jack Smith and not have been struck the next instant at his feet. But a woman—a woman, and Adrian's wife!

"Lady Landale," he said, after a silence during which the beating of her heart turned her sick and cold, and all her fever heat fell from her, leaving nothing but the knowledge of her shame, her misery, her hopeless love. "Lady Landale, let me bring you back to your cabin—it is late."

She went with him as one half-conscious. At the door she paused. The light from within fell upon his face, deeply troubled and white, but upon the lips and brows, what scorn ! He was a god among men. . . . . How she loved him, and he scorned her ! Poor Murthering Moll !

She looked up.

"Have you no word for me?" she cried passionately.

"Only this, Lady Landale : I will forget."

Back towards the distant northern light the schooner

clove her valiant way in spite of adverse winds and high seas.

The return journey was slower than the outward, and since the second day of it the lady kept much to her cabin, while the captain would pace the deck till far into the night, with unwonted uneasiness. To him the white wings of his *Peregrine* were bearing him all too slowly for endurance, while to the stormy woman's heart that beat through the night watches in passionate echo to his restless tread, every instant that passed but brought nearer the prospect of a future so intolerable that she could not bring herself to face it.

A gloom seemed to have come over the tight little craft, and to have spread even to the crew, who missed the ring of their captain's jolly laugh and the sound of his song.

When, within a day's sail of the goal, the planned disguise was finally carried out upon the schooner's fair sides and rigging, her beautiful stretch of sail curtailed, and her name (final disgrace), superseded by the unmeaning title of *The Pretty Jane*, open murmurs broke out which it required all Curwen's severity—and if the old martinet did not execute the summary justice he had threatened he was quite equal to the occasion nevertheless—and all Jack's personal influence to quell.

The dawn of the next day crept gloomily upon a world of rain ; with long faces the men paddled about the deck, doing their duty in silence ; Curwen's old countenance, set into grimmer lines than ever, looked as if it had just been detached from the prow of some vessel after hard experience of stress and storm. The spirits of the captain alone seemed to rise in proportion as they drew nearer land.

" The moon sets at half-past eleven," he said to Curwen, " but we need not fear her to-night. By half-past twelve I reckon on your having those twenty-five damned casks safe in the cave you took them from ; it is a matter of three journeys. And then the nose of the *Pretty Jane* must be pointed for the Orkneys. All's going well."

Night had fallen. "The gaudy bubbling and remorseful day" had "crept into the bosom of the sea." From the cross-trees the look-out man had already been able to

distinguish through the glass the faint distant glimmer of
Scarthey beacon, when Captain Jack knocked for admit
tance at Lady Landale's cabin for the last time, as he
thought, with a sigh of relief.

"In the course of an hour, Madam," he said in a grave
tone, "I hope to restore you to land. As for me, I shall
have again to hide in the peel, though I hope it will not
be for long. My fate—and by my fate I mean not only
my safety, but my honour, which, as you know, is now
bound up in the safety of the treasures—will be in your
hands. For I must wait at Scarthey till I can see Adrian
again, and upon your return to Pulwick I must beg you
to be the bearer of a message to ask him to come and
see me."

She replied in a voice that trembled a little:

"I will not fail you."

But her great eyes, dark circled, fixed upon him with a
meek, sorrowful look, spoke dumbly the troublous tale of
her mind. In her subdued mood the likeness to Madeleine was more obtrusive than it had ever yet been. He
contemplated her with melancholy, and drew a heavy
sigh.

Molly groaned in the depths of her soul, though her lips
tight set betrayed no sound. Oh, miserable chaos of the
human world, that such pent up love should be wasted—
wasted; that they, too, young and strong and beautiful,
alone together, so near, with such glorious happiness
within their reach, should yet be so perversely far asunder!

There was a long silence. They looked into each
other's eyes; but he was unseeing; his mind was far
away, dwelling upon the memory of that last meeting
with his love under the fir trees of Pulwick only ten days
ago, but now as irrevocably far as things seem that may
never again be. At length, she made a movement which
brought him back to present reality—a movement of her
wounded arm as if of pain. And he came back to Lady
Landale, worn with the fatigue of these long days in the
cramped discomfort of a schooner cabin, thinned by pain
and fevered thinkings, shorn of all that daintiness of appearance which can only be maintained in the midst of
luxury, and yet, by the light of the flickering lamp, more
triumphantly beautiful than ever.

His thoughts leaped to his friend with a pang of remorse.

" You are suffering—you are ill," he said. " Thus do I bring you back to him who last saw you so full of strength. . . . . But you will recover at Pulwick."

" Suffering, ill ! Ah, my God ! " As if suffocating, she pressed her hand upon her heart, and bowed her head till it rested on the table. And then he heard her murmur in a weary voice :

" Recover at Pulwick ! My God, my God ! The air at Pulwick will stifle me, I think."

He waited a moment in silence and saw that she was weeping. Then he went out and closed the door behind him with gentle hand.

Nearly all the lights of the ship were now extinguished, and in a gloom as great as that in which they had started upon their unsuccessful venture, the *Peregrine* and her crew returned to the little island which had already been so fateful to them.

Captain Jack had taken the helm himself, and Curwen stood upon his right hand waiting patiently for his commands. For an hour or so they hung off the shore. The rain fell close and fine around them ; it was as if sea and sky were merging by slow imperceptible degrees into one. The beacon light looming, halo encircled, through the mist, seemed, like a monster eye, to watch with unmoved contempt the restlessness of these pigmies in the grand solitude of the night.

Who shall say with what conflict of soul Molly, in her narrow seclusion, saw the light of Scarthey grow out of the dimness till its rays fell across the darkened cabin and glimmered on her wedding ring ?

At last the captain drew his watch, and by the faint rays upon the binnacle saw the hour had come.

" Boat loaded, Curwen ? " he asked in a low voice.

" This hour, sir."

" Ready to cast ? "

" Right, sir."

" Now, Curwen."

Low, from man to man, the order ran through the ship, and the anchor was dropped, almost within a musket shot of the peel. It was high tide, but no hand but Captain Jack's would have dared risk the vessel so close. She swung round, ready to slip at a moment's notice.

He left the helm; and in the wet darkness cannoned against the burly figure of his mate.

"You, Curwen? Remember we have not a moment to lose. Remain here—as soon as the men are back from the last run, sheer off."

He grasped the horny hand.

Curwen made an inarticulate noise in his big throat, but the grip of his fingers upon his master's was of eloquence sufficient.

"Let some one call the lady."

A couple of men ran forward with dark lanterns. The rest gathered round.

"Now, my lads, brisk and silent is the word."

The cabin door opened, and Molly came forth, the darkness hid the pallor of her face, but it could not hide the faltering of her steps. Captain Jack sprang forward and gave her his arm, and she leant upon it without speaking, heavily. For one moment she stopped as if she could not tear her feet from the beloved planks, but Curwen caught her by the other arm; and then she was on the swinging ladder. And so she left the *Peregrine*.

The gig was almost filled with barrels; there was only room for the four oarsmen selected, besides the captain and herself. The boat shoved off. She looked back and saw, as once before, the great wall of the ship's side rise sheer above the sea, saw the triangle of light again slide down to lie a span above the water-line. With what a leaping heart she had set forth, that black night, away from the hateful lighthouse beam to that glimmer of promise and mystery! And now! She felt herself grow sick at the thought of that home-coming; at the vision of the close warm rooms, of her husband's melancholy eyes. Yet, as she sat, the sleeve of the captain's rough sailor coat touched her shoulder, and she remembered she was still with him. It was not all death yet.

In less than three minutes they touched ground. He jumped into the water, and stretched out his arms for Molly. She rose giddily, and his embrace folded her round. The waves rolled in with surge and thud and dashed their spray upon them; and still the rain fell and beat upon her head, from which she had impatiently pushed her hood. But her spirit had no heed for things of the body this night.

Oh, if the sea would open sudden deeps before them! if even the quicksand would seize them in its murderous jaws, what ecstasy the hideous lingering death might hold for her, so that only she lay, thus, in his arms to the end!

It was over now; his arms had clasped her for the last time. She stood alone upon the dry sand, and her heart was in hell.

He was speaking; asking her pardon for not going at once with her to see her into the keep, but he dared not leave the beach till his cargo was landed, and he must show the men the way to the caves. Would she forgive him, would she go with him?

Forgive him! Go with him! She almost laughed aloud. A few poor moments more beside him; they would be as the drops of water to the burning tongue of Dives.

Yes, she would go with him.

One by one the precious caskets were carried between a couple of men, who stumbled in the darkness, close on their captain's heels. And the lady walked beside him and stood beside him without a word, in the falling rain. The boat went backwards and forwards twice; before the hour had run out, the luckless cargo was all once more landed, and the captain heard with infinite relief the last oar-strokes dwindling away in the distance, and saw the lights suddenly disappear.

"You have been very patient," he said to Molly then, with a gentle note in his voice.

But she did not answer. Are the souls of the damned patient?

"My Lady and Mr. the Captain! My God—my God! so wet—so tired! Enter—enter in the name of heaven. It is good, in verity, to have My Lady back, but, Mr. the Captain, is it well for *him* to be here? And Madam is ill? She goes pale and red by turns. Madam has the fever for sure! And her arm is hurt, and she is as wet as the first time she came here. Ah, Lord God, what are we coming to? Fire we must have. I shall send the wife."

"Ay, do so, man," cried Captain Jack, looking with concern at Lady Landale, who in truth seemed scarcely able to stand, and whose fluctuating colour and cracked fevered lips gave painful corroboration to René's surmise, "your mistress must be instantly attended to."

But Molly arrested the servant as he would have hurried past upon his errand.

"Your master?" she said in a dry whisper, "is he at Pulwick?"

"His honour! My faith, I must be but half-awake yet. Imbecile that I am, his honour—where is he? Is he not with you? No, indeed, he is not at Pulwick, My Lady; he has gone to St. Malo to seek you. Nothing would serve him but that he must go. And so he did not reach in time to meet you? Ah, the poor master—what anxiety for him!"

Captain Jack glanced in dismay at his friend's wife, met her suddenly illumined gaze and turned abruptly on his heel, with a grinding noise.

"See to your mistress," he said harshly, "I hear your women folk are roused overhead; hurry them, and when Lady Landale no longer requires you, I must speak with you on an urgent business of my own. You will find me in my old room."

"Go with the captain at once, René, since he wants you," interposed Molly quickly, "here comes Moggie. She will take care of me. Leave me, leave me. I feel strong again. Good-night, Captain Smith, I shall see you to-morrow?"

There was a wistful query in her voice and look.

Captain Smith bowed distantly and coldly, and hastened from the room, accompanied by René, while openmouthed and blinking, rosy, blowsy, and amazed, Mrs. Potter made her entry on the scene and stared at her mistress with the roundest of blue eyes.

"My good Renny," said the captain, "I have no time to lose. I have a hard hour's work to do, before I can even think of talking. I want your help. Your light will burn all safe for the time, will it not? Hark ye, man, you have been so faithful a fellow to my one friend that I am going to trust to you matters which concern my own honour and my own life. Ask no question, but do what I tell you, if you would help one who has helped your master long ago ; one whom your master would wish you to help."

Thus adjured, René repressed his growing astonishment at the incomprehensible development of events. And having, under direction, provided the sailor with a lantern, and himself with a wide tarpaulin and sundry carpenter's tools, he followed his leader readily enough through the ruinous passages, half choked up with sand, which led from the interior of the ruins to one of the sea caves.

Before reaching the open-mouthed rocky chamber, the captain obscured the light, and René promptly barked his shins against a barrel.

" *Sacrebleu*," he cried, feeling with quick hands the nature of the obstruction, " more kegs ? "

"The same, my friend ! Now hang that tarpaulin against the mouth of the cave and be sure it is close ; then we may again have some light upon the matter. What we must do will not bear interference, and moving glimmers on a dark night have told tales before this."

As soon as the beach entrance was made secure, the captain uncovered his lantern ; and as the double row of kegs stood revealed, his eyes rapidly scanned their number. Yes, they were all there : five and twenty.

"Now, to work, man ! We have to crack every one of these nuts, and take the kernels out."

Even as he spoke, he turned the nearest cask on end, with a blow of chisel and mallet stove in the head and began dragging out quantities of loose tow. In the centre of the barrel, secured in position on to a stout middle batten, was a bag of sail-cloth closely bound with cord. This he lifted with an effort, for it was over a hundred-weight, and flung upon the sand in a corner.

"That's the kernel you see," he said to René, who had watched the operation with keen interest. "And when we have shelled them all I will show you where to put them in safety. Now carry on—the quicker the better. The sooner we have it all upstairs, the freer I shall breathe."

Without another word, entering into the spirit of haste which seemed to fill his companion, and nobly controlling his seething curiosity, René set to work on his side, with his usual dexterousness.

Half an hour of speechless destructive labour completed the first part of the task. Then the two men carried the weighty bags into the room which had been Captain Jack's in the keep. And when they had travelled to and fro a dozen times with each heavy load, and the whole treasure was at length accumulated upstairs, René, with fresh surprise and admiration, saw the captain lift the hearthstone and disclose a recess in the heavy masonry—presumably a flue, in the living days of Scarthey peel—which, although much blocked with stony rubbish, had been evidently improved by the last lodger during his period of solitary residence into a convenient and very secure hiding-place.

Here was the precious pyramid now heaped up ; the stone was returned to its place, and the two stood in front of each other mopping their faces.

"Thank goodness, it is done," said Jack Smith. "And thank you too, Renny. To-morrow, break up these casks and add the staves to your firewood stack ; then nobody but you, in this part of the world, need be any the wiser about our night's work.—A smart piece of running, eh ?—Phew, I am tired ! Bring me some food, and some brandy, like a good fellow. Then you can back to your pillow and flatter yourself that you have helped Jack Smith out of a famous quandary."

René grinned and rushed to execute the order. He had less desire for his pillow than for the gratification of his hyper-excited curiosity.

But although pressed to quaff one cup of good fellow-ship and yet another, he was not destined to get his information, that night, from the captain, who had much ado to strangle his yawns sufficiently to swallow a mouthful or two of food.

"No one must know, Renny," was all he said, at last, between two gapes, kicking the hearthstone significantly, and stretching his arms, "not even the wife." Then he flung himself all dressed upon his bed.

"And my faith," said René, when he sought his wife a moment later, "he was fast asleep before I had closed the door."

CHAPTER XXVIII

THE END OF THE THREAD

MADELEINE had appeared greatly distressed at the thought that, through her, her sister was now in so doubtful and precarious a situation. It was part of her punishment, she told herself for her sins of deceit and unmaidenliness in encouraging and meeting a clandestine lover.

She had gone through some very bitter hours since her tryst at the ruins. The process of cutting off a malignant growth that has become part of oneself is none the less painful because the conviction is clear that it is for one's health to do so, and the will is firm not to falter. Not the less is the flesh mangled, do nerves throb, and veins bleed. But Madeleine was determined that nobody should even guess her sufferings.

Rupert had counted upon Sophia's old habit of obedience to him, and upon her superstitious terrors not to betray to the young girl the part he had played in the unmasking of her lover; but he had an unexpected, and even more powerful ally in Madeleine's own pride. When Miss Sophia had tremblingly endeavoured to falter out a few words of sympathy and sorrow, upon the distressing subject, Madeleine quickly interrupted her.

"Never speak even his name again, Sophia; all that is finished for me."

There was such a cold finality in her voice, that the poor confidant's expansiveness withered up within her beyond even the hope of blossoming again.

When Rupert heard of Captain Jack's latest doings, and especially of his sister-in-law's disappearance, he thought that the fates were propitious indeed. In his wildest schemes he could not have planned anything that would have suited his game more perfectly.

Though he thought it incumbent upon him to pull a face of desperate length whenever the subject was

touched, in his innermost soul he had hardly ever enjoyed so delightful a joke as this dénouement to his
brother's marriage and to his cousin's engagement. And,
strange to say, though he would most gravely protest
against any interpretation of his kinswoman's disappearance save the one which must most redound to her credit,
the story, started by the gossips in the village upon the
return of the revenue men, that Lady Landale had bolted
with the handsome smuggler, grew and spread apace all
over the county, more especially from such houses as
Rupert was wont to visit.

That all his hints and innuendoes should fail, apparently, to make Madeleine put upon the case the interpretation he would have liked, was at once a matter of secret
sneering and of admiration to his curiously complicated
mind.

The days went by, to all appearance placidly enough,
for the trio at Pulwick. Madeleine shunned none of the
usages of life in common, worked and talked with Sophia
of a morning, rode or walked out with Rupert of an
afternoon ; and passed the evening at her embroidery
frame meeting his efforts to entertain her as amiably as
before.

Rupert thought he knew enough of the human heart,
and more especially the feminine, to draw satisfactory
conclusions from this behaviour. For a girl to bear no
malice to the man who had taken it upon himself to
demonstrate to her the unworthiness of her lover, argued,
to his mind, that her affections could not have been very
deeply engaged in that quarter. It was clear that she felt
gratitude for a timely rescue. Nay, might he not go
further, and lay the flattering unction to his soul that she
would not be unwilling to transfer these same blighted
feelings to a more suitable recipient ?

A slight incident which took place a few nights later,
tended still more to increase the kindness of Madeleine's
manner to him upon the next day ; but this was for a
reason that he little suspected.

It had been an anniversary with Sophia—none less indeed than that of the lamented Rector's demise. When
her young cousin had retired to her room, the desire to
pursue her thither with a packet of old letters, and other
treasures exhumed from the depths of her cupboards, had

proved too strong for a soul burning for congenial sympathy ; and Sophia had spent a couple of very delightful hours pouring forth reminiscences and lamentations into the bosom of one who, as she said, she knew could understand her.

Madeleine a little wearied, stifling a sigh or a yawn as the minutes ticked by, was too gentle, too kind-hearted to repel the faithful, if loquacious mourner ; so she had sat and listened, which was all that Sophia required.

Upon the stroke of twelve, Miss Landale rose at length, collected her relics, and mopping her swollen eyes, embraced her cousin, and bade her good-night with much effusion, while with cordial alacrity the latter conducted her to the door.

But here Sophia paused. Holding the flat silver candlestick with one hand, with the other clasping to her bosom her bundle of superannuated love letters, she glanced out into the long black chasm of corridor with a shudder, and vowed she had not the courage to traverse it alone at such an hour. She cast as she spoke such a meaning glance at Madeleine's great bed, that, trembling lest her next words should be a proposal to share it for the night, the young girl hurriedly volunteered to re-conduct her to her own apartment.

Half way down the passage they had to pass the door of the picture gallery, which was ajar, disclosing light within. At the sight of Rupert standing with his back to them, looking fixedly at the picture upon the opposite wall, Sophia promptly thought better of the scream she was preparing, and seized her cousin by the arm.

"Come away, come away," she whispered, "he will be much displeased if he sees us."

Madeleine allowed herself to be pulled onward, but remembering Molly's previous encounter upon the same spot, was curious enough to demand an explanation of Rupert's nocturnal rambles when they had reached the haven of Sophia's bedroom. It was very simple, but it struck her as exceedingly pathetic and confirmed her in her opinion of the unreasonableness of her sister's dislike to Rupert.

He was gazing at his dead wife's picture. He could not bear, Sophia said, for any one to find him there ; could not bear the smallest allusion to his grief, but at night, as she had herself discovered quite by accident, he would often spend long spells as they had just seen him.

There was something in Madeleine's own nature, a susceptible proud reserve which made this trait in her cousin's character thoroughly congenial; moreover, what woman is not drawn with pity towards the man who can so mourn a woman.

She met him therefore, the next day, with a softness, almost a tenderness, of look and smile which roused his highest hopes. And when he proposed, after breakfast, that they should profit by the mild weather to stroll in the garden while Sophia was busy in the house, she willingly consented.

Up the gravel paths, between the gooseberry bushes, to the violet beds they went. It was one of those balmy days that come sometimes in early spring and encourage all sorts of false hopes in the hearts of men and vegetables. "A growing day," the farmers call them; indeed, at such times you may almost hear the swelling and the bursting of the buds, the rising of the sap, the throbbing and pushing of the young green life all around.

Madeleine grew hot with the weight of her fur tippet, the pale face under the plumy hat took an unusual pink bloom; her eyes shone with a moist radiance. Rupert, glancing up at her, as, bent upon one knee, he sought for stray violets amid the thick green leaves, thought it was thus a maiden looked who waited to be won; and though all of true love that he could ever give to woman lay buried with his little bride, he felt his pulses quicken with a certain æsthetic pleasure in the situation. Presently he rose, and, after arranging his bunch of purple sweetness into dainty form, offered it silently to his companion.

She took it, smiling, and carried it mechanically to her face.

Oh, the scent of the violets! Upon the most delicate yet mighty pinions she was carried back, despite all her proud resolves to that golden hour, only five days ago, when she lay upon her lover's broad breast, and heard the beating of his heart beneath her ear.

Again she felt his arm around her, so strong, yet so gentle; saw his handsome face bent towards her, closer— ever closer—felt again the tide of joy that coursed through her veins in the expectation of his kiss.

No, no, she must not—she would not yield to this degrading folly. If it were not yet dead, then she must kill it.

She had first grown pale, but the next moment a deep crimson flooded her face. She turned her head away, and Rupert saw her tremble as she dropped the hand that held the flowers close clenched by her side. He formed his own opinion of what was passing within her, and it made even his cold blood course hotly in his veins.

"Madeleine," he said, with low rapid utterance; "I am not mistaken, I trust, in thinking you look on me as a good friend?"

"Indeed, yes;" answered the girl, with an effort, turning her tremulous face towards him; "a good friend indeed."

Had he not been so five days ago? Aye, most truly, and she would have it so, in spite of the hungry voice within her which had awaked and cried out against the knowledge that had brought such misery.

He saw her set her little teeth and toss her head, and knew she was thinking of the adventurer who had dared aspire to her. And he gained warmer courage still.

"Nothing more than a friend, sweet?"

"A kind cousin; almost a brother."

"No, no; not a brother, Madeleine. Nay, hear me," taking her hands and looking into her uncomprehending eyes, "I would not be a brother, but something closer, dearer. We are both alone in the world, more or less. Whom have you but a mad-cap sister, a poor dreamer of a brother-in-law, an octogenarian aunt, to look to? I have no one, no one to whom my coming or my going, my living or my dying makes one pulse beat of difference— except poor Sophia. Let us join our loneliness and make of it a beautiful and happy home. Madeleine, I have learned to love you deeply!"

His eyes glowed between their narrowing eyelids, his voice rang changes upon chords of most exquisite tenderness; his whole manner was charged with a courtly reverence mingled with the subtlest hint of passion. Rupert as a lover had not a flaw in him.

Yet fear, suspicion, disgust chased each other in Madeleine's mind in quick succession. What did he mean? How could it be that he loved her? Oh! if *this* had been

23

his purpose, what motive was prompting him when he divided her from her deceiving lover? Was no one true then? Was this the inconsolable widower whose grief she had been so sympathetically considering all the morning; for whose disinterested anxiety and solicitude on her behalf her sore heart had forced itself to render gratitude? Oh! how terrible it all was . . . . what a hateful world!

"Well, Madeleine?" he pressed forward and slid his arm around her.

All her powers of thought and action restored by the deed, she disengaged herself with a movement of unconscious repulsion.

"Cousin Rupert, I am sure you mean kindly by me, but it is quite impossible—I shall never marry."

He drew back, as nonplussed as if she had struck him in the face.

"Pshaw, my dear Madeleine."

"Please, Cousin Rupert, no more."

"My dear girl, I have been precipitate."

"Nothing can make any difference. That I could never marry you, so much you must believe; that I shall never marry at all you are free to believe or not, as you please. I am sorry you should have spoken."

"Still hankering after that beggarly scoundrel?" muttered Rupert, a sneer uncovering his teeth betrayed hideously the ungenerous soul within. He was too deeply mortified, too shaken by this utter shattering of his last ambitions to be able to grasp his usual self-control.

Madeleine gave him one proud glance, turned abruptly away, and walked into the house.

She went steadily up to her room, and, once there, without hesitation proceeded to unlock a drawer in her writing-table and draw from it a little ribbon-tied parcel of letters—Jack's letters.

Her heart had failed her, womanlike, before the little sacrifice when she had unshrinkingly accomplished the larger one. Now, however, with determined hand, she threw the letters into the reddest cavern of her wood-fire and with hard dry eyes watched them burn. When the last scrap had writhed and fluttered and flamed into grey ash, she turned to her altar, and, extending her arm, called out aloud:

"I have done with it all for ever——"

And the next instant flinging herself upon her bed, she drew her brown ringlets before her face, and under this veil wept for her broken youth and her broken heart, and the hard cold life before her.

There is a kind of love a man can give to woman but once in his lifetime : the love of the man in the first flush of manhood for the woman he has chosen to be his mate, untransferable and never to be forgotten : love of passion so exquisite, of devotion so pure, born of the youth of the heart and belonging to an existence and personality lost for ever. A man may wed again, and (some say) love again, but between the boards of the coffin of his first wife—if he has loved her—lie secrets of tenderness, and sweetness, and delight, which, like the spring flowers, may not visit the later year.

But, notwithstanding this, a second wooing may have a charm and an interest of its own, even the wooing which is to precede a marriage of convenience.

So Rupert· found. The thought of an alliance with Madeleine de Savenaye was not only engrossing from the sense of its own intrinsic advantages, but had become the actual foundation-stone of all his new schemes of ambition.

Nay, more : such admiration and desire as he could still feel for woman, he had gradually come to centre upon his fair and graceful cousin, who added to her personal attractions the other indispensable attributes, blood, breeding and fortune. Mr. Landale was as essentially refined and fastidious in his judgment as he was unmeasured in his ambition.

His error of precipitancy had been pardonable enough ; and mere self-reproach for an ill-considered manœuvre would not have sufficed to plunge him into such a depth of bitter and angry despondency as that in which he now found himself. But the rebuff had been too uncompromising to leave him a single hope. He was too shrewd not to see that here was no pretty feminine nay, precursor of the yielding yea, not to realise that Madeleine had meant what she said and would abide by it. And, under the sting of the moment betrayed into a degradingly ill-mannered outburst, he had shown that he measured the full bearings of the position.

So, the wind still sat in that quarter!

Failing the mysterious smuggler, it was to be nobody with the Savenaye heiress—and least of all Rupert Landale.

And this, though the scoundrel had been thoroughly shown up; though he had started upon his illegal venture and was gone, never to return if he valued his neck, after murdering four officers of the crown and sinking a king's vessel; though he had carried away with him (ah! there was consolation in that excellent jest which had so far developed into Sir Adrian's wild goose chase to France and might still hold some delicate dénouement), had carried with him no less a person than Lady Landale herself (the fellow had good taste, and either of the sisters was a dainty morsel), he still left the baneful trail of his influence behind him upon the girl he had deluded and beguiled!

Rupert Landale, who, for motives of his own had pleased himself by hunting down Madeleine's lover, had felt, in the keenness of his blood-hound work, something of the blood-hound instinct of destruction and ferocity spring up within him before he had even set eyes on his quarry. And the day they had stood face to face this instinctive hatred had been intensified by some singular natural antagonism. Added to this there was now personal injury and the prey was out of reach. Impotence for revenge burned into the soul of him like a corrosive poison. Oh, let him but come within his grip again and he should not escape so easily.

Sits the wind still in that quarter?

The burthen droned in his head, angry conclusion to each long spell of inconclusive thought, as he still paced the garden, till the noon hour began to wane. And it was in this mood, that, at length, returning to his study, he crossed in one of the back passages a young woman enveloped in a brilliant scarlet and black shawl, who started in evident dismay on being confronted with him.

Rupert knew by sight and name every wench of kitchen and laundry, as well as every one of the buxom lasses or dames whom business brought periodically to the great hall. That this person was neither of the household nor one of the usual back-door visitors, he would have seen

at a glance, even had not her own embarrassment drawn
his closer attention. He looked keenly and recognised
the gatekeeper's daughter Moggie.

Having married Sir Adrian's servant and withdrawn to
take up her abode in the camp of the enemy, so to speak,
she was not one whom Mr. Landale would have regarded
with favour in any case ; but now, concentrating his
thoughts from their aimless whirl of dissatisfaction upon
the present encounter, he was struck by the woman's
manner.

Yes, she was most undoubtedly frightened. He examined her with a malevolent eye which still discoun-
tenanced her. And, though he made no inquiry, she
forthwith stammered out : " I—I came, sir, to see if there
be news of her Ladyship . . . . or of Sir Adrian, sir—
Renny can't leave the island, you know, and he be downright anxious."

" Well, my good woman, calm yourself. Nothing
wrong ; nothing to hide in this very laudable anxiety of
you and your good man ! No, we have no news yet—
that is quickly told, Mrs. Potter."

He kept her for a moment quailing and scared under
his cruel gaze, then went on his way, working upon the
new problems she had brought him to solve. No matter
was too small for Rupert's mind, he knew how inextricably
the most minute and apparently insignificant may be
connected with the most important events of life.

The woman was singularly anxious to explain, reflected
he, pausing at his chamber door, singularly ready with
her explanation—too ready. She must have lied. No
doubt she lied. Liar was written upon every line of the
terrified face of her. What was that infernal little French
husband of hers hatching now ? He had been in the
Smith plot, of course. Ah, curse that smuggling fellow :
he cropped up still on every side ! Pray the fates he
would crop up once too often for his own safety yet ;
who knew !

Meanwhile Mrs. Potter, the innocent news-gatherer,
must not be allowed to roam unwatched at her own
sweet will about the place. Hark ! what clumping,
creaking, steps ! These could only be produced by René's
fairy-footed spouse : the house servants had been too
well drilled by his irritable ear to venture in such shoe

leather within its range.   He closed his door, and gently walked back along the corridor.

As he passed Molly's apartment, he could hear the creaking of a wardrobe door ; and, a startling surmise springing into his brain, he quietly slipped into an opposite room and waited, leaving the door slightly ajar.

As he expected, a few minutes later, Moggie reappeared loaded with a bulky parcel, glancing anxiously right and left.   She tiptoed by him ; but, after a few steps, suddenly turning her head once more, met his eyes grimly fixed upon her through the narrow aperture.   With a faint squeal she paddled off as though a fiend were at her heels.

"Something more than anxiety for news there, Mrs. Potter," said Mr. Landale, apostrophising the retreating figure with a malignant, inward laugh!   Then, when the last echo of her stout boots had faded away, he entered his sister-in-law's room, looked around and meditatively began to open various presses and drawers. "You visited this one at any rate, my girl," thought he, as he recognised the special sound of the hinges.   "And, for a lady's maid, you have left it in singular disorder. As for this," pulling open a linen drawer half-emptied, and showing dainty feminine apparel, beribboned and belaced, in the most utter disorder—"why, fie on you, Mrs. Potter!   Is this the way to treat these pretty things ?"

He had seen enough.   He paused a moment in the middle of the room with his nails to his lips, smiling to himself.

"Ah, Mrs. Potter, I fancy you might have given us a little news, yourself!   Most unkind of my Lady Landale to prefer to keep us in this unnatural anxiety—most unkind indeed!   She must have singularly good reasons for so doing. . . .   Captain Smith, my friend, Mr. Cochrane, or whatever may be your name, we have an account to settle.   And there is that fool of an Adrian scurrying over the seas in search of his runaway wife!   By George! my hand is not played out yet!"

Slowly he repaired to his study.   There he sat down and wrote, without any further reflection, an urgent letter to the chief officer of the newly established Preventive Service Station.   Then he rang the bell.

" One of the grooms will ride at once to Lancaster with this," he said to the servant, looking at the missive in his hand.   But instead of delivering it he paused : a new idea had occurred.   How many of these servants might not be leagued in favour of that interloper, bribed, or knowing him, perhaps, to have been a friend of Sir Adrian, or yet again out of sheer spite to himself ?   No ;   he would leave no loop-hole for treachery now.

" Send the groom to me as soon as he is ready," he continued, and when the footman had withdrawn, enclosed the letter, with its tale-telling superscription, in another directed to a local firm of attorneys, with a covering note instructing them to see that the communication, on His Majesty's Service, should reach the proper hands without delay.

When the messenger had set forth, Mr. Landale, on his side, had his horse saddled and sallied out in the direction of Scarthey sands.

As from the top of the bluff he took a survey of the great bay, a couple of figures crossing the strand in the distance arrested his attention ; he reined in his horse behind a clump of bushes and watched.

" So ho ! Mrs. Potter, your careful husband could not leave the island ? " muttered he, as he marked the unmistakable squat figure of the one, a man carrying a burden upon his shoulder, whilst, enveloping the woman who walked briskly by his side, flared the brilliant-hued shawl of Moggie.   " That lie alone would have been sufficient to arouse suspicion.   Hallo, what is the damned *crapaud* up to ? "

The question was suggested by the man's movements, as, after returning the parcel to his consort at the beginning of the now bare causeway, he turned tail, while she trudged forward alone.

" The Shearman's house ! I thought as much.   Out he comes again, and not by himself.   I have made acquaintance with those small bare legs before.   I should have been astonished indeed if none of the Shearman fellows had been mixed up with the affair.   I shall be even yet with those creditable friends of yours, brother Adrian. So, it's you again, Johnny, my lad ; the pretty Mercury . . . . Can it be possible that Captain Smith is at his old games once more ? "

Mr. Landale's eyes shone with a curious eager light ;
he laughed a little mirthless laugh, which was neither
pleasant to hear nor to give.   "Dear me," he said aloud,
as he watched the pair tramp together towards Scarthey,
"for plotters in the dark, you are particularly easy to
detect, my good friends ! "

Then he checked himself, realising what a mere chance
it had been, after all—a fortuitous meeting in the passage
—that had first aroused his suspicions, and placed between his fingers the end of the thread he now thought it
so simple to follow up.   But he did hold the thread, and
depended no longer upon chance or guess-work, but on
his own relentless purpose to lay the plotters by the
heels, whatever their plot might be.

In the course of an hour and a half, Johnny Shearman,
whistling, lighthearted, and alone, was nearing his native
house once more, when the sight of a horseman, rapidly
advancing across the sands, brought him to a standstill,
to stare with a boy's curiosity.   Presently, however, recognising Mr. Landale—a person for whom he had more
dread than admiration—he was starting off homeward
again at a brisk canter, when a stern hail from the rider
arrested him.

"Johnny ! "   The boy debated a moment, measured
the distance between the cottage and himself, and
shrewdly recognised the advisability of obeying.
"Johnny, my boy, I want you at the Hall ; take hold of
my stirrup, and come along with me."

The boy, with every symptom of reluctance, demurred,
pleading a promise to return to his mother.   Then he
suddenly perceived a look in the gentleman's eye, which
gave him a frantic, unreasoned desire to bolt at once, and
at any cost.   But the horseman anticipated the thought ;
bending in the saddle, he reached out his arm and seized
the urchin by the collar.

"Why, you little devil, what is the matter with you ? "
he asked, grinning ominously into the chubby, terrified
face.   "It strikes me it is time you and I should come
to a little understanding.   Any more letters from the
smuggler to-day, eh ?   Ah, would you, you young idiot ! "
and Mr. Landale's fingers gave a sudden twist to the collar,
which strangled the rising yell.   "Listen, Johnny,"
tightening his grasp gradually until the brown face grew

scarlet, then purple, and the goggling eyes seemed to start out of their sockets ; " that is what it feels like to be hanged. They squeeze your neck so ; and they leave you dangling at the end of a rope till you are dead, dead, dead, and the crows come and eat you. Do you want to be hanged ? "

For some moments more he kept the writhing lad under the torture ; then loosening his grip, without however relinquishing his hold, allowed him to taste once more the living air.

" Do you want to be hanged, Johnny Shearman ? " he asked again gravely. The lad burst into gasping sobs, and looked up at his captor with an agony of fear in his bloodshot eyes. " No," continued Mr. Landale, " I am sure you don't, eh ? " with a renewed ominous contraction of the hand. " It's a fearful thing, is hanging. And yet many a lad, hardly older than you, has been hanged for less than you are doing. Magistrates can get people hanged, and I am a magistrate, you know. *Stop that noise !* "

" Now," continued the gentleman, " there are one or two little things I want to know myself, Johnny, and it's just possible I might let you off for this time if by chance you were able to tell them to me. So, for your sake, I hope you may be."

He could see that the boy's mind was now completely turned with fright.

" If you were to try to run away again I should know you had secrets to keep from me, and then, Johnny Shearman, it would go hard with you indeed ! Now come along beside me, up to the Hall."

Quite certain of his prey, he released him, and, setting his horse to a trot, smiled to note the desperate clutch of the lad upon his stirrup leather, as, with the perspiration dripping from his face, and panting breath, he struggled to keep up the pace alongside.

Marched with tremendous ceremony into the magistrate's study and directed to stand right opposite the light, while Mr. Landale installed himself in an arm-chair with a blood-curdling air of judicial sternness, Johnny Shearman, at most times as dare-devil a pickle of a boy as ever ran, but now reduced to a state of mental and physical jelly, underwent a terrible cross-examination. It was comparatively little that he had to say, and no doubt he wished most fervently he had greater revelations to make, and could thus propitiate the arbiter of the appalling fate he firmly believed might lie in store for him.   Meagre as his narrative was, however, it quite sufficed for Mr. Landale.

"I think, Johnny," he said more pleasantly, well knowing the inducement that a sudden relaxation from fear offers to a witness's garrulity, "I think I may say you will not hang this time—that is," with a sudden hardening of his voice, and making a great show of checking the answers with pen and ink in his most magisterial manner, "that is if you have really told me *all* you know and it be all *true*.   Now let us see, and take care.   You saw no one at the peel to-day but Renny Potter, Mrs. Potter and Mrs. Crackenshaw?"

"No, sir."

"But you heard other voices in the next room—a man's voice—whilst you were waiting?"

"Yes, sir."

"Then Renny Potter came back and gave you a message for your brothers.   This message they made you repeat, over and over again.   How did it go?"   And as Mr. Landale frowningly looked at his paper, the boy tremblingly repeated :

"I mun tell brothers Will an' Rob, that one or t'other mun watchen the light o' nights, to-night, to-morrow night, an' ontil woord coom again.   If light go out they mun setten forth in they ketch thot moment, fettled op for a two-three days' sailing.   If wind is contrairy like, they mun take sweeps.   This for the master's service— for Sir Adrian's service!"—amending the phrase with a sharp reading of the blackness of Mr. Landale's swift upward look.

"Yes," murmured the latter after a pause.   "And you were to tell no one else.   You were to keep it above all from getting to my ears.   Very good, Johnny.   If you have spoken the truth, you are safe."

There was a special cell, off the official study, with high windows, bolts and bars, and a wooden bench, for the temporary housing of such desperate criminals as might be brought to the judgment of Rupert Landale, Esquire, J.P.   There he now disposed of the young offender who snivelled piteously once more ; and having locked the door and pocketed the key, returned to his capacious arm-chair, where, as the twilight waned over the land, he fell to co-ordinating his scheme and gloating upon this unexpected turn of Fortune's wheel.

At that hour Madeleine, alone in her chamber, knelt before her little altar, wrestling with the rebellion of her soul and besieging the heavens with a cry for peace.

Sir Adrian having failed to hear aught of the *Peregrine* at St. Malo, filled with harassing doubt about its fate but clutching still at hope—as men will, even such pessimists as he—stood on the deck of his homeward bound ship, straining his eyes in the dusk for the coast line.

In the peel, the beacon had just been lighted by René, in whose company, up in his secluded turret, sat Captain Jack, smoking a pipe, but so unusually silent as to have reduced even the loquacious Frenchman to silence too. Below them Lady Landale, torn between the dread of a final separation from the loadstar of her existence and the gnawing anxiety roused in her bosom by Moggie's account of Mr. Landale's watchfulness, was pacing the long book-lined room with the restlessness of a caged panther.

On the road from Lancaster to Pulwick a posse of riding officers and a carriage full of hastily gathered preventive men were trotting on their way to the Priory.

CHAPTER XXIX

THE LIGHT GOES OUT

THE light of Scarthey had not been shining for quite an hour over the wilderness, when Lady Landale, suddenly breaking the chain of her restless tramp, ran to the door and called for Moggie.

There was so shrill a tone of anguish in the summons that the young woman rushed into the room in trembling expectancy : yet it was to find her mistress alone and the place undisturbed.

"Moggie," said Lady Landale, panting and pressing her hands upon her side as if in the endeavour to control the beating of her heart, "something is going to happen ; I know it, I feel it ! Tell Captain Smith that I must speak to him, here, at once."

Infected by the terror upon her mistress's face, Madame Lapôtre flew upon her errand ; a moment later, Captain Jack entered the room and stood before Lady Landale with a look of impatient inquiry.

"Oh, it is wicked, it is mad ! " cried she passionately ; "it is tempting God to remain here ! "

"Of whom are you speaking ? " he asked, with an involuntary glance of contempt at the distracted figure. "If it is of yourself, I entirely concur. How often these last days, and how earnestly have I not begged of you to return to Pulwick ? Was not the situation you placed me in with regard to Adrian already odious enough that it needed this added folly ? Oh, I know—I know what you would say : spare it me. My safety ? You fear for me ? Ah, Lady Landale, that you could have but left me in peace ! "

He had waxed hot with anger from his first would-be calmness, as he spoke. This dismal life of close but inharmonious proximity, started upon the seas and continued under his absent friend's own roof had tried his

364

impetuous temper to the utmost. Upon the morrow of their return he had, indeed, exercised all his powers of persuasion to induce Lady Landale to proceed to the Priory ; but, impelled by her frantic dread of the separation, and entrenching herself behind the argument that her mysterious re-appearance would awaken suspicion where people would otherwise believe the *Peregrine* still in foreign parts, she had declared her irrevocable determination not to quit the island until she knew him to be safe. And he had remained, actuated by the dual desire, first to exonerate himself personally in her husband's eyes from any possible suspicion of complicity in Molly's flight —the bare thought of which had become a horrible torment to him—then to encompass through that good friend's means an interview and full explanation with Madeleine, which not only the most ordinary precaution for his life, but likewise every instinct of pride forbade him now to seek himself.

Thus began a state of affairs which, as the days succeeded each other without news of Sir Adrian, became every moment more intolerable to his loyalty. The inaction, the solitary hours of reflection ; the maddening feeling of unavailing proximity to his heart's dearest, of impotency against the involving meshes of the present false and hateful position ; all this had brought into the young man's soul a fever of anger, which, as fevers will, consumed him the more fiercely because of his vigour and strength.

It was with undisguised hatred and with scorn immeasurable that he now surveyed the woman who had degraded him in his own eyes. At another time Molly might have yielded before his resentment, but at this hour her whole being was encompassed by a single thought.

"It is for you—for you !" she repeated with ashen lips ; "you must go before it is too late."

"And is it not too late?" stormed he. "Too late, indeed, do I see my treachery to Adrian, my more than brother ! Upon my ship I could not avoid your company, but here—Oh, I should have thought of him and not of myself, and done as my honour bade me ! You are right ; since you would not go, I should have done so. It was weak ; it was mad ; worse, worse—dishonourable!"

But she had no ears for his reproaches, no power to

feel the wounds he dealt her woman's heart with such relentless hand.

"Then you will go," she cried. "Tell René, the signal."

He started and looked at her with a different expression.

"Have you heard anything; has anything happened?" he asked, recovering self-restraint at the thought of danger.

"Not yet," she replied, "not yet, but it is coming."

Her look and voice were so charged with tragic force that for the moment he was impressed, and, brave man though he was, felt a little cold thrill run down his spine. She continued, in accents of the most piercing misery:

"And it will have been through me—it will have been through me! Oh, in mercy let me make the signal! Say you will go to-night."

"I will go."

There followed a little pause of breathless silence between them. Then as, without speaking, he would have turned away, a loud, peremptory knock resounded upon the door of the keep and echoed and re-echoed with lugubrious reverberation through the old stone passages around them.

At first, terror-stricken, her tongue clave to her palate, her feet were rooted to the ground; then with a scream she flung herself upon him and would have dragged him towards the door.

"They have come—hide—hide!"

He threw up his head to listen, while he strove to disengage himself. The blood had leaped to his cheek, and fire to his eye. "And if it be Adrian?" he cried.

Another knock thundered through the still air.

"It is but one man," cried René from his tower down the stairs. "You may open, Moggie."

"No—no," screamed Molly beside herself, and tighter clasped her arms round Captain Jack's neck.

"Adrian, it is Adrian!" said he. "Hush, Madam, let me go! Would you make the breach between me and my friend irreparable?"

Both his hands were on her wrists in the vain endeavour to disengage himself from her frenzied grip; the door was flung open and Rupert Landale stood in the opening, and looked in upon them.

"Damnation !" muttered Jack between his teeth and flung her from him, stamping his foot.

Rupert gazed from one to the other ; from the woman, who, haggard and dishevelled, now turned like a fury upon him, to the sailor's fierce erect figure. Then he closed the door with an air of grave deliberation.

"What do you want ?" demanded Molly—"you have come here for no good purpose. What do you want ?"

As she spoke she strove to place herself between the two men.

"I came, my dear sister-in-law," said Rupert in his coldest, most incisive voice, "to learn why, since you have come back from your little trip, you choose to remain in the ruins rather than return to your own house and family. The reason is clear to see now. My poor brother !"

The revulsion of disappointment had added to the wrath which the very sight of Rupert Landale aroused in Jack Smith's blood; this insinuation was the culminating injury. He took a step forward.

"Have a care, sir," he exclaimed, "how you outrage in my presence the wife of my best friend ! Have a care —I am not in such a hurry to leave you as when last we met !"

Mr. Landale raised his eyebrows, and again sent a look from Molly back to the sailor, the insolence of which lashed beyond all control the devils in the sailor's soul.

"We have an account to settle, it seems to me, Mr. Landale," said he, taking another step forward and slightly stooping his head to look the other in the eye. Crimson fury was in his own. "I doubt much whether it was quite wise of you, assuming that you expected to find me here, to have come without that pistolling retinue with which you provided yourself last time."

Rupert smiled and crossed his arms. Cowardice was no part of his character. He had come in advance of his blood-hounds, in part to assure himself of the correctness of his surmises, but also to feast upon the discomfiture of this man and this woman whom he hated. To have found them together, and thus, had been an unforeseen and delicious addition to his dish of vengeance, and he would linger over it while he could.

"Well, Captain Smith, and about this account ? Lady

Landale, I beg of you, be silent. You have brought sufficient disgrace upon our name as it is. Nay, sir," raising his voice, " it is useless to shake your head at me in this furious style ; nothing can alter facts. *I saw.* Who has an account to demand then—you, whose life is already forfeit for an accumulation of crimes ; you, screened by a conspiracy of bribed servants and . . . . your best friend's wife, as you dare call your paramour ; or I, in my brother's absence the natural guardian of his family, of his honour ? But I am too late. One sister I saved from the ignominy you would have brought upon her. The other I could not save."

With a roar Jack Smith would have sprung at the speaker ; but, once more, his friend's wife rushed between.

" Let him speak," she cried, "what matter what he says ? But you—remember your promise. I will make the signal."

The signal ! The mask of Rupert's face, sternly and sadly rebuking, was not proof against the exquisite aptness of this proposal. His men outside were waiting for the signal, surrounding the island from land and seaward, (for the prey was not to be allowed to escape them again) ; but how to make it without creating suspicion had not yet suggested itself to his fertile brain. Now, while he held her lover in play, Molly would herself deliver him to justice. Excellent, excellent ! Truly life held some delightful jokes for the man of humour !

The light of triumph came and went upon his countenance like a flash, but when the life hangs upon the decision of a moment the wits become abnormally sharp. Jack Smith saw it, halted upon his second headlong onslaught, and turned round.—Too late : Molly was gone. He brought his gaze back upon his enemy and saw he had been trapped.

Their gleams met like duelling blades, divining each other's purpose with the rapidity of thrust answering thrust. Both made a leap for the door. But Rupert was nearest ; he first had his hand on the key and turned it, and, with newly-born genius of fight, suddenly begotten of his hatred, quickly stooped, eluded the advancing grasp, was free for one second, and sent the key crashing through the window into the darkness of the night.

Baffled by the astounding swiftness of the act, the sailor, wheeling round, had already raised his fist to crush his feebler foe, when, in the midst of his fury, a glimmer of the all-importance of every second of time stayed his hand. He threw himself upon the heavy ladder that rested against Sir Adrian's rows of books, and, clasping it by the middle, swung it above his head. The battering blow would, no doubt, have burst panel, lock, and hinges the next instant, but again Rupert forestalled him, and charged him before the door could be reached.

Overbalanced by the weight he held aloft, Captain Jack was hurled down headlong beneath the ladder, and lay for a moment stunned by the violence of the fall.

When the clouds cleared away it was to let him see Rupert's face bending over him, his pale lips wreathed into a smile of malignant exultation.

"Caught!" said Mr. Landale, slowly, pausing over each word as though to prolong the savour of it in his mouth, "caught this time! And it is your mistress's hand that puts the noose round your neck. That is what I call poetical justice."

The prostrate man, collecting his scattered wits and his vast strength, made a violent effort to spring to his feet. But Rupert's whole weight was upon him, his long thin fingers were gripping him by each shoulder, his face grinned at him, close, detested, infuriating. The grasp that held him seemed to belong to no flesh and blood, it was as the grasp of skeleton hands, the grinning face became like a death's head.

"I shall come to your hanging, Captain Jack Smith, or rather, Mr. Hubert Cochrane of the Shaws."

These were the last words of Rupert Landale. A red whirl passed through the sailor's brain, his hands fell like lashes round the other's neck and drew it down. *If Hubert Cochrane dies so does Rupert Landale : that throat shall never give sound to that name again.*

Over and over they roll like savage beasts, but yet in deathly silence. For the pressure of the fingers on his gullet, fingers that seem to gain fresh strength every moment and pierce into his very flesh, will not allow even a sigh to pass Rupert's lips, and Jack can spare no atom of his energy from the fury of fight : not one to spare even for the hearing of the frantic knocks at the door, the

24

calls, the hammering at the lock, the desperate efforts
without to prise it open.

*But if Rupert Landale must die so shall Hubert Cochrane,
and by the hangman's hand, treble doomed by this.* The
same thought fills both these men's heads; the devil of
murder has possession of both their souls. But, true to
himself to the last, it is with Rupert a calculating devil.
The officers must soon be here : he will hold the scoundrel yet with the grasp of death, and his enemy shall be
found red-handed—red-handed !

His hatred, his determination of vengeance, the very
agony of the unequal struggle for life gave him a power
that is almost a match for the young athlete in his
frenzy.

The dying efforts of his victim tax Jack's strength more
than the living fight; but his hands are still locked in
their fatal clutch when at last, with one fearful and spasmodic jerk, Rupert Landale falls motionless. Then exhaustion enwraps the conqueror also, like a mantle. He,
too, lies motionless with his cheek on the floor, face to
face with the corpse, dimly conscious of the voluptuous-
ness of victory. But the dead grasp still holds him by
the wrists, and it grows cold now, and rigid upon them.
It is as if they were fettered with iron.

Lady Landale's dread of her once despised kinsman,
now that she knew what a powerful weapon he held in
his hands, this night, was almost fantastic.

As she darted from the room, she fell against René,
who, with a white face and bent ear, stood at the door,
eavesdropping, ready to rush to the help of Sir Adrian's
friend upon the first hint of necessity. But he had heard
more than he bargained for.

The scared, well-nigh agonised look of inquiry with
which he turned to his mistress was lost upon her. In
her whirlwind exit, she seized upon him and dragged him
with her to the ladder that led to the tower.

"Quick, René, the signal !"

And with the birdlike swiftness of a dream flight she
was up the steps before him.

Panting in her wake, ran the sturdy fellow, his brain
seething in a chaos of conflicting thought. Mr. the
Captain must be helped, must be saved : this one thing

was clear at any rate. His honour would wish it so—no matter what had happened. Yes, he would obey My Lady and make the signal. But, what if Mr. Landale were right? Not indeed in his accusation of Mr. the Captain, René knew, René had seen enough to trust him: he was no false friend; but as regarded My Lady? Alas! My Lady had indeed been strange in her manner these days; and even Moggie, as he minded him now, even Moggie had noticed, had hinted, and he had not understood.

The man's fingers fumbled over the catch of the great lantern, he shook as if he had the palsy. Goodness divine, if his master were to come home to this!

Impatiently Lady Landale pushed him upon one side. What ailed the fellow, when every second was crucial, life or death bringing? Medusa-like for one second her face hung, white-illumined, set into terrible fixity, above the great flame, the next instant all was blackness to their dazzled eyes. The light of Scarthey was out!

She groped for René; her hot fingers burnt upon his cold rough hand for a second.

"I will go down to the sands," she said, whispering as if she feared, even here, the keenness of Rupert's ear, "and you—hurry to him, stop with him, defend him, your master's friend!"

She flitted from him like a shadow, the ladder creaked faintly beneath her light footfall, and then louder beneath his weighty tread.

His master's friend!

Ay, he would stand by him, for his master's sake and for his own sake too—the good gentleman!—And they would get him safe out of the way before his honour's return.

Out upon the beach ran Molly.

It was a mild still night; through veils of light mist the moon shone with a tranquil bride-like grace upon the heaving palpitating waters and the mystery of the silent land.

A very night for lovers, it seemed; for sweet meetings and sweeter partings; a night that mocked with its great passionless calm at the wild anguish of this woman's impatience. Yet a night upon which sound travelled far.

She bent her ear—was there nothing to hear yet, nothing but the lap of the restless waters? Were those men false?

She rushed to and fro, from one point to another along the sands in a delirium of impotent desire.

Oh, hurry, hurry, hurry!

And as she turned again, there, upon the waters out in the offing, glimmered a light, curtseying with the swell of the waves; the sails of a ship caught the moonbeams. She could see the vessel plainly and that it was bearing full for the island. Alas! This might scarcely be the little Shearman boat manned by two fishermen only; even she, unversed in sea knowledge could tell that. It was as large as the *Peregrine* itself—certainly as large as the cutter.

The *cutter!*

She caught her breath, and clapped her hands to her lips to choke down the wild scream of fear that rose to them.

At the same instant, a dull thud of oars, a subdued murmur of a deep voice rose from the other side of the island.

They were coming, coming from the landward, these rescuers of her beloved. And yonder, with swelling canvas, came the hell ship from out the open sea, sent by Rupert's infernal malice and cleverness, to make their help of no avail; to seize him, in the very act of flight.

She ran in the direction of the sound, and with all her strength called upon the new-comers to speed.

"Here—here, for God's sake! Hasten or it will be too late!"

Her voice seemed to her, in the midst of the endless space, weak as a child's; but it was heard.

"Coming!" answered a gruff shout from afar. And the oar beat came closer, and fell with swifter rhythm. Stumbling, catching in her skirts, careless of pool or stone beneath her little slippered feet, Lady Landale came flying round the ruins: a couple of boats crashed in upon the shingle, and the whole night seemed suddenly to become alive with dark figures—men in uniform, with gleams upon them of brass badges and shining belts, and in their hands the gleam of arms.

For the moment she could not move. It was as if her knees were giving way, and she must fall.

None of them saw her in the shadow; but as they passed, she heard them talking to each other about the signal, the signal which they had been told to look for, which had been brought to them . . . . the signal *she* had made. Then with a wave of rage, the power of life returned to her. This was Rupert's work! But all was not lost yet. The other boat was coming, the other boat must be the rescue after all; the Shearman's boat, or— who knows?—if there was mercy in Heaven, the *Peregrine*, whose crew might have heard of their captain's risk.

Back she raced to the seaward beach, hurling—unknowing that she spoke at all—invectives upon her husband's brother.

"Serpent, blood-hound, devil, devil, you shall not have him!"

As she reached the landing-place, breathless, a boat was landing in very truth. Even as she came up a tall figure jumped out upon the sand, and crunched towards her with great strides.

She made a leap forward, halted, and cried out shrilly:

"Adrian!"

"Molly—wife! Thank God!" His arms were stretched out to her, but he saw her waver and shudder from him, and wring her hands. "My God, what has happened? The light out, too! What is it?"

She fastened on him with a sudden fierceness, the spring of a wild cat.

"Come," she said, drawing him towards the peel, "if you would save him, lose not a second."

He hesitated a moment, still; she tugged at him like one demented, panting her abjurations at him, though her voice was failing her. Then, without a word, he fell to running with her towards the keep, supporting her as they went.

The great door had swung back on its hinges, and the men were pressing, in a dark body, into the dim-lit recesses, when Sir Adrian and his wife reached the entrance.

The sight of the uniforms only confirmed the homecomer in his own forebodings anent the first act of the drama that was being enacted upon his peaceful island. He needed no further pushing from the frantic woman at his side. Lost in bringing her back, perhaps, his only friend! Lost by his loyalty and his true friendship!

They dashed up the stone stairs just as the locked door of the living-room burst with a crash, under the efforts of many stalwart shoulders; they saw the men crush forwards, and fall back, and herd on again, with a hoarse murmur that leaped from mouth to mouth.

And René came running out from the throng with the face of one that has seen Death. And he caught his mistress by the arm, and held her by main force against the wall. He showed no surprise at the sight of his master—there are moments in life that are beyond surprise—but cried wildly:

"She must not see!"

She fought like a tigress against the faithful arms, but still they held her, and Sir Adrian went in alone.

A couple of men were dragging Captain Jack to his feet, forcing his hands from the dead man's throat; it seemed as if they had grown as rigid and paralysed in their clasp like the corpse hands that had now, likewise, to be wrenched from their clutch of him.

He glanced around, as though dazed, then down at the disfigured purple face of his dead enemy, smiled and held out his hands stiffly for the gyves that were snapped upon them.

And then one of the fellows, with some instinctive feeling of decency, flung a coat over the slain man, and Captain Jack threw up his head and met Adrian's horror-stricken, sorrowful eyes.

At the unexpected sight he grew scarlet; he waved his fettered hands at him as they hustled him forth.

"I have killed your brother, Adrian," he called out in a loud voice, "but I brought back your wife!"

Some of the men were speaking to Sir Adrian, but drew back respectfully before the spectacle of his wordless agony.

But, as Molly, with a shriek, would have flung herself after the prisoner, her husband awoke to action, and, pushing René aside, caught her round the waist with an unyielding grip: his eyes sought her face. And, as the light fell on it, he understood. Aye, she had been brought back to him. But how?

And René, watching his master's countenance, suddenly burst out blubbering, like a child.

CHAPTER XXX

HUSBAND AND WIFE

Tout comprendre—
c'est tout pardonner.

Staring straight before her with haggard, unseeing eyes, her hands clasped till the delicate bones protruded, her young face lined into sudden agedness, grey with unnatural pallor, framed by the black masses of her dishevelled hair, it was thus Sir Adrian found his wife, when at length he was free to seek her.

He and René had laid the dead man upon the bed that had been occupied by his murderer, and composed as decently as might be the hideous corpse of him who had been the handsomest of his race. René had given his master the tale of all he knew himself, and Sir Adrian had ordered the boat to be prepared, determined to convey Lady Landale at once from the scene of so much horror. His own return to Pulwick, moreover, to break the news to Sophia, to attend to the removal of the body and the preparation for the funeral was of immediate necessity.

As he approached his wife she raised her eyes.

"What do you want with me?" she asked, with a stony look that arrested him, as he would gently have taken her hand.

"I would bring you home."

"Home!" the pale lips writhed in withering derision.

"Yes, home, Molly," he spoke as one might to a much-loved and unreasonable sick child—with infinite tenderness and compassion—"your own warm home, with your sister. You would like to go to Madeleine, would not you?"

She unclasped her hands and threw them out before her with a savage gesture of repulsion.

"To Madeleine?" she echoed, with an angry cry; and

375

then wheeling round upon him fiercely : " Do you want to kill me ? " she said, between her set teeth.

Sir Adrian's weary brow contracted. He paused and looked at her with profoundest sorrow.

Then she asked, hoarsely :

" Where have they taken him to ? "

"To Lancaster, I believe."

" Will they hang him ? "

" I pray God not."

" There is no use of praying to God, God is merciless. What will they do to him ? "

" He will be tried, Molly, in due course, and then, according to the sentence of the judges . . . . My poor child, control yourself, he shall be defended by the best lawyers that money can get. All a man can do for another I shall do for him."

She shot the sombre fire of her glance at him.

" You know that I love him," she said, with a terrible composure.

A sudden whiteness spread round Sir Adrian's lips.

"Poor child ! " he said again beneath his breath.

"Yes, I love him. I always wanted to see him. I was sick and tired of life at Pulwick, and that was why I went on board his ship. I went deliberately because I could not bear the dulness of it all. He mistook me for Madeleine in the dark—he kissed me. Afterwards I told him that I loved him. I begged him to take me away with him, for ever. I love him still, I would go with him still —it is as well that you should know. Nothing can alter it now. But he did not want me. He loves Madeleine."

The words fell from her lips with a steady, cruel, deliberateness. She kept her eyes upon him as she spoke, unpityingly, uncaring what anguish she inflicted ; nay, it seemed from some strange perversity, glad to make him suffer.

But hard upon a man as it must be to hear such a confession from his wife's lips, doubly hard to such a one as Adrian, whose heart bled for her pain as well as for his own, he held himself without departing for a second from his wonted quiet dignity. Only in his earnest gaze upon her there was perhaps, if possible, an added tenderness.

But she, to see him so unmoved, was moved herself to a sudden scorn.

What manner of man was this, that not love, nor jealousy, nor anger had power to stir?

"And now what will you do with me?" she asked him again, with superb contempt on eye and lip. "For a guilty wife I am to you, as far as the will could make me, and I have no claim upon you any more."

"No claim upon me!" he repeated, with a wonder of grief in his voice. "Ah, Molly, hush child! You are my wife. The child of the woman I loved—the woman I love for her own sake. You can no more put yourself out of my life now than you can out of my heart; had you been as guilty in deed as you may have been in purpose my words would be the same. Your husband's home is your home, my only wish to cherish and shelter you. You cannot escape my care, poor child, and some day you may be glad of it. My protection, my countenance you will always have. God! who am I that I should judge you? Is there any sin of human frailty that a human being dare condemn? Guilty? What is your guilt compared to mine for bringing you to this, allying my melancholy age with your bright youth?"

He fell into the chair opposite to her and covered his face with his hands. As, for a minute's space, his self-control wavered, she watched him, wearily. Her heat of temper had fallen from her very quickly; she broke into a moan.

"Oh, what does it matter? What does anything matter now? I love him and I have ruined him—had it not been for me he would be safe!"

After a little silence Sir Adrian rose. "I must leave you now, I must go to Pulwick," he said. His heart was yearning to her, he would have gathered her to his arms as a father his erring child, but he refrained from even touching her. "And you—what would you do? It shall be as you like."

"I would go to Lancaster," she said.

"The carriage shall be sent for you in the morning and Renny and his wife shall go with you. I will see to it. After Rupert's funeral—my God, what a night this has been!—I will join you, and together we shall work to save his life."

He paused, hesitated, and was about to turn away when suddenly she caught his hand and kissed it.

He knew she would as readily have kissed René's hand for a like promise ; that her gratitude was a pitiable thing for him, her husband, to bear ; and yet, all the way, on his sad and solitary journey to Pulwick, the touch of her lips went with him, bringing a strange sweetness to his heart.

There was a vast deal of wonder in the county generally, and among the old friends of his father's house in particular, when it became known that Sir Adrian Landale had engaged a noted counsel to defend his brother's murderer and was doing all he could to avert his probable doom. In lowered tones were whispered strange tales of Lady Landale's escapade. People wagged wise and virtuous heads and breathed scandalous hints of her power upon her infatuated husband ; and then they would tap their foreheads significantly. Indeed it needed all the master of Pulwick's wide-spread reputation for mental unsoundness to enable him to carry through such proceedings without rousing more violent feelings. As it was, it is to be doubted whether his interference had any other effect than that of helping to inflame the public mind against the prisoner.

The jury's verdict was a foregone conclusion ; and though the learned lawyer duly prepared a very fine speech and pocketed some monstrous fees with a great deal of complaisance, he was honest enough not to hold out the smallest hope of being able to save his client.

The conviction was too clear, the " crimes " the prisoner had committed were of " too horrible and bloody a character, threatening the very foundations of society," to admit of a merciful view of the case.

As the trial drew near, Sir Adrian's despondency increased ; each day seemed to bring a heavier furrow to his brow, an added weight to his lagging steps. He avoided as much as possible all meetings with his wife, who, on the contrary, recovered stronger courage with the flight of time, but whose feverish interest in his exertions was now transferred to some secret plans that she was for ever discussing with René. The prisoner himself showed great calmness.

"They will sentence me of course," he said quietly to Adrian, " but whether they will hang me is another question. I don't think that my hour has come yet or that the cord is twisted which will hang Jack Smith."

In other moods, he would ridicule Sir Adrian's labours in his cause with the most gentle note of affectionate mockery. But, from the desire doubtless to save one so disinterested and unworldly from any accusation of complicity, he was silent upon the schemes on which he pinned his hopes of escape.

The first meeting of the friends after the scene at Scarthey had been, of course, painful to both.

When he entered the cell, Adrian had stretched out his hand in silence, but Captain Jack held his own pressed to his side.

"It is like you to come," he said gloomily, "but you cannot shake the hand that stifled your brother's life out of him. And I should do it again, Adrian! Mark you, I am not repentant!"

"Give me your hand, Jack," said Adrian steadfastly. "I am not of those who shift responsibility from the dead to the living. You were grievously treated. Oh, give me your hand, friend, can I think of anything now but your peril and your truth to me?"

For an instant still the younger man hesitated and inquiringly raised his eyes laden with anxious trouble, to the elder man's face.

"My wife has told me all," said Sir Adrian, turning his head to hide his twitching lip.

And then Jack Smith's hand leaped out to meet his friend's upon an impulse of warm sympathy, and the two faced each other, looking the words they could not utter.

The year eighteen hundred and fifteen which delivered England at last from the strain of outlandish conflict saw a revival of official activity concerning matters of more homely interest. The powers that were awoke to the necessity, among other things, of putting a stop by the most stringent means to the constant and extensive leakage in the national revenue proceeding from the organisation of free traders or smugglers.

After twenty years of almost complete supineness on the part of the authorities, the first efforts made towards a systematic "Preventive" coast service, composed of customs, excise and naval officials in proportion varied

according to the localities, remained singularly futile.
And to the notorious inability of these latter to cope with
the experience and the devilish daring of the old established free traders, was due no doubt to the ferocity of
the inquisitional laws presently levelled against smuggling and smugglers—laws which ruthlessly trenched
upon almost every element of the British subjects' vaunted
personal freedom, and which added, for the time, several
new " hanging cases " to the sixty odd already in existence.

That part of the indictment against Captain Jack Smith
and the other criminals still at large, which dealt with their
offences against the smuggling act, would in later times
have broken down infallibly from want of proper evidence :
not a tittle of information was forthcoming which could
support examination.   But a judge of assizes and a jury
in 1815, were not to be baulked of the necessary victim by
mere circumstantiality when certain offences against
society and against His Majesty had to be avenged ; and
the dispensers of justice were less concerned with strict
evidence than with the desirability of making examples.
Strong presumption was all that was required to them to
hang their man ; and indeed the hanging of Captain Jack
upon the other and more serious counts than that of unlawful occupation, was, as has been said, a foregone
conclusion.   The triple charge of murder being but too
fully corroborated.

Every specious argument that could be mooted was of
course put forward by counsel for the defence, to show
that the death of the preventive men and of Mr. Landale
on Scarthey Island and the sinking of the revenue cutter must be looked upon, on the one hand, as simple man-
slaughter in self-defence, and as the result of accidental
collision, on the other.   But, as every one anticipated, the
charge of the judge and the finding of the jury demanded strenuously the extreme penalty of the law.   Besides this the judge deemed it advisable to introduce
into the sentence one of those already obsolete penal-
ties of posthumous degradation, devised in coarser ages
for the purpose of making an awful impression upon the
living.

" Prisoner at the bar," said his lordship at the conclusion of the last day's proceedings, " the sentence of the

law which I am about to pass upon you and which the court awards is that you now be taken to the place whence you came, and from thence, on the day appointed, to the place of execution, there to be hanged by the neck until you be dead, dead, dead. And may God have mercy on your soul!"

Captain Jack, standing bolt upright, with his eyes fixed upon the speaker, calm as he ever had been when awaiting the enemy's broadside, hearkened without stirring a muscle. But when the judge, after pronouncing the last words with a lingering fulness and impressiveness, continued through the heavy silence: "And that, at a subsequent time, your body, bound in irons, shall be suspended upon a gibbet erected as near as possible to the scenes of your successive crimes, and shall there remain as a lasting warning to wrong-doers of the inevitable ultimate end of such an evil life as yours," a wave of crimson flew to the prisoner's forehead, upon which every vein swelled ominously.

He shot a glance of fury at the large flabby countenance of the righteous arbiter of his doom, whilst his hands closed themselves with an involuntary gesture of menace. Then the tide of anger ebbed; a contemptuous smile parted his lips. And, bowing with an air of light mockery to the court, he turned, erect and easy, to follow his turnkey out of the hall.

CHAPTER XXXI

IN LANCASTER CASTLE

ALL that his friendship for the condemned man, all that his love and pity for his almost distracted wife, could suggest, Sir Adrian Landale had done in London to try and avert Captain Jack's doom. But it was in vain. There also old stories of his peculiar tenets and of his well-known disaffection to the established order of things, had been raked up against him. Unfavourable comparisons had been drawn between him and Rupert; surprise and disapproval had been expressed at the unnatural brother, who was displaying such energy to obtain mercy for his brother's murderer. Finally an influential personage, whom Sir Adrian had contrived to interest in the case, in memory of an old friendship with his father, informed the baronet that his persistence was viewed with extreme disfavour in the most exalted quarter, and that His Royal Highness himself had pronounced that Captain Jack was a damned rascal and richly deserved his fate.

From the beginning, indeed, the suppliant had been without hope. Though he was resolved to leave no stone unturned, no possibility untried in the effort to save his friend, well-nigh the saddest part of the whole business to him was the realisation that the prisoner had not only broken those custom laws (of which Sir Adrian himself disapproved as arbitrary) but also, as he had been warned, those other laws upon which depend all social order and security ; broken them so grievously that, whatever excuses the philosopher might find in heat of blood and stress of circumstances, given laws at all, the sentence could not be pronounced otherwise than just.

And so, with an aching heart and a wider horror than ever of the cruel world of men, and of the injustices to which legal justice leads, Sir Adrian left London to hurry back to Lancaster with all the speed that post-horses

could muster. The time was now drawing short. As
the traveller rattled along the stony streets of the old
Palatine town, and saw the dawn breaking, exquisite,
primrose tinted, faintly beautiful as some dream vision
over the distant hills, his soul was gripped with an iron
clutch. In three more days the gallant heart, breaking
in the confinement of the prison yonder, would have
throbbed its last! And he longed, with a desire futile
but none the less intense, that, according to that doctrine
of Vicarious Atonement preached to humanity by the
greatest of all examples, he could lay down his own weary
and disappointed life for his friend.

Having breakfasted at the hotel, less for the necessity
of food than for the sake of passing the time till the morning should have worn to sufficient maturity, he sought on
foot the quiet lodgings where he had installed his wife
under René's guard before starting on his futile quest.
Early as the hour still was—seven had but just rung
merrily from some chiming church clock—the faithful
fellow was already astir and prompt to answer his master's
summons.

One look at the latter's countenance was sufficient to
confirm the servant's own worst forebodings.

"Ah, your honour, and is it indeed so. *Ces gredins!*
and will they hang so good a gentleman?"

"Hush, Renny, not so loud," cried the other with an
anxious look at the folding-doors, that divided the little
sitting-room from the inner apartment.

"Oh, his honour need have no fear. My Lady is gone,
gone to Pulwick. His honour need not disquiet himself;
he can well imagine that I would not allow her to go alone
—when I had been given a trust so precious. No, no, the
old lady, Miss O'Donoghue, your honour's aunt and her
ladyship's, she has heard of all these terrible doings, and
came to Lancaster to be with My Lady. *Ma foi*, I know
not if she be just the person one would have chosen, for
she has scolded a great deal, and is as agitated—as agitated as a young rabbit. But, after all, she loves the poor
young lady with all her heart, and I think she has roused
her a little. His honour knows," said the man, flushing
to the roots of his hair, whilst he shifted nervously from
one foot to another, "that My Lady has been much upset about the poor captain. After his honour went, she

would sit, staring out of the window there, just where the street turns up to the castle, and neither ate nor slept, nor talked to speak of. Of course, as I told the old Demoiselle, I knew it was because My Lady had taken it to heart about the signal that she made—thinking to save him—and which only brought the gabelous on him, that his honour's infernal brother (God forgive me, and have mercy on his soul) had set to watch. And My Lady liked to see me coming and going, for she sent me every day to the prison ; she did not once go herself."

Sir Adrian drew a long breath. With the most delicate intuition of his master's thoughts, René avoided even a glance at him while he continued in as natural a tone as he could assume :

"But the day after the old miss came, she, My Lady, told me to find out if he would see her. He said no ; but that the only kindness any one could do him now would be to bring him Mademoiselle Madeleine, and let him speak to her once more. And My Lady, when she heard this, she started off that day with the old one to fetch Mademoiselle herself at Pulwick. And she left me behind, your honour, for I had a little plan there."

René faltered and a crestfallen look crept upon his face.

Sir Adrian remembered how before his departure for London his servant had cheerily assured him that Mr. the Captain would be safe out of the country long before he returned, "faith of him, René, who had already been in two prisons, and knew their ways, and how to contrive an escape, as his honour well knew." A sad smile parted his lips.

"And so you failed, Renny," he said.

"Ah, your honour, those satanic English turnkeys ! With a Frenchman, the job had been done ; but it is a bad thing to be in prison in England. His honour can vouch I have some brains. I had made plans—a hundred plans, but there was ever something that did not work. The captain, he too, was eager, as your honour can imagine. My faith, we thought and we thought, and we schemed and contrived, and in the end, there was only one thing to complete our plot—to bribe the jailer. Would your honour believe—it was only that one little difficulty. My Lady had given me a hundred

guineas, I had enough money, your honour sees.   But
the man—I had smoked with him, drunk with him, ay,
and made him drunk too, and I thought all was going
well, but when I hinted to him what we wanted—Ah ! he
was a brute—I tell you I had hard work to escape the
prison myself, and only for my leaving him with some of
the money, I should now be pinched there too.   I hardly
dare show my face in the place any more.   And my poor
Lady builds on the hope, and Mr. the Captain—I had to
tell him, he took it like an angel.   Ah, the poor gentleman !   He looked at me so brave and kind !   'I am as
grateful, my poor friend, as if you had done it,' said he,
'and perhaps it is all for the best.'   All for the best—ah,
your honour ! "

René fairly broke down here, and wept on his sleeve.
But Sir Adrian's eyes, circled and worn with watching
and thought, shone dry with a far deeper grief, as, a few
moments later, he passed along the street towards the
walls of the castle.

There was in those days little difficulty in obtaining
admission to a condemned prisoner ; and, in the rear of
the red-headed, good-tempered looking jailer—the same,
he surmised, whose sternness in duty had baffled the
Breton's simple wiles—he stepped out of the sweet morning sunshine into the long stone passages.   The first
tainted breath of the prison brought a chill to his blood
and oppression to his lungs, and the gloom of the place
enveloped him like a pall.

With a rattle of keys a door dismally creaking on its
hinges was swung back at last, and the visitor was ushered
into the narrow cell, dark for all its whitewashed walls,
where Captain Jack was spending his last hours upon
earth.   The hinges groaned again, the door slammed,
and the key once more grated in the lock.   Sir Adrian
was alone with his friend.

For a moment there was silence ; the contraction of
the elder man's heart had brought a giddiness to his brain,
a dimness of his eyes, through which he was ill able to
distinguish anything.

But then there was a clank of fetters—ah, what a sound
to connect with lucky Jack Smith, the gayest, freest, and
most buoyant of men !   And a voice cried :

25

" Adrian ! "

It had a joyful ring, well-nigh the old hearty tones.   It struck Adrian to the soul.

He could have borne, he thought, to find his friend a broken man, changed out of all recognition, crushed by his misfortunes ; but to find him the same, a little pale, indeed, and thinner, with a steady earnestness in the sea-blue eyes instead of the old dancing-light, but still gallant and undaunted, still radiating vigorous life and breezy energy by his very presence, this was a cruelty of fate which seemed unendurable.

"I declare," the prisoner had continued, " I declare I thought you were only the incorruptible jailer taking his morning survey. They are desperately careful of me, Adrian, and watch me with maternal solicitude lest I should strangle myself with my chains, these pretty bracelets which I have had to wear ever since poor Renny was found out, or swallow my pillow—dash me ! it's small enough—and spoil the pretty show for Saturday ! Why, why, Adrian, old friend ? "

There was a sudden change of tone to the warmest concern, for Sir Adrian had staggered and would have fallen had not Jack, as nimbly as his fetters would allow him, sprung to support him and conduct him to the bed.

A shaft of light struck through the tiny barred window on to the elder man's face, and showed it against the surrounding darkness deathly white and wet with anguish.

" I have done all I could, Hubert," he murmured, in an extinguished voice, " but to no avail."

" Ay, man, I guessed as much.   But never fret for me, Adrian : I have looked death too often in the face to play the poltroon, now.   I don't say it's the end I should have chosen for myself; but it is inevitable, and there is nothing, as you know, my friend, that a man cannot face if he knows it must be faced."

The grasp of his strong warm hands, all manacled as they were, upon the other's nerveless clammy fingers, sent, more than the words, something of the speaker's own courage to his friend's wrung heart.   And yet that very courage was an added torment.

That from a community, so full of evil, feeble, harmful wretches, this noble soul, no matter how it had sinned, should be banished at the bidding of justice—what mockery of right was this? The world was out of joint indeed. He groaned aloud.

"Nay, I'll have none of it," cried Jack. "Our last talk, Adrian, must not be spoiled by futile regrets. Yes, our last talk it is to be, for "—the prisoner's face became transfigured with a tenderness so exquisite that Adrian stared at its beauty, amazed—" I have begged her, Madeleine, to come and see me once more. I think she can be here to-day, at latest to-morrow. And after that I would not see any of those I love again, that I may fit myself to meet my God."

He spoke with the utmost simplicity. Adrian bowed his head silently. Then averting his eyes, he said : "My wife has gone to Pulwick to fetch her."

Captain Jack crimsoned. "That is kind," he answered, in a low voice ; and, after a pause, pursued : " I hope you do not think it wrong of me to wish to see her. But you may trust me. I shall distress her as little as is possible in the circumstances. It is not, as you can fancy "—his face flushed again as he spoke—"to indulge in a pathetic parting scene, or beg from her sweet lips one last kiss—that would be too grossly selfish, and however this poor body of mine, so soon to be carrion, may yearn to hold her once more closely, these lips, so soon to touch death, shall touch hers no more. I have risen so far above this earthliness, that in so many hours I am to shake off for ever, that I can trust myself to meet her soul to soul. She must believe me now, and I would tell her, Adrian, that my deceit was not premeditated, and that the man she once honoured with her love is not the base wretch she deems. I think it may comfort her. If she does mourn for me at all—she has so proud a spirit, my princess, as I used to call her—it may comfort her to know that I was not all unworthy of the love she once gave me, of the tears she may yet give to its memory and mine."

Sir Adrian pressed his hand, but again could not speak, and Captain Jack went on :

"You will give her a happy home, will you not, till she has one of her own? You and your old dragon of an aunt, whose bark is so much worse than her bite, will watch and guard her. Ah, poor old lady ! she is one of

those that will not weep for Jack Smith, eh, Adrian ?
Well, well, I have had a happy life, barring one or two
hard raps of fate, and when only I have seen Madeleine
once more, I'll feel all taut for the port, though the passage there be a rough one."

Sir Adrian turned his gaze with astonishment upon him.
The sailor read his thoughts :

" Don't think," he said, while a sudden shadow crossed
his face, " don't think that I don't realise my position,
that I have not had to fight my battle.   In the beginning
I had hopes ; never in the success of your mission, but,
absurd as it was, in Renny's scheme.   The good fellow's
own hopefulness was infectious, I believe.   And when
that fell through—well then, man, I just had to make up
my mind to what was to be.   It was a battle, as I told
you.   I have been in danger of death many a time upon
the brave old *St. Nicholas*, and my *Cormorant*—death from
the salt sea, from musket ball and cannon shot, fearful
deaths of mangling and hacking.   But death on the gallows, the shameful death of the criminal ; to be hung ; to
be executed—Pah ! Ay ! it was a battle—two nights and
one day I fought it.   And I tell you, 'tis a hard thing to
bring the living flesh and the leaping blood to submit to
such as that.   At first I thought indeed, it could not be
borne, and I must reckon upon your or Renny's friendship
for a secret speed.   I should have had the pluck to starve
myself if need be, only I am so damned strong and
healthy, I feared it could not have been managed in the
time.   At any rate, I could have dashed my brains out
against the wall—but I see it otherwise now.   The
prison chaplain, a good man, Adrian, has made me realise that it would be cowardly, that I should accept my
sentence as atonement, as deserved—I *have* deserved to
die."

It had been Sir Adrian's own thought ; but he broke
out now in inarticulate protest.   It seemed too gross, too
monstrous.

" Yes, Adrian, I have.   You warned me, good friend,
in your peaceful room—ah, how long ago it seems now !
that night, when all that could make life beautiful lay to
my hand for the taking.   Oh, man, why did I not heed
you ! You warned me : he who breaks one law will end
by breaking many.   You were right.   See the harm I

wreaked—those poor fellows, who were but doing their
duty bravely, whose lives I sacrificed without remorse!
Your brother, too, whose soul, with the most deliberate
vindictiveness, I sent before its Maker, without an instant's preparation! A guilty soul it was; for he hounded
me down, one would almost think for the sport of it. . . .
God! when I think that, but for him, for his wanton interference—but there, the devils are loose again! I must
not think on him. Do I not deserve my fate, if the Bible
law be right? 'He who sheds blood, his blood shall be
shed.' Never was sentence more just. I have sinned, I
have repented; I am now ready to atone. I believe the
sacrifice will be accepted."

He laid his hand, for a minute, upon the Bible on the
table, with a significant gesture.

But Sir Adrian, the philosopher, though he could find
no words to impeach the logic of his friend's reasoning,
and was all astir with admiration for a resignation as
perfect as either Christian or Stoic could desire, found his
soul rising in tumultuous rebellion against the hideous
decree. The longing that had beset him in the dawn,
now seized upon him with a new passion, and the cry
escaped his lips almost unwittingly:

"Oh, if I could die for you!"

"No, no," said Jack, with his sweet smile, "your life
is too valuable, too precious to the world. Adrian, believe me, you can still do much good with it. And I
know you will be happy yet."

It was the only allusion he had made to his friend's
more personal sorrows. Before the latter had time to
reply, he hastened to proceed:

"And now to business. All the gold entrusted to me
lies at Scarthey and, faith, I believe it lies as weightily
on my mind as if it was all stored there instead! Renny
knows the secret hiding-place. Will you engage to restore it to its owners, in all privacy? This is a terribly
arduous undertaking, Adrian, and it is asking much of
your friendship; but if I know you, not too much. And
it will enable my poor bones to lie at rest, or rather," with
a rueful laugh, "hang at rest on their gibbet: for you
know I am to be set up as a warning to other fools, like
a rat on a barn door. I have, by the kindness of the
chaplain, been able to write out a full schedule of the

different sums, and to whom they are due.   He has taken
charge of the closed packet directed to you, and will give
it to you intact, I feel sure.   He is a man of honour, and
I trust him to respect the confidence I have placed in
him. . . . . Egad! the poor old boys will be right glad
to get their coin back in safety.   A couple of them have
been up here already, to interview me, in fear and trembling.   They were hard set to credit me when I assured
them that they would be no losers in the end, after all
—barring the waiting.   You see, I counted upon you."

"I shall never rest until it is done," said Sir Adrian,
simply.   And Captain Jack as simply answered : "Thank
you.   Among the treasure there is also £10,000 of my
own ; the rest of my laboriously acquired fortune is forfeit to the Crown, as you know—much good may it do
it !   But this little hoard I give to you.   You do not want
it, of course, and therefore it is only to be yours that you
may administrate it in accordance to my wishes.   Another charge—but I make no apology.   I wish you to
divide it in three equal shares : two to be employed as
you see best, for the widows and families of those poor
fellows of the preventive service, victims of my venture ;
the third, as well as my beautiful *Peregrine*, I leave to
the mate and men who served me so faithfully.   They
have fled with her, and must avoid England for some
time.   But Renny will contrive to hear of them ; they
are bound to return in secret for tidings, and I should like
to feel that the misery I have left behind me may be
mitigated. . . . . And now, dear Adrian, that is all.   The
man outside grows impatient.   I hear him shuffling his
keys.   Hark ! there he knocks ; the fellow has a certain
rude feeling for me.   An honest fellow.   Dear Adrian,
good-bye."

"My God ! this is hard—is there nothing else—nothing
—can indeed all my friendship be of no further help ?—
Hubert !"

"Hush, hush," cried Jack Smith hastily, "Adrian, you
alone of all living beings now know me by that name.
Never let it cross your lips again.   I could not die in peace
were it not for the thought that I bring no discredit upon
it.   My mother believes me dead—God in His mercy has
spared me the crowning misery of bringing shame to her
white hairs—shame to the old race.   Hubert Cochrane

died ten years ago. Jack Smith alone it is that dies by the hangman's hand. One other," his voice softened and the hard look of pain left his face, "one other shall hear the secret besides you—but I know she will never speak of it, even to you—and such is my wish."

It was the pride of race at its last and highest expression.

There was the sound, without, of the key in the lock.

"One last word—if you love me, nay, as you love me—do not be there on Saturday ! This parting with you—the good-bye to her—that is my death. Afterwards what happens to this flesh," he struck at himself with his chained hands, "matters no more than what will happen to the soulless corpse. I know you would come to help me with the feeling of your love, your presence—but do not—do not—and now good-bye !"

Adrian seized his friend by the hands with a despairing grip, the door rolled back with its dismal screech.

The prisoner smiled at him with tender eyes. This man whom, all unwillingly he had robbed of his wife's heart, was broken with grief that he could not save the life that had brought him misery. Here was a friend to be proud of, even at the gate of death !

"God be with you, dear Adrian ! God bless you and your household, and your children, and your children's children ! Hear my last words : *From my death will be born your happiness, and if its growth be slow, yet it will wax strong and sure as the years go by.*"

The words broke from him with prophetic solemnity ; their hands fell apart, and Adrian, led by the jailer, stumbled forth blindly. Jack Smith stood erect, still smiling, watching them : were Adrian to turn he should find no weakness, no faltering for the final remembrance.

But Adrian did not turn. And the door closed, closed upon hope and happiness and life, shut in shame and death. Out yonder, with Adrian, was the fresh bright world, the sea, the sunshine, the dear ones ; here the prison smells, the gloom, the constraint, the inflicted dreadful death. All his hard-won calm fled from him ; all his youth, his immense vitality woke up and cried out in him again. He raised his hands and pulled fiercely at his collar as if already the rope were round his neck strangling him. His blood hammered in his brain. God

—God—it was impossible—it could not be—it was a dream !

Beyond, from far distant in the street came the cry of a little child :

" Da-da—daddy."

The prisoner threw up his arms and then fell upon his face upon the bed, torn by sobs.

Yes, Adrian would have children ; but Hubert Cochrane, who, from the beautiful young brood that was to have sprung from his loins would have grafted on the old stock a fresh and noble tree, he was to pass barren out of life and leave no trace behind him.

CHAPTER XXXII

THE ONE HE LOVED AND THE ONE WHO LOVED HIM

On the evening of the previous day Lady Landale and her Aunt had arrived at Pulwick. The drive had been a dismal one to poor Miss O'Donoghue. Neither her angry expostulations, nor her tender remonstrances, nor her attempts at consolation could succeed in drawing a connected sentence from Molly, who, with a fever spot of red upon each cheek only roused herself from the depth of thought in which she seemed plunged to urge the coachman to greater speed. Miss O'Donoghue tried the whole gamut of her art in vain, and was obliged at last to desist from sheer weariness and in much anxiety.

Madeleine and Sophia were seated by the fireside in the library when the unexpected travellers came in upon them. Sophia, in the blackest of black weeds, started guiltily up from the volume of "The Corsair," in which she had been plunged, while Madeleine, without manifesting any surprise, rose placidly, laid aside her needlework—a coarse flannel frock, evidently destined for charity—and bestowed upon her sister and aunt an affectionate though unexpansive embrace.

She had grown somewhat thinner and more thoughtful-looking since Molly and she had last met, on that fatal 15th of March, but otherwise was unchanged in her serene beauty. Molly clutched her wrist with a burning hand, and, paying not the slightest attention to the other two, nor condescending to any preamble, began at once, in hurried words to explain her mission.

"He has asked for you, Madeleine," she cried, her eyes flaming with unnatural brilliance as they sought her sister's mild gaze. "He has asked for you, I will take you back with me, to-morrow, not later than to-morrow. Don't you understand?" shaking her impatiently as she held her, "he is in prison, condemned to death, he has

393

asked for you, he wants to see you.   On Saturday—on
Saturday——" Something clicked in her throat, and she
raised her hand to it with an uneasy gesture, one that
those who surrounded her had grown curiously familiar
with of late.

Madeleine drew away from her at this address, the
whole fair calm of her countenance troubled like a placid
pool by the casting of a stone.   Clasping her hands and
looking down : "I saw that the unfortunate man was
condemned," she said.   "I have prayed for him daily,
I trust he repents.   I am truly sorry for him.   From my
heart I forgive him the deception he practised upon me.
But——" a slight shudder shook her, "I could not see
him again—surely you could not wish it of me."

She spoke with such extreme gentleness that for a
minute the woman before her, in the seething turmoil of
her soul, failed to grasp the meaning of her words.

"You could not go!" she repeated in a bewildered
way, "I could not wish it of you—!" then with a sort of
shriek which drew Tanty and Miss Sophia hurriedly towards her, "Don't you understand—on Saturday—if it
all fails, they will hang him?"

"A-ah!" exclaimed Madeleine with a movement as if
to ward off the sound—the cry, the gesture expressive,
not of grief, but of shrinking repugnance.   But after a
second, controlling herself :

"And what should that be now, sister, to you or to
me?" she said haughtily.

Lady Landale clapped her hands together.

"And this is the woman he loves !" she cried with a
shrill laugh.   And she staggered, and sank back upon a
chair in an attitude of utter prostration.

"Molly, Molly," exclaimed her sister reprovingly,
while she glanced in much distress at Miss O'Donoghue,
"you are not yourself; you do not know what you are
saying."

"Remember," interposed Sophia in tragic tones, "that
you are speaking of the murderer of my beloved brother."
Then she dissolved in tears, and was obliged to hide her
countenance in the folds of a vast pocket-handkerchief.

"Killing vermin is not murder !" cried Molly fiercely,
awakening from her torpor.

Miss O'Donoghue, who in the most unwonted silence

had been watching the scene with her shrewd eyes, here
seized the horrified Sophia by the elbow and trundled
her, with a great deal of energy and determination, to the
door.

"Get out of this, you foolish creature," she said in a
stern whisper, "and don't attempt to show your nose here
again till I give it leave to walk in !" Then returning to
the sisters, and looking from Molly's haggard, distracted
face to Madeleine's pale one : "If you take my advice,
my dear," she said, a little drily, to the latter, "you will
not make so many bones about going to see that poor lad
in the prison, and you'll stop wrangling with your sister,
for she is just not able to bear it. We shall start to-
morrow, Molly," turning to Lady Landale, and speaking
in the tone of one addressing a sick child, "and Madeleine will be quite ready as early as you wish."

"My dear aunt," said Madeleine, growing white to the
lips, "I am very sorry if Molly is ill, but you are quite
mistaken if you think I can yield to her wishes in this
matter. I could not go ; I could not ; it is impossible !"

"Hear her," cried the other, starting from her seat.
"Oh, what are you made of? Is it water that runs in
your veins ? you that he loves"—her voice broke into a
wail—"you who ought to be so proud to know he loves
you even though your heart be broken ! You refuse to
go to him, refuse his last request ! . . . . Come to the
light," she went on, seizing the girl's wrists again ; "let
me look at you. Bah ! you never loved him. You don't
even understand what it is to love . . . . But what could
one expect from you, who abandoned him in the moment
of danger. You are afraid ; afraid of the painful scene,
the discomfort, the sight of the prison, of his beautiful
face worn and changed—afraid of the discredit. Oh ! I
know you, I know you. But mind you, Madeleine de
Savenaye, he wishes to see you, and I swore you would
go to him, and you shall go, if I have to drag you with
these hands of mine."

Her grip was so fierce, her eyes so savage, the words
so strange, that Madeleine screamed faintly, "She is
mad !" and was amazed that Miss O'Donoghue did not
rush to the rescue !

But Miss O'Donoghue, peering at her from the depths
of her arm-chair, merely said snappishly : "Ah, child,

can't you say you will go, and have done! Oughtn't
you to be ashamed to be so hard-hearted?" and mopped
her perspiring and agitated countenance with her kerchief.
Then upon the girl's bewildered mind dawned a glimmer
of the truth; and, blushing to the roots of her hair, she
looked at her sister with a growing horror.

"Oh, Molly, Molly!" she said again, with a sort of
groan.

"Will you go?" cried Molly from between her set
teeth.

Again the girl shuddered.

"Less than ever—now," she murmured. And as Molly
threw her from her, almost with violence, she covered
her face with her hands and fell, weeping bitter tears,
upon the couch behind her.

Lady Landale, with great steps, stormed up and down
the room, her eyes fixed on space, her lips moving; now
and again a word escaped her then, sometimes hurled at
her sister, sometimes only in desperate communing with
herself.

"Base, cowardly, mean! Oh, my God, cruel—cruel!
To go back without her."

After a little, with a sudden change of mood, she halted
and stood a while, as if in deep reflection, holding her
hand to her head, then crossing the room hurriedly,
she knelt down, and flung her arms round the weeping
figure.

"*Ma petite Madeleine*," she said in a voice of the most
piteous pleading, "thou and I, we were always good
friends; thou canst not have the heart to be so cruel to
me now. See, my darling, he must die, they say—oh,
Madeleine, Madeleine! And he asked for you. The
one thing, he told René, the only thing we could do for
him on earth was to let him see you once more. My
little sister, you cannot refuse: he loves you. What has
he done to offend you? Your pride cannot forgive him
for being what he is, I suppose; yet such as he is you
should be proud of him. He is too noble, too straight-
forward to have intentionally deceived you. If he did
wrong, it was for love of you. Madeleine, Madeleine!"

Her tones trailed away into a moan.

Miss O'Donoghue sobbed loudly from her corner.
Madeleine, who had looked at her sister at first with

repulsion, seemed moved ; she placed her hands upon her shoulders, and gazed sadly into the flushed face.

" My poor Molly," she said hesitatingly, "this is dreadful ! But I too—I too was led into deceit, into folly." She blushed painfully. "I would not blame you ; it was not your fault that you were carried away in his ship. You went only for my sake : I cannot forget that. Yet that he should have this unhappy power over you too, you with your good husband, you a married woman, oh, my poor sister, it is terrible ! He is a wicked man ; I pray that he may yet repent."

" Heavens," interrupted Molly, her passion up in arms again, loosening as she spoke her clasp upon her sister, and rising to her feet to look down on her with withering scorn, "have I not made myself clear ? Are you deaf, stupid, as well as heartless ? It is you—you—*you* he loves, *you* he wants. What am *I* to him ? " with a curious sob, half of laughter, half of anguish. " Your pious fears are quite unfounded as far as he is concerned—the wicked man, as you call him ! Oh, he spurns my love with as much horror as even you could wish ! "

" Molly ! "

" Ay—Molly, and Molly—how shocked you are ! Yes, I love him, I don't care who hears it. I love him— Adrian knows—he is not as virtuous as you, evidently, for Adrian pities me. He is doing all he can, though they say it is in vain, to get a reprieve for him—though I *do* love him ! While you—you are too good, too immaculate even to soil your dainty foot upon the floor of his prison, that floor that I could kiss because his shoe has trod it. But it is impossible ! no human being could be so hard, least of all you, whom I have seen turn sick at the sight of a dead worm—Madeleine—— ! "

Crouching down in the former imploring manner, while her breast heaved with dry tearless sobs : " It cannot hurt you, you who loved him." And then with the old pitiful cry, " it is the only thing he wants, and he loves you."

Madeleine disengaged herself from the clinging hands with a gesture almost of disgust.

" Listen to me," she said, after a pause, " try and compose yourself and understand. All this month I have had time to think, to realise, to pray. I have seen what the world is worth, that it is full of horror, of sin, of trouble, of dreadful dissensions—that its sorrow far out-weighs its happiness. I *have* suffered," her pretty lips quivered an instant, but she hardened herself and went on, "but it is better so—it was God's will, it was to show me where to find real comfort, the true peace. I have quite made up my mind. I was only waiting to see you again and tell you—next week ⁚ am going back to the convent for ever. Oh, why did we leave it, Molly, why did we leave it!" She broke down, and the tears gushed from her eyes.

Lady Landale had listened in silence.

"Well—is that all ?" she said impatiently, when her sister ceased speaking, while in the background Tanty groaned out a protest, and bewailed that she was alive to see the day. "What does it matter what you do after-wards—you can go to the convent—go where you will then ; but what has that to say to your visit to *him* now ?"

"I have done with all human love," said Madeleine solemnly, crossing her hands on her breast, and looking upward with inspired eyes. "I did love this man once," she answered, hardening herself to speak firmly, though again her lips quivered—"he himself killed that love by his own doing. I trusted him ; he betrayed that trust ; he would have betrayed me, but that I have forgiven, it is past and done with. But to go and see him now, to stir up in my heart, not the old love, it could not be, but agitation, sorrow—to disturb this quietness of soul, this calm which God has given me at last after so much prayer and struggle—no, no—it would not be right, it cannot be ! Moreover, if I would, I could not, indeed I could not. The very thought of it all, the disgrace, that place of sin and shame, of him in chains, condemned—a criminal—a murderer ! . . . ."

A nervous shudder shook her from head to foot, she seemed in truth to sicken and grow faint, like one forced to face some hideous nauseating spectacle. "As for him," she went on in low, feeble tones, "it will be the best too. God knows I forgive him, that I am sorry for him, that I regret his terrible fate. But I feel it would be worse for him to see me—if he must die, it would be wrong to distract him from his last preparations. And it would only be a useless pain to him, for I could not pre-

tend—he would see that I despise him.   I thought I loved
a noble gentleman, not one who was even then playing
with crime and cheating."

The faint passionless voice had hardly ceased before,
with a loud cry, Molly sprang at her sister as if she would
have strangled her.

" Oh, unnatural wretch," she exclaimed, " you are not
fit to live ! "

Tanty rushed forward and dragged the infuriated woman
away.

Madeleine rose up stiffly—swayed a moment as she
stood—and then fell unconscious to the ground.

Next day in the dawn Lady Landale came into her
sister's bedroom.   Her circled eyes, her drawn face bespeaking a sleepless night.

Madeleine was lying, beautiful and white, like a broken
lily, in the dim light of the lamp ; Sophia, an unlovely
spectacle in curl papers, wizened and red-eyed from her
night's watch, looked up warningly from the arm-chair
beside her.   But Molly went unhesitatingly to the window,
pulled the curtains, unbarred the shutters, and then
walked over to the bed.

As she approached, Madeleine opened her blue eyes
and gazed at her beseechingly.

" There is yet time," said Molly in a hollow voice.
" Get up and come with me."

The wan face upon the pillow grew whiter still,
the old horror grew in the uplifted eyes, the wan lips murmured, " I cannot."

There was an immense strength of resistance in the
girl's very feebleness.

Molly turned away abruptly, then back again once
more.

"At least you will send him a message ? "

Madeleine drew a deep breath, closed her eyes a moment and seemed to whisper a prayer ; then aloud she
said, while, like a shadow so faint was it, a flush rose to
her cheeks :

" Tell him that I forgive him, that I forgive him freely
—that I shall always pray for him."   The flush grew
deeper.   " Tell him too that I shall never be any man's
bride, now."

She closed her eyes again and the colour slowly ebbed away. Molly stood, her black brows drawn, gazing down upon her in silence.—Did she love him after all? Who can fathom the mystery of another's heart?

"I will tell him," she answered at last. "Good-bye, Madeleine—I shall never see you or speak to you again as long as I live."

She left the room with a slow, heavy step.

Madeleine shivered, and with both hands clasped the silver crucifix that hung around her neck ; two great tears escaped from her black lashes and rolled down her cheeks. Miss Sophia moaned. She, poor soul, had had tragedy enough, at last.

When the jailer brought in the mid-day meal after Adrian's departure, he found the prisoner seated very quietly at his table, his open Bible before him, but his eyes fixed dreamily upon the space of dim whitewashed wall, and his mind evidently far away.

Upon his guardian's entrance he roused himself, however, and begged him, when he should return for the dish, to restore neatness to the bed and to assist him in the ordering of his toilet which he wished to be spick and span.

"For I expect a visitor," said Captain Jack gravely.

When in due course the fellow had carried out these wishes with the surly good-nature characteristic of him, Jack set himself to wait.

The square of sky through his window grew from dazzling white to deepest blue, the shadows travelled along the blank walls, the street noises rose and fell in capricious gusts, the church bells jangled, all the myriad sounds which had come to measure his solitary day struck their familiar course upon his ear ; yet the expected visitor delayed. But the captain, among other things, had learnt to possess his soul in patience of late ; and so, as he slowly paced his cell after his wont, he betrayed neither irritation nor melancholy. If she did not come to-day, then it would be to-morrow. He had no doubt of this.

The afternoon had waned—golden without, full of grey shadows in the prison room—when light footfalls mingled with the well-known heavy tread and jangle of keys, along the echoing passage.

There was the murmur of a woman's voice, a word of gruff reply, and the next moment a tall form wrapped in a many-folded black cloak and closely veiled, advanced a few steps into the room, while, as before, the turnkey retired and locked the door behind him.

His heart beating so thickly that for the moment utterance was impossible, Captain Jack made one hurried pace forward with outstretched hands, only to check himself, however, and let them fall by his side. He would meet her calmly, humbly, as he had resolved.

The woman threw back her veil, and it was Molly's dark gaze, Molly's brown face, flushed and haggard, yet always beautiful, that looked out of the black frame.

An ashen pallor spread over the prisoner's countenance.

" Madeleine ? " he asked in a whisper ; then, with a loud ring of stern demand, " *Madeleine !* "

" I went for her, I went for her myself—I did all I could —she would not come."

She would not come !

It is a sort of unwritten law that the supremely afflicted have the right, where possible, to the gratification of the least of their wishes. That Madeleine could refuse to come to him in his last extremity, had never once crossed her lover's brain. He stood bewildered.

"She is not ill ? "

" Ill ! " Lady Landale's red lips curved in scorn, " No— not ill—but a coward ! " She spat the word fiercely as if at the offender's face.

There fell a minute's silence, broken only by a few labouring deep-drawn breaths from the prisoner's oppressed lungs. Then he stood as if turned to stone, not a muscle moving, his eyes fixed, his jaw set.

Molly trembled before this composure, beneath which she divined a suffering so intense that her own frail barriers of self-restraint were well-nigh broken down by a torrent of passionate pity.

But she braced herself with the feeling of the moment's urgency. She had no time to lose.

" Hear me," she cried in low hurried tones, laying a hand upon his folded arm and then drawing it away again as if frightened by the rigid tension she felt there. " Waste no more thought on one so unworthy—all is not

26

lost—I bring you hope, life. Oh, for God's sake, wake up and listen to me—I can save you still. Captain Smith, Jack—*Jack!*"

Her voice rose as high as she dare lift it, but no statue could be more unhearing.

The woman cast a desperate look around her; hearkened fearfully, all was silent within the prison; then with tremulous haste she cast off her immense cloak, pulled her bonnet from her head, divested herself of her long full skirt and stood, a strange vision, lithe, unconscious, unashamed, her slender woman's figure clad in complete man's raiment, with the exception of the coat. Her dark head cropped and curly, her face, with its fever-bloom, rising flower-like above the folds of her white shirt.

With anxious haste she compared herself with the prisoner.

"René told me well," she said; "with your coat upon me none would tell the difference in this dark room. I am nearly as tall as you too. Thanks be to God that he made me so. *Jack,*" calling in his ear, "don't you see? Don't you understand? It is all quite easy. You have only to put on these clothes of mine, this cloak, the bonnet comes quite over the face; stoop a little as you go out and hold this handkerchief to your face as if in tears. The carriage waits outside and René. The rest is planned. I shall sit on the bed with your coat on. It is a chance— a certainty. When I found René had failed. I swore that I would save you yet. Ever since I came from Pulwick this morning he and I have worked together upon this last plan. There is not a flaw; it must succeed. Oh, God, he does not hear me! Jack—Jack!"

She shook him with a sort of fury, then, falling at his feet, clasped his knees.

"For God's sake—for God's sake!"

He sighed, and again came the murmur:

"She would not come——" He lifted his hand to his forehead and looked round, then down at her, as if from a great height.

She saw that he was aroused at last, sprang to her feet, and poured out the details of the scheme again.

"I run no risk, you see. They would not dare to punish me, a woman—Lady Landale—even if they could. Be quick, the precious moments are going by. I gave the man some gold to leave us as long as he could, but any moment he may be upon us."

"Poor woman," said Jack, and his voice seemed as far off as his gaze ; "see these chains."

She staggered back an instant, but the next, crying :

"The file—the file—that was why René gave it to me." She seized the skirt as it lay at her feet, and, striving with agonised endeavours to control the trembling of her hands, drew forth from its pocket a file and would have taken his wrist. But he held his hands above his head, out of her reach, while a strange smile, almost of triumph, parted his lips.

"The bitterness of death is past," he said.

She tore at him in a frenzy, but, repulsed by his immobility, fell again broken at his feet.

In a torrent of words she besought him, for Adrian's sake, for the sake of the beautiful world, of his youth, of the sweetness of life—in her madness, at last, for her own sake ! She had ruined him, but she would atone, she would make him happy yet. If he died it was death to her. . . . .

When at length her voice sank away from sheer exhaustion, he helped her to rise, and seated her on the chair ; then told her quietly that he was quite determined.

"Go home," said he, "and leave me in peace. I thank you for what you would have done, thank you for trying to bring Madeleine," he paused a moment. How purely he had loved her—and twice, twice she had failed him. "Yet, I do not blame her," he went on as if to himself ; "I did not deserve to see her, and it has made all the rest easy. Remember," again addressing the woman whom hopelessness seemed for a moment to have benumbed, "that if you would yet do me a kindness, be kind to her. If you would atone—atone to Adrian."

"To Adrian ? " echoed Molly, stung to the quick, with a pale smile of exceeding bitterness. And with a rush of pride, strength returned to her.

" I leave you resolved to die then ? " she asked him, fiercely.

" You leave me glad to die," he replied, unhesitatingly.

She spoke no more, but got up to replace her garments. He assisted her in silence, but as his awkward bound hands touched her she shuddered away from him.

As she gathered the cloak round her shoulders again, there was a noise of heavy feet at the door.

The jailer thrust in his rusty head and looked furtively from the prisoner to his visitor as they stood silently apart from each other ; then, making a sign to some one whose dark figure was shadowed behind him without, entered with a hesitating sidelong step, and, drawing Captain Jack on one side, whispered in his ear.

"The blacksmith's yonder. He's come to measure you, captain, for them there irons you know of—best get the lady quietly away, for he wunnut wait no longer."

The prisoner smiled sternly.

"I am ready," he said, aloud.

"I'll keep him outside a minute or two," added the man, wiping his brow, evidently much relieved by his charge's calmness. "I kep' him back as long as I could—but happen it's allus best to hurry the parting after all."

He moved away upon tiptoe, in instinctive tribute to the lady's sorrow, and drew the door to.

Molly threw back her veil which she had lowered upon his entrance, her face was livid.

"What is it?" she asked, articulating with difficulty.

"Nothing—a fellow to see to my irons."

He moved his hands as he spoke, and she understood him, as he had hoped, to refer only to his manacles.

She drew a gasping breath. How they watched him ! Yet all was not lost after all.

"I will leave the file," she said, in a quick whisper ; "you will reflect ; there is yet to-morrow," and rushed to hide it in his bed. But he caught her by the arm, his patience worn out at length.

"Useless," he answered, harshly. "I shall not use it. Moreover, it would be found, and I am sure it is not your wish to bring unnecessary hardship upon my last moments. I should lose the only thing that is left to me, the comfort of being alone. And to-morrow I shall see no one."

The door groaned apart :

"Very sorry, mum," came the husky voice in the opening, "Time's up."

She turned a look of agony upon Captain Jack's determined figure. Was this to be the end ? Was she to leave him so, without even one kind word?"

Alas, poor soul! All her hopes had fallen to this—a parting word.

He was unpitying; his arms were folded; he made no sign.

She took a step away and swayed; the turnkey came forward compassionately to lead her out. But the next instant she wheeled round and stood alone and erect, braced up by the extremity of her anguish.

"I *have* a message," she cried, as if the words were forced from her. "I could not make her come, but I made her send you a message. She told me to say that she forgave you, freely; that she would always pray for you. She bade me tell you too that she would never be any man's bride now."

It had been like the rending of body and soul to tell him this. As she saw the condemned man's face quiver and flush at last out of its impassiveness, she thought hell itself could hold no more hideous torment.

He extended his arms:

"Now welcome death!" he exclaimed.

And she turned and fled down the passage as though driven upon this last cry.

"E-h, he be a strange one!" said the jailer afterwards to his mate. "If ye'd heard that poor lady sob as she went by! I've seen many a one in the same case, but I was sore for her, I was that. And he—as cool—joking with Robert over the hanging irons the next minute. 'New sort of tailor I've got,' says he. 'Make them smart,' he says, 'since I'm to wear them in so exalted a position.' So exalted a position, that's what he says. 'And they've got to last me some long time, you know,' says he."

"He'll be something worth looking at on Saturday. I could almost wish he could ha' got off, only that it's a fine sight to see a real gentleman go through it. Ah, it's they desperate villains has the proper pluck!"

CHAPTER XXXIII

LAUNCHED ON THE GREAT WAVE

Sir Adrian made, at first personally, then through Miss O'Donoghue, two attempts to induce his wife to return to Pulwick, or at any rate to leave Lancaster on the next day. But the contempt, then the fury, which she opposed to their reasoning rendered it worse than useless.

The very sight of her husband, indeed, seemed to exasperate the unfortunate woman to such a degree that, in spite of his anxiety concerning her, he resolved to spare her even to the consciousness of his presence, and absented himself altogether from the house.

Miss O'Donoghue, unable to cope with a state of affairs at once so distressing and so unbecoming, finally retired to her own apartment with a book of piety and some gruel, and abandoned all further endeavour to guide her unruly relations. So that Molly found herself left to her own resources, in the guardianship of René, the only company her misery could tolerate.

Three times she went to the castle, to be met each time with the announcement that, by the express wish of the prisoner, no visitors were to be admitted to him again. Then in restless wandering about the streets—once entering the little chapel where the silent tabernacle seemed, with its closed door, to offer no relenting to the stormy cry of her soul, and sent her forth uncomforted in the very midst of René's humble bead-telling, to pace the flags anew—so the terrible day wore to a close for her; and so that night came, precursor of the most terrible day of all.

The exhaustion of Lady Landale's body produced at last a fortunate torpor of mind. Flung upon her bed she fell into a heavy sleep, and Tanty who announced her intention of watching her, when René's guardianship had of necessity to cease, had the satisfaction of informing Adrian, as he crept into the house, like one who had no business there, of this consoling fact before retiring herself to the capacious arm-chair in which she heroically purposed to spend the night.

The sun was bright in the heavens, there was a clatter and bustle in the street, when Molly woke with a great start out of this sleep of exhaustion. Her heart beating with heavy strokes, she sat up in bed and gazed upon her surroundings with startled eyes. What was this strange feeling of oppression, of terror? Why was she in this sordid little room? Why was her hair cut short? Ah, my God! memory returned upon her all too swiftly. It was for to-day—*to-day ;* and she was perhaps too late. She might never see him again!

The throbbing of her heart was suffocating, sickening, as she slipped out of bed. For a moment she hardly dared consult the little watch that lay ticking upon her dressing table. It was only a few minutes past seven ; there was yet time.

The energy of her desire conquered the weakness of her overwrought nerves.

Noiselessly, so as to avoid awakening the slumbering watcher in the arm-chair, but steadily, she clothed herself, wrapt the dark mantle round her ; and then, pausing for a moment to gaze with a fierce disdain at the unconscious face of Miss O'Donoghue, which, with snores emerging energetically and regularly from the great hooked nose, presented a weird and witchlike vision in the frame of a night-cap, fearfully and wonderfully befrilled, crept from the room and down the stairs.

At René's door she paused and knocked.

He opened on the instant. From his worn face she guessed that he had been up all night. He put his finger to his lips as he saw her, and glanced meaningly towards the bed.

The words she would have spoken expired in a quick-drawn breath. Her husband, with face of deathlike pallor and silvered hair abroad upon the pillow, lay upon the poor couch, still in his yesterday attire, but covered carefully with a cloak. His breast rose and fell peacefully with his regular breath.

The scorn with which she had looked at Miss O'Don-

oghue now shot forth a thousand times intensified from
Molly's circled eyes upon the prostrate figure.

"Asleep!" she cried.

And then with that incongruity with which things
trivial and irrelevant come upon us, even in the supremest
moments of life, the thought struck her sharply how old
a man he was. Her lip curved.

"Yes, My Lady—asleep," answered René steadily—it
seemed as if the faithful peasant had read her to her
soul. "Thank God, asleep. It is enough to have to
lose one good gentleman from the world this day. If his
honour were not sleeping at last, I should not answer
for him—I who speak to you. I took upon myself to
put some of the medicine, that he has had to take now
and again, when his sorrows come upon him and he
cannot rest, into his soup last night. It has had a good
effect. His honour will sleep three or four hours still,
and that, My Lady, must be. His honour has suffered
enough these last days, God knows!"

The wife turned away with an impatient gesture.

"Look, Madame, at his white hairs. All white now—
they that were of a brown so beautiful, all but a few
locks, only a few months past! Well may he look old.
When was ever any one made to suffer as he has been,
in only forty years of life? Ah, My Lady, we were at
least tranquil upon our island!"

There was a volume of reproach in the quiet simplicity
of the words, though Lady Landale was too bent on her
own purpose to heed them. But she felt that they lodged
in her mind, that she would find them there later; but
not now—not now.

"It is to be for nine o'clock, you know," she said, with
desperate calmness. "I must see him again. I must
see him well. Alone I shall not be able to get a good
place in the crowd. Oh, I would see all!" she added,
with a terrible laugh.

René cast a glance at his master's placid face.

"I am ready to come with My Lady," he said then,
and took his hat.

A turbulent, tender April day it was. Gusts of west
wind, balmy and sweet with all the sweet budding life of
the fields beyond, came eddying up the dusty streets and
blowing merrily into the faces of the holiday crowd that

already pressed in a steady stream towards the castle courtyard to see the hanging. In those days there were hangings so many after assizes that an execution could hardly be said to possess the interest of novelty. But there were circumstances enough attending the forthcoming show to give it quite a piquancy of its own in the eyes of the worthy Lancastrian burghers, who hurried with wives and children to the place of doom, anxious to secure sitting or standing room with a good view of the gallows-tree.

It was not every day, indeed, that a *gentleman* was hanged. So handsome a man, too, as the rumours went, and so dare-devil a fellow ; friend of the noble family of Landale, and a murderer of its most respected member. Could justice ever have served up a spicier dish whereon to regale the multitude ?

First the courtyard, then, the walls, the roofs of the adjoining houses, swarmed with an eager crowd. Every space of ground and slate and tile, every ledge and window, was occupied. As thick as bees they hung—men, women, and children ; a sea of white faces pressed together, each still, yet all as instinct with tremulous movement as a field of corn in the wind ; while the hoarse, indescribable murmur that seizes one with so strange and fearsome an impression, the voice of the multitude, rose and fell with a mighty pulsation, broken here and there by the shriller cry of a child.

Overhead the sky, a delicious spring blue sky, flecked with tiny white clouds, looked down like a great smile upon the crowd that laughed and joked beneath.

No pity in heaven or on earth.

But as the felon came out into the air, which, warm and fickle, puffed against his cheek, he cast one steady glance around upon the black human hive and then looked up into the white flecked ether, without the quiver of a nerve.

He drew the spring breath into his lungs with a grateful expansion of his deep chest. How fresh it was ! And the sky, how fair and blue !

As the eagerly expected group emerged from the prison door and was greeted by a roar that curdled the blood in at least one woman's heart there, an old Irish hag, who sat in a coign of vantage, hugging her knees and crooning. a little black pipe held in her toothless jaws, ceased her dismal hum to concentrate all her attention upon the condemned man.

The creature was well known for miles around as a constant attendant at such spectacles, and had become in the course of time a privileged spectator. No one would have dreamt of disputing the first place to old Judy. Since the day when, still a young woman, she had seen her two sons, mere lads, hanged, the one for sheep-stealing, the other for harbouring the booty, she had, by a strange freak of nature, taken a taste for the spectacle of justice at work, and what had been the cause of her greatest sorrow became the only solace of her life. Judy and her pipe had become as familiar a figure at the periodical entertainment as the executioner himself—more so, indeed, for she had seen many generations of these latter, and could compare their styles with the judgment of a connoisseur.

But as Captain Jack advanced, the pallor of his clean shorn, handsome face illumined not so much by the morning sun without it seemed as by the shining of the bright spirit within ; as gallantly clad as he had ever been, even in the old Bath days when he had been courting fair Madeleine de Savenaye ; his head proudly uplifted, his tread firm, strong of soul, strong of body—some chord was struck in the perverted old heart that had so long revelled in unholy and gruesome pleasure. She drew the pipe from her lips, and broke out into screeching lamentations.

"Oh, me boy, me boy, me beautiful boy ! Is it hang him they will, and he so beautiful and brave ? The murthering villains, my curse on them—a mother's curse—God's curse on them—the black murtherers ! "

She scrambled to her feet, and shook her fist wildly in the face of one of the sheriff's men.

A woman in the crowd, standing rigid and motionless, enveloped in mourning robes, here suddenly caught up the words with a muttering lip.

"Murderers, who said murderers ? Don't they know who murdered him ? Murdering Moll, Murdering Moll ! "

"For heaven's love, Madam," cried a man beside her, who seemed in such anxiety concerning her as to pay little heed to the solemn procession which was now attracting universal attention, "let me take you away!"

But she looked at him with a distraught, unseeing eye, and pulled at the collar of her dress as if she were choking.

Old Judy's sudden expression of opinion created a small disturbance. The procession had to halt; a couple of officials good-naturedly elbowed her on one side.

But she thrust a withered hand expanded in protest over their shoulders, as the prisoner came forward again.

"God bless ye, honey, God bless ye : it's a wicked world."

He turned towards her ; for the last time the old sweet smile sprang to lip and eye.

"Thank you, mother," he said, and raised his hand to his bare head with courteous gesture.

The crowd howled and swayed. He passed on.

And now the end ! There is the cart ; the officers draw back to make way for the man who is to help him with his final toilet. The chaplain, too, falls away after wringing his hand again and again. Good man, he weeps and cannot speak the sacred words he would. Why weep? We must all die ! How blue the sky is : he will look once more before drawing down the cap upon his eyes. His hands are free, for he is to die as like a gentleman as may be. Just the old blue that used to smile down at him upon his merry *Peregrine*, and up at him from the dancing waves. He had always thought he would have liked to die upon the sea, in the cool fresh water . . . . a clean, brave death.

It is hard to die in a crowd. Even the very beasts would creep into cave or bush to die decently—unwatched.

A last puff of sweeping wind in his face ; then darkness, blind, suffocating. . . . .

Ah, God is good ! Here is the old ship giving and rising under his feet like the living creature he always thought her, and here is dazzling brilliant sunshine all around, so bright he scarce can see the free white-crested waves that are dashing down upon him ; but he is upon the sea indeed, upon the sea alone, and the waves are coming. Hark how they roar, see how they gather ! The brave *Peregrine* she dips and springs, she will weather the breakers with him at the helm no matter how they rear.

On, on they come, mountain high, overwhelming, bitter drenching.

A great wave in very truth, it gathers and breaks and onward rolls, and carries the soul of Hubert Cochrane with it.

The woman in the black cloak falls as if she had been struck, and as those around her draw apart to let her companion and another man lift her and carry her away, they note with horror that her face is dark and swollen, as if the cord that had just done its evil work yonder had been tightened also round her slender throat.

CHAPTER XXXIV

THE GIBBET ON THE SANDS

Woman! take up thy life once more
Where thou hast left it;
Nothing is changed for thee, thou art the same,
Thou who didst think that all things
Would be wholly changed for thee.
Luteplayer's Song.

PULWICK again.   The whirlwind of disaster that upon
that fatal fifteenth of March had burst upon the house of
Landale has passed and swept away.   But it has left deep
trace of its passage.

The restless head, the busy hand, the scheming brain
of Rupert Landale lie now mouldering under the sod of
the little churchyard where first they started the mischief
that was to have such far reaching effects.   Low, too, lies
the proud head of the mistress of Pulwick, so stricken,
indeed, so fever-tortured, that those who love her best
scarce dare hope more for her than rest at last under the
same earth that presses thus lightly above her enemy's
eternal sleep.

There is a great stillness in the house.   People go to
and fro with muffled steps, the master with bent white
head; Miss O'Donoghue, indefatigable sick nurse: Madeleine, who may not venture as far as the threshold of her
sister's room, and awaits in prayer and tears the hour of
that final bereavement which will free her to take wing
towards the cloister for which her soul longs; Sophia,
crushed finally by the sorrows she has played at all her
days.   Seemingly there is peace once more upon them
all, but it is the peace of exhaustion rather than that of
repose.   And yet—could they but know it, as the sands
run down in the hour-glass of time there are golden grains
gathering still to drop into the lives of each.

But meanwhile none may read the future, and Molly

fights for her life in the darkened room, the gloom of which, to the souls of the dwellers at Pulwick, seems to spread even to the sunny skies without.

When Lady Landale was brought back to her home from Lancaster, it was held by every one who saw her that Death had laid his cold finger on her forehead, and that her surrender to his call could only be a matter of hours.

The physician in attendance could point out no reasonable ground for hope. Such a case had never come within his experience or knowledge, and he was with difficulty induced to believe that it was not the result of actual violence.

"In every particular," said he, "the patient's symptoms are those of coma resulting from prolonged strangulation or asphyxia. These spectacles are very dangerous to highly sensitive organisations. Lady Landale no doubt felt for the miserable wretch in the benevolence of her heart. Imagination aiding her, she realised suddenly the horror of his death throes, and this vivid realisation was followed by the actual simulacrum of the torture. We have seen hysterical subjects simulate in the same manner diverse diseases of which they themselves are organically free, such as epilepsy, or the like. But Lady Landale's condition is otherwise serious. She is alive; more I cannot say."

According to his lights, he had bled the patient, as he would have bled, by rote, to recall to life one actually cut down from the beam. But, although the young blood did flow, bearing testimony to the fact that the heart still beat in that deathlike frame, the vitality left seemed so faint as to defy the power of human ministration.

The flame of life barely flickered; but the powers of youth were of greater strength in the unconscious body than could have been suspected, and gradually, almost imperceptibly, they asserted themselves.

With the return of animation, however, came a new danger: fever, burning, devastating, more terrible even than the almost mortal syncope; that fever of the brain which wastes like the rack, before which science stands helpless, and the watcher sinks into despair at his impotence to screen a beloved sufferer from the horrible, ever-recurring phantoms of delirium.

Had not Sir Adrian intuitively known well-nigh every
act of the drama which had already been so fatal to his
house, Molly's frenzied utterances would have told him
all.   Every secret incident of that storm of passion which
had desolated her life was laid bare to his sorrowing
heart :—her aspirations for an ideal, centred suddenly
upon one man ; her love rapture cruelly baulked at every
step ; the consuming of that love fire, resisting all frustra-
tion of hope, all efforts of conscience, of honour ; how
her whole being became merged into that of the man she
loved and whom she had ruined, her life in his life, her
very breath in his breath.   And then the lamentable, inevitable end : the fearful confrontation with his death.
Again and again, in never ceasing repetition, was that
fair, most dear body, that harrowed soul, dragged step by
step through every iota of the past torture, always to fall
at last into the same stillness of exhaustion—appalling
image of final death that wrung Adrian with untold
agonies of despair.

For many days this condition of things lasted unaltered.
In the physician's own words it was impossible that life
could much longer resist such fierce onslaughts.   But one
evening a change came over the spirit of the sufferer's
vision.

There had been a somewhat longer interval between
the paroxysms ; Sir Adrian seated as usual by the bed,
waiting now with a sinking heart for the wonted return
of the frenzy, clamouring in his soul to heaven for pity
on one whom seemingly no human aid could succour,
dared yet draw no shadow of hope from the more prolonged stillness of the patient.   Presently indeed, she
grew restless, tossed her arms, muttered with parched
lips.   Then she suddenly sat up and listened as if to some
deeply annoying and disquieting sound, fell back again
under his gentle hands, rolling her little black head wearily
from side to side, only however to start again, and again
listen.   Thus it went on for a while until the haunted,
weary eyes grew suddenly distraught with terror and
loathing.   Straining them into space as if seeking something she ought to see but could not, she began to speak
in a quick yet distinct whisper :

" How it creaks, creaks—creaks ! Will no one stop
that creaking ! What is it that creaks so ? Will no one

stop that creaking ! " And again she placed her cheek on
the pillow, covering her ear with her little, wasted hand,
and for a while remained motionless, moaning like a
child. But it was only to spring up again, this time with
a cry which brought the physician from the adjacent
sleeping room in alarm to her bedside.

"Ah, God," she shrieked, her eyes distended and staring as if into the far distance through walls and outlying
darkness. "I see it ! They have done it, they have
done it ! It is hanging on the sands—how it creaks and
sways in the wind ! It will creak for ever, for ever. . . . .
Now it spins round, it looks this way—the black face !
It looks at *me* ! " She gave another piercing cry, then her
frame grew rigid. With mouth open and fixed eyeballs
she seemed lost in the frightful fascination of the image
before her brain.

As, distracted by the sight of her torments, Adrian hung
over her, racking his mind in the endeavour to soothe her,
her words struck a chill into his very soul. He cast a
terrified glance at the doctor who was ominously feeling
her pulse.

"There is a change," he faltered.

The doctor shrugged his shoulders.

"I have told you before," he retorted irritably, "that
you should attach no more importance to the substance
of these delirious wanderings than you would to the ravings of madness. It is the fact of the delirium itself which
must alarm us. She is less and less able to bear it."

The patient moaned and shuddered, resisting the gentle
force that would have pressed her down on her pillow.

"Oh the creaking, the creaking ! Will no one stop
that creaking ! Must I hear it go on creak, creak, creak
for ever, and see it sway and sway. . . . . Will no one
ever stop it ! "

Sir Adrian took a sudden resolution. "I will," he said,
low and clear into her ear. She sank down on the
instant and looked at him, back from her far distance,
almost as if she understood him and the pitiful cry for the
help he would have given his heart's blood to procure
for her, was silent for the moment upon her lips.

"I will prepare an opiate," said the physician in a
whisper.

"And I," said Sir Adrian to him, with a strange expression upon his pale face, "am going to stop that creaking."

The man of medicine gazed after him with a look of intense astonishment which rapidly changed to one of professional interest.

"It is evident that I shall soon have another mentally deranged patient to see to," he remarked to himself as he rose to seek the drugs he meant to administer.

Downstairs, Sir Adrian immediately called for René, and being informed that he had left for the island early in the afternoon and had announced his return before night, cast a cloak over his shoulders and hurried forth in the hope of meeting him upon his homeward way. His pulses were beating well-nigh as wildly as those of the fever stricken woman upstairs in the house. He dared not pause to reflect on his purpose, or seek to disentangle the confusion of his thoughts, for fear of being confronted with the hopelessness of their folly. But the exquisite serenity of the night sky, where swam the moon, "a silver splendour;" the freshness of the sweeping breeze that dashed, keen from the east, over the sea against his face; all the glorious distance, the unconsciousness and detachment of nature from the fume and misery of life, brought him unwittingly to a calmer mood.

He had reached the extreme confine of the pine wood, when, across the sands that stretched unbroken to the lips of the sea, a figure advanced towards him.

"Renny!" called Sir Adrian.

"Your honour!" cried the man, breaking into a run to meet him. O God! how ghostly white looked the master's face in the moon-flood!

"My Lady——?"

"Not worse; yet not better—and that means worse now. But there is a change. Renny," sinking his voice and clasping the man's sturdy arm with clammy hand, "is it true they have placed him on the sands to-day?"

The man stared.

"How did your honour know? Yes—they have done so. It is true: the swine! not more than an hour, in verity. How could it have come so soon to your honour's ears? This morning, indeed, they came from the town in a cart, and planted the great gibbet on Scarthey Point, at low water. And to-night they brought the body, all bound in irons, and from a boat, for it was high tide, they riveted it on the chain.   And it is to remain for ever, your honour—so they say."

"Strange," murmured Sir Adrian to himself, gazing seaward with awestruck eyes.   "And did you," he asked, "hear its creaking, Renny, as it swayed in the wind?"

Again René cast a quick glance of alarm at his master. The master had a singular manner with him to-night! Then edging closer to him he whispered in his ear :

"They say it is to hang for ever.   There is a warning to those who would interfere with this justice of theirs. But, your honour, there came one to the island to-day, I do not know if your honour knows him, the captain's second on that vessel of misfortune.   And I believe, your honour, the dawn will never see that poor, black body hanging over yonder like a scarecrow, to spoil our view. This man, this brave mariner, Curwen is his name, he is mad furious with us all !   He has just but come from hearing of his captain's fate, and he is ready to kill us, that we let him be murdered without breaking some heads for him.   Faith, if it could have done any good, it is not I that would have balanced about it !   But, as I told him, there was no use running one's own head into a loop of rope when that would please nobody but Mr. the Judge. But he is not to be reasoned with.   He is like a wild animal.   When I left him," said René, dropping his voice still lower, "he was knocking a coffin together out of the old sea wood on Scarthey.   He said his captain would rest better in those boards that were seasoned with salt water.   And when I went away, your honour, and left him hammering there—faith, I thought that the coffin was like to be seasoned by another kind of salt water too."

His face twitched and the ready tears sprang to his own eyes which, unashamed, he now wiped with his sleeve after his custom.   But Sir Adrian's mind was still drifting in distant ghastly companionship.

"How the wind blows !" he said, and shuddered a little.   "How the poor body must sway in the wind, and the chains creak."

"If it can make any difference to the poor captain he will lie in peace to-night, please God," said René.

"Ay," said Sir Adrian, "and you and I, friend, will go too, and help this good fellow in his task.   I hope, I believe, that I should have done this thing of my own thought, had I had time to think at all. But now, more hangs upon those creaking chains than you can dream of. This is a strange world—and it is full of ghosts to-night. But we must hurry, Renny."

*   *   *   *   *

Bound even to the tips of her burning little fingers by the spell of the opiate, Lady Landale lay in the shadowed room as one dead, yet in her sick brain fearfully awake, keenly alive.

At first it was as if she too was manacled in chains till she could not move a muscle, could not breathe or cry because of the ring round her breast ; and she was hanging with the black figure, swaying, while the rusty iron links went creak, creak, creak, with every swing to and fro. Then suddenly she seemed to stand, as it were, out of herself and to be seeing with the naked soul alone. And what she saw was the great stretch of beach and sea, white, white, white, in the moonlight and spreading, it seemed, for leagues and leagues, spreading till all the world was only beach and sea.

But close to her in the whitest moonlight rose the great gibbet, gaunt and black, cutting the pale sky in two and athwart ; and hanging from it was the black figure that swayed and swung. And though the winds muttered and the waves growled, she could not hear them with the ears of the soul, for that the whole of this great world of sea and sand was filled with the creaking of the chains.

But now, across the bleak and pallid spaces came three black figures. And, as she looked and watched and they drew nearer, the dreadful burthen of the gibbet swung round as if to greet them, and she too, felt in her soul that she knew them all three, though not by names, as creatures of earth know each other, but by the kinship of the soul. This man with hair as white as the white beach, hair that seemed to shine silver as he came ; and him yonder who followed him as a dog his master ; and yonder again the third, in the seaman's dress, with hard face hewn into such rugged lines of grief and fury—she knew them all. And next they reached the gibbet : and one swarmed up the black post, and hammered and filed and prised, and then, oh merciful God ! the creaking stopped at last !

Now she could hear the wash of the waves, the rush of the wholesome wind !

A mist came across her vision ; faintly she saw the stiffened disfigured corpse which yet she felt had once been something she had loved with passion, laid reverently upon a stretcher, its irons loosened and cast away, and then covered with a great cloak. Then the sea, the beach, the white moon faded and waved and receded. Molly's soul went back to her body again, while blessed tears fell one by one from her hot eyes. She breathed ; her limbs relaxed ; round the tired brain came, with a soft hush like that of gentle wings, dark oblivion.

Bending over her, for he was aware that for good or evil the crisis was at hand, the physician saw moisture bead upon the suddenly smoothed brow, heard a deep sigh escape the parted lips. And then with a movement like a weary child's she drew her arms close and fell asleep.

Having laid his friend to his secret rest, deep in the rock of Scarthey, where the free waves that his soul had revelled in would beat till the world's end, Sir Adrian returned to Pulwick in the early morning, spent with the long and heavy night's toil—for it had taxed the strength of even three men to hollow out a grave in such a soil. On the threshold he was greeted by the physician.

"How beautiful upon the mountains are the feet of the messengers of glad tidings !" From afar, by the man's demeanour, he knew that the tidings were glad. And most blessed they were indeed to his ears, but to them alone not strange. Throughout every detail of his errand his mind had dwelt rather with the living than the dead. What he had done, he had done for her ; and now, the task achieved, it seemed but natural that the object for which it had been undertaken should have been achieved likewise.

But, left once more with her, seeing her once more wrapt in placid sleep, whom he had thought he would never behold at rest again save in the last sleep of all, the revulsion was overpowering. He sat down by her side, and through his tears gazed long at the lovely head, now in its pallor and emaciation so sadly like that of his dead love in the sorrowful days of youth ; and he thanked heaven that he was still of the earth to shield her with his devotion, to cherish her who was now so helpless and bereft.

And with such tears and such thoughts came a forget-fulness of that anguish which in him, as well as in her, had for so long been part of actual existence.

When Tanty entered on tiptoe some hours later, she saw her niece motionless upon her pillow, sleeping as easily and reposefully as a child. And close to her head, Sir Adrian, reclining in the arm-chair, asleep likewise. His arm was stretched limply over the bed and, on its sleeve still stained with the red mud of the grave in Scar-they, rested Lady Landale's little, thin, ivory-white fingers.

Thus ended Molly's brief but terrible madness.

"Then you have hope, real hope ?" asked Sir Adrian, of the physician as they met again that day in the gallery.

"Every hope," replied the man of science with the proud consciousness of having, by his wisdom, pulled his patient out of the very jaws of death. "Recovery is now but a question of a time ; of a long time, of course, for this crisis has left her weaker than the new-born babe. Repose, complete repose, sleep : that is almost every-thing. And she will sleep. Happily, as usual in such cases, Lady Landale seems to have lost all memory. But I must impress upon you, Sir Adrian, that the longer we can keep her in this state, the better. If you have rea-son to believe that even the sight of *you* might recall dis-tressing impressions, you must let me request of you to keep away from the sick room till your wife's strength be sufficiently restored to be able to face emotions."

This was said with a certain significance which called the colour to Sir Adrian's cheek. He acquiesced, how-ever, without hesitation ; and, banished from the place where his treasure lay, fell to haunting the passages for the rest of the day and to waylaying the privileged at-tendants with a humble resignation which would have been sorrowful but for the savour of his recent relief from anguish.

But the next morning, Lady Landale, though too weak

of body to lift a finger, too weak of mind to connect a
single coherent phrase, nevertheless took the matter into
her own hands, and proved that it is as easy to err upon
the side of prudence as upon its reverse.

Miss O'Donoghue, emerging silently from the room
after her night's vigil, came upon her nephew at his post,
and, struck to her kind heart by his wistful countenance,
bade him with many winks and nods enter and have a
look at his wife.

"Don't make a sound," she whispered to him, "and
then she won't hear you. But, faith she's sleeping so
well, it's my belief if you danced a jig she would not stir
a limb. Go in, child, go in. It's beautiful to see her!"

And Adrian, pressed by his own longing, was unable
to resist the offer. Noiselessly he stepped across the forbidden threshold and stood for a long time contemplating
the sleeper in the dim light. As he was about to creep
out at length, she suddenly opened her eyes and fixed
them wonderingly upon him. Fearful of having done the
cruel deed against which he had been warned, he felt
his heart contract and would have rushed away, in an
agony of self-accusation, when there occurred what
seemed to him a miracle.

A faint smile came upon the pale lips, and narrowed
ever so little the large sunken eyes. Yes; by all that
was beautiful, it was a smile—transient and piteous, but
a smile. And for him!

As he bent forward, almost incapable of believing, the
lips relaxed again and the lids drooped, but she shifted
her hands upon the bed, uneasily, as if seeking something. He knelt, trembling, by her side, and as with
diffident fingers he clasped the wandering hands he felt
them faintly cling to his. And his heart melted all in joy.
The man of science had reasoned astray; there need be
no separation between the husband who would so dearly
console, and the wife who needed help so sorely.

For a long while he remained thus kneeling and holding her hands. It seemed as though some of the life
strength he longed to be able to pour from himself to her,
actually passed into her frame: as though there were indeed a healing virtue in his all encompassing tenderness;
for, after a while, a faint colour came to the sunken
cheeks. And presently, still holding his hand, she fell

once more into that slumber which was now her healing.

After this it was found that the patient actually became fretful and fevered again when her husband was too long absent from her side; and thus it came to pass that he began to supersede all other watchers in her room. Tanty in highest good humour, declared that her services were no longer necessary, and volunteered to conduct Madeleine to the Jersey convent, whither (her decision being irrevocable) it was generally felt that it would be well for the latter to proceed before her sister's memory with returning strength should have returned likewise.

This memory, without which the being he loved would remain afflicted and incomplete, yet upon the working of which so much that was still uncertain must hinge—Sir Adrian at once yearned for, and dreaded it.

Many a time as he met the sweet and joyful greeting in those eyes where he had grown accustomed to find nought but either mockery or disdain, did he recall his friend's prophetic words : "Out of my death will grow your happiness." Was there happiness indeed yet in store in the future? Alas, happiness for them dwelt in oblivion ; and, some day, "remembrance would wake with all her busy train, and swell at *her* breast," and then——

Meanwhile, however, the present had a sweetness of its own. There was now free scope for the passion of devotedness which almost made up the sum of this man's character—a character which, to the Molly of wayward days, to the hot-pulsed, eager, impatient "Murthering Moll," had been utterly incomprehensible and uncongenial. And to the Molly crushed in the direst battle of life, whom one more harshness of fate, even the slightest, would have straightway hurled back into the grave that had barely been baulked of its prey, it gave the very food and breath of her new existence.

Week after week passed in this guise, during which her natural healthiness slowly but surely re-established itself ; weeks that were happy to him, in later life, to look back upon, though now full of an anxiousness which waxed stronger as recovery drew nearer.

There was little talking between them, and that kept by him studiously on subjects of purely ephemeral, childish interest. Her mind, by the happy dispensation of nature which facilitates healing by all means when once healing has begun, was blank to any impressions save the luxury of rest, of passive enjoyment, indifferent to ought but the passing present. She took pleasure in flowers, in the gambols of pet animals, in long listless spells of cloud-gazing when the heavens were bright, in the presence of her husband in whom she only saw a being whose eyes were always beautiful with the light of kindness, whose touch invariably soothed her when fatigue or irritation marred the even course of her feelings.

She had ever a smile for him, which entered his soul like the radiance of sunshine through a stormy sky.

Thus the days went by. Like a child she ate and slept and chattered—irresponsible chatter that was music to his ear. She laughed and teased him too, as a child would ; till sad, as it was, he hugged the incomplete happiness to his heart with a dire foreboding that it might be all he was to know in life.

But one evening, in sudden freak, she bade him open the shutters, pull the curtains, and raise the window that she might, from her pillow, look forth upon the night, and smell the sweet night air.

She had been unusually well that day, and on her face now filling out once more into its old soft oval, bloomed again a look of warm life and youth. Unsuspecting, unthinking Sir Adrian obeyed. It was a dim, close night, and the blush-roses nodded palely into the room from the outer darkness as he raised the sash. There was no moon, no stars shone in the mist hung sky ; there was no light to be seen anywhere except one faint glimmer in the distance—the light upon Scarthey Island.

"Is that a star?" said Molly, after a moment's dreamy silence.

Sir Adrian started. A vision of all that might hang upon his answer flashed through his brain. With a trembling hand he pulled the curtain. It was too late.

Molly sat up in bed, with a contracted brow and hands outstretched as one who would seize a tantalising escaping memory.

"I used to watch it then, at night, from this window," she whispered. "What was it? The light of Scarthey?" Then suddenly, with a scream ; "The light of Scarthey !"

Adrian sprang to her side but she turned from him, shrank from him, with a look of dread which seared him to the soul.

"Do not come near me, do not touch me," she cried.

And then he left her.

Miss O'Donoghue was gone upon her journey with Madeleine. There was none in whom he might confide, with whom seek counsel. But presently, listening outside the door in an agony of suspense, he heard a storm of sobs. In time these gradually subsided; and later he learnt from Moggie, whom he had hurriedly ordered to her mistress's side, that his wife was quiet and seemed inclined to rest.

On the next day, she expressed no desire to see him and he dared not go to her unsought. He gathered a great dewy bunch of roses and had them brought to her upon her breakfast tray instead of bringing them himself as had been his wont.

She had taken the roses, Moggie told him, and laid them to her cheek. "The master sent them, said I," continued the sturdy little matron, who was far from possessing the instinctive tact of her spouse; "an' she get agate o'crying quiet like and let the flowers fall out of her hands on the bed—Eh, what ever's coom to her, sin yesterday? Wannut you go in, sir?"

"Not unless she sends for me," said Sir Adrian hastily. "And remember, Moggie, do not speak my name to her. She must not be worried or distressed. But if she sends for me, come at once. You will find me in the library."

And in the library he sat the long, long day, waiting for the summons that did not come. She never sent for him.

She had wept a good deal during the day, the faithful reporter told him in the evening, but always "quiet like;" had spoken little, and though of unwonted gentleness of manner had persistently declined to be carried to the garden as usual, or even to leave her room. Now she had gone back to bed, and was sleeping peacefully.

An hour later Sir Adrian left his home for Scarthey once again. It is to be doubted whether, through all the vicissitudes of his existence he ever carried into the sheltering ruins a heart more full of cruel pain.

When Tanty returned to Pulwick from her travels
again, it was to find in Miss Landale the only member of
the family waiting to greet her. The old lady's displeasure
on learning the reason of this defection, was at first too
intense to find relief in words. But presently the strings of
her tongue were loosened under the influence of the usual
feminine restorative ; and, failing a better listener, she began to dilate upon the situation with her wonted garrulity.

"Yes, my good Sophia, I will thank you for another
cup of tea. What should we do without tea in this weary
world? I declare it's the only pleasure left to me now—
for, of all the ungrateful things in life, working for your
posterity is the most ungrateful. Posterity is born to
trample on one . . . . And now, sit down and tell me
exactly how matters stand. My niece is greatly better,
I hear. The doctor considers her quite convalescent?
At least this is very satisfactory. Very satisfactory
indeed ! Just now she is resting. Quite so. I should
not dream of disturbing her ; more especially as the
sight of me would probably revive painful memories,
and we must not risk her having a bad night—of
course not. Ah, my dear, memory, like one's teeth,
is a very doubtful blessing. Far more trouble than
pleasure when you have it, and yet a dreadful nuisance
when you have not—But what's this I hear about Adrian?
Gone back to that detestable island of his again ! I left
him and Molly smiling into each other's eyes, clasping
each other's hands like two turtle-doves. Why, she could
not as much as swallow a mouthful of soup, unless he
was beside her to feed her—And now I am told he has
not been near her for four days. What is the meaning of
this? Oh, don't talk to me, Sophia ! It's more than flesh
and blood can bear. Here am I, having been backward
and forward over nine hundred miles, looking after you
all, at my age, till I don't know which it is, Lancashire
or Somerset I'm in, or whether I'm on my head or my
heels, though I'm sure I can count every bone of my
body by the aching of them ;—and I did think I was
coming back to a little peace and comfort at length.
That island of his, Sophia, will be the death of me ! I
wish it was at the bottom of the sea : that is the only
thing that will bring your brother to his senses, I believe. Now he might as well be in his grave at once,

like Rupert, for all the good he is ; though, for that matter it's more harm than good poor Rupert ever did while he was alive——"

" Excuse me, Aunt Rose," here exclaimed Sophia, heroically, her corkscrew ringlets trembling with agitation, " but I must beg you to refrain from such remarks—I cannot hear my dear brother. . . . ."

But Miss O'Donoghue waved the interruption peremptorily away.

" Now it's no use your going on, Sophia. *We* don't think a man flies straight to heaven just because he's dead. And nothing will ever make me approve of Rupert's conduct in all this dreadful business. Of course one must not speak evil of those who can't defend themselves, but for all that he is dead and buried, Rupert might argue with me from now till doomsday, and he never would convince me that it is the part of a gentleman to act like a Bow Street runner. I *hope*, my dear, he has found more mercy than he gave. I *hope* so. But only for him my poor dear grand-niece Molly would never have gone off on that mad journey, and my poor grand-niece Madeleine would not be buried alive on that other island at the back of God's speed. Ah, yes, my dear, it has been a very sad time ! I declare I felt all the while as if I were conducting a corpse to be buried ; and now I feel as if I had come back from the dear girl's funeral. We had a dreadful passage, and she was *so* sick that I'm afraid even if she wanted to come out of that place again she'd never have the courage to face the crossing. She was a wreck—a perfect wreck, when she reached the convent. Many a time I thought she would only land to find herself dead. *I* wanted her to come to the hotel with me, where I should have popped her into bed with a hot bottle ; but nothing would serve her but that she must go to the convent at once. ' I shall not be able to rest till I am there,' she said. ' And it's precious little rest you will get there,' said I. ' if it's rest you want ?—What with the hard beds, and all the prayers you have to say, and the popping out of bed, as soon as you are asleep, to sing in the middle of the night, and those blessed little bells going every three minutes and a half. There is no rest in a convent, my dear.' But I might as well have talked to the wall.

"When I went to see her the next day, true enough, she declared that she was more content already, and that her soul had found what it yearned for—peace. She was quite calm, and sent you all messages to say how she would pray for you and for the repose of the souls of those you loved—Rupert, your rector and all—that they may reach eternal bliss."

"God forbid!" exclaimed the pious Protestant, in horrified tones.

"God forbid?—You're a regular heathen, Sophia. Oh, I know what you mean quite well. But would it not have been better for you to have been praying for that poor fellow who never lived to marry you, all these years, than to have been wasting your time weeping over spilt milk? Tell me *that*, miss. Please to remember, too, that you could not have come to be the heretic you are, if your great grandfather had not been the time-server he was. Any how, you need not distress yourself. I don't think Madeleine's prayers will do any one any harm, even Rupert; though, honestly, I don't think they are likely to be of much good in *that* quarter. However, there, there, we won't discuss the subject any more. Poor darling; so I left her. I declare I never liked her so much as when I said good-bye, for I felt I'd never see her again. And the Reverend Mother—oh! she is a very good, holy woman—a Jerningham, and thus, you know, a connection of mine. She was an heiress but chose the cloister. And I saw the buckles sable on a memorial window in the chapel erected to another sister—also a nun—they are a terribly pious family. I knew them at once, for they are charges I also am entitled to bear, as you know, or, rather, don't know, I presume; for you have all the haziest notion of what sort of blood it is that runs in your veins. Well, as I said, she is a holy woman! She tried to console me in her pious way. Oh, it was very beautiful, of course :—bride of heaven and the rest of it. But I had rather seen her the bride of a nice young man. Many is the time I have wished I had not been so hasty about that poor young Smith. I don't believe he *was* purely Smith after all. He must have had some good blood in his veins! Oh, of course, of course, he was dreadfully wicked, I know; but he was a fine fellow, and all these complications would have been avoided.

But, after all, it was Rupert's fault if everything ended in tragedy. . . . . there, there, we won't speak another word about your brother ; we must leave him to the Lord —and," added Miss O'Donoghue, piously under her breath, " if it's not the devil, He is playing with him, it's a poor kind of justice up there !—Alas, my poor Sophia, such is life.   One only sees things in their true light when they're gone into the darkness of the past.   And now we must make the best of the present, which, I regret to find, seems disposed to be peculiarly uncomfortable.   But I have done what I could, and now I owe it myself to wash my hands of you and look after my own soul.—I'll take no more journeys, at any rate, except to lay my bones at Bunratty ; if I live to reach it alive."

CHAPTER XXXV

THE LIGHT REKINDLED

Look not upon the sky at eventide,
For that makes sorrowful the heart of man;
Look rather here into my heart,
And joyful shalt thou always be.
Luteplayer's Song.

It was on the fifth day after Sir Adrian's return to his island home. Outwardly the place was the same. A man had been engaged to attend to the lighthouse duties, but he and his wife lived apart in their own corner of the building and never intruded into the master's apartments or into the turret-room which had been Captain Jack's.

From the moment that Sir Adrian, attended by René, had re-entered the old rooms, the peel had resumed its wonted aspect. But the peace, the serenity which belonged to it for so many years, had fled—fled, it seemed to Sir Adrian, for ever. Still there was solitude and, in so far, repose. It was something to have such a haven of refuge for his bruised spirit.

The whole morning of this day had been spent in counting out and securing, in separate lots, duly docketted and distinguished, a portion of that unwieldy accumulation of wealth, the charge of which he had accepted, against the time when it should be called for and claimed by its depositors.

The task was by no means simple, and required all his attention; but there is a blessing even in mere mechanical labour, that soothes the torment of the mind. In the particular occupation upon which he had been engaged there was, moreover, a hidden touching element. It was work for the helpless dead, work for that erring man but noble soul who had been his loyal friend. As Sir Adrian tied up each bag of gold and labelled it with the name of some unknown creditor who had trusted Jack, dimly the

thought occurred that it would stand material proof, call
for recognition that this Captain Smith, who had died the
death of a felon, had been a true man even in his own
chosen lawless path.

On the table, amid the papers and books, a heap of
gold pieces yet untold, remainder of his allotted day's
task, awaited still his ministering hand. But he was
tired. It was the dreamy hour of the day when the
shadows grow long, the shafts of light level; and Sir
Adrian sat at his open window, gazing at the distant view
of Pulwick, while his thoughts wandered into the future,
immediate and distant. With the self-detachment of his
nature these thoughts all bore upon the future of the
woman whom he pictured to himself lying behind those
sunlit windows yonder, framed by the verdure of leafy
June, gathering slowly back her broken strength for the
long life stretching before her.

Unlike the musings which in the lonely days of old had
ever drifted irresistibly towards the past and gathered
round the image of the dead, all the power of his mind
was now fixed upon what was to come, upon the child,
still dearer than the mother, who had all her life to live.
What would she do? What could *he* do for her, now that
she required his helping hand no more? Life was full of
sorrow past and present; and in the future there lurked
no promise of better things. The mind of man is always
fain, even in its darkest hour, to take flight into some
distant realm of hope. To those whom life has utterly
betrayed there is always the hope of approaching death—
but this, even, reason denied to him. He was so strong;
illness had never taken hold of him; he came from such
long-lived stock! He might almost outlive her, might
for ever stand as the one ineluctable check upon her
peace of mind. And his melancholy reflections came
circling back to their first starting-point—that barren rock
of misery in a vast sea of despondency—there was nothing to be done.

The barriers raised between them, on his side partly by
the poisonous words of his brother, partly by the phantom of that old love of which the new had at first been
but an eluding reflex, and on hers, by the chilly disillusion which had fallen so soon upon her ardent nature;
these sank into insignificance, contrasted to the whirl of

baulked passion which had passed over her life, to leave it utterly blasted, to turn her indifference to hate.

Yes, that was the burden of his thoughts : she hated and dreaded him. His love, his forbearance, his chivalrousness had been in vain. All he had now to live upon was the memory of those few days when, under the spell of oblivion the beloved child had smiled on him in the unconscious love born of her helplessness and his care. But even this most precious remembrance of the present was now, like that of the past, to be obscured by its abrupt and terrible end.

Death had given birth to the first and last avowal of love in her who had perished between his arms under the swirling waters of the Vilaine—but it was Life itself, returning life and health of mind, which had changed looks of trust and affection into the chilly stare of dread in the eyes of her whom with all the strength of his hoarded manhood he now loved alone. The past for all its sorrows had held sweetness : the present, the future, nothing but torment. And now, even the past, with its love and its sorrow was gone from him, merged in the greater love and sorrow of the present. How long could he bear it ?—Useless clamour of the soul ! He must bear it. Life must be accepted.

Sir Adrian rose and, standing, paused a moment to let his sight, wandering beyond the immense sands, seek repose for a moment in the blue haze marking the horizon of the hills. The day was pure, exquisite in its waning beauty ; the breeze as light and soft as a caress. In the great stillness of the bay the sisters sea and land talked in gentle intermittent murmurs. Now and then the cries of circling sea-fowl brought a note of uncanny joy into the harmony that seemed like silence in its unity.

A beautiful harmonious world ! But to him the very sense of the outer peace gave a fresh emphasis to the discordance of his own life. He brought his gaze from afar and slowly turned to resume his work. But even as he turned a black speck upon the nearer arm of sea challenged his fleeting attention. He stood and watched —and, as he watched, a sensation, the most poignant and yet eerie he had ever known clutched him by the heart.

A boat was approaching : a small row-boat in which

the oars were plyed by a woman. By the multi-coloured, glaring shawl (poor Jack's appreciated gift) he knew her, but without attaching name or personality to his recognition ; for all his being was drawn to the something that lay huddled, black and motionless, in the stern. He felt to the innermost fibre of him that this something was a woman too—this woman Molly. But the conviction seized him with a force that was beyond surprise. And all the vital heat in him fled to his heart, leaving him deadly cold.

As her face grew out of the distance towards him, a minute white patch amid the dark cloud of silk and lace that enwrapt it, it seemed as though he had known for centuries that she was thus to come to him. And the glow of his heart spread to his brain.

When the boat was about to land, he began, like one walking in his sleep, to move away ; and, slowly descending the stairs of the keep, he advanced towards the margin of the sea. He walked slowly, for the body was heavy whilst the soul trembled within its earthly bounds.

Molly had alighted and was toiling, with her new born and yet but feeble strength upon the yielding sand, supported between René and Moggie. She halted as she saw him approach, and, when he came close, looked up into his face. Her frail figure wavered and bent, and she would have fallen on her knees before him, but that he opened his arms wide and caught her to him.

An exclamation rose to Moggie's lips, to die unformed under an imperious glance from René who, with shining eyes and set mouth, had stood apart to watch the momentous issue.

Adrian felt his wife nestle to him as he held her. And then the tide of his long-bound love overflowed. And gathering her up in his arms as if she were a child, he turned to carry the broken woman with him into the shelter, the silence of the ruins.

At the foot of the outer wall, just out of reach of high water, yet within reach of its salt spray, a little mound of red stony soil rose very slightly above the green turf ; at its head, a small stone cross, roughly hewn, was let into the masonry itself. The grave of Hubert Cochrane was not obtrusive : in a few months it would have merged again into the greensward, and its humble memorial

28

symbol would be covered with moss and lichen like the matrix of stone which encompassed it.

Involuntarily as he passed it, the man, with his all too light burden, halted. A flame shot through him as Molly turned her head to gaze too : he shook with a brief agony of jealousy—jealousy of the dead ! The next instant he felt her recoil, look up pleadingly and cling to him again, and he knew into the soul of his soul that the words spoken by those loyal lips—now clay beneath that clay —were coming true, that, out of his house laid desolate to him was to rise a new and stately mansion.

Grasping her closer he hurried into the sanctuary of the old room, where he had first seen her bright young beauty.

At the door he gently suffered her to stand, still supporting her with one arm about her waist. As they entered, she cast a rapid glance around : her eyes, bedewed with rising tears, fell upon the heap of gold glinting under the rays of the sinking sun, and she understood the nature of the task her coming had interrupted. Her tears gushed forth ; catching his hand between hers, and looking up at him with a strange, wonderful humility, she pressed it to her lips.

What need for words between them, then ?

He stood a little while motionless in front of her, entranced yet still almost incredulous, as one suddenly freed from long intolerable pain, when there rose once more, for the last time, before his mind's eye the ideal image that had been the companion of twenty years of his existence. It was vivid almost as life. He saw Cécile de Savenaye bend over her child with grave and tender look, then turn and smile upon him with the old exquisite sweetness that he had adored so madly in that far off past. And then, it was as if she had merged into Molly. Behold, she was gone ! there was no Cécile, only Molly the woman he loved. Molly, whom now he seized to his heart, who smiled at him through her tears as he bent to kiss her lips.

Twilight was waning and the light of Scarthey beamed peacefully over the yellow sands ; and the waves receded, dragging away sand and shingle from the foot of the hidden grave.

THE END

www.ingramcontent.com/pod-product-compliance
Lightning Source LLC
Chambersburg PA
CBHW031825270326
41932CB00008B/552